SEP   - 1997

BREAKING POINT

BREAKING
POINT

Why Women Fall Apart and
How They Can Re-create Their Lives

Martha N. Beck, Ph.D.

TIMES ⒯ BOOKS

RANDOM HOUSE

Grateful acknowledgment is made to the following for permission to
reprint previously published material: *Common Courage Press:*
Excerpts from *Patriarchy: Notes of an Expert Witness* by Phyllis
Chesler. Reprinted by permission of Common Courage Press.
· *Crown Publishers, Inc.:* Excerpts from *Backlash* by Susan Faludi.
Copyright © 1991 by Susan Faludi. Reprinted by permission of
Crown Publishers, Inc. · *Good News Publishers/Crossway Books:*
Excerpts from *The Way Home: Beyond Feminism and Back to Reality*
by Mary Pride (pp. 91–92). Copyright © 1985 by Mary Pride.
Reprinted by permission of Good News Publishers/Crossway
Books, Wheaton, Illinois. · *Phyllis Schlafly:* Excerpt from *The Phyllis
Schlafly Report,* October, 1973, Section 2. Reprinted by permission
of Phyllis Schlafly.

Library of Congress Cataloging-in-Publication Data

Beck, Martha Nibley
Breaking point :
why women fall apart and how they can re-create their lives /
Martha N. Beck. —1st ed.
p.   cm.
ISBN 0-8129-6375-X (acid-free paper)
1. Women—United States—Psychology.
2. Women—United States—Social conditions.
3. Stress (Psychology).   4. Sex role—United States.   I. Title.
HQ1206.B32   1997
305.42'0973—dc21

Random House website address: http://www.randomhouse.com/

Book design by M. Kristen Bearse

Printed in the United States of America on acid-free paper

2   4   6   8   9   7   5   3

First Edition

To my mother, my sisters, and my daughters;
and to all the other women who have been
my mothers, sisters, and daughters throughout my life

Acknowledgments

I HAVE LITERALLY been working to develop the ideas in this book since I was a child. To thank everyone who helped in its production would be a virtually infinite task. The following acknowledgments are therefore incomplete; I ask those I have left out to pardon my sins of omission.

My dear friend Karen Gerdes was midwife to this book from conception to completion. She has my undying gratitude for her insights, encouragement, and support.

John Beck, my husband, demonstrated an astonishing capacity for comforting and cheerleading during the difficult years when I combined the research for this book with graduate school, work, and the births of our children. Without his loving optimism, I would now be living in a rubber room. Our children, Katie, Adam, and Elizabeth, have also given me love and long-suffering beyond their years during the times when I have buried myself in my work.

My family of origin, particularly my mother and sisters, helped enormously during my preliminary research. Their intelligent commentary was key in developing my analysis.

I owe another debt of gratitude to Ruth Killpack, whose life, philosophy, and guidance are inspirational to me. I would also like to thank the extraordinary women I met through Dr. Killpack. Their stories helped me move out of my own biases and see through the eyes of other women.

Aage Sørensen, Annemette Sørensen, and Lenore Weitzman, my advisers at Harvard, each played a different but essential role in the development of my ideas. I would also like to thank Professor Orlando Patterson for his invaluable instruction in qualitative research methods and the sociological analysis of modernization.

Marie Cornwall and others at the Women's Research Institute at Brigham Young University found financial support and professional encouragement for me during the initial phases of my research. Laura Marwick was a dedicated research assistant. Many thanks to them.

My friends and fellow writers Annette Rogers, Dawn Swanson, and Thora Knight gave me unstintingly honest and helpful advice during the writing of this book. Without them, I could never have begun to write it, let alone managed to get it published. I am deeply grateful for their friendship and direction.

Much of my motivation to propose this book came from the support, advice, and incisive criticism of my agent, Susan Schulman. Her enthusiasm and honesty made the process of writing more fun than I would ever have expected.

Elizabeth Rapoport, my editor at Times Books, has been an invaluable coach and ally during the writing of *Breaking Point*. Her suggestions on both the style and content of the book were invaluable. It has been a privilege to work with someone of such intelligence and sensitivity.

Last but most, I want to thank the women I interviewed, whose stories were the basis for all my conclusions. I can only hope that I have represented these women fairly, and that I can give back something to the people who have given so much to me.

Author's Note

I am extraordinarily grateful to the hundreds of women whose voices appear in this book. In order to protect their privacy, I have changed their names and identifying characteristics.

Contents

PHASE FOUR **Transcendence**

PHASE FIVE **Re-creation**

AFTERWORD

BREAKING POINT

Introduction:
The Process of Moving Through
the Breaking Point

When Random House decided to publish this book, they faxed me a copy of their standard twelve-page contract. It began like this:

> AGREEMENT made this 8th day of March, 1996, between TIMES BOOKS, A DIVISION OF RANDOM HOUSE . . . (referred to as the Publisher), and Martha Beck, Ph.D. . . . . (referred to as the Author and designated by the masculine singular pronoun) WHEREAS the parties wish respectively to publish and have published a work (referred to as the work) of non-fiction provisionally titled DEADLOCK.

Is it just me, or is there something a tiny bit odd about that paragraph, aside from the fact that it has the same snappy readability as the list of ingredients for a multisymptom cold remedy? Clearly, the lawyers at Random House (referred to as Lawyers) didn't think so. My agent (referred to as Susan) didn't notice it either, and to be perfectly honest, neither did I (the author). It was my husband, John Beck, Ph.D. (referred to as Muffincakes, but only when we're alone), who first called attention to the gender-bender in the contract. The fax was lying next to my computer when John wandered in and picked it up.

"*Masculine* singular pronoun?" he said. "Good lord, Martha! You never told me you're a man!"

"Gimme that," I responded with my customary wit and charm.

"Geez!" said John. "You live with someone for twelve years, you have children together, you think you know her—"

"Him," I corrected, scanning the contract.

For there it was, in the most excruciatingly legal black and white. One clause required me (the author) to "covenant and agree that *he* is the sole author of the work." "*He* will not," said another line item, ". . . publish or permit to be published" any competing work. In addition, the contract stated, "the Author agrees to submit to the Publisher a proposal for *his* next book-length work."

By the time I had read through twelve pages of this, I was entering a twilight zone where I was beginning to think of *myself* in terms of "he," "him," and "his." Clearly, everyone who dealt with this standard publishing-contract format had gotten used to the wording years before. It wasn't as if the Lawyers couldn't have changed the word "he" to the more politically correct "he or she"—after all, the contract isn't exactly a model of concise prose. Or they could simply have called me "the Author" all the way through, and left the pronouns out of it altogether. But they didn't. If Martha Beck, Ph.D., was going to sign a contract with Times Books, she was going to do it as a he.

Mind you, this should not have surprised me. After years of interviewing American women to determine what they think about gender roles, I'd heard "she-man" stories from many people: a successful executive who was invariably referred to as "Mr. Daniels" on office memos; a military officer by the name of Jennifer who had earned the right to be called "sir"; a high school vice-principal who had received an award for being the principal's "right-hand man." Perhaps I should have felt grateful that I had finally done something that put me, along with these impressive women, in the ranks of the masculine.

The problem is that neither I nor any of the other "she-men" I knew was quite sure whether we were being complimented or insulted. On one hand, you could argue that treating a woman like a man, in a society where men have always been the more privileged gender, is an admirable move toward equality. On the other hand, you could say that requiring a woman to fit a male mold—right down to the pronouns—is to grossly neglect the fact that women are making a unique, female contribution to society, and that women, even in the most feminine manifestations, are quite capable of doing things that were once thought to require male expertise.

This is the problem with discussing women's roles in the United States of America. There are always two sides to the argument, always two ways to evaluate anything a woman does, or anything done to her. Are women helpless victims of male oppression? That makes us seem pathetically weak, which we aren't. Well, then, are we *not* victims? That implies that we're wholly responsible for our own historical subordination to men, which we aren't. Do we require special treatment because of our role in bearing children? Saying so opens the way for people to discriminate against us and call it "protection," which isn't fair. Do mothers *not* require any special treatment? That means that a father and a mother should be required to perform exactly the same work on the day their child is born, which isn't fair either. The fact is that in hundreds of ways, in millions of lives, the role of women in today's United States takes the form of *paradox*—a problem or question that cannot be solved without leading directly to another problem or question.

The paradoxical language in my book contract is a trivial example, a semantic quirk that has little impact on the way I live my life. But it is symptomatic of a social approach to gender that has powerful—and overwhelmingly negative—consequences for millions of women. American society has set up a no-win scenario in which to win approval women must be and do irreconcilable things. Thus, the mother who cares for her children in her home is not seen as "supporting" them; if she works to "support" them, she is not giving them enough care. A husband may "allow" his wife to take a job, as though he were doing her a favor; but when he goes out to work at a similar job, she is not seen as doing him a favor, but as having yet another favor done for her. A woman who spends all her days doing housework holds a lowly social status; but if she does anything else, she is neglecting her "proper" responsibilities and receives social censure. And the problem does not end with frustrating social attitudes and judgments. Sometimes, as we shall see, the common paradoxes of everyday female roles create situations that literally destroy women's lives.

THE MANY FACES OF THE BREAKING POINT

In the following pages, I'll be telling the stories of dozens of women who have been trapped—at the breaking point—by forces stemming directly from our culture's paradoxical definition of female roles. On the surface, these women's problems seem infinitely varied, but the paradox of being female in American society underlies all of them. Here are a few examples:

◆ Mariko, thirty-five, has just received a promotion at the TV news station where she works. She is now making more money than her husband, allowing the family to get out of debt for the first time in years. But instead of making things smoother at home, Mariko's promotion has led to tension and stress. "My husband and I have been fighting more," she says. "It's not good for the kids or for us. I'm working so hard to make things better for my family, but no matter what I do, things seem to get worse. I feel so defeated, and I'm *so* tired. I can't make sense of it all."

◆ Alessandra is eighty years old. On the day I speak to her, she is suffering from heart disease, loneliness, and wrenching confusion. "I've cared for people all my life," she says. "And I wouldn't have done it any other way. But somehow, I always thought that I was making a kind of investment, that caring for others would create a caring that would come back to me. I spend a lot of time being afraid for my future. I try to figure out what I did wrong in the past. But I can't figure it out. Everything just seems wrong, somehow."

◆ Brenda is twenty-five and engaged to be married. She loves her fiancé "madly," but has been suffering dramatic mood swings as her marriage approaches. "Half of the time I feel like all my dreams are about to come true," she says, "and the other half of the time I feel as though they're all about to end. I'm very conflicted; I'm not quite sure what's wrong with me."

◆ Yarro was born in Cuba and emigrated to the United States in the 1980s. She married an American and bore two children before her husband left her, with no money and an uncertain grasp of English. "I work so hard since I get divorced," she tells me. "Because I [did] work so hard, we didn't starve. But I feel so guilty, so sad for my children. This is not the way I want[ed] to be a mother. Sometimes I think, 'I should be proud, raise two children alone.' But their life is not what I wanted. It is very hard, for my children and for me. It is very hard."

◆ When I interview Jenny, she has just given birth to her first child, a daughter. As she cradles her week-old infant, she finds herself flooded with mixed feelings. "I look at her and I think how wonderful it is that she is a girl," Jenny tells me. "I think about the great women I have known, how much they enrich the world and my life. And yet, at the same time, I know she'll face a lot of barriers. I think about women I know who have been in situations where they were defenseless and powerless. The weird thing is that the strongest women I know and the ones with the most problems are often the same people. What does that mean? How should I teach my daughter what it means to be female? Sometimes I look at her and I get so confused that I end up crying, and I'm not even sure why."

At first glance, it may seem that each of these women is suffering from a separate ailment. Brenda has the "cold feet" experienced by many an engaged person, Yarro is suffering from culture shock, Jenny probably has a touch of postpartum depression, and so on. All of these terms are accurate and useful, but they mask the fact that the same social forces are also at work in all these cases. These forces are so deeply entrenched in our cultural mind-set that we must look closely at our society to understand how they emerged—but their effects are easy to see in the lives of all the women mentioned above. Each of these women, in her own way, is feeling similar things: exhaustion, sadness, low self-esteem, lack of trust in her own instincts, and a peculiar, unassailable, overwhelming bewilderment.

Many women share these symptoms—ailments that come not from mental illness or personal weakness, but from a pervasive double-mindedness in our basic value system, a profound paradox in the way our society defines its women. The effects of this paradox are not limited to women; they are dragging our entire culture into an infinite variety of baffling conundrums. In this book, I'll describe the basic paradoxes of American culture in detail, and show you why and how it is making more and more women's lives extraordinarily difficult. As we'll see, there is a way to move beyond the problems, a way to transcend the conflicting demands American society is making of its female members. Before we can move on into a saner way of life, however, we must recognize and articulate the elements of our culture's *in*-sanity.

THE BEST OF TIMES, THE WORST OF TIMES

The basic values underlying our society have led to dizzyingly rapid changes in American women's roles over the past few decades. In less than the span of a human lifetime, women's roles have changed more than in all of history prior to now. As a result, this is now the very best of times for women in the United States of America. It is also the very worst. How can I say such a thing? Well, consider the following facts:

POINT	COUNTERPOINT
American women's personal earnings have risen dramatically over the past thirty years. The average American woman today earns more money than any other "average woman" at any time or place in human history.	The rate of poverty among American women is at an all-time high. Women and children constitute a higher percentage of the American poor than ever before. As one researcher puts it, poverty in America "wears a feminine face."

POINT	COUNTERPOINT
In a country where education is the key to occupational success, women are now better educated than men. American girls are more likely than American boys to graduate from high school, and American colleges now accept more women than men.	American women are still pooled in low-ranking, low-prestige jobs, and men average higher earnings than women in every age group, every educational level, and every occupational category.

POINT	COUNTERPOINT
American women have more control over their own biological life cycles than ever before. In particular, the availability of effective reproductive technologies has reached unprecedented levels.	Unwanted pregnancy is also more common than ever before, and obtaining day care is one of the most pressing problems faced by many American women.

POINT	COUNTERPOINT
Women have gone beyond the old, rigid, feminine role that limits females to domestic work and social nurturing. The freedom to choose a career is more real for American women than it has ever been for women anywhere. Most have jobs, and most stay in the workforce regardless of their marital status.	Women still do the vast bulk of domestic work in this country, whether or not they have careers outside their homes. In addition, the average American woman can expect to spend seventeen years as the primary caregiver for children, and eighteen years caring for elderly or incapacitated relatives.

If these sets of information seem strangely inconsistent to you, you're in good company. Scholars, policymakers, activists, and ordinary people often wade into "women's issues" determined to understand and correct the problems that beset America's female population—only to impale themselves on the horns of dilemmas more complex than they ever anticipated. Examples are everywhere. Laws passed to free women from unsatisfactory marriages end up damaging the quality of those women's lives. Equal-rights programs unfortunately exacerbate inequality. Schemes to free women from social bondage turn out, in practice, to entrap them. Confusion about women's roles permeates American society, from our political institutions to our legal codes to the actions and attitudes of individual citizens.

PARADOX:
WHY AMERICAN WOMEN CAN'T WIN FOR LOSING

At the root of the confusion about women's roles is a contradictory definition of what it means to be a "good person" in American society. Our value system contains two ways to measure human value. One side of the definition requires a "good" person to sacrifice individual rewards for the benefit of the group. The other requires the opposite: resisting the pressure of the group in preference to personal independence and achievement. Throughout American history, structures and institutions have been built up around these two measures of human worth in such a way that they have become *mutually exclusive, yet absolutely indispensable.*

Women are the group in American society that has been saddled with the task of resolving this little paradox; of reconciling the irreconcilable value system of their entire culture. The result is that in the United States, women's roles are becoming steadily more contradictory, self-refuting, and impossible to fulfill. An American woman can't succeed at one set of responsibilities without failing by another set of criteria.

Like any paradoxical demand, this contradictory social role can lead to a situation of utter impossibility, for when you are at the breaking point, you can't go on with anything—*including staying where you are.* This is where the definition of female social roles is taking American women. Many of us have encountered it already, and as time goes by, a higher and higher percentage of women are becoming entangled in its baffling convolutions. I have interviewed scores of women who know the breaking point from the inside out. I have spent most of my life trying to understand it from the outside in.

HOW I CAME TO STUDY THE BREAKING POINT

This book combines the things I have learned through research and sociological training with the stories I heard from some three hundred American women over a ten-year period, from 1986 to 1996. I have actually been interviewing women throughout my adult life. In 1983, the year I reached legal drinking age, I had just completed my first two years as an undergraduate at Harvard. Like many Harvard students, I decided to spend my junior year of college overseas, studying a foreign culture. At least, this is the official version of the story, the one I tell to polite acquaintances and possible employers. The unofficial version is that during my sophomore year, I fell hopelessly in love with my future husband, who was headed to Singapore to complete a Rotary scholarship. In a leap of faith that seems absolutely insane to me in retrospect, I married John one fine spring day and boarded a plane with him, headed for the Far East, the next. Fortunately, the marriage turned out rather well, and for the next fourteen months, I developed my multicultural skills by peering at flash cards of Chinese characters, unintentionally breaking the etiquette rules of many exotic cultures, and getting hopelessly lost in almost every major city of the Far East.

To make all of this sound good to the Harvard officials who would decide whether or not my year in Asia would count toward my college degree, I decided to do some research on Chinese society. I knew that as a woman I would have a hard time doing up-close cultural observations of traditional Chinese men—to them, women did not belong in male company outside their own families.

Accordingly, I decided to focus on women. I began to interview Chinese women in Singapore, then won a fellowship that took me to China to complete my research. I used a nondirective, reflective style of interviewing, a style recommended by feminist social scientists to avoid imposing the researcher's way of thinking on the women they interview. I loved this interview style, not only because I agreed with its logic but because it allowed me to get by with minimal questioning. This was just dandy with me, since my Chinese skills were something less than rock-solid at the best of times, and deteriorated alarmingly when I was in unfamiliar circumstances.

I eventually found my way to an airport, returned with John to Harvard, finished my last year as an undergraduate, and went on to do graduate work in sociology. The whole time, I kept right on interviewing women, although I switched from the Chinese to the American variety. Interviewing had proved so interesting to me that I was almost addicted to it. It also seemed useful to keep interviewing, since I knew that I eventually wanted to write a dissertation on women's social roles, looking at some of the contradictions I'd seen in the "modernization" of female roles in China.

To be honest, though, the most compelling motivation for my research was that as I moved into my late twenties, the confusion and stress in my own life were reaching intolerable levels. After concluding that it would be easier to have children during those flexible-schedule graduate school years than later in our careers, John and I had three children while working toward our Ph.D.'s at Harvard, a strategy that deserves a place in the history of bad planning right up there with, say, the Bay of Pigs invasion. If you are thinking of doing anything similar, I strongly advise you to seek therapy. Due largely to the tolerance and goodwill of the Harvard sociology faculty, I managed to finish my coursework and complete a dissertation on the responses of a very traditional American subculture (the Church of the Latter-Day Saints, or Mormons) to changes in women's roles. I emerged from my graduate school years with a Ph.D., three adorable children, innumerable stress-related health problems, and one remaining goal: to sleep at least twelve hours every night for the rest of my life. Plus naps.

By that time, I had also interviewed hundreds of American women—and this was one aspect of my professional life that gave me more than it took. No matter how tired I was, or how many life stories I had heard, I found myself fascinated by virtually every interview I conducted. It was in other women's stories that I began to find answers for the problems and conflicts I faced in my own life—and some that I hadn't been able to face, or even conceptualize, until more insightful women shared their thoughts and experiences with me. After yet a few more years of interviews, I came to see the experience of women in American culture in terms of paradox, the breaking point, and transcendence; elements I will describe in this book.

During the past ten years, aside from all this interviewing, I've done many other forms of research on women's issues. I've read hundreds of thousands of pages of academic and journalistic analyses, watched endless hours of debates both live and televised, listened to dozens of speakers at conferences and gatherings focused solely on understanding female social roles. But that's not where I found the ideas that helped me understand what was happening to me, or how I might think about being female in ways that were helpful rather than hurtful. I found those precious things in the stories of real women's real lives; stories they shared with me over restaurant tables, babies' car seats, hardwood desktops, quilting frames, cups of tea, stacks of paperwork, kitchen sinks, and the thousands of other spaces where the work of women's lives takes place.

I've included many of their stories in this book—some of them verbatim. I have two reasons for this. The first is that I have learned that breaking points have the most power to harm when they are not *articulated*—when the voices of ordinary women are belittled, ignored, or silenced. Right now, there are tremendous pressures on American women (sometimes from surprising sources) that work to keep them from articulating their own experiences, and opinions. Some of the most powerful stories I heard during my interview research had never been told before, and far more had never really been heard. Until such stories become part of the foundation on which we base our conception of women's roles, American women will continue to be misunderstood, and sometimes mistreated.

A second reason for recounting real-world experiences is to demonstrate the *patterns* that emerged as the personal stories of many women came together. Those patterns were nothing like what I expected to see when I began studying American women. Everything I had read or heard, in academic journals or weekly newsmagazines, in Harvard seminars and daytime talk shows, made me expect to see women moving from "traditional" roles into "modern" ones—or at least fighting with each other about whether a "traditional" or "modern" role was best. Instead, what I saw among American women was a *process* in which women absorbed a paradoxical way of looking at themselves, carried that paradox to the breaking point, and then somehow made transformative sense of seemingly impossible situations. Those who went through the process emerged on the other side with a different way of defining themselves, the people around them, and ultimately society itself.

THE PHASES OF THE BREAKING-POINT PROCESS

The way women move through the breaking point is unique to every individual, but in general the process breaks down into five recognizable phases. I've devoted a couple of chapters in this book to describing each one. Before we go into the detailed descriptions, though, I'd like you to have a "road map" of this process and the logic behind it. I hope that this will give you a sense of the whole journey, a sense that, while we may be going off all the beaten tracks open to women today, we are still headed for a very real and attainable destination.

Of course, you may already have been through the entire breaking-point process, in which case you will recognize all the pit stops, detours, and scenic wonders of the journey sketched out below. You will remember exactly what each phase looked and felt like as it happened to you. If you are currently at a midpoint on the journey, you will recognize *some* of the phases, but only the ones you've already experienced. The rest may seem unfamiliar, and perhaps downright strange. If none of the "Phases of the Breaking Point" looks familiar to you, my advice is simply to wait awhile. You may be one of the lucky women in the United States who live long, happy lives without ever experiencing it. You may also have won over ten million dollars in the Publishers Clearing House Giveaway.

But I doubt it.

PHASE ONE: SOCIALIZATION

An individual woman's trip to the breaking point begins the moment she is born into American culture, which idealizes two incompatible value systems. As she grows up, she absorbs the core values of her culture. The problem is that these core values are contradictory. Each woman's family and friends, the American educational system, the media, and other social structures collaborate to reinforce the idea that women's roles must incorporate mutually exclusive elements.

◆ *Chapter 1. Some History* To move forward through the logic of transcending the breaking point, we first need to look back at the history that has put every modern woman in a position that is at best precarious, and at worst impossible. In this chapter, we'll see where our ideas about what a woman should be originated—and why some key ideas born hundreds of years ago are still tearing so many American women apart.

◆ *Chapter 2. Lurching Through Herstory* Women's history is a novel development in Western thought—until recently, the story of the world has been "his story," an account of the male experience. This chapter will look at the way women's roles have developed, how the idea of the perfect woman has become more and more insanely contradictory as the herstory of the United States has unfolded. The rather chilling evidence of this herstory suggests that at the moment you are reading this book, the American definition of women's roles is more paradoxical, more impossible to realize, than it has ever been before.

PHASE TWO: ENCOUNTERING PARADOX

As an American girl grows, she begins to encounter society's paradoxical expectations. Over time, it becomes harder and harder for her to fulfill her role definition. She feels pressure both from the variety of things she is expected to do, and from the strong judgments placed on her by other people. Increasingly, virtually everything an American female does is likely to be judged—and judged very harshly—as a statement of her position on women's roles.

◆ *Chapter 3. Strange Loops and Double Binds* The concept of *paradox* is crucial to understanding what American women are going through today. A paradox consists of two ideas that refer to, and contradict, each other. The way paradox operates, the harder a person tries to obey one set of directives, the more pressure she experiences to *disobey* them. Sound confusing? Oh, believe me, it is. And if you're an American woman, you live with it every day. Being caught in a paradox leads many women to a characteristic array of behaviors and feelings: confusion, exhaustion, difficulty making decisions, and many more. Americans tend to think of these behaviors as female—characteristic of women, part and parcel of their feminine nature. Actually, they are the normal reactions of *anyone* stuck in a paradoxical social role.

◆ *Chapter 4. Refugees from the Holy War* The conflict between the two polar opposites of American attitudes is being played out in a holy war between very loud and strident factions of Americans. The soldiers in this war believe that all women should be completely committed *either* to individual equality *or* to traditional values and institutions. Each side of this conflict feels that the other is threatening, evil, and must be eradicated. Unbeknownst to these holy warriors, the battles they are fighting *cannot be won by either side.* Furthermore, the vast majority of women in the United States do not want to participate in this "war." Unfortunately, the noncombatant views of the majority are instantaneously labeled and judged by the holy warriors, until women have begun to mute their voices and doubt their basic instincts for fear of getting caught in the crossfire.

PHASE THREE: REACHING THE BREAKING POINT

The longer a woman navigates through the world according to a paradoxical set of directions, the more inadequate she feels and the less respect she has for her own judgment. At some point, she may encounter a situation in which she believes she *must do* at least two things that cannot be reconciled. At this point the woman begins to experience the symptoms of the breaking point, including physical and mental exhaustion, depression, irritability, anxiety, a sense of impending doom, and an inability to act or make decisions.

◆ *Chapter 5. Hitting the Breaking Point*   Chapter 5 will tell the stories of women who are or have been at the breaking point. I'll describe how they reached this horrific situation, and what it is like from their perspective. A typical woman tries to fill all her culture's demands without paying much attention to the fact that these demands are incompatible—until the fateful day when, encountering a situation that requires her to act on paradoxical directives, she ends up in crisis. Often, this occurs following a "life accident"—some unpredictable change in a woman's life that finally brings her to the point where she is paralyzed by the contradictory requirements she feels she must fulfill. But more and more, women are reaching the breaking point simply by living in a society where paradoxical demands on women are constantly increasing.

◆ *Chapter 6. The Age Factor*   The change in American women's roles has been so rapid that people of different ages, even those born only a decade apart, have been affected by that change in very different ways. Although women of all ages in the United States are facing paradoxical demands, the *way* in which these factors bring them to the breaking point is often different depending on when they were born. In Chapter 6, we'll look at how different cohorts of women, born in different decades, are experiencing this phase.

PHASE FOUR: TRANSCENDENCE

A woman may be at the breaking point for a long time. The nature of paradox means that as she struggles to free herself from this impossible situation, the conflict in her self-definition actually intensifies. Inevitably, the woman enters the process I call "meltdown," in which her vision of herself, her relationships, her purpose in life, and other key ingredients of her worldview begin to break apart. When this process is complete—just when things seem to be at their worst—the woman may experience a sudden, involuntary "leap" to a completely different way of viewing herself and the demands being made of her. In one memorable moment, she literally moves outside of her culture and social conditioning. This event is almost indescribable, since it lies outside our society's range of shared concepts. Nevertheless, it has a powerful, transformative effect on the woman who experiences it.

◆ *Chapter 7. Meltdown* This chapter describes one of the most alarming things that can happen to a person: the meltdown of her worldview. Once a woman arrives at the breaking point, the paralysis and confusion of the situation begin to "spread backward" into the ideas, concepts, and values that brought her there. The woman begins to feel that everything she thought she knew about herself, along with her culture's version of reality, is disintegrating. This is so painful and terrifying that a woman at this stage of the process often feels that she is literally about to die. She may put up a valiant fight, but at some point she simply runs out of strength and stops fighting. It is then that she may experience the next, almost indescribable step.

◆ *Chapter 8.* Satori: *The Paradigm Shift* *Satori* is a Japanese word, used by Zen masters to describe a moment of enlightened awareness, a breakthrough to a new way of seeing. The English phrase *paradigm shift* comes close to the same meaning, but it doesn't capture the whole range of what women feel at the moment of transcending the breaking point. *Satori* occurs when a breaking point becomes so intense that it pushes a woman out of the entire system of logic that created her view of herself. In essence, the woman is forced to think outside her society's reality. This is like seeing a hitherto undiscovered color or tasting a new flavor; you can't adequately explain it to someone who's never experienced it.

However a woman describes her own *satori*, she links it with a profound sense of discovering her true self, a self free to move out of a no-way-out situation. This new self often comes up with startling, creative solutions to a woman's problems—but more important is her completely different way of seeing the problems in the first place.

PHASE FIVE: RE-CREATION

After a woman has experienced *satori*, she begins to rebuild the structures of her own life, and her own identity, according to a unique, original blueprint. At first glance such a woman may not appear unusual—not particularly different from her former self, or from any other woman. However, because she is dealing with an agenda different from that of her society, she will occasionally do unusual things, until other people begin to see her behavior as unpredictable, inconsistent, perhaps even bizarre. While no two women will make exactly the same choices, the *way* they make those choices is characterized by a calm detachment that, to observers, makes them all the more baffling. Fortunately, at this stage the woman doesn't spend much time wondering what other people think about her. She is too busy re-creating herself, her social environment, her universe.

◆ *Chapter 9. Caring for the True Self* Before going through the breaking-point process, most women have a worldview based on their society's values. The final phase of the process begins with a woman's realization that the demands and judgments our society imposes on women are unworkable, and that she needs to become essentially independent of her culture. This requires a tremendous level of honesty (by which a woman stays connected to her true self) and compassion (by which she nurtures it). Many women who commit themselves to these two basic means of caring for the true self end up wreaking a sort of beneficent havoc on the social systems around them. Nevertheless, women who have been through it, often repeatedly, understand that caring for the true self is the only way to maintain a steady course through the bewildering paradoxes of their society.

◆ *Chapter 10. Changing the Rules of the Game* Women who have been through the process realize that most social "rules" have the arbitrary nature of a game. The woman who has been through the breaking point is quite willing to participate in social games that do not require her to violate the principles of honesty and compassion. However, when she is pressured to play a game that violates these standards, she will either refuse to play or begin to change the rules. This type of behavior is anathema to people who are deeply invested in playing social games as they now exist. A woman who stands firm in her resolve to care for her true self may find herself being branded a traitor, a threat to civilization as we know it. As we will see, this is not an inaccurate perception. Many women who have set out to do nothing more than care for their true selves end up literally changing the world. Ultimately, the logical conclusion of this whole process is the transformation of a society that is presently heading for self-destruction.

◆ *Chapter 11. The "Emergent" Society* When the (formal or informal) rules of their society dictate that people should betray their true selves by dishonesty or cruelty, women who have been through the entire breaking-point process typically refuse to conform. Their actions tend to have a ripple effect on the social groups around them, making deception and lack of compassion awkward and difficult to sustain. This ripple effect may extend no further than a woman's immediate set of relatives and acquaintances. However, when women act to care for their true selves in the context of a social group that is already strained (as is the present United States), they may spark a uniquely powerful sort of revolution—a revolution that comes from the heart and conscience of a massive and diverse group, rather than from one or two established ideologies. Great women and men have created this kind of revolution at many important historical moments. The paradox of American society has brought it to one such moment now. Women who have been through the breaking point are charting a course to a new way of understanding individual identity and human life.

HOW TO READ THIS BOOK

I'd like to point out here that the "Phases of the Breaking-Point Process" is a *descriptive* list, not a *prescriptive* one. In other words, this book describes what happens when a woman has reached the breaking point and passed beyond it, but it's not a procedure you can run out and do deliberately, like a fitness program or a craft project. Think of the book in the same category as those guides to natural childbirth for expectant mothers. Just because the birth process follows recognizable steps doesn't mean that the mother can control when her water breaks or her contractions become intense. She has no idea what variations on the theme of childbirth will be played out when her baby is born. The point of reading about it is that the whole birth process tends to go better, and cause the mother less distress, when she knows what is happening to her.

As a matter of fact, in a number of ways, transcending the breaking point is like giving birth. For instance, it is usually excruciating,* rarely convenient, and practically never lets up when you decide that you're tired and would like to quit, or at least take a coffee break. On the other hand, the pain, fear, and exhaustion are not wasted. Through them, someone wonderful comes into the world; someone utterly unique, whom no one has ever seen before. A woman who enters and transcends this phase "gives birth" to her own true self—and that true self, in turn, can create new and healing directions for society.

Once you have walked through a step-by-step description of transcending the breaking point, as I did when I listened to women's stories and as you will do as you read this book, the whole process makes as much logical sense as the process by which a woman's body creates life from life. When you encounter your own breaking points (I say *when*, not *if*), you will be able to see where the problems come from and what to expect. But as with any birth, no matter how much logic you apply to it, you cannot watch it happen—much less experience it—without feeling that you have been present at something wonderful, something miraculous, something that, in the final analysis, makes it all worthwhile.

---

* I should acknowledge that I have read treatises that argue that the so-called pain of labor and delivery is a myth, invented by male doctors as an excuse to dominate the birth process. One book claimed that the *real* reason some women scream and grimace while having babies is that they are experiencing orgasm. If you are one of these women, I don't know whether to envy you for having a truly fabulous childbirth experience or pity you for having horrible sex, but you might want to trash the whole "birth" analogy and substitute some other protracted and difficult procedure, like boot camp or junior high school.

PHASE ONE:

SOCIALIZATION

PHASE TWO:

ENCOUNTERING PARADOX

PHASE THREE:

REACHING THE BREAKING POINT

PHASE FOUR:

TRANSCENDENCE

PHASE FIVE:

RE-CREATION

PHASE ONE

Socialization

CHAPTER ONE

✦

Some History:
The Foundation of a House Divided

ANNIE LEONARD

Annie Leonard came completely unwrapped at her husband Jeff's forty-third birthday party, and it was all because of seventeenth-century European philosophy. Not that Annie ever thinks about seventeenth-century European philosophy. During my years in academia, I've met people who dwell on the topic the way others dwell on baseball statistics or the story line of their favorite soap opera, but Annie isn't one of them. She is many other things: a gracious, warm woman with a wonderful sense of humor, the mother of five happy children, the wife of a successful executive, the center of a devoted group of friends, and an astonishingly competent homemaker. In her chosen field, Annie is as high-achieving, self-motivated, and accomplished as any corporate president who ever led a Fortune 500 company. That's why her behavior at Jeff's birthday party was so unsettling to Annie's family, her friends, and, most of all, Annie herself.

Annie, 42

Everything started out just fine. Jeff's boss had invited the four top district managers and their wives to dinner. It just happened to be Jeff's birthday, and we thought it would be a great way to celebrate.

Annie knew that it was a tremendous compliment for Jeff to be invited to dinner with the CEO of his company, a man I'll call Norman Manchester. She was happy to accompany Jeff to the event, even though corporate functions were not her favorite way to spend her time. The problem started at about the time dessert was served. Norman Manchester tapped on his wineglass with a fork to draw everyone's attention, lifted the glass, and made a toast. According to Annie, it went something like this:

"I want to congratulate everyone here on your success. You people have done more in less time than almost anyone else in the company. I've been told that Jeff is just turning forty-three, and the rest of you aren't much older. Most of the men at your level are too old to be considered for further promotion, but you four are not."

Annie looked at her husband, who was positively glowing under Manchester's approval, and tried to smile. Oddly, she couldn't. "My stomach felt all tight," she told me later. "Like a fist I couldn't unclench." She struggled to compose herself as Manchester went on:

"Most people don't *make* things happen," he said. "Most people just *let* things happen—and sometimes they get in the way. You people are different. You make your dreams come true. You have the loyalty and respect of your coworkers, the company, and the world. And if that's not enough, you can always think about the size of your Christmas bonuses."

Everyone laughed. Annie put down her spoon and gripped her hands together in her lap.

"And of course," Manchester concluded, "I'd like to thank you ladies for the support you give us all. We know that we wouldn't be here today without the ladies." All the men at the table began to applaud politely.

At that moment, without any warning, Annie burst into tears. I don't mean a little drip-and-sniffle affair. This was serious weeping, complete with loud sobbing and muddy little rivers of mascara running down Annie's cheeks. It came on like a tornado, and with just as unsettling an effect. Everyone at the table stared, aghast, at Annie.

> Oh, God, I thought I was going to die from embarrassment. I mean, can you imagine? This was one of the most important nights in Jeff's life, and I was coming apart. It was like . . . I could see it happening, but I really truly couldn't stop it. I'd been crying a lot at home, in the year or two before that, but . . . I could always control it. Until that one night.

Mumbling an apology, Annie got up from the table and rushed toward the women's room. Jeff was right behind her. He adored Annie, and her sudden outburst scared him badly. He caught up with her in front of the rest-room doors.

> He was so sweet, so worried. I tried to think what to tell him, about why I was crying. I realized that it was nothing he could understand. It was about my whole life. . . . It was about getting up every day and helping Jeff and the kids get ready to go do something important, and never having to get dressed to do anything important myself. It was about listening to people like Manchester say, "Oh, all you people are so wonderful," and then saying, "And we could never do it without the ladies." As though "the ladies" weren't "people."
>
> I mean, I was going to be forty-three in a few months, too—and what did I have to show for it? Twenty years of dishwashing, cooking, cleaning floors that were going to be dirty again tomorrow. How could Jeff understand that? . . . He kept asking me what was wrong, what he could do for me. I thought about trying to explain it all, but finally I just told him what it all boiled down to. I said, "I'm not sure I even exist."

Jeff Leonard didn't have a clue what his wife was talking about, but when she related the incident to me a few months later, I knew what Annie meant. I understood partly because I am female myself, partly because I had interviewed dozens of other women who had said approximately the same thing, and partly because I knew something about seventeenth-century European philosophy.

You see, Annie's strange sense of invisibility, of nonexistence, did not simply descend upon her from nowhere. Nor did it come from her own mind. It wasn't a hysterical fit, a bad mood, a severe case of PMS, or a chemical imbalance. It was a *deliberate human invention*, created by certain people at a certain time and in a certain place.

◆ *The Invention of the Invisible Woman* The things we usually think of as "inventions" are objects that we can see and touch, or perhaps processes we can use (like a new way to take the salt out of seawater). But the biggest human inventions, the ones that have the most powerful impact on our daily lives, are hardly ever recognized as human constructions. They are the *systems of behavior* we use to interact with one another, to get our physical, emotional, and social needs met. Every culture on earth has developed certain ways to regulate human behavior: laws, customs, traditions, and the unofficial rules sociologists refer to as "norms."

The members of each culture begin to absorb these rules about human life almost from the moment of birth—and because the rules are so deeply learned, they often aren't recognized as human inventions. When a child asks why she should follow these cultural rules, the only answer may be "Because that's how it's done." By the time we reach adulthood, we have absorbed millions and millions of "rules" about how we should behave, and we have been trained not to question them—they are just *how it's done*. Should the rules ever stop working or become counterproductive, we may not even realize that other options exist. We may not be able to see that our way of life is not an immutable law of nature, but simply a set of constructions devised by human beings; an invention that may be adjusted or tinkered with just as deliberately as any mechanical device.

In Annie Leonard's case, she, her husband, and every other person at the infamous Dinner of Tears were operating on a set of social constructs and assumptions that were last "adjusted" during a particularly innovative time in the history of our culture. The time was about four hundred years ago, during a period known as the Enlightenment. The place was Western Europe, and the "inventors" were a group of remarkable philosophers, the thinkers who shape a society's view of the world. In the next few pages, I'll go into some detail about the way Enlightenment thinkers perceived society, because knowing how they set up the constructs of our culture *then* and *there* is the only way to understand what's happening to women like Annie Leonard here and now.

THE DARK AGES AND THE ENLIGHTENMENT

We all know that the government of the United States was founded by European pilgrims who came to the New World to realize the ideals of freedom and equality. The reason these ideals meant so much to early Americans is that along with their egalitarian ideals, they had inherited a culture of *in*equality and subjugation that went back to early European history. The Enlightenment got its name from the fact that it "lit up" the Western world after the grim period of history known as the Dark Ages.

One thing that always impresses me, when I read books or watch documentaries about the Dark Ages, is the amount of flogging that went on. You'd think that in the Dark Ages, it was hard to take a stroll through an average European village without seeing a couple of floggings in progress, and possibly getting flogged yourself. This is why I sometimes refer to the social structure of the Dark Ages as the Flogging Order. Old European societies were arranged in a hierarchy, like the "pecking orders" among chickens. There were several levels to the social pyramid. Your level in this pyramid determined which people you were entitled to flog, and which were entitled to flog you. Upper-level aristocrats could flog lower-level aristocrats. Lower-level aristocrats could flog freemen. Freemen flogged serfs. The king could flog anyone except possibly the clergy, who flogged themselves. And of course, all men were considered well within their rights when they flogged "their" women.

The belief that women "belonged" to men was related to the way Dark Age Europeans thought about social power in general, not only gender roles. In the Dark Ages, most Europeans were thought to be "owned" by their social superiors. Each nobleman had "his" own peasants, who grew crops on his land. The nobleman was entitled to live on these crops, and to more or less dictate how "his" peasants lived. In return, the upper classes were supposed to offer protection and sustenance to the people who "belonged" to them.

When this system worked, it created a symbiosis that functioned fairly well. The problem was that it was wide open to corruption. While powerful rich people had plenty of ways to make sure the weak and impoverished served them, the weak and impoverished didn't have any way to claim their part of the deal (sustenance and protection) if someone in the upper classes decided not to cooperate. If a bad king or aristocrat decided to tax "his" people until they starved, overwork them, flog them unmercifully, or in some other way break the code of social conduct, he could do so without much risk to himself. This made abuse of power all too common in the Dark Ages.

During the Enlightenment, which began in the sixteenth century, many of Europe's best thinkers began to question the underlying philosophy of the Flogging Order. Over the next few centuries, these "social philosophers" would slowly popularize some ideas that would become the foundation of the modern United States, shape a large portion of each of our lives, and eventually cause Annie Leonard to burst into tears at a restaurant table in 1993. I'm going to go through some of these ideas quite carefully, because, as we will see, they still impact each of us, every day of our lives. They underlie the pressures that you face every day as you go out into your social environment. Some of these ideas may seem utterly obvious to you, because you've been familiar with them practically since you were born. But at the historical moment when they were introduced, they were new and revolutionary.

Enlightenment Idea #1: Observation Is Better Than Inspiration

The view of reality that powered the social hierarchy of Dark Age Europe was based on faith—faith in a combination of religious doctrines, ancient scholarship, and superstition. The society worked because everyone believed that its structure was divinely appointed, and that terrible things would (and *should*) happen to anyone who questioned it. Medieval Europeans believed that God had put the king and other aristocrats at the head of society, and that God expected the lower classes to stay in their place. Women occupied a lower social position than men because they were "the devil's gateway," the descendants of Eve who brought about Adam's fall from grace. Anyone—especially a woman—who stepped out of position in the Flogging Order, or even spoke out against inequality, was violating not only the law but also God's will.

The echoes of this belief still reverberate in the lives of American women. Consider this comment from Gretchen, a college student from New Jersey.

Gretchen, 21

I played Joan of Arc in my high school's production of *Saint Joan* [a play by George Bernard Shaw]. There's this scene at the beginning of the play where God is speaking to Joan and telling her that she is the only person who can save France from its enemies. She's terrified. She talks about being at the foot of this huge mountain and not knowing how to start climbing.

I was going through this scene in rehearsal one day and all of a sudden I started crying for real. Everyone thought, "Wow, she's really getting into character." But right then I was crying for myself, not just for Joan of Arc. I realized that even though she lived hundreds of years ago, I still had to deal with some of the same things she did. Here was this woman who desperately wanted to make a positive change in the world, and . . . as if it wasn't enough to have to do this job, she was going to be condemned for doing it. And of course that's what happened. She saved France, and [the English] burned her at the stake for being a witch.

Things aren't that different for a woman who wants to change the world today. It's so much harder for a woman to really change things than it is for a man. So many people still think strong women are witches. They may not burn us at the stake, but I still think there are a lot of people who would try to destroy a powerful woman for getting "out of her proper place." And they'd still think they were doing it for God and country.

As Gretchen observed, there is an unbroken cord running from Dark Age Europe to the present-day United States. In both societies, some people believe that women should remain in a subordinate position because God and tradition decree it. However, in the United States, another very powerful way of looking at life, the Enlightenment perspective, counterbalances the Dark Age veneration for tradition.

Toward the end of the sixteenth century, an English aristocrat named Francis Bacon put forward the radical idea that people should believe only what they see, rather than seeing only what they believe. In other words, Bacon said that people's idea of truth should be based on what they can observe with their physical senses, rather than what they are told by established traditions. Observation, he said, is better than inspiration.

This idea became the foundation for the modern scientific method. Eventually it would lead to the development of everything from modern medicine to space travel. In Bacon's day, it inspired more and more educated upper-class men to think and write like modern scientists, and the information base of European society began to expand rapidly.

The belief in "observation over inspiration" still affects women today, just as the belief in the old Flogging Order still affects us. I interviewed women who clung to Bacon's ideas just as fervently as any European nobleman of the Enlightenment.

For example, since 1965, Eloise has been the only female biology professor at a small but elite college in the American Northeast. She has taught very little in recent years, having turned most of her attention to running a career-counseling center for women graduates. Eloise firmly believes that the only way to help her students achieve their potential is to rely strictly on the scientific method.

Eloise, 66

The reason I went into science, back when women were only taking courses in literature and art, is that in science, there are clear answers that you can see, right there in front of you. If I create an experiment that helps move knowledge forward, and if other scientists find that the experiment can be successfully replicated, nobody can argue with the results just because a woman found them first. That's why Marie Curie's work still stands, even though she was way ahead of her time. She was using the modern scientific method, and nobody has been able to fault her research.

I tell my female students, "Stick to things you can prove." I tell them that people have tried to "put me in my place" for years, but in science, the results are right there. Solid. Visible. The only way to make any change is by sticking to what you can see.

♦ *"Modern" and "Traditional" Thinking* Eloise used the term "modern scientific method" to describe her approach to life. The word "modern" is a very important marker for the new way of thinking and behaving that emerged during the European Enlightenment. The word entered the English language in the late sixteenth century, just about the time Francis Bacon's ideas were becoming popular. All the social and philosophical changes that followed the "observational" method of looking at the world were called "modern" innovations—as opposed to religiously based, hierarchically organized "traditional" society.

In this book, I'll be using the words "modern" and "traditional" in this very specific sense. In everyday speech, these words are used to mean several different things. All those shades of meaning are valid. But in these pages, for the purposes of understanding the world American women are living in, I'd like to use the word "modern" to refer to the way of thinking that emerged from the Enlightenment, and the word "traditional" to refer to the worldview in which human beings "belonged" to one another and were obligated to remain interdependent.

Enlightenment Idea #2: Rationality Is God

Once European scholars set out to discover truth by observation, instead of inspiration, they soon found themselves drawing logical conclusions about the things they observed. These conclusions didn't always agree with the existing, "orthodox" view of the world, and traditional authorities were not pleased by them. For example, Galileo observed the motions of the planets and calculated that the only explanation for what he saw was that the sun, not the earth, was the center of our solar system. This directly contradicted the contemporary religious belief that human beings were at the center of God's universe.

The Catholic Church didn't formally accept Galileo's version of the solar system until the 1980s. In his own time, only the most radical Enlightenment scholars agreed with him. Those who believed Galileo did so because they had come to accept logical calculation—reason, or rationality—as more powerful than the existing, scripturally based versions of reality.

The battle between these two worldviews still continues in American culture. You can see it in our educational system. Modern views about things like the earth's creation and the development of species are still being contested by people who accept the biblical premise that God created the earth in seven days, and put various species (including humans) on it without involving evolution.

Modern thinkers today, just like their counterparts in the European Enlightenment, dispute the biblical account in favor of what they observe and calculate. In their worldview, reason, or "rational" thinking, plays the same role that God plays for traditionalists: it is the ultimate source for discovering and validating truth. In the modern view, a person can challenge any idea, even religious belief, *as long as that person is thinking and behaving rationally.* This is exactly the reason that Eloise insists her female students learn "scientific" ways of thinking. As long as the "rational" rules of logic and reason are followed to the letter, she believes, no one can negate a woman's conclusions just because she's female. For a thoroughgoing modern thinker, "rational" thought and action cancel out all the possible contradictions anyone may have against a given argument.

Because "rationality" was the cornerstone of truth for modern thinkers, the scholars of the Enlightenment were careful to define exactly what "rationality" was. The way Enlightenment philosophy came to define it, "rational" thought and action were *thought or action based on physical observation and logical calculation, designed to improve the material well-being of the individual.*

Enlightenment Idea #3: The Individual over the Group

In traditional society, people's status and well-being had been tied to the status and well-being of the person to whom they "belonged." If the king was wealthy, the kingdom was wealthy. If one knight was better off than another, the peasants in his little village were supposed to have a higher standard of living than the other peasants. The servant of a great noble could look down his nose at the servant of a poorer master. If a husband was part of the nobility, his wife and children were nobility as well. Everyone's place in society was measured by the position of the leader—the person God had placed at the head of the social group.

If you think this idea has no impact on your life, think again. Many surveys and censuses in the United States still measure individual well-being in terms of the money earned by the "HOH"—the Head Of Household. Most American women are still renamed when they marry, so as to establish that they now "belong to" their husbands rather than their fathers. The invitation Annie Leonard received to the famous Dinner of Tears referred to her as "Mrs. Jeff Leonard," not even acknowledging that she had a name apart from Jeff's. Nowadays some American women, thinking along modern lines, decide to use their own names even after they are married, to emphasize the fact that they do not "belong" to their husbands. But if you check your telephone book, you will still see most families listed as a single, male name.

Enlightenment philosophers questioned this kinship-based, group-oriented way of assigning social position. After all, if observation and rational calculation are the ultimate source of truth, then anyone who can observe and calculate has equal access to truth. If that is so, then there is no need to defer to special, privileged people whom God has appointed as leaders. Every rational person should be able to think things out individually. In modern thinking, the rational individual, not the clan or group, became the unit of society.

Enlightenment Idea #4: Equality over Hierarchy

If any rational person is equally able to access truth, the staggering political implication is that *all rational individuals in a society should be considered equal under the law.* "Rational individual" is another key term I'll be using throughout this book. You see, Enlightenment scholars most emphatically didn't say that *all the people* in a society should be equal. Being considered a full-fledged individual, with the right to equality, was tied directly to being "rational." Since rationality had taken the place of God for Enlightenment scholars, acting rationally had the same impact on them as being born into a God-given hierarchy had on their traditional forebears. (Not coincidentally, the capacity to think rationally was assumed to belong only to people who were at the white, educated intellectual's social level or above.)

Americans still venerate traditional ideas about belonging to families and establishing hierarchies of respect and interdependence. On the other hand, we also believe that if a young person, like Albert Einstein, comes up with a great rational idea, people who are older, have fancier titles, or wield more power should listen to that young person simply because his ideas are more rational than theirs. The right to be considered equal to people who are higher in the traditional Flogging Order still rests on an individual's ability to think rationally.

This was much more obvious during the European Enlightenment than it is today. Americans tend to have two misconceptions about the phrase "all men are created equal" in our Declaration of Independence. The first misconception is that Thomas Jefferson came up with the phrase. The second is that it was meant to refer to all people, male or female, rich or poor, Caucasian or not.

Actually, the words "all men are created equal" was originally written by a British philosopher named John Locke, some time before the Revolutionary War. *And when Locke wrote "all men are created equal," it was with the understanding that he, like the Enlightenment scholars who went before and after him, was referring not to all people, but only to people like him: property-owning adult white males.* Women and people of color were most definitely *not* included—for reasons we shall see. This is the key to understanding why Jeff Leonard has been so richly rewarded for his contribution to society, while Annie's equally important life's work gains her almost nothing in the way of money, prestige, or power.

ENLIGHTENMENT ASSUMPTIONS: HOW JEFF GOT TO BE A LOT MORE EQUAL THAN ANNIE

Almost every human being takes some things for granted. To a well-tended baby, for example, having a parent respond to every fuss and whimper seems to represent the correct and natural functioning of the universe. Moreover, young children assume that their life situation is pretty much the same as everybody else's. I remember going to a friend's house when I was about three and wondering why my friend's family did not have normal silverware. "Normal" silverware, of course, was silverware in the same pattern as the silverware in my parents' house. It had never occurred to me that even in such a trivial detail, other people's lives might differ from my own.

This kind of assumption is exactly what Enlightenment thinkers made when they designed their model of a perfect society. To be a modern scholar in Enlightenment Europe, you pretty much had to be an aristocratic man. Peasants had no education, and religious authorities, such as monks and priests, studied the Bible rather than modern philosophy.

Naturally, the men who became modern scholars were most aware of the social inequalities that affected *them* negatively. Specifically, they weren't crazy about having other men, from higher strata of the society, rule over them. Their modern alternative to traditional society was designed to prove that *they* were equal to the men who were higher up than they were in the Flogging Order.

At the same time, however, these scholars were benefiting from the traditional labor of those who occupied a social position *below* them. Very few modern scholars ever had to do any domestic work, such as household cleaning and maintenance, and they were not expected to spend much time caring for other people, either physically or emotionally. All of that sort of lowly, "subrational" work was done *for* them. Most Enlightenment thinkers lived in economies enriched by slavery, many had servants, and virtually all of them could rely on the unpaid, constant, supportive labor of women.

When the Enlightenment philosophers outlined their ideal society, then, it was a society where every rational individual would do rational work (the kind of work philosophers did), and be equal to every other rational individual. *This model of society assumed, as a matter of course, that all rational individuals would have all their traditional work done for them, by people who did not work for money, but for the traditional rewards of protection and sustenance.*

This is why Annie Leonard's life's work could simply be overlooked as though it were invisible by the "professional" side of her society. The work Jeff Leonard does at his company is directly descended from the kinds of work male aristocrats did during the Enlightenment. Annie's daily labors, on the other hand, are closer to the work done by the *servants* of those aristocrats. When Jeff spends ten hours in the office, everyone agrees that he is doing a Real Job. When Annie spends ten hours cleaning, cooking, and helping her children grow up to be productive human beings, she doesn't even show up on the radar screen of Modern Careers.

THE INVISIBLE MAJORITY

The way Enlightenment philosophers reconciled the idea of social equality with their own desire to hold on to the advantages they got from the traditional system was this: they simply believed that everyone below them in the social order was incapable of rational behavior. To us, the idea of human equality and the idea that some human beings are "subrational" seem completely incompatible. But the Enlightenment philosophers came from a society where the idea of different "types" of human being had never been challenged. God had created the human race with a clear hierarchy in mind, and He simply hadn't given rational minds to women or people of color. Non-Caucasians often weren't even considered "human," and women were simply "incomplete" or "corrupt" forms of human life that served as vehicles for bringing fully human beings (white males) into being. Lower-class men were in lowly circumstances because God had put them there, and literally made them different from kings and princes and other noblemen.

In short, the Enlightenment definition of free-and-equal citizens made a huge stride toward equality by claiming that all rational beings should be equal under the law, but it didn't include lower-class men, people of color, or women, any more than it included hunting dogs or workhorses. The philosophers didn't expect that women and servants would ever even think to ask for equality, any more than you would expect your cat to march up to you shouting, "Catch your own damn mice—I'm running for Congress!" No, the scholars of the Enlightenment just assumed that the people who did traditional work for them did so because it was part of their intrinsic nature. Women and servants couldn't be rational individuals—would never even *want* to be—because they were incapable of thinking or acting rationally.*

The society of the United States was based on this Enlightenment social model, complete with the assumption that there will always be a large pool of competent adults who are not free-and-equal citizens, but subrational creatures whose only role in life is to provide for the traditional needs of rational men. This belief was taken so much for granted that it didn't even bear mentioning in most philosophers' descriptions of a perfect civilization. But it was most definitely there.

What this means is that in the philosophical ideal on which our nation

---

* To illustrate this further, consider that many scientists who believe firmly in the theory of evolution—that we are literally related to other life-forms—still consider it scientific heresy to suggest that animals have consciousness, or even emotions. If you own a cat or a dog, you know darn well when your pet feels anxious, sad, angry, happy. But many people still insist that the inner life of animals is utterly different from that of humans—or that animals have no "inner life" at all. This makes it easy to dismiss moral issues such as whether or not killing animals is a form of murder, or the eradication of a species a form of genocide. In order to feel comfortable chewing one's steak, it helps to think of cattle as completely devoid of feelings. This is exactly the way early rationalists kept themselves comfortable with the idea of relying on the menial labor of others—by claiming that specific groups of "others" had no ability or desire to appreciate the world the way a "rational man" could.

is based, the people, the time, the effort, and the skill required to do traditional work are not considered a part of the ideal society. The people have to be there, mind you, but neither they nor their work is ever really credited; they are a sort of invisible support staff for modern society. As far as society itself is concerned, they simply do not bear mentioning. They are there the way sunshine and rain are there, as necessary natural phenomena that operate in the background of rational individuals' lives.

By now you should have some idea why Annie Leonard began to wonder whether she even existed. Her husband, Jeff, his coworkers, the CEO Norman Manchester, are all part of the cultural heritage of Enlightenment Europe. In their worldview—a worldview older than the United States itself—society is composed of rational men who work and succeed in certain narrowly defined segments of human activity. Traditional work, such as the maintenance of domestic life and the care of people who are not fully independent, is "nonrational."

This is why Norman Manchester could sit with a group of eight people, use the phrase "all of you," and still refer only to the four *men* at the table. Descendants of the Enlightenment tradition have always used the language of universal equality ("all men," "mankind," "humanity," etc.) to refer to the narrow segment of the population they considered rational. This is why, for example, the United States government was set up to fulfill "democratic" ideals—government by, for, and of the people— but initially prohibited women, the poor, and people of color from voting. It is why American medical and psychological scholars still publish articles on health and disease "in humans," when in fact the researchers have studied only men. It is why huge segments of our "free-and-equal society" have never been free or equal. And it is the reason that no matter how diligent, competent, and successful Annie Leonard may be at the crucially important, extremely demanding task of maintaining her family's well-being, she will never be rewarded with the recognition, money, or power her husband earns at the office.

The deep-rooted assumptions of Enlightenment philosophy also explain why Jeff, as loving and well intentioned as he is, simply doesn't understand why Annie feels unhappy in her "invisible" role. He is in the position of the well-cared-for child who has never questioned that his parents' lives just naturally revolve around him. Neither Jeff nor Annie realizes that the ways they think about gender, work, status, and wealth are not simply laws of nature. They have never articulated the fact that their attitudes, social roles, and ideas about "proper behavior" were constructed and taught to them as human inventions; the process was so much a part of their bedrock life experience that they never even noticed it.

This works well for Jeff, who is able to fit into the Enlightenment ideal of the rational individual *because his gender and social position put him pretty close to the position of an Enlightenment scholar*. But Annie's life is not so simple. She is part of a system that speaks in terms of "equality for all individuals," and yet assumes that women are not included in this all-inclusive phrase. Our society has deeply internalized two opposite systems—modern egalitarianism and traditional hierarchy—without ever clearly articulating the contradiction between them.

Annie, like all Americans, has been educated and socialized in the Enlightenment-based ethic of individual achievement, which says that all rational individuals are created equal. But her society also expects her to serve as the "invisible" support system for rational individuals. And no matter how much Annie achieves in that task, the work she does disappears into the fuzzy background of perceptions, into the mass of "sub-rational" labor done, not by full members of the society, but by Somebody Else. No wonder Annie is haunted by the feeling that she doesn't exist. In the major philosophical system that underlies our society, she literally doesn't.

FELICIA WOODMAN

To get an image of how profoundly American society operates on the contradictory system of modern and traditional ideals, we need to take a closer look at how our Founding Fathers built contradictory ideas about equality into the laws, policies, and structures of United States society. To introduce that topic, let's take a look at another story from an American woman's life.

Felicia Woodman seems to have little in common with Annie Leonard, but in fact the two women share personal histories complicated by the United States' dual value system. Felicia is a beautifully statuesque, articulate, thoughtful African-American woman who confronts the stressful issues in her own life not by disrupting birthday parties, but by writing startling, fiery, highly original poetry. Despite the fact that she never got good grades and had dropped out of high school at fifteen, Felicia was angrily eloquent when I interviewed her in 1988.

Felicia, 20

The way I see it, this whole country runs on broken promises. They tell you you're supposed to have equality. They tell you you're supposed to be supported as a mother. They tell you your color and your sex don't matter, that everybody's got the same chance to succeed. They make you think you're free, you know—free to do anything and have the life you want. But they're lying. You try to live on those promises, and you find out that this country breaks every one of them.

Once you've heard some of her story, it isn't hard to see why Felicia is so bitter. She grew up in a rundown neighborhood in New York City. By the time she was five years old, Felicia had heard every discriminatory label and stereotype that had ever been assigned to people of her race. She struggled to maintain her self-esteem, but it was hard for Felicia to accept herself as she slowly realized that the color of her skin was a major disadvantage in U.S. society.

At thirteen, Felicia was sullen and depressed much of the time, and her grades in school dropped off. She was often sent to study hall in the school library for lack of attention and unfinished homework. While she was there, she read books and articles about the history of African-Americans and the struggle for equality, past and present. There were no easy answers for her in anything she read. The history of slavery, and the marks it had left on her own experience, made Felicia feel steadily more disenchanted with American society and discouraged about her own future.

When I was about fifteen, they sent me to this guidance counselor who was visiting our school. This woman started telling me that the only way I was going to be successful in my life was by studying hard and staying in school. I told her that I could study 'til the end of the world, and I still wouldn't have a snowball's chance in hell of being successful in this country.

Discouraged and overwhelmed, Felicia began to skip school and hang around with her boyfriend, who had dropped out the year before. This was a move she would come to regret, but as she told me, "That was where I was at that time. It felt like I was at the starting point on this long road, where people like me had to start way behind everybody else."

By sixteen, Felicia was pregnant. A month before her baby was born, her boyfriend left New York to work in his older brother's auto-body shop in Chicago. He promised to send money back and eventually have Felicia and the baby move to Illinois to join him. Felicia smiled wryly when she told me that. "The guy was history," she said. "I knew I'd never hear from him again." She never did. She continued to live with her mother and an older sister in Brooklyn, and got a job as a floor clerk at Sears.

The night she went into labor, Felicia related, she was struck with an overwhelming sense of sadness and fear.

> It wasn't so much the labor pains, you know. It was this feeling like, "Oh my God, I'm bringing this tiny person into the world and I don't have any way to keep this baby safe." It was like I didn't want to let her be born, because she was safe as long as she was inside me, but the outside world—no, that just wasn't safe enough for her. I knew what she was getting into, you know. After she was born I looked at her and I thought, "She's so little, and she don't know anything about what she's up against. She don't know that the little newborn white boy baby in the next little crib is any different from her. And he don't know it either. But they're gonna find out, you know. They're gonna find out all that stuff, way too soon."

After her daughter, Serena, was born, Felicia's life became even more difficult. Her desire to keep her daughter safe touched with anxiety everything she did. "It's one thing to be poor . . . when you're on your own," she said, "but when there's a baby to take care of, it gets scary." Felicia's sister had just had a baby of her own, and their mother couldn't give up her job to help with child care. Felicia tried to find affordable day care, but soon discovered that after paying for it, she couldn't stretch her salary far enough to pay for food.

She tried leaving little Serena with a neighbor, who offered to baby-sit for very little money. "The first day I came home, and Serena was lying in the corner, screaming, just shaking. Her diaper hadn't been changed all day." Felicia quit her job and became the full-time caretaker for her daughter and her six-month-old nephew. She also applied for welfare for the first time in her life.

> I want to get off welfare, but if I work at the kind of jobs I can get and I earn a little money, they take away the welfare support. Then I got nothing to spend on taking care of Serena. If I stay home and get wel-

fare, I got someone to care for my baby—me—*and* a little money. Not enough, but some. If I got a job, paid for day care, and tried to live on the rest, we would starve.

Felicia, like Annie Leonard, is suffering the consequences of a culture that claims to offer universal equality, but does so from an incomplete and unrealistic model of human needs, one that requires an "invisible" domestic support system for every individual. For Felicia, however, the problem of gender is compounded by race. Her problems are based in seventeenth-century European philosophy just as Annie Leonard's are, but in Felicia's case, the historical process that created her dilemmas have been vastly complicated by the taste of sugar and the texture of underwear.

HOW SWEET FOOD AND SOFT CLOTHES DEEPENED THE CONTRADICTION IN AMERICAN VALUES

We've already seen how the scholars of the European Enlightenment created a model of an ideal society in which "everybody" (meaning all white, property-owning adult males) would be considered free-and-equal rational individuals. They oriented their philosophy around two sets of deep core values.

Core values are beliefs we hold so dear that they influence every action and decision; ideas we live by and, if need be, are willing to die for. The ideal of universal equality and freedom was one of the core values the Enlightenment thinkers built into their vision of a perfect society. The other major core value is the idea that each individual is entitled to a traditional family life and all the advantages it held for adult upper-class males. In other words, the society of the United States was "programmed" by these deeply internalized cultural values to strive toward two ideals—one traditional and one modern—which were *designed to be fundamentally incompatible*.

In retrospect, the behavior of the early Americans who adopted this contradictory value system often seems almost unbelievably hypocritical. Consider the fact that while Thomas Jefferson wrote the stirring words "We hold these truths to be self-evident; that all men are created equal . . . ," his own slaves (one of whom was his wife's half-sister) were tending his garden, cleaning his house, cooking his food, and caring for all his other traditional needs. Slavery is an outrageous violation of the rational ideal of equality—unless you can convince yourself that certain individuals aren't "rational," and therefore do not truly belong in society. And the more people stand to gain from such an idea, the easier it is for them to accept.

Here's where the texture of underwear and the taste of sugar come in. One of the ways American colonists could get rich quick was to grow cash crops that didn't thrive in the climate of Western Europe but loved the hot, humid environment of southern North America. Of all these crops, the biggest sellers by far were cotton and sugarcane. Up until the eighteenth century, most Europeans wore a lot of wool and linen, and the wealthier people dressed in silk. But silk was prohibitively expensive for most commoners, and wool and linen, in case you haven't noticed, are scratchy. The commercials are right. Nothing else feels like cotton.

As for sugar, well, I think that should be self-explanatory to anyone who has ever sampled a dessert. Every human baby is born preferring sweet above all other tastes, and a lot of Americans never seem to grow out of it. In the eighteenth and nineteenth centuries, Asian writers commented with astonishment on what they saw as the white race's insatiable lust for sugar. The only thing they could compare it to was opium addiction. (Actually, that analogy is close enough to the truth to make me feel very uncomfortable about my own eating habits. I think I'll go have some Oreos to calm myself down.) The point is that when people realized they could buy sugar in large quantities from farmers in the southern American colonies, both Europeans and European-Americans started consuming the stuff like crazy.

All of this would eventually have a huge impact on the life of Felicia Woodman. If it hadn't been for cotton and sugar, Felicia probably wouldn't even have been born on the American continent. You see, not only do these crops require heat and humidity to grow, they also require an enormous amount of cultivation and processing before consumers can use them. In the eighteenth century, when American farmers began growing sugar and cotton in large quantities, the process had not been mechanized; it had to be done by people, and the less those people were paid, the bigger the farmer's profits were. The economic system of the American South was intimately, inextricably, connected to slavery.

DARK AGE AMERICA

To get the biggest possible profit from plantation farming, colonists in the southern United States established a culture not unlike the old European Flogging Order. This culture was more courtly and hierarchical than anything developed in the northern states. An upper-class southern gentleman held huge tracts of land, which were worked by "his" people. While the aristocrat's family bore his surname ("Scarlett O'Hara" became "Mrs. Rhett Butler"), his slaves were referred to with the same name, in the possessive ("O'Hara's Joe," or "Butler's Sally").

To justify owning and living off the labor of unpaid human beings, the aristocrats of the South developed a strong cultural belief that "subrational" people such as blacks and women not only accepted but *needed* a traditional social position, where their work for a rational individual would be rewarded by protection and sustenance. This is why chivalry toward women and the infantilization of non-Caucasians was a much stronger cultural norm in the southern colonies than in the North. Women were seen as fragile creatures in need of a male protector, and any nonwhite was seen as an overgrown child fit only for manual labor and other forms of servitude.

It is no coincidence that many of the problems in Felicia's life, and in the African-American community (lack of self-esteem and hope for the future, low level of education, broken relationships, absentee fathers, poverty), are exactly the conditions *created* by slave owners to keep slaves from organizing the kind of solidarity necessary for a successful revolt. The Enlightenment idea that rational individuals should be able to maximize their own well-being works a lot better for people who are born into a culture that nurtures their independence. Felicia did not have this privilege. More than a century after slavery was abolished in the United States, the social patterns it created are still operating in her life—as another African-American woman, Rohanna, told me.

Rohanna, 60

We think slavery was so long ago, but it really wasn't. My great-grandparents were slaves. My grandma still lived in the shack where she was born, off to the side of the owner's mansion. I'd go there when I was little, and she'd tell me stories about her parents' lives. You just go ahead and try to tell me that our society has left that time so far behind that it never affects us. I'm telling you, it affects us every day.

Because of its role in the economy, the grotesque double standard that led some Americans to believe in both equal rights and slavery was difficult to challenge. For example, the first time Thomas Jefferson publicly used the phrase "all men are created equal" was in court, defending the rights of a slave. However, Jefferson received such negative feedback for extending the idea of equality to a black man that he seems to have decided to pull back, focusing his energy on gaining American independence from monarchical England. He worried that the issue of slavery would divide the United States, and of course he was right.

Most of the policymakers who established the United States government shared Jefferson's uneasiness about speaking out against slavery and risking division within the ranks of American leaders. And so, in the United States, the subordination of "subrational" people was accepted as part of the national culture and encoded (or at least permitted) in legal, political, and economic systems. The upshot was that *at the same time American statesmen were creating the most egalitarian government on earth, they were concretizing economic, legal, and political structures that assumed the inferiority of women and people of color.*

THE GREAT AMERICAN LOOPHOLE

Some of the Founding Fathers of the United States truly seem to have wanted their new government to run on the principle of universal equality. Others seem to have assumed, at a very deep psychological level, that women and non-Caucasians were innately subrational and had no desire or ability to become "free-and-equal" citizens. As George Bernard Shaw would write, "The American forces the black slave to shine his boots; and concludes from this that the black is capable of nothing but bootshining."[1] The same could (and later would) be said of American attitudes toward women.

In fact, the assumption that women are subrational was even more deeply ingrained in the American consciousness than the idea of racial inequality. You see, while only some Americans, mostly Southerners, profited from slavery, virtually every American citizen (read "property-owning white male") benefited from the unpaid traditional labor of women. From the very beginning, a few people applied Enlightenment thinking to females, arguing that women were rational beings who deserved equality with men. Very few influential policymakers paid any attention to this idea. This was partly because the female perspective was almost entirely absent from the debates on the definition of "equality," partly because women themselves usually accepted their "subrational" status as *the way it's done*, but mainly because bringing women into the category of "rational individual" would have required an immense shift in both the worldview and the economy of the nascent United States.

We'll look more closely at early movements toward establishing women's political equality in the next chapter. Right now it's enough to know that female equality wasn't taken very seriously in a nation where most women's lives were wholly bound up in traditional labor (including the "labor" of frequent childbirth); where all the leaders were men who assumed that women would always take care of their traditional needs; and where a much more volatile disagreement over the issue of slavery was leading straight to the Civil War.

The important thing to remember is that the language of the United States' most basic governmental documents, such as the Declaration of Independence and the Constitution, is phrased in terms of *universal* equality. Intentionally or not, the framers of American government set the country up in such a way that, if they could prove themselves "rational," people of any race or gender could claim equal rights under the Constitution. Since traditional behavior gains few rewards in American culture, every American has strong incentives to qualify as a rational individual and gain equal rights under the law. As Tiesha, an American lawyer of Chinese ancestry, put it:

Tiesha, 35

The way things were written down in the laws of the United States isn't the way they are done. In practice, Americans act in ways that are racist and sexist all the time. The only good thing about it is that the way things were *written down* in the United States, the country has this basic commitment to equality. When you get trapped by the way Americans actually behave, you still have a little hope, because you can go back to the things they wrote down and demand your rights.

WHY ENLIGHTENMENT-STYLE EQUALITY WILL NEVER BE ENOUGH

The ideal of a society where every person is a free-and-equal citizen, doing rational things and enjoying the lifestyle of an Enlightenment gentleman, is a wonderful one. The only problem with it is that it doesn't work. The Enlightenment model of a "free-and-equal" citizen is a man who has all his social and domestic needs met by Someone Else.

If everyone qualified as a free-and-equal rational individual on the Enlightenment model—that is, if we all pursued our own material well-being by rational calculation, all the time—society would simply collapse. Nobody would be left to take care of the traditional work that makes our existence viable. The assumptions of the early American policymakers are still a part of our national culture. They are still encoded in our institutions. *Our society's structures still assume that a pool of free labor will always be available for each and every citizen.*

Because this ideal isn't workable, the ideas that justified slavery during the Colonial period not only survived the Civil War, but still thrive in the United States today—racism is one of the most volatile social issues in this country. Because American social structures also rely on the unpaid, invisible work of women, sexism is also alive and well in the United States. Any American woman knows this from experience. Any non-Caucasian American knows it. And women of color, like Felicia Woodman, know it (as Felicia told me) "way deep down in my bones."

THE INDUSTRIAL REVOLUTION
AND THE CRISIS OF THE YUPPIE PARENT

Whatever its drawbacks, the philosophy of the European Enlightenment created a framework that allowed society to move forward into unprecedented prosperity. The modern scientific method continued the rapid expansion of our knowledge base and spawned an amazing array of new technologies. Scientists operating on modern ideas found ways to lengthen human life, reduce the time and labor necessary to produce food and other necessities, and generally make people healthier and wealthier.

The United States, founded on and devoted to Enlightenment ideals, developed very rapidly from a backward frontier society to a booming modern economy. As modernization progressed, it created different ways of thinking about the work people do and the way they spend their time. The net effect on gender roles was to narrow the social role considered acceptable for American men, and to devalue "women's work" more than ever. This wasn't anyone's specific intention so much as the inevitable result of adopting modern ideals, and it ended up being hard on men and women alike. Let me show you what I mean.

GAYLE PERRY

Gayle Perry and her husband, Don Cordell, don't particularly like being referred to as Yuppies, but there's really no other way to describe them. They met as undergraduates at Boston University, where Don majored in psychology with a minor in economics, and Gayle, mindful of the lack of women in the hard sciences, was a computer science major. Don and Gayle were very committed to the idea of universal equality, including gender equality. They were the very model of the politically correct American couple.

For four years after their marriage, Gayle and Don were not only Yuppies, they were the Yuppiest kind of Yuppies; a Double Income, No Kids couple, known as "Dinks" in American parlance. Gayle did software development for a computer company. Don worked for a Boston securities firm. Each of them put in the time and energy it took to do well in their respective jobs, and they were rewarded for their diligence with promotions and raises. By the time they were both twenty-nine years old, they had saved enough money to put a down payment on a small but handsome brownstone apartment on Boston's fashionable Beacon Hill. They had an idyllic Yuppie lifestyle, meeting friends after work to attend plays and concerts, experimenting with the kinds of recipes that call for three different types of vinegar, decorating their apartment in a bold, contemporary style, complete with original ceramic sculptures and a lot of glass. Gayle thoroughly enjoyed her life, but as she approached her thirtieth birthday, she found herself growing restless.

Gayle, 32

I started to think about having a baby. All my friends were having kids, and you know, the old biological clock is always ticking. I used to go shopping and spend all my time at the Baby Gap store. They have the cutest outfits there. I'd look at the clothes and imagine dressing my own baby in them.

Don was a little surprised when Gayle brought up the subject of having a baby. He had always imagined he'd have children someday, but he hadn't expected the day to arrive quite so soon. It took him a couple of months to get used to the idea. Then one evening, on his way home from work, Don drove past Fenway Park and had a sudden image of himself sitting in the stands with an adoring son or daughter, eating hot dogs and showing the world of baseball to a child's wondering eyes. He bought a dozen roses and a bottle of good champagne, took them home to Gayle, and announced that he, too, was ready for parenthood.

A year later, Gayle and Don's son, Kevin, was delivered in a hospital birthing room, by a midwife, after a natural, drug-free labor. Don had coached Gayle through her Lamaze breathing exercises and played tapes of whale songs in the birthing room. Kevin was a beautiful baby, with

Don's blond hair and Gayle's delicate features. Everything was exactly the way Gayle had dreamed it would be. For about a week. After that, as Gayle succinctly put it, "everything went straight to hell."

Kevin slept about twenty hours a day during that first week. We thought that's how it would be forever, you know—until he left for college or something. . . . Looking back on it now, I think he was just resting up for a career in screaming.

The pediatrician told Gayle that Kevin was "a little colicky." This mild-sounding affliction translated into massive sleep deprivation for both Don and Gayle. Kevin slept in half-hour naps, revving his engines for another hour of bellowing.

I didn't know that a human being could function without sleeping more than thirty minutes at a stretch. Come to think of it, I'm not sure we can. Don and I got crazy after a month of not sleeping. We stopped cooking, we stopped talking, we stopped just about anything but wishing we were asleep.

As soon as she learned she was pregnant, Gayle had arranged three months of maternity leave and booked Kevin into a well-run day-care center near the apartment. She planned to leave a supply of breast milk with the center each day, so that Kevin could have the benefits of mother's milk and Gayle would still be free to go back to her job. Her coworkers had been impressed by the efficiency with which she had set about combining motherhood with her intense, high-pressure career.

The first day I tried to go back to work was a nightmare. I thought you could arrange child care the way I arranged everything else in my life. I got up at five to get everything ready to go, put Kevin in this Baby Gap outfit, and drove to the day-care center. I gave my frozen breast milk to the kitchen worker and went to the newborn center.
When I got there, there were five babies crying. The workers were trying to deal with all of it at once. Of course, Kevin started screaming too. Then I realized he'd messed his diaper, and it had gotten all over his clothes. I didn't have a spare outfit. I had to borrow one from the staff. Then, while I'm changing Kevin, the kitchen worker comes in and says they tried to thaw my breast milk in the microwave, and the plastic containers melted. They wanted more breast milk from me right

then. Gayle, the Dairy Queen. I was so tired and frustrated that I started crying. . . .

In the end, the day-care thing didn't work out the way we thought it would. I left Kevin there for a week or so, but he screamed the whole time and I was miserable leaving him. Plus, by the time I got to the office I felt like I'd already worked a full day. I'd figured out how long it would take me to do everything, but I hadn't figured on how tired I would be. It was like saying, "Okay, I can walk ten miles in two hours, so I should be able to walk about a hundred and twenty miles every day." It worked on paper, but not in real life.

Gayle decided to cut back to half-time work. She went in to the office in the evenings, when Don was home. That way, Gayle could stay with Kevin until a little after five, then leave for the office and work until nine, returning home by ten. They could dispense with day care altogether, which was a good thing, because the drop in Gayle's income was making things rather tight financially. It looked like a pretty good plan.

The problem was that Don wasn't used to being home by five o'clock sharp. Even though everyone at his company had "nine-to-five" jobs, they actually worked late almost every night. It was just expected.

Before Kevin was born, Don worked late most nights, like everybody else. Now he was watching the clock every day, and leaving at five o'clock. When he explained that he was going home to take care of his son—well, let's just say that wasn't an excuse his boss respected.

When Kevin was six months old, Don received his first negative performance report. Both Don and Gayle were stunned. The firm where Don worked was notoriously cutthroat. Those who didn't climb tended to lose their jobs rather quickly.

We were terrified. We'd been on top of the world, and now all of a sudden we were seriously looking at losing our apartment. We sat down and had a serious talk. I decided to take a leave of absence from my job so that Don could "prove himself" to his company. It seemed like the only thing we could do. After all, I was breast-feeding. It was harder for me to work full-time because of that. And we needed Don's job to survive. But right after we made the decision, I woke up one night and I thought, "God help us, we've turned into our parents!"

Neither Don nor Gayle was content with their lifestyle. Gayle felt cooped up and exhausted by taking care of the baby twenty-four hours a day, and she missed her colleagues and her work. For his part, Don missed being intimately involved with Kevin's infancy. "Sometimes," he told me, "I have dreams that Kevin had grown up and left home, and I never even knew what he looked like." In their gloomier moments, it seemed to Gayle and Don that they were trapped in a predestined family curse.

As I sat in their brownstone apartment listening to Gayle, I could certainly understand why they might feel this way. But of course the problem didn't start with Gayle's childhood, or Don's. It started with the Industrial Revolution.

THE INDUSTRIAL REVOLUTION AND THE CREATION OF THE SLEEPLESS PARENT

The Industrial Revolution was yet another result of modernization, and it got rolling early in those countries where modern ideas about thought, science, and politics first took hold. Before the Industrial Revolution, most people lived on farms, where they grew their own food and hand-made most of their clothing, housing, and tools. Gradually, the production of these things moved to factories, where it was easier and cheaper to turn out consistent, reliable products at a low cost. In order to buy these factory-made goods, people needed cash, and manufacturers paid in cash for labor. As modernization progressed, the United States gradually switched from an agricultural to a manufacturing economy.

This dramatically changed the way most American families operated. In an agricultural economy, extended families lived and worked together, on the same land. In a manufacturing economy, men would leave for the workplace early in the day, returning home when the day's work was done. This made it essential for women to remain at home, caring for children and property. The labor of men and women became more and more "split," in terms of both geography (where they worked) and function (what they did). The effect of this was to accentuate the difference between the lifestyle of rational men, who were free to go out and sell their labor to the highest bidder on the public market, and that of "sub-rational" females, who were taking over more and more of the U.S.'s domestic, private, traditional work.

This was not an unmixed blessing for American men. Competition for jobs meant that the men who were willing to devote the most time and energy to their jobs won out over men who had more varied interests. Naturally, the industrial workplace did not expect a workingman to need time to do things like care for children, cook, or clean house. The typical American job that evolved during the Industrial Revolution was designed for a worker who had a full-time domestic support staff that freed him from all traditional responsibilities. In other words, *the whole structure of the American economy was built on the assumption that every single worker has a wife.*

This is true of American jobs to this day. As Sibyl, a line worker in an automobile plant, told me:

Sibyl, 41

My husband works in the same building I do, and his job is pretty much like mine. Let me tell you, by the end of the day on a job like that, you're tired. Me and Hal go home together, and we're both pooped out. But he expects me to take care of him and fix him a hot meal. I don't have the energy for it. The job takes the day's work all out of you.

Because the modern worker's job was designed to require every bit of effort from someone who had a free, full-time support staff, the ever-widening division between men's and women's work during the Industrial Revolution created a good deal of stress *for both sexes.* Men did earn cash, but their jobs demanded all of their time and narrowed the focus of their lives to the unromantic purpose of increasing their employer's revenues. A preindustrial farmer worked extremely hard, but he also had the freedom to set his own schedule, watch his children grow up, and take an occasional nap. Farming has a rhythmic quality: during the fallow periods, such as midwinter, an early American farming man would repair tools but also swap stories with his family, learn to play the guitar, hunt, whittle, or just sit and think. A worker in the industrial economy lost the variety and autonomy of these activities, often in workplaces that were about as exciting and energizing as a lump of lead.

WHY *WALDEN* WASN'T WRITTEN BY THOREAU'S MOTHER

In the nineteenth century, observers of the American scene were horrified to see what the Industrial Revolution was doing to men's lives. I learned about this the summer before I started my first year at Harvard.

Like all incoming freshmen, I received a list of books I was supposed to have read by the time school started in the autumn. Since I was not a prep-school graduate with Ivy League parents and infinite *savoir-faire*, but an extremely nervous seventeen-year-old from a small town in the boondocks, I read all of them. I thought there was going to be some kind of quiz the day I arrived in Massachusetts—perhaps a checkpoint at the airport: "Please lay your bags on their sides on the conveyor belt and discuss the implications of X-ray machines in terms of Plato's Cave." As it turned out, no one ever asked me about these books, but clearly Harvard thought every well-educated young American should know them.

One of the classics on the list was *Walden*, by Henry David Thoreau. Thoreau lived in the American Northeast in the early to mid-1800s. Watching the effect of grinding, constant, mindless industrial labor on his fellow American men, Thoreau wrote that most of them "live lives of quiet desperation." To prove that there was no need for men to be absorbed by the great machine of industry, Thoreau set out alone into the New England forest and built a small cabin at the edge of one Walden Pond. He lived there for a solid year. *Walden* is his diary from this time. It is full of poetic commentary about the simplicity of living in accord with nature, and the ease with which Thoreau was able to meet all his own needs without having to give up all his time and energy to Industry.

Like millions of Americans before me, I was both moved and convinced by Thoreau's masterpiece. I'm sure every Harvard freshman who actually got around to reading *Walden* was equally persuaded that human needs are simple and easily met, and that we should all devote our lives to enriching our experience and thinking deep thoughts.

Imagine my surprise when, some years later, I discovered that the "ease and simplicity" of Thoreau's life had a lot to do with the fact that his mother and sister had brought in prepared food and taken away his laundry for washing and repair almost every day during the entire time he was at Walden. His neighbors in the Walden Pond vicinity were quoted as saying that poor old Henry would have starved to death in a week without the staunch support of his female relatives.

I felt deeply betrayed by this revelation. It occurred to me that perhaps Thoreau's mother could have written an equally moving treatise on the ease and simplicity of human life if she hadn't been cooking, cleaning, and mending for Henry and the other Thoreaus day in and day out. *Walden*, while without doubt a terrific book, perpetuated exactly the same idea that had characterized Enlightenment thinking centuries earlier: that the lives of rational men must be rescued from social bondage, whereas the lives of women simply didn't enter into the equation. A man supported by the constant labor of women was the equivalent of a man living in noble and self-sufficient isolation.

THE DISAPPEARING FEMALE

By sharpening the division between "men's work" and "women's work," the Industrial Revolution not only narrowed the scope of male life; it also made women's lives even more invisible than they had been before. Now men worked at job sites where women were rarely even seen. Men earned cash for their labor in an economy that was becoming more cash-based all the time. Unpaid work, in a cash economy, doesn't count as "productive" work, no matter how essential it may be to sustaining society. Women were excluded from "public" work, and the absence of men in the "private" world of the home increased the necessity for women to do a larger and larger share of traditional labor.

"Women's work" was unpaid; therefore, as the United States switched to a cash economy, it came to be seen as worthless. Women were working harder than ever, at precisely the same time that their work was almost totally devalued.

And how did this eventually lead to serious sleep deprivation for Gayle Perry and Don Cordell, young Yuppie parents extraordinaire? It did so by creating cultural structures and expectations that every employee will have *both* a traditional family *and* complete freedom from any aspect of traditional work. Both Don and Gayle were in jobs designed on this assumption. As long as they were able to act like the Enlightenment model of a rational individual, they both reaped rich rewards from their social system. But when their traditional responsibilities suddenly increased, they found that the well-ordered, predictable modern workplace didn't leave room for the messy, unpredictable demands of parenthood. Little Kevin didn't act at all like a rational individual, and he protested in a most inconsiderate manner when his parents tried to act like rational individuals themselves.

Gayle and Don would have encountered similar difficulties if they had tried to care for a sick parent, fallen ill themselves, suffered an accidental injury, or even had a profound loss, like the death of a relative. The modern workplace expects people to operate very much like machines. It leaves precious little room for fatigue, grief, sickness, or time to care for other people.

Because Gayle and Don inherited the mind-set of Enlightenment scholars, they deeply believe that their status as free-and-equal citizens depends on excelling in this "rational" world. However, because they have also inherited the Enlightenment scholar's appreciation for his traditional family, Gayle and Don naturally think they should have that, too. The assumption that Somebody Else will always be available to do the traditional work has lasted well into an era when most adults, both male and female, are employed. This is creating tremendous stress on all Americans—but especially on women.

THE WOMEN'S ISSUES THAT AREN'T

The Enlightenment image of modern life works well as long as only *some* people try to enact it and the rest of the population does traditional work. But at heart, the United States' political, legal, and economic structures are directly antithetical to the needs of traditional institutions like the family *because they were designed to be that way.* Remember, way back in the sixteenth century, Enlightenment scholars proposed their rational model *in opposition to* traditional social structures. As society modernizes according to this model, traditional institutions become harder and harder to sustain.

This is not a gender issue. Originally, all lower-class people were expected to do traditional labor. Later, the United States granted rational-individual status to all adult white males, turning over traditional work to women and nonwhite men. When the Emancipation Proclamation granted full citizenship to American men of all races (in a strict legal sense, if not in practice), traditional responsibilities were left to the only group of adults still considered "subrational": women. The reason issues like child care, domestic work, and birth control have been labeled "women's issues" is not that they don't affect men, but that women don't have any other group to whom they can pass the buck of caring for the traditional needs of society.

I often hear social analysts, from highly trained experts to talkative cabdrivers, pointing out that a number of problems are on the rise because American women are "leaving the home." Actually, *all* American adults have left the home under economic and social pressure to act as rational individuals. Ironically, *women get the blame not because they bailed out of traditional responsibilities early on, but because they are the last to go.*

I have never counted the exact number of women who have told me that they feel guilty and culpable for "leaving" their homes to take paid employment, but the number is well into the hundreds. On the other hand, I rarely hear anyone complaining that men should "get back to the home" in order to keep the family running—not even the women who have told me how difficult it is to manage as the only adult present in the home. I have heard vivid descriptions of women's loneliness, exhaustion, worry, and sometimes terror as they dealt with sick children, ruptured water pipes, invading prowlers, broken hips, car accidents, house fires, and a huge array of other catastrophes while their husbands were away (either out of town or at the office), doing "real work." None of them has ever suggested that men have "abandoned" the home by taking paying jobs.

In this respect, American women are following the trend of the culture in general. For example, you'd be hard-pressed to come up with a dozen studies investigating the relationship between, say, children's tendency to juvenile delinquency, or emotional illness, or failure to thrive, and "fathers working outside the home." Almost all such studies—and trust me, there are plenty of them—focus on *women's* "abandonment" of the traditional family. But the truly traditional family had at least *two* adults at home, and often many more than two.

In preindustrial days, grandparents, aunts and uncles, hired hands, and a variety of other adults might be present in the home at any time. Children were raised by *groups* of adults, not isolated caretakers. Most adults were able to provide for their own survival needs, and gain community respect, without leaving the family property. In a modern environment, however, where there is virtually no economic or social reward attached to domestic work or the care of others, even the most devoted grandmothers, aunts, or sisters (much less grandfathers, uncles, or brothers) now have fewer incentives to help solidify a traditional family. Instead, time taken to shore up family ties must be *subtracted* from time spent securing one's own well-being. In addition, the geographical mobility of our culture means that many friends and relatives who might *want* to pitch in and help a mother raise her children aren't in the same vicinity. All of these factors have been eroding the true traditional family—the group of interested adults raising children as part of a home economy—for some time now. As the last vestiges of that "typical" family have begun to fragment, women have taken more and more of the blame for things they cannot control, and received less and less of the credit for holding their families together in the face of enormous social and economic pressures.

DOUBLE MESSAGES

The core values that were built into United States culture at its inception are still firmly in place. A 1989 Gallup poll found that the desire for a modern, individual career and the desire for a traditional family are the two top priorities for Americans. This is hardly surprising. Who wouldn't want to live like a European gentleman, like Thomas Jefferson or Henry David Thoreau? Who wouldn't want to be free to focus all their attention on their personal well-being, yet still enjoy the emotional and psychological benefits of a traditional system that is cared for by Someone Else?

Over the course of our history, as modern ideals have granted this rational-individual status to more and more people, American women have increasingly been saddled with the task of maintaining our two contradictory core values. The more traditional work has been pushed into the invisible background of society, the more of it women have been expected to do. The more modern ideals have been rewarded and glorified, the more incentive women have to get out of their assigned position and claim equality for themselves.

Since before the United States became a nation, some Americans have argued that women, too, deserve the rights of a free-and-equal citizen. The dream they have is to give Annie Leonard a life's work as visible and remunerative as Jeff's, so that she, too, can have large Christmas bonuses and dinners with the CEO. The dream is to free Felicia Woodman from her captivity in the cycle of poverty and help her earn the same social status and income as her white male counterparts. It is to free Gayle Perry from traditional "women's work" so that she, like her husband, can have a successful career. It is to extend to women all the privileges, powers, and rights enjoyed by the Enlightenment philosophers who created our national culture.

This ideal is more than commendable. It is noble, inspiring, revolutionary in the best sense of the word. It has only one problem. It's impossible. The goal of universal Enlightenment-style equality, *equality as Americans have been taught to think of it and define it*, involves the achievement of two contradictory models, each of which negates the other. The process of history has narrowed men's roles to include only one side of this equation. American males grow up hearing the social message "Modern and traditional behavior are incompatible, and you must be modern." This has impoverished the life experience of many men, depriving them of the chance to explore much of the range of human behavior. But American women are in an even more difficult situation. We are being told, "Modern and traditional behavior are incompatible, and *you must do both.*" We have inherited a paradox, an assignment that is literally impossible to fulfill.

Because Americans' paradoxical goals are based on assumptions we hold deep in our core values, the conflict between them is rarely articulated. In fact, attempts to "free" American women are usually grounded in this same unexamined paradox. As a result, these attempts have not moved female roles forward in a single, unified direction. They have simply joined the forces that are splitting American women in two.

In this chapter, we've looked at historical events that are still affecting women in the United States. But in "standard" history, as in every other science or discipline, the lives of women are often invisible. The next chapter will look at "herstory," the process by which women themselves have absorbed the paradox of the American value system, incorporated it into their lives, and set out in two opposite directions at once.

CHAPTER TWO

✦

Lurching Through Herstory

"All the world's a stage," wrote Shakespeare, "and all the men and women merely players. They have their exits and their entrances, and one man in his time plays many parts." I was in a high school production of *As You Like It*, so I learned this line when I was fifteen—never suspecting that years later, I would be required to read thousands of pages of boring sociological treatises to reach exactly the same conclusion.

A social "role" is just like a role in a play, and whether or not we think we're acting, we put on our costumes and play our parts every day. I behave, dress, and speak quite differently depending on whether I'm teaching a roomful of college students, going shopping with a friend, or watching TV with my kids. You probably have at least a couple of roles yourself. You have different "costumes" hanging in your closet for each role, and you know just how to get into character when you're "on."

Gender roles are some of the strongest "parts" human beings play. Most of us know whether we're male or female,* and we all know a *lot* about how to "play the part" of a man or a woman. Of course, the particulars of gender roles are different from one culture to the next, and they change over time. For example, in our present culture a man who wears a skirt is considered ridiculous, but in old Scotland or Samoa the right skirt was essential to a warrior's macho image. On the other hand, in the nineteenth century even the thought of wearing pants was enough

---

* I say "most of us" because there are people who feel their gender identity doesn't match their physical sex, which can be very confusing.

to give a "real lady" the vapors. Today an American woman in pants won't draw a second glance (unless there is something highly unusual about the woman, the pants, or both).

THE UNEXPECTED PATTERN
OF FEMALE ROLE DEVELOPMENT

Costumes are only one aspect of gender roles. Without even knowing it, we all notice and react to the constant subtle changes in the way our culture expects men and women to act. We make choices about our own behavior in the context of these cultural expectations. In the two-hundred-plus years of United States history, the roles of both men and women have changed a great deal. As American society modernized, the status of rational individual was extended to include more and more males; first all classes, and then all races. But for a long time that part was not offered to both genders. The rational-individual role was written for a male actor, and women were supposed to fill in the supporting parts.

Once men of all classes and races had legally been given equal status in the United States, a lot of people expected to see women's roles modernize in exactly the same way. In fact, many social scientists, who have been educated to think like Enlightenment scholars, still do expect this. They see women as one more group destined to move out of an oppressive, Dark Age hierarchy into the status of real, true, rational individuals. According to this way of looking at the world, changes in women's roles should follow exactly the same pattern as changes in men's roles.

But that isn't what's happening.

What *is* happening is that while American men's roles have been developing like this:

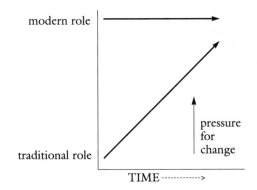

American women's roles have been developing like this:

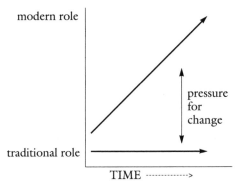

What these graphs show is that *while there has been steadily increasing pressure for American women to move into a more modern role, it has always been accompanied by steadily increasing pressure to remain in a traditional role.* Society's expectations of American women have simultaneously changed to demand more modern, individualistic, economically calculated behavior *and* more traditional, noneconomic, relationship-oriented behavior. They are likely to continue on this course as long as our cultural assumptions remain unchallenged. This means that men's roles will continue to become more narrow and constricted—but also more uniform. Women's roles, on the other hand, are under constant pressure to become more traditional *and* more modern. Expectations of females will continue to intensify in opposite directions, becoming ever more fragmented and impossible to integrate.

The result of this paradoxical pressure has been that American women's roles have evolved in an odd, lurching, ambivalent sort of way. Some analysts have described it as a series of steps toward modernization, with each step followed by a "backlash" to more traditional roles—a sort of "two steps forward, one step back" pattern. But if you look closely at the social ideals about women throughout American history, you'll actually see constantly increasing distance between the two aspects of women's roles—not "two steps forward, one step back," but "two steps forward and back at the same time." If this sounds confusing, that's because it is. Probably the best way to clarify it is to take a closer look at the "herstory" of American women's roles.

"HERSTORY" IN THE EARLY UNITED STATES

American women's roles maintained a strictly traditional form for decades after the United States became a nation. Women's rights don't even enter into most descriptions of early American society. But that's not because women were totally unaware of the implications of Enlightenment philosophy. Just as men were inspired by that philosophy to build a nation where they could all be equal, some women seized on the ideas of the Enlightenment to argue for free-and-equal status.

For example, in the late 1700s, an Englishwoman named Mary Wollstonecraft wrote a book entitled *A Vindication of the Rights of Woman*, which was published first in London, but was also very popular in the new United States. Wollstonecraft's book used Enlightenment equal-rights logic to argue against the idea that a woman's only function was to please and serve men.[1] Wollstonecraft called this "nonsense," and argued that the role of rational individual applied to women every bit as much as it did to men.

Motivated by the same kind of thinking that inspired *A Vindication of the Rights of Woman*, some American women pushed hard for equal rights to be encoded in the laws and policies of the United States. In 1777, statesman John Adams's wife, Abigail, wrote him a letter reminding him that when he participated in drafting the laws of the United States, he should "remember the ladies and be more generous and favorable to them than your ancestors.

"All men would be tyrants if they could," said Abigail, and followed up with a blunt threat: "If particular care and attention is not paid to the ladies, we are determined to foment a rebellion, and will not hold ourselves bound by any laws in which we have no voice or representation."[2]

Despite this warning, the lawmakers who set up the U.S. government went ahead and made laws according to which, to paraphrase Orwell, some people were a lot more equal than others. Certainly women weren't given equality with men. The new laws made sure that all *households* were considered equal—but within the household, white men still literally ruled over their slaves, their children, and their wives. In fact, some historians argue that the new Enlightenment-based laws and policies were the first legal regulations to specifically *bar* American women from participating in public life. During the period after the Revolutionary War and before the routinization of the United States government, the absence of concrete laws and policies, along with the presence of egalitarian philosophy, left a lot of unanswered questions about women's status. Once the U.S. government had adopted a canon of law, women were explicitly barred from full citizenship, including the right to vote, certain privileges of ownership and inheritance, and many other aspects of public life. By assigning relatively equal rights to all white, property-owning adult males, the American government set up a society far more egalitarian than those of the European aristocracies. But by specifically barring women from these rights, they created *race and gender barriers* to replace what had originally been *class* barriers. In other words, *at exactly the same time that new egalitarian laws offered American women a way to argue they were equal to men, those same laws pushed them further away from equality than they had been before.*

At this point, you may be wondering why women like Abigail Adams didn't "foment a rebellion" the way she had warned her husband they would. Part of the answer is that the women who were arguing for equality were few and far between, and lived very privileged lives. They were upper-class and white, they had servants (just like the upper-class males of the Enlightenment), and they had the time and resources to become well educated. Abigail Adams also had a husband who sat around thinking about equal rights all day every day. Mary Wollstonecraft was even more unusual in her day, although she would have fit right in at a feminist retreat in the 1990s. She was an Adult Child of an Alcoholic, which probably contributed to her Codependent Relationship with the essayist William Godwin. She was also a Single Parent by Choice, preferring to raise an illegitimate daughter by herself rather than marry.[3] Women like Adams and Wollstonecraft, who had the leisure to consider Enlightenment philosophy, also had a great many advantages that made their lives relatively comfortable, compared to those of poorer women. The very money and resources that put them in a position to idealize equality also meant that they were less motivated to seek changes in their lifestyle.

In contrast to people like Adams and Wollstonecraft, the average woman on the street at the time of the American Revolution didn't have the time, the money, or the education to put Enlightenment egalitarianism at the center of her daily life, let alone run around fomenting revolution or anything else. Voting rights tend to fade into insignificance when you're scrabbling out a living based on subsistence agriculture, caring for sick people with primitive medical techniques, having babies every year during your entire adult life, and so on.

The thing to remember is that from the very beginning, the structure of the United States government did two contradictory things, which are still affecting your daily life. First: In order for men to attain Enlighten-ment-style equality without giving up the rewarding aspects of tradi-tional society, *American government separated women's roles from men's roles more sharply than ever before, and explicitly limited women to a role within the household.* Second: By adopting that same Enlightenment phi-losophy as its logical basis, *the U.S. government gave women a logical basis for claiming equal rights if they could fit the Enlightenment definition of "rational individuals."* As we will see, the constriction of men's roles and the division of women's roles that began during this period have been operating ever since.

THE "HERSTORY" OF THE INDUSTRIAL REVOLUTION

In the last chapter, we saw how the Industrial Revolution separated men's and women's roles in the economy. Men's work, which was grow-ing more different from women's work all the time, was seen as the mod-ern extension of the gentleman's occupation—in other words, "real" work.

To this day, Americans still make the distinction between "real" work, which means paid work, and the traditional work that women are sup-posed to do for free. Nancy, one of the women I interviewed, made a comment I heard from dozens of women in one way or another.

Nancy, 44

I get so sick of people asking me, "Do you work?" Of course I work! I've got five children under ten—I work twenty-four hours a day! But of course that's not what it means when people say, "Do you work?" They mean do you work for pay, outside your home. Sometimes I hear myself say, "No, I don't work," and I think: "That's a complete lie! I work harder than anyone I know!"

Women who are doing a tremendous amount of domestic work (in order to free their husbands' time for "real" jobs) often feel this kind of anger and defensiveness—and no wonder. Following the Enlightenment worldview, American society gives much higher status to people who work for money than to people who work for love. Millions of American women (including yours truly) can tell you that most of the high-paying, high-prestige jobs they have held are nowhere near as grueling and diffi-cult as the work they've done in their own homes, for no money and low prestige. But since the Industrial Revolution redefined the concept of "work," the traditional labor of women has never been seen as "real."

The clear separation between men's work (outside of the home, high prestige, paid for in cash money) and women's work (inside the home, low prestige, paid for in room and board) gave American women much more incentive to prove they could fit the definition of a "rational individual." If they could claim equal rights, they could access the same advantages men got from their position in the economy. The egalitarian values of the Enlightenment gave women a foundation on which to build the argument for equality.

As the Industrial Revolution progressed and the American economy was centered more and more on cash, women increasingly depended on male wage earners to give them access to the currency their culture favored. It was the Dark Ages all over again: a woman was expected to work for her husband, in return for protection and sustenance. Since she needed money to live and her husband was her only source of cash, she was dependent on his good graces to survive. If he was stingy or abusive, there wasn't much she could do about it. Fortunately, there were still some laws and strong social customs that required a man to protect and provide for his dependents. Women who belonged to a household (in other words, the vast majority of American women) relied more and more heavily on these traditional values to protect their own quality of life.

Do you see what the last two paragraphs just spelled out? *As the Industrial Revolution progressed, it created stronger and stronger pressures on American women to support both modern equal-rights values and traditional, hierarchical values.*

THE BIRTH OF THE FEMINIST MOVEMENT

Let's look first at the equal-rights side of this equation. As the Industrial Revolution transformed American society, egalitarian thinkers produced a constant trickle of essays and speeches advocating women's rights. The feminist cause was aided by the nineteenth-century idea that it would be good for American children (particularly boys) if their mothers weren't completely unschooled. Americans gradually decided that girls should be educated, at least in the three R's—basic reading, writing, and arithmetic.

By the 1820s, a few women's seminaries were beginning to offer higher education for women. The country's first coeducational college opened in 1833. And what was taught in these seminaries and colleges? Why, of course, none other than the Enlightenment-style thinking which underlay the whole structure of modern Western civilization. So American families who sent their daughters off to learn to be better wives and mothers were actually exposing them to the idea that no rational person should have to do traditional labor. As the American economy grew richer, more and more women had both the leisure and the educational background to understand and care about equal rights. Mabel, a graceful elderly woman I interviewed, remembered what an impact this had caused in her own family.

Mabel, 82

My grandmother went to a seminary in Massachusetts, not all that long after the Civil War. She'd always been sort of fiery, had a strong disposition. Her father thought that if he sent her to the seminary, she would learn to be more of a lady. Instead, she got more and more opinionated all the time. By the time she graduated, she really thought she could tell her father where to get off. She raised my mother to give no ground to a man, and that's how I was raised, myself. My great-grandfather would probably be horrified to know that he created a whole line of feminists. He's probably spinning in his grave!

Around the middle of the nineteenth century, the first great leaders of the women's rights movement began agitating for equality. Lectures were a major part of an American society that had no radio or television, and women's rights advocates went on the lecture circuit to deliver their egalitarian message. Their major focus was the demand that women be given voting rights. In 1873, Susan B. Anthony was arrested, tried, and convicted for the terrible crime of trying to vote.

Again, Americans' resistance to the idea of granting women equal rights was not only a plain and simple prejudice against females, but also embodied the underlying fear that if everybody became an "equal citizen" in modern terms, the United States would have no one left to do traditional labor. A heckler at one of Susan B. Anthony's speeches put it very clearly. "The lady goes in for taking women away from the washtub," the man argued, "and in the name of heaven, who is going there, if they don't?"[4]

It was a good question.

While upper-class American women had the education and leisure to agitate for the vote, and even for female participation in the labor force, poor women were already out there in the public sector—and they were not having a good time. Women worked in the sweatshops and textile factories of the large American cities for pennies a day, coming home completely exhausted only to find their domestic chores still undone. They were paid less than men, partly because any woman poor enough to have to work was desperate enough to accept miserable wages, and partly because the general consensus among Americans, from employers to the women themselves, was that the work men did was worth more than "women's work." Many of the employed women of this period would undoubtedly have preferred to stay at home and have their financial needs met by husbands or fathers. Because of this, working women were not the enthusiastic supporters of feminism that you might expect.

Only those Americans who were most devoted to Enlightenment ideals were really enthusiastic about the arguments of women's rights advocates. In 1848, a group of feminist thinkers set up a conference known as the Seneca Falls Convention, at which they read a "Declaration of Sentiments and Resolutions." This document was modeled after the Declaration of Independence, but with statements about women's full equality thrown in. The Seneca Falls Convention was organized not only by women, but also by men who believed deeply in the ideals of the Enlightenment.

Just like the original Enlightenment thinkers, the Seneca Falls Convention organizers were mainly highly educated, upper-class people who were working toward the goal of modern equality for all rational beings. The convention didn't attract much notice outside the intellectual circles; in fact, it is far better known among Americans today than it was when it actually occurred. However, the central message of the Seneca Falls Convention was a powerful one, and in the long run the convention would be seen as a turning point. It was the first time a group of Americans gathered to affirm that women are as capable of rational behavior as men, and deserve the same rights and privileges granted to all rational individuals. Keep that in mind as we look at the other side of women's role development during the Industrial Revolution.

THE "CULT OF TRUE WOMANHOOD" IN THE NINETEENTH-CENTURY UNITED STATES

At the same time that the feminist movement was gathering steam, a movement later dubbed the Cult of True Womanhood was transforming the American ideal of the Perfect Female in *exactly the opposite direction*.

Prior to the Industrial Revolution, a woman in the New World had to be tough and resilient just to survive. Frontier life required hard physical labor and as many helping hands as possible. This meant that for all but the richest families, the best sort of woman was one who could bear a grundle of children while working like a plowhorse. But as the Industrial Revolution brought new prosperity to the country, reduced people's need to carve a life out of the land, and increased the separation between men's work and women's work, the image of the ideal female changed. In order to justify the way work was assigned to the different genders, women came to be seen as delicate flowers, physically and psychologically unable to cope with the rough, tough world outside the home.

So it was that while American feminists were claiming that women were rational beings just like men, a lot of other women were teaching each other how to appear nonrational and utterly *different* from men. The idea was that females should be virtuous, helpless, innocent, and weak. The fashions of the day included various types of restrictive clothing that cinched in women's torsos and accentuated their hips and busts, making them appear wasp-waisted and curvaceous—as "female" as possible. The tight waists inhibited breathing, as well as movement, and caused women to faint easily. The ladylike swoon became a hallmark of True Womanhood. There were actually instruction manuals on how to faint properly in order to maximize one's feminine image. It is a testament to the fact that humans believe what they want to that when a nineteenth-century woman keeled over, most Americans attributed it to the delicacy of the female sex, and not to the fact that she was wearing a whalebone corset that would have strangled a bull elephant.

According to the Cult of True Womanhood, females should be shielded from such dangers as bad language, adventure novels, newsworthy events, all musical instruments except harps and keyboards (other instruments required unladylike postures or gestures), sex in any form, and of course nondomestic work. The reason a man would devote his energy to protecting such a hothouse flower was that females were also supposed to embody everything lovely and virtuous about humankind. A man therefore desperately needed a woman around, or he would sink into depravity. The True Woman perched prettily on her pedestal (except for the brief intervals when she was unconscious), accepting a man's adulation, protection, and whatever money she could convince him to shell out. Not a bad gig, if you like pedestals.

THE DELICATE BALANCE:
SUSTAINING A PARADOXICAL VALUE SYSTEM

It may seem puzzling that modern feminism and this ultratraditional view of women arose at the same time. Actually, it is perfectly logical. If something like the Cult of True Womanhood had not come in to counterbalance the spread of modern ideals, the traditional aspects of American culture would have disappeared very rapidly. Remember the Enlightenment definition of rational behavior? It stipulated that a rational person *always* acts to maximize his own material advantage.

If everyone behaved this way, women would stop taking care of children, and men would stop giving up part of their earnings either to their children or to their wives. The ideal society of the Enlightenment imagination was one with *no* kinship obligations, in which *no one* had to do traditional work. This is simply not a workable social system, since every human being is in some way, at some point, dependent on the unpaid care of others. The Cult of True Womanhood arose because Americans sensed this. They needed to counterbalance the steady push toward "rational" behavior that had been built into the American political, legal, and economic system.

TWENTIETH-CENTURY WOMEN'S ROLES:
LURCHING FROM LEFT TO RIGHT

The tension between the idea of female equality and traditional women's roles was present in the United States from the beginning. In the twentieth century, though, this tug-of-war has become downright violent. Depending on whose side you're hearing, our whole century has been *either* one long series of attacks on traditional morality by rabid feminists, bravely countered by people with good old-fashioned traditional values, *or* an endless struggle for female equality in which the valiant work done by feminists has been countered by surges of opposition from male-dominated reactionary bigots.

Because Americans have a contradictory set of "core values," neither side of this argument ever really wins. Instead, *the intensity of each side increases to balance the intensity of the other*, so that in the end, American culture can stay precariously, wobblingly balanced between its egalitarian and traditional value systems.

As the twentieth century progressed, American opinions about women's roles became more and more split between the modern ideal of a perfectly equal, rational society, and the intimate, cooperative, hierarchical relationships of an idealized traditional society. We speak about these two ideals in terms of opposite directions: the modern, egalitarian side of the argument is usually seen politically as being the liberal "left," while the traditional side is seen as the conservative "right." Our society has been lurching from left to right more and more drastically since the twentieth century began. Let me show you what I mean.

SWING TO THE LEFT

◆ *Women Get the Vote* By the dawn of the twentieth century, the pressure to give women voting rights was becoming intense. We've already seen that more American women were becoming educated, feminist lecturers were spreading the ideals of the Enlightenment, and the country was becoming wealthier and more technologically advanced. All of these trends accelerated as the century got under way, pushing the cause of universal suffrage to the forefront of American political thought and popular culture. My father, who was born in 1910, used to sing this verse from a popular song he learned as a child:

> I should worry, I should fret,
> I should marry a Suffragette.
> She should die,
> I should cry,
> Then I'd marry some other guy.

This pretty much sums up how Americans felt about the suffrage movement in the early years of the century. They didn't really hate suffragettes (after all, there is the part about crying when one of them dies), but the whole idea of women doing something as manly as voting made most Americans nervous.

This mood was similar to the feeling Abraham Lincoln had once said white Americans had about slaves: "It's like having a tiger by the ears. You're afraid to hang on, but you're more afraid to let go." What would happen if male Americans "let go of the tiger's ears" by allowing the subordinate 50 percent of the population to have its own say in a democratic government? This question made a lot of men jumpy. Politicians, in particular, got positively queasy at the thought of women voting.

And yet, because the U.S. government was founded in Enlightenment philosophy, which granted equality to all rational individuals, the only way Americans could logically deny women the vote was to continue to deny that they were rational. By this time, women were writing books, conducting research, getting degrees, and doing a slew of other things that made it very hard to deny their capacity for rationality. Enlightenment logic is clear: if it looks like a rational individual and it quacks like a rational individual, then it should be allowed to vote like a rational individual.

Ironically, though, it was the Cult of True Womanhood, as much as the feminist movement itself, that finally got American women the vote. As long as the feminists based their arguments on the idea that they were "rational individuals" and therefore had a right to act like men, the majority of Americans—*both male and female*—balked at their ideas. Men worried about losing their dominant position in the society. Women worried that they would no longer be able to occupy a protected traditional role. Both sexes worried about the nurturing aspects of traditional society disappearing from American culture. But then, moderate feminists began to wave the banner of True Womanhood. They pointed out that since women were such pure, noble, and maternal creatures, in whom were vested all the best aspects of traditional humanity, women would naturally vote in ways that supported traditional values.

It was on the strength of this argument that the states finally began enfranchising women in the first couple of decades of the twentieth century. As long as they talked about individual rights, the suffragettes had alarmed Americans with the specter of a society without support for traditional institutions like the family. Once they claimed to have the intention of *strengthening* those institutions, Americans were willing to let women vote. Again, it was not merely male hatred of women that delayed enfranchisement, but a much more universal fear of losing the traditional aspects of life valued by *all* Americans.

The first state to enfranchise women was Wyoming, in 1869. The other states followed until finally, in 1918, the Constitution was amended to include women as voting citizens of the United States. This was a huge coup for feminists. Everyone expected the nature of American politics to change drastically. Politicians rushed to curry favor with female voters. Republicans and Democrats alike appointed women as members of their national committees. Congress pushed through a flurry of legislation to support health care and education for mothers and infants. Everyone braced for the impact newly enfranchised female voters would have on the government of the United States. People were ready for almost anything.

But no one expected what actually happened.

SWING TO THE RIGHT

◆ *The Great Anticlimax of Enfranchisement*   What happened after American women finally won the vote was this:

Not a whole lot.

As the first full-suffrage elections ended, American politicians scrambled to see what women *as a group* were doing with their new voting rights. The answer was that women didn't vote as a group. Different policies sounded good to women of different income levels, races, lifestyles, and social positions. Women (surprise, surprise) often disagreed with each other. In other words, women didn't act like the members of a single class with common interests. Instead, they tended to vote almost exactly like their husbands.

This came as a shock to people—especially feminists—who had become used to speaking of women as a united, oppressed mass. Analysts at the time (and since then) have offered a number of speculative reasons why the female vote tended to align so closely with the voting patterns of their male family members. Maybe, some said, American women just weren't conscious enough of their collective interests. Maybe they weren't educated enough, maybe they were dominated by their husbands, maybe they were so used to following male orders that even in the privacy of the voting booth they were ruled by their husbands' opinions and demands.

All of these explanations may have some truth to them. But the major reason women voted like their husbands is much simpler, and it makes perfect sense if you look at the way American society was put together.

Think, for example, about what a typical American woman in the early 1920s would have been thinking as she went off to vote. Let's suppose that this voter—I think I'll call her Gladiola Snodgrass—is married with children, like the vast majority of American women. At the time, Gladiola has three boys and a girl at home, all under the age of eight. Her period is late, and as she walks along she wonders if she's pregnant again. Her husband, Biff, works at a sawmill, bringing home a wage that barely supports the family. Gladiola is concerned. There's been talk of laying off men at the sawmill because new machines are faster and cheaper than human workers. The Snodgrass children are growing like kudzu, costing a fortune in food and shoes alone. Gladiola and Biff have been fantasizing about buying a car, but the money is still too tight. If Gladiola has another baby, how will they afford it? All these things are worrying her as she shows up at the voting booth.

Now Gladiola stands in the booth, ready to vote. Because the development of American society has split the pressures on women's roles, there are two clear—and opposite—ways Gladiola might think about her life, and the issues that will improve it. One way is to identify herself with all women, seeing her gender as the primary cause of her life problems. If Gladiola thinks this way, she will cast a vote to free women from a domestic role, which may ultimately allow her to get a job and earn her own money. This sounds good to Gladiola—but there are a lot of uncertainties that go with it. For example, if she did get a job, she and Biff would have to get some kind of domestic help with child care and housekeeping to replace Gladiola's labor in her home. The domestic help also has to cost less than Gladiola can earn; otherwise, it would be cheaper for her to stay home exactly as she is doing now. If all women are free to act like men, and everyone in America wants a high-paying, high-prestige job, where is this cheap domestic help going to come from? And even if Gladiola votes for these changes, who knows how long it will be before American society can implement them all?

The other way Gladiola can look at her ballot is to evaluate which vote will help Biff hang on to his job, or if worse comes to worst, get another one that pays a good wage and offers some kinds of benefits. She can think about issues that might cut down taxes on Biff's salary, leaving more money for the Snodgrass family. She can vote for people who will strongly support the traditional beliefs that a woman *shouldn't* work for money, and that therefore a man *must* protect and provide for his wife and children. A vote for these issues will require much less change and has much more potential to benefit Gladiola, in the short run, than a vote that separates women's interests from those of men.

At this point in history, Gladiola's immediate concerns are much more closely aligned with her husband's interests than with the interests of women as a political group. Whatever Gladiola's views on equality, her children need shoes *now*, she thinks she is pregnant *now*, and her only source of income (her husband's job) needs some shoring up *now*. Not because she is irrational or slavishly devoted to male power, but because she is a very rational person who thinks quite clearly about her own best interests, Gladiola picks up her pencil and votes just like Biff.

In the opening decades of the twentieth century, most American women were in Gladiola's position, or something fairly similar. The vote that was most likely to ensure their own security was a vote for policies that benefited their husbands and fathers. When it became clear that women did vote this way, and not as a unified group lobbying for their interests as a gender, American politicians heaved a collective sigh of relief. The laws they had passed to support women's participation in the society as rational individuals expired one by one, leaving things much as they had been before universal suffrage.

SWING TO THE LEFT

◆ *World War I Turns "Men's Work" into "Women's Work"*   The First World War took a lot of men out of the American economy altogether. The need for women to make up for the shortage of male labor during the war led to a number of changes in the way Americans viewed women's roles. The True Womanhood ideal of the ethereal, fragile female took some solid hits. Being healthy and ready to work was once again considered a desirable thing for a woman. Distorting underwear fell out of fashion. Fainting was no longer a badge of female grace. During the war, women were hired to "fill in" for men at specific tasks, such as secretarial work and telephone operation, and these jobs ultimately became part of what Americans considered "women's work." More than ever before, females—in particular those who were single, divorced, or widowed—gained a small but stable niche in the American employment structure.

Cecelia, 86

We started to use the words "career girl." No one had ever thought of such a thing, but there really were women who were deciding to work, and we had to call them something. Of course, they weren't looked at with approval. No one in my school ever wanted to be called a "career girl." It meant you were sort of pushy, and probably not attractive to men.

During the early decades of the twentieth century, it was still presumed that only an unmarried woman (who probably had some sort of personality disorder) would become a "career girl"—but the category was recognized. And the modernization of the whole culture made the idea of women working seem less outlandish and more logical than ever before.

SWING TO THE RIGHT

◆ *Women's Rights Get "Depressed"*   When the First World War ended and American soldiers came home, the support for women's participation in public life and labor quickly faded. However, no one took back the advances toward egalitarianism that had already been achieved. Women stayed in "pink-collar" jobs such as typing and answering phones. They could vote, live independently more easily than before, and claim at least some of the respect they deserved for helping the country survive a crisis.

As the United States moved through the 1920s and then entered the horrific economic catastrophe of the Depression, the issues of women's equality were overshadowed by overwhelming economic problems. Millions of American men lost jobs, farms, and other ways of making a living—and that meant their wives and children suffered, too.

Esther, 75

Now, listen—there wasn't *time* to think about women's lib when I was a child. There wasn't the freedom. We were *that* close to starving. My father was out of work, and he'd go off looking for a job, sometimes for weeks. We would run out of food, and my mother would have nothing to feed us except the vegetables she grew in our little garden. I remember my little brother bringing home food he'd found in garbage cans. My mother would have smacked him silly if he'd done that before the Depression. As it was, she just put it on the table, and no one said a word about it. When you're living that way, you don't think about things like equal rights. You think about whatever you can do to keep the family alive.

During these years the feminist movement, which had been booming during the fight to win the vote, lost much of its momentum. When human beings are hungry and threatened, they tend to forget philosophical abstractions and concentrate on behaviors that help families support and protect each other. During the Great Depression and in the period leading up to World War II, then, most Americans' goal was not to get women out of the traditional household, but to *strengthen* the household and get men back in the position of earning a decent wage to support their families.

SWING TO THE LEFT

◆ *World War II—A Riveting Era for Women's Roles*   War is hell for human beings, but it's heaven for manufacturing industries. An all-out war effort requires huge amounts of just about everything human beings make, from low-tech items like food and textiles to the most sophisticated gadgetry engineers can invent. In particular, the nature of war in the 1940s required a huge number of mechanical devices: trucks, ships, tanks, jeeps, planes, and so on. At the same time demand for these things went through the ceiling, creating a need for millions of workers to manufacture them, the pool of available male employees was shipping out for Europe and Asia.

World War I had brought a lot of women into comparatively genteel jobs like typing and answering telephones. During World War II, the difference between the demand for laborers and the number of available men was even bigger. After decades of firm belief in women's inability to work outside the home, many Americans suddenly realized female workers could do just about anything men could do—even heavy manufacturing. There's nothing like necessity to break down stereotypes.

Edna, 70

It makes me laugh to think about it. I mean, here women had been doing hard manual work for hundreds of years—I mean, I'd like to see any man try washing a load of diapers in a tub, or making twenty loaves of bread from scratch! But somehow, until the war, men just managed to *not notice* that women could do hard work.

As American women were hired to do everything from shipping linens to building airplanes, the last lingering image of the feeble, idealized True Woman fell off her pedestal, busting her bustle and bursting the busks from her bust.[5] She got back up wearing denim overalls and carrying a ten-pound monkey wrench. Posters of her, with ruddy cheeks, strong muscles, and the name "Rosie the Riveter," were put out by the government to deliberately create a shift in American attitudes about women's roles.

The famous riveters were only the tip of the iceberg. Now that there has been a popular movie about it (*A League of Their Own*), you probably know that female baseball teams replaced some of the absent male ballplayers—and drew respectable audiences. Women spearheaded fundraising drives, healed the sick and wounded, ran schools, put out fires, got food and supplies to both American troops and the civilians of war-torn countries. Contrary to the theories of True Womanhood, women were good at all these jobs, and they enjoyed them. Earning their own money and receiving the respect that goes with "real" work felt just as good to women as it did to men.

SWING TO THE RIGHT

◆ *The Postwar Era—The Good Old Days Are Here at Last*   When the war finally ended and American troops came home, the U.S. economy really got booming. So did the population. In the late 1940s and early 1950s, *for the very first time,* typical Americans were prosperous enough to create the ideal of the suburban nuclear family. The woman's role in this scenario was very clear. The men home from the war needed all the jobs they could get; a "proper" woman stayed home, looked pretty, and had babies.

She also cleaned house like a maniac. Another common misperception Americans have is that modern appliances reduced the time American women spent cleaning and cooking. *Au contraire, mes chères.* What happened, as vacuum cleaners and washer-dryers and Fuller brush salesmen spread throughout the land, was not that the time spent doing housework went down, but that American standards of minimum cleanliness went up—and up and up.

Lilian, 63

When I was little, we didn't expect everything to be so spic-and-span. My mother washed clothes on Monday, and I only had a few dresses. I'd wear something two or three days in a row without washing it. Everybody did. But my children would rather have died than wear the same thing to school on Monday and Tuesday. It seems like the more machines we got to help with the housework, the cleaner things had to be.

Lilian's suspicions were correct. By some estimates, an American woman in the 1950s actually spent *more* time doing housework than her counterpart in the 1890s. The images of strong, ruddy women throwing on overalls and leaving home for the job site vanished without a trace. The images that replaced Rosie the Riveter in the American media had something of the overdressed, narrow-waisted True Woman of the nineteenth century. Advertisers pushing appliances and cleaning products helped reinforce the idea that woman's happiness and social acceptability revolved around making everything in her house immaculately clean.

And so, in the postwar period, American women's roles were simultaneously experiencing more pressure to become modern—*and to remain purely traditional*—than ever before. Women voted, had jobs, participated in civil and military defense. They were highly educated, they'd proved their ability to work outside the home—and yet they were expected to stay alone with small children in isolated "nuclear family" dwellings, buffing their linoleum in high heels, A-line skirts, full makeup, and pearls. This situation was supposed to be the realization of an ideal lifestyle, but, in retrospect, doesn't it look a little weird?

Isabelle, 50

To me, the TV series *Bewitched* sums up everything about that period of the fifties and early sixties. Here's a show about this intelligent, competent woman who can go anywhere and do anything. If she wants to she can spit-shine her entire house in a split second—with her nose, no less. She's married to this drippy ad man who can barely stumble his way through a day at the office.

And how does this woman spend her time? Pretending not to have any of her powers, so that she can stay home cleaning the drippy ad man's house. I mean, *WHY?* Why did Samantha use a vacuum cleaner? Why did Darrin get so hysterical if she used her powers? And what did Americans get out of watching this show? I think the whole society was just obsessed with trying to keep women from using their power.

These were the same issues that began to grow in a lot of American women's minds as the war grew more distant in time and the hours they spent waiting for their respective ad men to come home ticked on.

One scholarly analyst of popular media, Susan Douglas, has written that Samantha, the innocent-looking young wife whose half-repressed powers so unnerved her husband in *Bewitched*, "embodied important contradictions" in the lives and psyches of American women in the years after World War II. "[S]he was a happy, respectable suburban housewife who exerted power beyond the kitchen or the living room," says Douglas. "She was at once traditional and modern." [6] Beneath the light-hearted media images and laugh tracks lay a tension that troubled many American women, and scared many men half to death. As women became more educated, more conversant with and capable of the modern tasks that had been seen as masculine territory, the social expectation that they would use these powers only in behalf of a traditional role reached an all-time high. The paradox of women's role definition was becoming extreme to the point of absurdity.

SWING TO THE LEFT

◆ *The Sixties and Seventies—The Women's Movement Takes Off* The feminist movement of the 1960s virtually exploded out of the artificial, idealized housewifery of the post–World War II era. The book that struck a match to the volatile mixture of high education and heavy restrictions on women's roles was Betty Friedan's *The Feminine Mystique*. Friedan interviewed a lot of American women and found that they suffered from a growing sense of boredom, low self-esteem, and hopelessness. She called this "the problem that has no name" and convincingly pointed out that any intelligent, active person would begin to feel this way if restricted to a narrow, nonintellectual, low-prestige, nonremunerative social role. It was essentially the reaction of a rational individual to being locked in a cage—even though the "cage" of women's roles in the fifties had lovely plush carpets.

Linda, 52

The feminist movement hit me like an electric shock. It was the same with all my friends. Suddenly people were articulating what we had been feeling for years, without even knowing it. There was this surge of hope that we didn't have to be stereotypes anymore—we could be real people at last. I had a copy of *The Feminine Mystique* that I kept under my pillow. I never let my husband see it. It was like we were rebels.

American women like Linda and her friends read feminist writings and responded with a tidal wave of unorthodox behavior. They joined consciousness-raising groups, burned their bras, left their husbands, signed up for graduate school, and demanded all the modern rights American men enjoyed.

This period is always described in books about women's rights as "a heady time for feminism." If you were alive during the women's movement of the 1960s and early 1970s, you probably have some war stories to tell about your own confrontations with sexism, feminism, and change. I certainly do. I came on the American scene at about the same time as *The Feminine Mystique*, and from the moment I got a handle on the English language, everything the "women's lib" people were saying made darn good sense to me. I was a little confused about the bra-burning issue until I figured out (1) what a bra was, and (2) that you were supposed to take it off before you burned it. Other than that, I joined the feminist movement with all the fervor one could expect of someone who still had no permanent teeth.

For example, in the first grade my best friend, Joan, and I demanded a turn raising our school's American flag in the mornings, a ceremony that had always been reserved for boys. After a fierce debate among the school administrators, we got our chance.

I will never forget the morning, during a record-setting cold snap, when Joan and I discovered that the flagpole chain had frozen to the pole, preventing us from pulling the flag into place. Joan jumped up and grabbed the chain, swinging on it with her whole weight, which was probably about fifty pounds. Her hands froze to the metal. We discussed this problem, me standing in the snow in my galoshes, Joan dangling from the chain, and resolved that whatever happened, we would not besmirch our sex's reputation by failing at our task. I sat down in the snow by the flagpole so that Joan could support herself by standing on my shoulders, and the two of us waited there for the temperature to rise (which seemed to take about an hour) rather than go back into the school and acknowledge defeat. Right on, sisters!

In the United States during the 1960s and 1970s, society contained a massive pool of young women and girls, like Joan and me, who had been educated to be just as rational, just as individualistic, just as ambitious—in short, just as modern—as their brothers. But while a typical American male could look forward to a prestigious, remunerative career of his own choosing, women were expected to act like the witch Samantha Stephens, tucking most of their abilities and interests under a dust ruffle (except when they could be useful to their husbands' careers) and becoming full-time domestic caretakers.

Lori, 50

It was insane! I had gotten better grades than any of the boys in my family, and I'd gotten into a better college. But my father wouldn't let me go, because he felt very strongly about women "staying in their place." He paid for my brothers to limp through junior college, while I turned down a scholarship. What kind of sense does that make?

Once the population bulge of the Baby Boom reached the age of early adulthood, and a huge group of women were facing this kind of discrimination, they balked. Collectively, vigorously, articulately, angrily, the Baby Boom women demanded their rights as full free-and-equal individuals, the identity it had taken them almost four hundred years to win.

The feminists of the 1960s operated on the same Enlightenment model of equality that underlay the basic structure of American society. Naturally, one of their chief demands was that women should be allowed the same access to wealth, power, and prestige that American men enjoyed, thereby freeing them from dependency on men. But remember, the male role in the workplace had long since come to absorb the bulk of a human being's time—and that's assuming that each worker had Somebody Else doing all the physical and emotional work of traditional social structures.

ROLE COMBINATION:
BRING HOME THE BACON, FRY IT UP IN A PAN . . .

Because there was no one else available to do this work if women moved into the modern workplace, the feminists of the 1960s and '70s simply adopted the Enlightenment philosophers' assumption that traditional work was so trivial and easy as to be inconsequential. It would just *get done*, while rational individuals did "real" work outside the home. In *The Feminine Mystique*, Betty Friedan made it clear that any woman with an ounce of intelligence and determination should be able to fulfill all the needs of the traditional household while also succeeding at the kind of career designed for a man with a full-time wife.

> In actual fact, it is not as difficult as the feminine mystique implies, to combine marriage and motherhood and even the kind of lifelong personal purpose that once was called "career." It merely takes a new life plan—in terms of one's whole life as a woman.[7]

This idea went over big with educated Americans in the 1960s and '70s. After all, they were well versed in the political ideas formulated by Enlightenment thinkers. Both male and female scholars eagerly supported the idea that women should be able to do both traditional and modern work at the same time. They loved this idea *because it solved the problem of finding Somebody Else to sustain the society's traditional institutions while everyone became equal rational individuals in the modern economy.* The assumption that traditional work is not only low-class, but also trivial and easy, was an implied part of every liberal-arts education in the United States.

I saw some truly amazing examples of how deeply the most educated Americans believe in the trivial nature of "women's work" when I was a student at Harvard expecting my first child. On one occasion, a brilliant sociology professor, who had spent his long life studying and teaching human behavior at the best educational institutions in the United States, assured me that I would have no trouble at all caring for a baby while I finished a Ph.D. This world-famous expert on human behavior told me quite seriously (and I quote), "Babies don't really take any time until they're five years old. After that, you have to drive them to school." Like the Enlightenment scholars who went before him, this man was simply generalizing from his own experience. The important point here is that *nothing in his extensive training in Western social science had challenged his belief that Somebody Else raises the children of all rational individuals.*

At about this same time another Harvardian—this one a student in a class I taught—asked me if I would be working through the whole academic year. I answered that I'd be taking a semester off because I'd be having my baby right around midterms. The student responded incredulously, "You're taking the whole semester off for something that only takes *one day?*"

You must understand that neither this student nor the professor was an insensitive or stupid person. They were simply doing their very best to be enlightened feminist thinkers. At Harvard in the early 1980s, it was considered politically correct to assume that a woman who had a baby would be no more inconvenienced by the process than a man whose child was being born. Even hinting that *anything* might make it hard for females to participate in the rational labor force, *exactly as it had been designed for males with free traditional support,* was considered a terrible breach of etiquette.

If it was true, as many feminists of this era claimed, that doing both women's work and men's work was easy and energizing, then any woman who couldn't bring home the bacon, fry it up in a pan, and never let you forget you're a man was just being a wimp. If she pointed out anything that made it hard for her to put in the kind of working day that had been designed for a man with a full-time wife, she was seen as supporting the old Cult of True Womanhood that had kept women in a subordinate position. She was not only a weakling, but a traitor to the entire female sex.

PARADOX CATCHES UP WITH THE
AMERICAN FAMILY

If nothing else, the women's movement showed how many American females were unhappy with their traditional family situations. Between the
mid-1960s and the late 1970s, more and more couples split up, until
well over a third of all American marriages could be expected to dissolve.
In the vast majority of cases, it was the wife, not the husband, who filed
for divorce.

This flew in the face of the belief that all an American woman wanted
was a man to depend on, and that women were innately devoted to traditional institutions. It reflected a social fact that had been smilingly ignored by Americans right up through the 1950s: that marriage was a
very different thing from male and female perspectives—and that generally speaking it was great for men, lousy for women. The way gender
roles had developed in the United States meant that when an American man got married, he would henceforth have personal service for
all his traditional needs while he spent his time maximizing his importance and income in the modern labor force. A woman who got married moved *down* from the status of free-and-equal individual to the role
of a Dark Age peasant—economic dependency on a social "superior,"
endless days of unpaid domestic labor, low prestige, and virtually no
autonomy.

TECHNOLOGICAL LIBERATION

Along with the consciousness-raising that came from the women's movement, some technological breakthroughs helped women move away
from their domestic role into the labor market. Effective birth control
was now readily available to American women. The industrial society was
developing into a "postindustrial" phase, which meant that the jobs
done by most Americans were in service, not manufacturing, and did not
depend on physical strength or anything else that could make them ex-
clusively "male" tasks.

From the perspective of feminism, with its Enlightenment base, the
statistics for American women during the sixties, seventies, and early
eighties looked terrific. American women were earning more than ever
before, even though they still got paid much less than American men for
doing the same work. Millions of women had left unhappy marriages,

freeing themselves from traditional stereotypes and male domination. Women were moving into career areas where only men had gone before. As French feminist Simone de Beauvoir once said, "A woman must do twice as well as a man to be considered equally as good. Fortunately, this is not difficult." The modern woman of the late 1970s was pictured as someone who could Do It All, and love every minute of it.

SWING TO THE RIGHT

◆ *The Eighties—Antifeminist Backlash*   The Baby Boomers had been raised in the wealthiest economy in the world. Their parents, who supported them until they were adults, were still hale and hearty. They had postponed marriage and childbearing longer than previous generations, gone to college in unprecedented numbers, and moved into good jobs. In the 1980s, the Boomer's typical lifestyle was summed up in the acronym YUP or Yuppie, short for "young, upwardly mobile professional." Women, as well as men, were part of the Yuppie crowd. As the women's movement mowed down barriers that had excluded women from power, prestige, and wealth, women became accepted parts of the modern workforce. The Baby Boomers didn't really start to worry about the possible conflicts between their modern and traditional value systems until about the mid-1980s. At this point, a number of issues came to the forefront of national attitudes toward women's roles.

1. Late Marriage

By the 1980s, divorce and the tendency to stay single longer than previous generations had increased the average age at which Americans married. In the 1980s, many single women began to worry that their chances of marrying were going down with age. Researchers (and I use the term loosely) began making wild, speculative "calculations" that American women over the age of thirty-five had a better chance of being kidnapped by terrorists than getting married. The notable thing about such claims was that American women seemed to take them seriously.

Robin, 40

I admit it. When I was thirty-two and not married I was scared. And I was frustrated. Yes, I wanted a career—but why shouldn't I have a marriage and a family as well? Men have all those things!

2. Infertility

Even if they were married, American women who had put off childbearing (usually in order to compete better in the workforce) began to worry that their chance to have children might zip right past them. Since women's fertility decreases with age, dropping off rather quickly after thirty-five, many of the Baby Boomers who delayed starting families in order to succeed in the modern workplace had less luck than they expected becoming pregnant.

Lynnette, 44

I had always been so worried about making sure I *didn't* get pregnant. I'd panic if I forgot to take one of my pills, or if my period was a day late. I guess I just came to think that the instant I stopped preventing it, I'd be pregnant. I decided to have my first when I was thirty-eight, and after a year of trying, we weren't pregnant. We went for help at that point.

An enormous "fertility industry" grew up in American medicine: new methods of ensuring conception were devised, and test-tube babies became a reality. Even though most couples who went for such treatments were still not able to conceive a child, millions of dollars continued to pour into fertility research and treatment as the first wave of feminists set out to have babies.

3. Role Strain

By the time I was a teenager, I was a devoted feminist who believed absolutely in women's ability to compete on an equal footing with men while accomplishing every traditional task females had ever done. Most of the Americans born during the Baby Boom agreed with me. But by the late 1970s, a small but rising grumble could be heard from America's working women. I remember a *Saturday Night Live* skit from this period. A housewife with a grocery bag bounces into a sunny kitchen announcing that she has three children, a full-time job, a beautifully clean house, and multicourse dinners on her table every night. "How do I do it?" She beams into the camera. Then she pulls a syringe from her grocery bag, holds it up, and says, "I take speed!" Comedy, always the first area of popular culture to speak forbidden truths, was beginning to reflect the deep, dark secret of many American women.

They were getting tired.

The studies done on role combination in the 1970s tended to find that women who combined roles were healthier and more robust than women who did only traditional or only modern work. Researchers were thrilled by these politically correct findings. One much-cited article explained that women could "do it all" because human energy was "elastic"—when women had more work to do, they simply became more energetic. This was a lovely thought for feminist analysts who had been claiming all along that women's work in the home wasn't "real" and that they should be able to throw in a "masculine" career without any trouble at all. What these researchers rarely considered was that maybe they were finding amazingly healthy, robust women combining career and family because *only the healthiest and most robust women could do all that work.*

Tanya, 47

I have two kids and I work full-time as a nurse. The other day I came home from work and jumped right into cleaning the house, cooking dinner, and helping the kids with their homework. All day I'd been noticing that I felt a little uncomfortable in my abdominal area, but I hadn't really stopped to think about it. It got worse and worse as the day wore on. When I finally got the kids to bed and cleaned up, I let myself pay attention to the discomfort. Then I realized what the problem was—I hadn't had time to go to the bathroom all day long! It sounds so silly, but I have to tell you I was pretty proud of myself. I don't think there are many people who can work that hard and hang in that long. You have to have a lot of endurance to live like I live!

By the 1980s, not just a select few, but *most* American mothers were in the workforce. This was partly because of new opportunities for women and their desire to obtain the money, wealth, and status reserved for "working" Americans. But that wasn't the whole story. For one thing, the huge number of divorced mothers were expected to provide at least some of the money to raise their children—and even when fathers were supposed to pay alimony and child support, many of them didn't.

Then there was the fact that, because women had moved into the workforce in such numbers, many American families had two wage earners. That meant that employers had been able to reduce the average single wage relative to the cost of living. Instead of men demanding, "You've got to give me a raise—I can't support a family on this!" they could reason, "I can't support a family on this—but we'll get by if the wife and I both work." By the 1980s, many American mothers didn't just *choose* to work, they *had* to work.

Erma, 60

I hear all this stuff about women getting the "privilege" of working. Well, I had two children to raise on my own, and it sure didn't feel like a "privilege" to me. I didn't feel "liberated" because I had a job—I hated it! I was worn out! All I ever wanted was to stay home and have a man take care of the bills. But that's not the way it worked out.

Contrary to their predictions, when social scientists went out to talk to actual American working mothers like Erma, they did not find that combining modern jobs and traditional domestic work was filling these women chock-full of vibrant health and energy. In the 1980s, one sociologist who studied working mothers wrote, "These people talked about sleep the way a starving person talks about food."[8] Another said that she found working mothers "torn apart" by the demands on their time and energy.[9] Even when they were coping pretty well physically, a lot of American women were beset by guilt, confusion, and a sense of being overwhelmed.

Angela, 40

If you don't work, in our society, you're looked down on; you're "just a housewife." But if you *do* work, you're not a good mother. Sometimes I get so torn up thinking about how people are judging me.

Margaret, 38

The guilt is just tremendous. It's huge. Whenever the sitter comes in and I go to work, I feel like I've deserted my kids. My husband goes to work, and he feels like he's being virtuous.

In the 1980s, a distraught woman accosted feminist Gloria Steinem at a banquet celebrating the progress of American feminism.

"Why didn't you tell us?" the woman implored. "Why didn't you tell us it was going to be like this?"

Steinem's characteristically honest answer summed up the one-sidedness inherent in a purely modern view of life.

"Well," she said, "we didn't know." [10]

4. The Feminization of Poverty

A lot of the distress American women were feeling in the 1980s wasn't quantifiable. You can't really measure how tired someone is, or how "torn apart" she feels—you can only take her word for it. But in the 1980s, people who studied gender began to see a clear, measurable pattern that did not bode well for American women.

It was labeled "the feminization of poverty"; for the first time in history, a clear connection had been established between gender and standard of living. A larger and larger percentage of America's poor were women and children who lived in female-headed households. In the year after a divorce, an ex-husband's income went up substantially, while an ex-wife's plummeted.[11] By 1986, an unprecedented 48 percent of America's poor families were composed only of women and children. Conversely, a larger percentage of American women lived in poverty than ever before.

The middle to late 1980s saw an upsurge in concern about the "feminization of poverty." The tone in popular and scholarly media turned against the idea of working women, and showcased those who returned to a more traditional role. Glowing articles were written about high-achieving women who quit their jobs and went home to raise children in a revitalized version of domestic bliss (many gave the impression that this was a national trend, when in fact most working women couldn't afford to quit their jobs, and didn't want to in any case). A *Harvard Business Review* article proposed that a separate "mommy track" be instituted in corporations, for women who wanted to have children while continuing their careers. In short, Americans were realizing that their headlong rush to achieve a perfect Enlightenment equality had pushed them farther than they wanted to go toward destroying traditional institutions. As the swing to the left began to yield unwanted results, American society had come to a creaking halt and surged back toward the right. But of course that wouldn't last for long.

SWING TO THE LEFT

♦ *The 1990s "Second Wave" of Feminism Rises Against the Backlash*
In the 1990s, the generation of American women born *after* the Baby
Boomers reached the same life stage the Boomers had in the 1960s. The
young adult women of the nineties were schooled in the same old Enlightenment tradition that had fueled their older sisters' bid for equality.
Not yet enmeshed in the logistical complexities of trying to care for society's traditional institutions, they were inspired by the rhetoric of earlier
feminists and disgusted by the way American women were backing away
from egalitarian ideals. They created what has been called the second
wave of feminism. Standing on the shoulders of their predecessors, they
were even more willing to push for major social changes and more determined to gain equality with men.

It was very clear to the members of the second wave that they were
fighting a more complicated battle than earlier feminists had realized.
The first major bid for equality had been followed by a swing to the right
that was deeply disappointing and quite baffling to the second wave.
Everyone had an explanation for the backlash against feminism that had
occurred during the 1980s. Here are some of the favorites:

1. *The "All Men Are Ruthless Domineering Brutes" Axiom* According to this theory, whenever American women begin to modernize,
   or become more like the Enlightenment ideal of a rational individual, American men feel threatened and launch a calculated effort to
   shove women back into a traditional role. American women don't
   like this, but so far, they've been too weak to resist.
2. *The "Most Women Are Completely Clueless" Hypothesis* This explanation is based on the idea that the majority of American women
   have accepted traditional social roles because they just don't know
   any better—they've been duped into submission. American women
   will hold on to this belief, the theory goes, until their consciousness
   is raised (forcibly, if need be) by the minority of women who are rational. Then they will get fighting mad and rush out with a roar, in
   numbers too big to ignore, and claim free-and-equal status.
3. *The "Evil Plot to Keep Women Down" Scenario* This is a combination of the first two theories. It goes like this: First, women's roles
   begin to modernize. Then, men launch an attack to push women
   "backwards." Some women are too dim-witted to figure out what's

wrong; others are too weak to fight back. But there is a third group of women, who are neither stupid nor feeble—they're just downright wicked. Recognizing that they will win out if they cater to the interests of powerful males, these treacherous females actually join with the men to push the rest of American women back to a traditional role.

Now, all these explanations have undoubtedly been accurate at certain times and places. There have been plenty of brutal, domineering men in American history, and probably a lot of deluded, helpless, or scheming women as well. But to say that any of these scenarios accounts for the perplexing ambivalence toward women's roles, in any broad general way, gives far too little credit to Americans of both sexes. The real reason for the staggered, left-right-left-right pattern of American women's role development is that for four hundred years, no one has questioned the incomplete and problematic Enlightenment definition of "equality."

So where has the "herstory" of female role definition brought American women? Certainly not to solutions for all our problems. The women of the United States are still discriminated against in both public and private life—the legacy of a traditional hierarchy. They also have ended up with the most painful and destructive elements of modern roles. Instead of being progressively "liberated," American women as a group, over the course of our nation's development, have been saddled with the literally impossible responsibility of balancing two opposite and mutually exclusive core value systems.

The sensation many women described to me, of being caught up in a maelstrom of contradictory structures and ideals, is not the feeling people have as they move smoothly into a modern role. It is the result of being trapped in paradox, of being brought to the breaking point. The next chapter will look more closely at this phenomenon, examining the nature and dynamics of paradox. Only by understanding these things can we even begin to make sense of the forces that have been splitting women's roles in contradictory directions since the founding of our nation—forces that impact every American woman today more drastically than they have at any previous time in "herstory."

PHASE ONE: SOCIALIZATION
PHASE TWO: ENCOUNTERING PARADOX
PHASE THREE: REACHING THE BREAKING POINT
PHASE FOUR: TRANSCENDENCE
PHASE FIVE: RE-CREATION

PHASE TWO

✦

Encountering Paradox

CHAPTER THREE

Strange Loops and Double Binds:
The Nature of Paradox

Terry Estridge is the youngest of four daughters born into the family of Colonel and Mrs. Dennis P. Estridge, of Jacksonville, Florida. She is also their only son. If you think that sounds confusing, you should try being Terry. After having three daughters, Dennis Estridge did everything he could, including seeking medical advice, to make sure his fourth and last child would be male. It didn't work.

Terry, 36
My mom says Dad could hardly look at me when I was born. He wanted a boy so bad. But then he sort of switched. He started thinking maybe a girl could do the things he'd wanted a boy to do.

It seemed to Colonel Estridge that Terry, as she grew, was stronger and more active than her sisters, more like a soldier. One day he brought home a toddler-sized camouflage suit and dressed her in it. She pointed an imaginary gun and shouted "Bang! Bang!" like a miniature Rambo. From then on, Terry was her father's favorite.

. . . it was a little weird, the way he always bought my sisters dolls, and I got baseball mitts and trucks. But I liked the attention. I got to be good at a lot of things my sisters never did. Dad put me in Little League and taught me how to box.

Sally Estridge was ambivalent about Terry's "tomboy" personality. In Sally's world, men were strong, bold, authoritative warriors, and women were sugar and spice and everything nice. The two sets did not intersect. For her part, Terry found her parents extremely confusing, their approval and disapproval double-edged. Sally, as well as Dennis, seemed proud when Terry was chosen as captain of her Little League team. Dennis, as well as Sally, agreed that Terry should "act like a lady." The Estridges didn't argue about what Terry should do and be. Instead, they sent her a daily blizzard of contradictory messages: "Play to win, Terry!" "Don't be so competitive, Terry!" "Learn not to throw like a girl, Terry!" "Try to be more ladylike, Terry!" "You can be anything you want to be, Terry!" "Someday you'll have to settle down and be a wife and mother, Terry!"

> I remember reading *Dr. Dolittle* when I was about ten. There's an animal in the book called a "push-me-pull-you." It had two heads, one on each end, and it was always trying to go in two different directions at once. When I read that, it was like this light went on in my head: "That's my life! That's me! I'm a push-me-pull-you!"

I met Terry when she was thirty-six, and the first word that came to my mind when I tried to describe her was "haunted." She was an extremely accomplished person who constantly apologized for the very things she worked desperately hard to achieve. She told me she was a research biologist, then added that I probably thought that was "weird." She spoke lovingly about the three children she had borne during her five-year marriage to a Marine lieutenant, then hastened to assure me that she never let motherhood interfere with her career. She had put her older children in day care while she finished her schooling, and she felt guilty about it. On the other hand, she felt equally guilty for keeping her youngest child at home until he was nearly six before sending him off to kindergarten. I couldn't see anything wrong with any of these things, but Terry seemed to expect negative judgment from me and everyone else.

Not all of us live with such explicit contradictions as Terry Estridge, but Terry's case exemplifies the paradoxical role definition that affects all American women. In order to understand this, we're going to look more closely at the dynamics of paradox in general, and the paradox of female roles in particular.

RECIPE FOR PARADOX

To make a paradox, take one strong, directive idea. Add an equal amount of any other idea that cancels out the first one. Mix well until the two are completely blended. For an example of what the finished paradox will look like, consider the following sentence:

This statement is a lie.

If the above statement is true, then it must be a lie, because it says it is. But if we can believe that it's a lie, that means it must be true. If it's false, then it isn't a lie, which means it's true, in which case it must be a lie, which makes it true, which makes it false, which makes it true, which makes it false. . . .

This dizzying circular logic is the hallmark of a true paradox. Sentences like "This is a lie" or "I am lying" are paradoxical because they have two contradictory elements. All true paradoxes have this structure; at least two elements that are both supposed to be equally true, but that cancel each other out. The confusing, back-and-forth reasoning that is set in motion by a paradox is called a strange loop by mathematicians. That phrase perfectly describes the sense of disorientation and self-contradiction that emerges when one is struggling to resolve a paradox. The problem is that, since both the contradictory elements of the paradox are supposed to be *equally true*, there is actually no way to "solve" a paradoxical dilemma the way one might solve a different kind of problem.

The more important it is for us to solve a paradoxical problem, the more we get stuck in the strange loop it creates. A paradox that is very important to us, to the extent that we can't just walk away and forget about it, can get us deeply engaged in the strange loop of reasoning. With those concepts in mind, let's take a look at how our society "paradoxes" its female members.

THE "PARADOXING" OF THE AMERICAN FEMALE

From the moment she was born, Terry Estridge continually received at least three powerful, distinct messages from her parents, which created a paradox in Terry's own concept of what and who she was. To different degrees, these same three messages filter through our culture to influence every baby girl born in the United States. The first message is that boys and girls are, and should be, completely different from each other. The second is that being a girl is the inferior role, and that to win praise or attention, one has to achieve in areas that fit the definition of "male" achievement. The third message is that if you are born female, you must conform to our society's model of a "proper" girl.

This mixture of messages leaves many American girls, like Terry Estridge, with the deep, often unconscious conviction that in order to be "good," they have to become two things that contradict each other. The nature of paradox means that no matter how hard a person tries to fulfill such expectations—to be a "good girl" or a "good woman"—she will always be perceived, *at the very same time*, as doing something "bad," inferior, or inappropriate.

◆ *Babes in Paradox*   Terry's socialization in the paradox of gender began early—but so does everyone else's. To avoid being affected by the paradoxical definitions of female roles, an infant girl would have to be raised by robots, preferably in a subterranean salt mine or a space capsule. From the moment someone says, "It's a girl!" the people around the baby are already assigning stereotypical interpretations to her behavior.

A female baby's understanding of the world, and her self-concept, are formed largely by the "mirroring" she gets from the people around her. Infants are like little socialization sponges, incredibly adept at soaking up other people's expectations and conforming to them. Babies pick up their ideas about what it means to be male and female by watching the way adults respond to them—and adults react very differently to a baby depending on whether they think the child is male or female. For example, when experimenters ask volunteers to guess what a crying baby is feeling, the volunteers who think the baby is a boy say that "he" is definitely angry, while those who have been told the baby is a girl say that "she" is obviously sad.[1] Same baby, same crying, totally different social interpretations.

These stereotypes will last a lifetime, and help create what they expect. By the time most boys reach adulthood, they will have deeply internalized the idea that anger is more permissible for them than sadness. Girls, on the other hand, will have learned that for them, sadness is more permissible than anger. Our prisons are full of men who need to grieve but can only rage; our psychologists' offices are full of women who need to rage but can only grieve. Gender stereotyping robs *both* of the full range of their emotional and psychological lives.

◆ *The Paradoxical Child*   The Enlightenment assumption that boys do "real" things, while girls, in order to be considered feminine, should refrain from achievement, is communicated throughout childhood in an infinite variety of ways. For example, consider American media productions designed for children. Male characters outnumber females in books and television programming for all age levels, from preschool to high school. The male characters are depicted as leading more interesting, adventurous lives, as being more capable than female characters, and as earning more rewards for their behavior.[2] This is true even in the most lauded and intelligent children's programs (as one woman asked me, "Have you ever noticed how incredibly lame-o the girl muppets on *Sesame Street* are?").

Try this little experiment yourself: browse through the children's book section at a bookstore or watch some children's shows, from cartoons to educational programs, on TV. Then simply count how many major characters are male and how many are female. Many books and programs are becoming increasingly alert to the idea that the two genders should get equal "airtime," but over the course of a whole morning's reading or watching, you'll be amazed (well, anyway, *I* always am) at how strongly the scale still tips in favor of male characters.

Think about what this does to a typical little girl in the United States. She may simply decide that she isn't a "real person," and that she can't do any of the exciting things most of the characters in her stories are doing, because such activities are only for boys. Many of the women I interviewed told me something like this:

Camille, 33

I remember going to the Walt Disney version of *The Jungle Book* when I was a kid. I sat there and watched Mowgli live this wild life with bears and wolves, climbing trees and swimming in rivers and doing all kinds of wonderful things. Then, at the end of the movie, Mowgli falls in love with this little girl his own age. She's out getting water for cooking. She sings this song about how she's going to get the water every day until she grows up, and then she'll have a daughter and she'll stay home and cook while her daughter gets the water, etc., etc. I sat and listened to that song and just felt sick. How come she didn't get to have any fun adventures? Why was her life so mapped out for her, and so boring? Well, obviously, because she was a girl.

You can probably give your own examples of this kind of "role shaping," whether you are male or female. I can. When I was in the first grade, my teacher gave the class a special assignment. We were all supposed to choose a famous person from history as our own personal role model. We were to hang pictures of our heroes in our rooms, find out everything we could about them, and deliver oral reports about them to the class.

Without the slightest sense of impropriety, I chose Abraham Lincoln as my hero. When the time for our oral presentations came around, I went up to the front of the classroom and taped my picture of Honest Abe to the blackboard. Much to my surprise, the whole first-grade class went into fits of laughter. My teacher took the picture down and gently suggested that I spend a little extra time and do my report on *Mrs.* Lincoln. I tried, I really did, but with all respect to Mrs. Lincoln, the idea of emulating a clinically depressed syphilitic who spent the last years of her life in a dark room crying for her deceased children just didn't float my boat. With characteristic perversity I went ahead and did my report on Abraham Lincoln, leading to dire predictions that I would sprout whiskers at puberty, turn every man I ever met into a soprano, and die unmarried.

Speaking of grade school, the double message that girls must aspire to individual achievement, but also *not* aspire, has been observed in classroom dynamics for years. A large part of every American child's life is spent in an education system where boys and girls are overtly told to aim for the same goals, at the same time that girls are subtly discouraged from achieving them.

In study after study, researchers have found that teachers treat boys and girls differently. Boys are usually punished for rambunctious behavior, girls for academic mistakes. Girls get praise for tidiness and appearance, boys for doing well in their schoolwork. In fact, girls often don't get any feedback at all on their academic performance, while teachers tend to give boys more comments and work harder with them to come up with alternative solutions when they make mistakes.[3] All of this takes place in a setting where *every student is supposed to be competing against every other student for identical goals.* The message that girls should try to perform as well as boys is accompanied by constant messages, both subtle and blatant, that girls should *not* excel in "masculine" things.

Most researchers who study these dynamics describe them as straightforward inequality. But the problem is more complex than that. Girls are not simply less supported than boys in their efforts to achieve. They are given powerful incentives to achieve in the manner of a rational individual while *also* being pressured to behave in stereotypically female ways. This is not just discouragement. It is *paradox*, and it means that most American girls are deeply engaged in a fragmenting and disorienting strange loop as they try to enact an impossible, internally contradictory ideal. Every girl who goes through the American school system will almost certainly be affected by these paradoxical demands.

♦ *The "Real World": Paradox in the American Workforce*   As many problems as it has, the educational system in the United States is a model of Enlightenment egalitarianism compared with what happens in the "real world" of the American job market. From kindergarten up through college, most American students are enjoying a lifestyle that makes it relatively easy for them to define female roles paradoxically without seriously disrupting the fabric of their lives. Parents or other caretakers do the students' laundry, buy and cook food, pay the gas bill, and so on. In other words, most young Americans—including girls—have approximately the same kind of lifestyle as Enlightenment gentlemen scholars. There are inequalities in the ways boys and girls are treated, but the consequences of violating stereotypes aren't life-threatening. This is why I often heard this kind of sentiment expressed by the young, single women students I interviewed:

Jill, 18

I really don't think we have any more discrimination problems in the United States. I know it was bad in the past, but all my friends at college are equal. It doesn't matter whether you're a man or a woman or what race you are or anything. I think everybody in America gets treated pretty equally nowadays.

These are the words of a person who has lived the protected lifestyle of the rational individual, Enlightenment-style. As long as they are single, supported by their parents, and going to school, American women really may be treated approximately like men in their age group. Outside the educational system, however, the paradox of female role definition can be much more disruptive. In the workplace, many American women find themselves confronted with paradoxical demands that have profound effects on their careers, and ultimately the quality of their lives. Tamara Holt's story is an example of how the paradox of being female affected one woman's career.

TAMARA HOLT

Tamara Holt was twenty-three and fresh out of college when she was hired as the assistant office manager for the law firm of Grossett, Dunnell, Hertzig, Spencer & Webb.

Tamara, 35

I was sort of a glorified receptionist. I did a lot of filing and stayed overtime to help with paperwork whenever a lawyer was pushing a deadline—which was always.

Tamara was an ideal assistant office manager. She was intelligent, efficient, and outgoing. The first face potential clients saw when they walked through the law firm's door was well-sculpted and clear-skinned, with naturally blond hair, large green eyes, and a dazzling smile. The smile alone probably brought in hundreds of thousands of dollars in revenues for Grossett, Dunnell, and the rest of them. Tamara was an asset to the firm, and she knew it. What she didn't know, when she got her job, was that she was a feminist waiting to happen.

I'd never really thought much about women's issues. I always did pretty much everything I wanted in school. I even played coed doubles tennis. All my friends were pretty much the same, whether they were boys or girls. We all wanted careers, and we all wanted families. And we all thought we would have both.

The women's movement of the sixties and seventies had done away with a sizable chunk of the discrimination faced by female students only a few years older than Tamara. She felt grateful to her feminist benefactors, but pretty much forgot about them as she planned for a bright future of equal opportunity at Grossett, Dunnell, Hertzig, Spencer & Webb.

After about six months I was handling more work than half the young guys in the firm. I was doing research, finishing briefs for people, the whole thing. I knew I was a lot sharper than most of the people in the office . . . but nobody seemed to notice. They treated me just about the way they treated the copier—nobody noticed me unless I did something wrong. Or at least they didn't notice the *work*. They noticed me, all right. The men were always hitting on me. Finally, I just got sick of it.

Tamara, her consciousness rising by the minute, went to the firm's founder, Edward Grossett himself, to lodge a complaint about her working conditions. She told him she wanted and deserved a lot more respect than she was getting. She was tired of being overworked and undercompensated just because she was a woman.

Grossett laughed gently and explained to Tamara that she was laboring under a misconception. The way she was treated had more to do with her behavior and her lack of qualifications than it did with the simple fact of being female.

> He said he knew it wasn't fair, but women just weren't used to "playing hardball" the way male attorneys do. He said a woman had to learn to act more authoritative in the office if she wanted respect. He also said I didn't realize what the lawyers in the firm had been through in order to become attorneys . . . [that] if I had been through the same thing, I would have earned their respect, and they would treat me just like any other lawyer. So I decided right then that I would go to law school.

Tamara proved to be a legal eagle. She graduated fifth in her class, sailed through her bar exam, and took her diploma straight to Ed Grossett. Impressed, Grossett gave Tamara a job as a junior attorney.

> I can't tell you how good it felt to walk past the receptionist's desk, where I used to sit, and then on to my own office. I'd almost forgotten how unpleasant it had been to work there as an office manager. I figured that now that I was an attorney, things would be different. . . . Well, they were. They were about twenty times worse.

The idea of a beautiful young blond woman with a law degree seemed to have some sort of aphrodisiac effect on the men of Grossett, Dunnell, Hertzig, Spencer & Webb. Besides the fact that Tamara already had a steady boyfriend, she had decided years before that it would be wise not to date any of the men she worked with. She explained this patiently to the many attorneys and legal assistants, old and young, who stopped by her office to casually mention that they had two tickets to the opera or a free day to take her windsurfing. Tamara maintained a cordial but professional distance from all her male colleagues, and concentrated on the grueling work it took to succeed in the firm.

> One night I was in the office late, working on a complicated case. I overheard a conversation from the next office. There were three men's voices. One of them said something like "Did she turn you down too?" and then this other guy said yes, and then they all laughed. And then somebody said, "Well, you know she's screwing Grossett. That's

how she got the job." He was saying things like "You don't think they hired her for her brains, do you?" As if they all understood I was some kind of airhead.

. . . At first I wasn't sure they were talking about me. There were two other women in the firm, and one of them was single, so I thought it might be her. But then they started talking about how they could get promoted too if they had the blond hair and—you know, breasts and everything. And then the first guy said something about how he wouldn't go out with a bitch like that no matter what, because women like that are just waiting to stab you in the back.

It's still very confusing to me, thinking about it, because they were degrading me for exactly the same reasons they wanted to date me. I still can't quite get a handle on it. How did they want me to act?

Stunned and frightened, Tamara went back to Grossett, whom she had come to think of as her mentor. She told him part of what she had overheard (leaving out the rumor that she and Grossett were having an affair). She asked her boss to reprimand the men and possibly institute some sensitivity training. Grossett responded with the same soft, dismissive chuckle he had used to soothe Tamara years before.

He told me I just had to expect that kind of behavior from the other attorneys, because it was so new to them to have to work with women as peers. He said if I wanted to get along, I should try to act more like "other women." He said he wished I would act a little more like I used to, that it was more appropriate for a woman. This is the same guy who told me that my problem was being *too much* like other women.

Two weeks later, one of the junior lawyers with whom Tamara had become friends knocked on the door of her office and said he had something to tell her.

He told me he thought I should know that the women in the secretarial staff were really ticked off at me. I'd known all these people when I'd been the office manager, and I thought we were friends, but he said that wasn't true. According to him, the women on the office staff said I acted superior and went out of my way to put them down.

Tamara felt besieged, confused, and alone. "It was a nightmare," she told me. "I felt as though I were being punished for some strange crime that I'd committed without knowing it. No trial, no jury, just a whole lot of judges."

After only three months, Tamara quit her job at the law firm.

The work wasn't a problem—I actually liked the work. The whole issue was that in that firm there was no way for me to *be*. After a while, I just didn't want to deal with it anymore.

Tamara never did figure out exactly what the people at Grossett, Dunnell, Hertzig, Spencer & Webb had really expected of her. "It stays with me," she said. "Since then, I've never felt like I can really be sure what people are thinking about me, or if I'm on the right track."

DOUBLE BINDS AND TORMENTED MINDS

Tamara Holt's law firm, like Terry Estridge's family (and most other American institutions, large and small), had a paradoxical definition of female roles firmly embedded in its culture. Any woman who didn't achieve in exactly the way men did was treated as a subordinate, unimportant female, but women who could compete with men on their own professional turf were castigated for not acting feminine enough. In this environment, Tamara simply could not win. As Tamara herself pointed out, the office culture demanded that she *be* two incompatible things. When paradox is incorporated into social roles and expectations this way, psychologists call it a double bind.

Double binds occur whenever a person receives contradictory instructions about how to act, think, or feel. The more powerful the source of the paradoxical demands, and the more we believe we should fulfill them, the more "deeply engaging" double binds become. A minor double-bind situation may merely put us in a bad mood, but when the double bind comes from a high authority or is accepted by the majority of the people we see as powerful, it can lock us into a strange loop that seems inescapable.

For example, when a contradictory instruction comes from a small child, it isn't likely to be terribly destructive for an adult. Each of my own children passed through a stage where he or she insisted that I do more than one thing at a time, such as making a peanut butter sandwich and pouring a glass of milk. Even coming from my own toddler-age offspring, this contradictory expectation was enough to frustrate me into some grumpy behavior, but I didn't take it seriously enough to get really bent out of shape. As children grow, the contradictory expectations they have of their caretakers become more mature, more aligned with adult value systems, and therefore more deeply engaging. For example, the teenager who wants the security, assistance, and financial support of a child *as well as* the complete independence of an adult can put a parent in a fairly serious double bind.

For their part, parents exercise tremendous authority in their children's eyes. A parent who demands contradictory behaviors of their children ("Be my little girl forever, but get a life of your own"; "Be successful enough to make me proud, but never more successful than I am") can unintentionally bend well-meaning offspring into psychological pretzels.

Double binds are most destructive *when they come from sources whose authority we trust, and when we don't have enough distance from the source to articulate what is happening.* This is often the case when children are receiving paradoxical demands from their caretakers. For example, Terry Estridge first started getting mixed messages from her parents when she was about two minutes old. She was in no position to question the way her parents viewed the world, their own identities, or Terry herself. Infants don't see their parents' way of looking at the world as a limited, imperfect struggle to understand the universe, but as the Way the Universe Really Is.

THE CULTURE OF PARADOX

Culture, the combination of actions, values, expectations, definitions, and beliefs that are considered normal in a given society, is the ultimate "parent," the most powerful, authoritative source we rely on to tell us how to live. From the moment we are born, we begin to accept our culture's way of seeing and thinking, usually without much criticism. That means that if culture looks at women through a paradoxical lens, *women learn to look at themselves in exactly the same way.*

A classic example of how strongly American culture prescribes paradoxical roles for women is the famous Broverman study, conducted in the late 1960s. In this study, a research team led by one I. K. Broverman asked a group of mental health professionals (psychiatrists, psychologists, and the like) to write down three lists of adjectives. One list would contain all the qualities that characterize a psychologically healthy man. Another would list the qualities of a healthy woman. On the third list, the participants were supposed to write down the traits of a healthy adult.

I'm sure you've already guessed what happened. The subjects in the Broverman study listed similar qualities for a healthy adult and a healthy man. According to these experts, both healthy men and healthy adults are assertive, forceful, independent, self-reliant, and individualistic, among other things. But *under the "healthy woman" heading, they listed qualities that were not characteristic of a healthy adult.* Indeed, the healthy woman described by the subjects in the Broverman study is much more attuned to others' assertions, ambitions, and forceful behaviors than to her own. A healthy woman was supposed to be gentle, kind, "able to devote [her]self completely to others," "aware of others' feelings," and "helpful to others."[4] So, according to the perceptions of these highly trained mental health specialists—one of our culture's most respected sources of role definition—a person *cannot be* both a healthy adult and a healthy woman.

INTERNALIZING THE DOUBLE BIND

Without realizing it, all Americans, male and female, absorb these contradictory ideas about women's roles into our most basic "maps of the world," our ways of conceptualizing reality. When this happens, the double bind of female role definition can become nightmarish for a woman. It is confusing enough to think about a hypothetical paradox, like the sentence "I am lying." But imagine how incapacitating it would be for me if I *really believed* that I was lying! I would not be able to trust my own words or thoughts, and I would be stuck so completely in the strange loop of trying to figure out my own reality that I wouldn't know what to do next. This is what happens to women who absorb the contradictory role definition of the surrounding culture.

Doris, 50

It seems to me that all I ever do is apologize. I'm sorry I don't think for myself enough, I'm sorry I don't agree with other people's opinions enough, I'm sorry I'm not strong enough, I'm sorry I'm too strong. I'm sorry, sorry, sorry. I ought to just wear a sign that says I'M SORRY, and people could attach it to everything I do.

Melody, 30

When I go to see my parents, all my mother ever asks about is how I'm doing with my little boy. All my father ever asks about is how my degree program is going. He doesn't like it when I talk about being a housewife, she doesn't like it when I talk about being a student—it's fine as long as the three of us are never in a room together. When that happens, I just stare at them and keep my mouth shut.

Consider the results of another psychological study done in the 1960s. Student volunteers were asked to complete the story of a young woman, Anne, who "finds herself at the top of her medical school class." Here are some of the things that female students wrote about Anne:

Anne starts proclaiming her surprise and joy. Her fellow classmates are so disgusted with her behavior that they jump on her in a body and beat her. She is maimed for life.

Anne doesn't want to be number one in her class. . . . She drops down to ninth in the class and then marries the boy who graduates number one.

Anne feels guilty. . . . She will finally have a nervous breakdown and quit medical school and marry a successful young doctor.

These responses convinced researchers that in our culture "a bright woman is in a double bind." They had a very good point, but they also assumed that these paradoxical ideals would be "more characteristic of women who are capable of success and who are career oriented" than of "less successful" women.[5] The tendency for the scholars of the twentieth century, like those of the sixteenth, was to focus on people like themselves and to assume that success refers only to activities that were valued by Enlightenment scholars. But the paradox of female role definition reaches far beyond the female doctors and lawyers of our society. You don't have to be a college valedictorian or the president of your own company to run up against a paradoxical gender definition in our culture. You don't have to be in a leadership position. You don't have to be employed. You don't have to be bright. You barely even have to be conscious. All you have to be is female.

In my research, I found that *all* types of women, not just college-educated or career-oriented individuals, were struggling with double binds. As our society moves closer and closer to the impossible dream of achieving total individual equality *without giving up* traditional hierarchy, women are defined and judged by more and more contradictory standards. Our society's laws, policies, and institutions are designed around this paradoxical definition of women's roles. As a result, American women in all sorts of social situations—rich, poor, old, young, black, white, married, single—are finding themselves caught in the strange loop of paradox. Our society has "modernized" to the point where, if you don't go out and find a situation that locks you in a double bind, a double bind is more and more likely to come find you.

In my research I heard hundreds of possible examples, ranging from the trivial to the truly horrendous. I'm going to present three of these stories at some length. Colette Bingham, Bernice Llewelyn, and Lee Nguyen are very different from one another—and very different from the college students who wrote the tales of Anne's destruction. Although, like Anne, all three of these women are very intelligent, most experts would think that they would be in no danger of confronting the double binds American women face when they move into "masculine" roles. Nevertheless, each of them faced a true double bind and reflected the experience of dozens more women I interviewed whose ordinary lives had brought them extraordinary conflict. As you read through their stories, notice the differences and the similarities among these three women.

COLETTE BINGHAM

Colette Bingham is a high school dropout who worked as a waitress until she married Harvey, a steel-plant worker from her neighborhood. The couple have two children. Colette quit her job as soon as the first child was born, staying home until the younger one was old enough to go to school. Once she had some free time, Colette began to think about returning to work in order to get out of the house and earn extra money.

◆   Colette, 28

He didn't like that at all. Harvey's family is real traditional. So he feels like it would be wrong if I didn't stay at home and look after the house. . . . Well, then he hurt his back and he was on disability for two weeks. It scared him, because the doctor said he was going to have to watch out for his back all the time—it could give out and need surgery and who knows what. So then he says, "Okay, Colette, you win. Go ahead, get a job."

Well, I did. I went back to the coffee shop, and they really liked me before and the manager took me back on right away. So then I kind of relaxed at home, you know? Because I sort of thought Harvey would pick up some of the housework after that, because now I was putting food on the table too.

But after I'd been working about two weeks, Harvey's furious at me. He talks to his mother, and she calls me and says, "Colette, you have to take care of the house. Harvey says he can't even expect to find his socks in their drawer anymore. After all, he is letting you go out and have a job like you wanted. The least you can do is keep the house clean. Otherwise he may not put up with all this stuff you're pulling, working and everything."

So here I am. I go to work all day, and I work just as hard as Harvey. They made him a supervisor now, so he just gets to sit on his butt most of the day. I'm on my feet all day. But when I come home, guess who has to do all the housework and watch out for the kids and go to all the teacher conferences and stuff? I'll tell you, it isn't Harvey.

I'm real tired. I like work, but it's like I have to start over when I get home. It feels crazy to me. It's like if Harvey works, that means I owe him, and if I work, that means I still owe him! That doesn't make sense. I don't understand the way people think about this.

BERNICE LLEWELYN

When I interviewed her, Bernice was a charming, thoughtful woman with prematurely snow-white hair. She carried pictures of her five grown children and her seven grandchildren in her purse, ready to display. She also carried a simmering anger that contrasted with her sweet, grandmotherly appearance.

Bernice grew up in the Midwest. She married a handsome young executive named Eric Llewelyn and moved with him to Chicago, where he began a job with an advertising agency and Bernice happily set up house. Over the next fifteen years, the couple had five children, two boys and three girls.

Eric Llewelyn climbed steadily up the career ladder in his agency. The more responsibilities he assumed, the more his time went to the job and the less Bernice and the children saw of him. He worked most nights and weekends. He also traveled a great deal, leaving Bernice alone with the children for one to three weeks each month. "It was lonely," Bernice said. "I didn't get out much. But it was very important to Eric to succeed in his job, and I wanted to support him."

Bernice, 50

A real "company man" needed a full-time wife. Eric always expressed appreciation for the way I was willing to stand behind him. I tried not to ever bother him at work. I took care of everything at home, and I had my lipstick on and the house clean and his dinner hot for him no matter how late he came home.

Eric said that a lot of other men in his company weren't doing as well as he was because they didn't have wives like me. Some of the wives were even into "women's lib," and they were absolutely poison for their husband's careers. Eric said he was so glad I wasn't like that. That made me feel really good.

After seventeen years at the firm, Eric was promoted to vice president of the company. His workload and travel increased to the point where Bernice hardly saw him at all. At about the same time, Bernice's mother had a cerebral hemorrhage that left her too weak to speak with her daughter on the phone.

At this point, Bernice went into a severe clinical depression. She knew almost nothing about the condition, and did not understand her own overwhelming sadness, fatigue, and loss of interest in life.

Back on my daddy's farm, the word "depression" meant what happened in 1929. There wasn't time to be depressed. When you felt a little low, why, you just got yourself moving and worked your way out of it.

Bernice couldn't "work her way out" of her depression in 1969. She began to let the housework slip. She found herself crying uncontrollably when Eric called to say he wouldn't be home until after midnight or that one of his trips had been extended for a week. Bernice gained twenty pounds in six months and began to sleep late in the mornings, sometimes lacking the energy to dress herself until the children were due home from school. The year she turned forty, Bernice's hair changed almost overnight from rich auburn to completely gray.

Eric, who had only one more hurdle to clear before he could have a chance at the presidency of his company, was horrified by the change in his wife's behavior, and even more so by the changes in her appearance. A year after her mother's stroke, Bernice received the biggest shock of her life. Eric returned from a month-long trip to Europe and announced that he was filing for divorce.

I was just numb. I couldn't believe it. My whole life had been supporting him, waiting until he retired so we could spend time together. I had never been anything but a wife and mother. I had no job skills. My self-esteem was nonexistent. I had five kids who needed me, and I hadn't been functioning at all because I was so depressed. I'd given my life to Eric's career, and now that he didn't need me he was throwing me away.

The reason for Eric's decision came as another shock. He had met another woman, an advertising executive from another agency. She was ten years younger than Bernice, tall and slim, with a college degree and an M.B.A.

Eric said she understood him better than I ever could, because she knew what his life was all about, and all I knew was babies and housework. . . . He felt she understood the pressures he was under, and how hard his work was. He said I should have made something of myself, gone back to school, taken a job. He said that in this day and age, any woman who had any brains would be out doing something with her life. I wasn't interesting to him anymore. He wanted a "liberated woman."

For another year Bernice tried desperately to win back Eric's affection. She had her hair dyed, tried to lose weight, and started taking correspondence courses in business. But her husband's abandonment deepened her depression, and she became even less functional than before. She was hospitalized briefly, began psychotherapy, and eventually accepted the fact that her marriage was over. She and her children moved back to Bernice's hometown, where Bernice managed to get a job at the nursing home where her mother now lives. According to Bernice, her children were "torn apart" by their parents' divorce, and are struggling to adjust to another new environment and a great deal less money. Bernice herself is feeling somewhat better, although she was forced to quit therapy because of her low income and the loss of Eric's insurance.

I take it one day at a time. I get up in the morning, and I do my work during the day, and I go to bed at night. I still don't understand what happened. For eighteen years I was the best wife I could be, and then somehow that turned out to be wrong. Someday, I'll stop and look back and try to figure out what happened. Right now, it's just too much for me.

LEE NGUYEN

Lee Nguyen, a delicate, soft-spoken thirty-eight-year-old, comes from a poor but proud family who fled South Vietnam during the war and took refuge in San Francisco. Lee, who was eight years old at the time, learned English quickly and became her parents' connection to the world outside the Vietnamese American community. Intelligent and hardworking, Lee planned to be the first person in her family to graduate from high school. She was thrilled when a popular boy in her high school asked her to the homecoming dance her senior year. After the dance, the boy drove to a secluded area and suggested that they have sex. When Lee refused, he raped her.

Lee told no one about the incident. Since she had gone out with the boy willingly, it never even occurred to her that she might not be responsible for the rape. She became timid and depressed, and took to hiding in the girl's rest room between classes to avoid encountering her "boyfriend." In Lee's eyes, the situation was her own fault. "Vietnamese girls have to be virgins," she told me. "Nobody cares whether she wanted to lose her virginity or not. If it happens, she's ruined."

Two months after the dance, Lee realized she was pregnant.

Her first thought was to commit suicide: "But," she told me sadly, "I didn't have the nerve." She was terrified that her parents would find out about the pregnancy and disown or punish her. She searched her mind for any way out of the situation. In Vietnam, Lee had known women who had had abortions. Lee loved children and had never thought she would even consider such an operation—but then she had never expected to become pregnant against her will, by a person who now appeared regularly in her nightmares. After a sleepless week, Lee went to the emergency room of a hospital near her home and asked a nurse how much an abortion would cost.

Lee, 38

She told me there was no such thing as abortion in the United States. I said they must know how to do it here, because even in Vietnam I knew women who had one. She said that they could do it, but it was illegal. Like murder.

The nurse said it didn't matter what they did in Vietnam, my baby would be born on American soil and so it was an American citizen. She said the American government protects all its citizens, even before they are born. I was so ashamed. I always wanted to be the right kind of American, and now I was the worst—I was a tramp, a slut, and a murderer. I wanted to die.

Desperate, Lee bought a bus ticket to Los Angeles, where her sister lived with her husband and two children. Lee's sister was shocked by her arrival, but grudgingly accepted Lee's story about how the pregnancy had begun. She called their parents, explained the situation, and told them Lee would be staying with her for a while. For the next seven months, Lee cleaned house and delivered newspapers to contribute to her sister's family income. By the time her baby was due, she was more or less resigned to her new life.

Lee planned to have her baby at home, with only her sister to help. But things did not go well. After twenty hours of excruciating labor, Lee's sister and brother-in-law took her to the hospital, where doctors determined that the baby's head was too large to fit through the opening in Lee's pelvis. Without immediate action, both mother and child would die. Lee was put under general anesthesia and her son, Tran, was born by cesarean section.

The cost of the operation was more than Lee's parents earned in four years. She had no insurance. Her sister and brother-in-law generously offered to pay for part of the medical bills, but even after they had drained their small savings, the remaining costs were more than Lee could imagine. Moreover, the difficult labor and the surgery left her so weak that she could not walk, and she had to give up her housecleaning and paper route. Her sister's family could not afford to support Lee and her baby. Although Lee was extremely reluctant to apply for welfare, she could see no other option.

When Tran was a month old I went to the welfare agency and asked if I could get help. They gave me a lot of papers to fill out. I didn't even know most of the answers. I had to take the papers home and study them like a school assignment. I got them all filled out, and then I went back to the agency. Then they told me that I didn't qualify for assistance because my brother-in-law had been providing for me, paying medical bills and things like that.

I remembered what the woman at the hospital told me when I wanted an abortion. I said, "Okay, maybe you can't give me any help, but what about my baby? He is American, he was born on American soil." I said, "I thought the American government takes care of all its citizens."

The caseworker smiled at me like I was so dumb she just had to feel sorry for me. She said I was talking about a Communist country. I tried to tell her I am from South Vietnam, not North Vietnam, but she didn't act like she even heard me. She said, "In America, we believe that parents are responsible for their own children." Like she was explaining it to a stupid person. She said, "If you knew you couldn't take care of a baby, you shouldn't have had a baby."

In order to become eligible for welfare, Lee had to move out of her sister's house into the only apartment she could afford: a tiny, run-down studio room in one of L.A.'s worst neighborhoods. She took a series of jobs, leaving her son with generally unreliable caretakers. Tran was the victim of racial prejudice that ran two ways; both the white and the Vietnamese communities looked down on him because he had the chocolate-brown hair and oval eyes of a Eurasian. By the time he was fourteen, Tran had joined a gang. By nineteen, he was in prison. As usual, Lee blames herself.

I tried to be a good mother, but I wasn't good enough. Tran had a hard life. Every time I looked at him, I could see he looked like his father. And I always know that I didn't want to have this baby. I love him, but I didn't want to have him. I think in this situation, maybe two lives went wrong. Mine and Tran's. I think about the reasons why all the time. But really, I don't understand. I think maybe I never can truly be an American, because I don't understand how things work here.

PARADOXICAL MORALS

Tamara Holt, Colette Bingham, Bernice Llewelyn, and Lee Nguyen all used the same three words to describe their reactions to the stories of their lives: "I don't understand." The events I've described in this chapter left each woman with a strong sense of injustice and injury, but also with an inability to articulate the exact nature of her problem. Each felt ashamed and lost confidence in herself and the people around her. None could see a clear argument against the inexplicable forces that were damaging her life, and so each woman experienced her anger as a vague, inescapable, unjustifiable distress, rather than a motivation to act in her own behalf.

As different as these women are, the problem they all share is that their own moral systems include the same paradoxical values by which American society judges its women. Because there are two sets of standards, one based on traditional, hierarchical values, the other on modern, egalitarian values, the people around any given woman can judge, overwork, abandon, condemn, belittle, or betray her no matter what she does—*and justify their actions by citing her own deepest core values.* Because women share these values, they often don't protest the injustices done to them. Instead, they agree with them, developing massive stores of guilt and a devastating loss of trust in themselves. In effect, a woman who has been "double-bound" by her own culture's value system ends up believing that she is "always lying" and taking full blame for it. Let's take a closer look at how this happens.

HOW TO DOUBLE-BIND A WOMAN

Since our society's development pattern has left women with the task of fulfilling American society's incompatible modern and traditional goals, it is exceptionally easy to put any female American in a double bind. Here are the instructions: First, you figure out whether the woman in question is doing something that follows traditional values or modern ones. Then use the opposite set of values to show her that she's wrong or inadequate. If she responds to this by changing her behavior to conform with the values you're preaching, you simply hop back to the other set of values and condemn her for not following *them.* You can keep up the game *forever*, because this is a paradoxical strange loop; it goes on and on without ever ending. This can be wonderfully useful for you, because using this simple double-bind technique, you can get a woman to do just about anything you want her to do—and still feel as though she owes you more! Talk about a handy-dandy tool for getting things done!

Consider how this elegant strategy operated in the cases of Colette, Bernice, and Lee. Colette's family members relied on the traditional morality that says a woman should act as a man's domestic support system while he works. The woman *owes* her labor to the man, just as a traditional serf owed a lifetime's servitude to his lord or king, because the more powerful person provides protection and sustenance for the less powerful. Her family and her culture emphasized to Colette that when a man works, he is providing for his wife, who is morally bound to repay this service by taking a subordinate status.

Then Colette got a job. Immediately, her family switched from the traditional model to the other core value of American society, the modern idea of freedom and equality. In this model, the individual secures personal advantages by earning money. The job is a *privilege*, not a burden; freedom, not responsibility. Working on this model, Harvey and his mother can claim that Colette is receiving a tremendous benefit by being "allowed" to work for money.

Do you see how nicely this works for Harvey? When he goes to work, he feels that he is doing Colette a favor (traditional values). But when Colette takes a job, Harvey can think of himself as the one who has enabled Colette to achieve individual material advantages (modern values), and once again, he is her benefactor. Either way, just as Colette said, *she feels she owes him.*

The same strategy worked for Bernice's husband, Eric. His corporate job was designed on the traditional assumption that every worker has a full-time wife taking care of all his domestic needs. In fact, having a wife who was willing to play this role to the hilt was a clear consideration in deciding which men would be promoted. Men whose wives were "into women's lib" were out of the running; they would obviously be unable to devote as much energy to their jobs as men whose wives pitched in to free them from every noncareer concern. During his rise through the corporate ranks, Eric continually reinforced Bernice's role as the ideal corporate wife. He thanked and praised her for doing whatever it took to facilitate his success, and made no bones about disliking "liberated women." Any inclination Bernice might have had to develop her own nondomestic interests and skills was nipped very effectively in the bud.

Then Eric's promotion, the health crisis of Bernice's mother, and Bernice's own clinical depression. As her manner and appearance changed, Bernice became more and more unsuitable as a corporate wife. Eric was clearly appalled. Since I heard the story only from Bernice's point of view, it isn't really fair to guess exactly what went through her husband's mind in the next few months. What we do know is that he decided to divorce Bernice and become involved with a younger, more glamorous woman in his own profession.

All Eric had to do in order to justify this choice was shift over from the traditional side of American core values to the modern, egalitarian side. According to this individualistic set of values, a man would want companionship from someone who understands the things that interest him, and who has the personal wealth, status, and influence to make her a "real" rational individual. In an egalitarian society, Eric told Bernice, nothing is stopping any woman from becoming this sort of person. A woman who spends all her time cleaning house and raising children doesn't even know what it's like to be a full-fledged rational individual—and why should a man want to pair off with such a low achiever? From Eric's perspective, he deserved more. When Eric discouraged Bernice from being anything but a corporate wife, mother, and homemaker, his opinions resonated with Bernice's own values. But later, when Eric switched over to a modern set of rules, which discounted Bernice and her life's work, *that, too, resonated with Bernice's own values.* Instead of feeling righteous indignation, she accepted Eric's low opinion of her housewifely status and put up a desperate, eleventh-hour attempt to become a rational individual on the Enlightenment model.

Lee Nguyen's case is even more tragic. She wasn't born into the American value system, but as a young refugee she had an intense desire to become "the right kind of American." The boy who raped her was certainly responsible for the damage done to Lee and for the resulting pregnancy, but the problems he caused were simply destructive, not paradoxical. The double bind, in Lee's case, came from an *institutionalized* version of paradoxical values; from the policies and laws of the very United States Lee so passionately revered.

Unfortunately, Lee's experience was not particularly unusual. In many areas of life, American institutions claim a philosophical grounding in traditional values when it suits a given economic, political, or ideological purpose, only to wave the banner of egalitarianism as soon as the traditional values become inconvenient. In 1970, as the nurse told Lee, the American government reserved the right to make the choice about abortion, on the grounds that even the unborn should have full constitutional rights to protection as an individual. Lee was denied an abortion on the grounds that individual rights have more validity than traditional, hierarchical values, in which dependent children "belong" to their parents. However, once her baby was born, the welfare system disavowed any responsibility to care for the baby, on the traditional grounds that Lee and her extended family were solely responsible for the child's existence: "Parents are responsible for their own children."

AS THE STRANGE LOOP TURNS

The farther United States society travels on its ambivalent journey toward traditional and modern ideals, the more people and policies take on the character of paradox. The examples in this chapter barely hint at the variety of ways in which American women are becoming trapped in the strange loop of their paradoxical role definition. Perhaps you can think of ways in which your own life is affected by the strange blend of opposites that require an American woman to be two incompatible things. If not, you probably don't have long to wait.

Suppose you had read this chapter only as far as the sentence "This statement is a lie" and stopped there until you could puzzle out a clear meaning. You would still be staring at that page, because the nature of paradox means that such a problem has no solution from within the system of logic that created it. The same is true of a paradoxical social role. Many of the women I interviewed had reached a point where paradoxical expectations had come to rule their lives. Instead of merely trying to *think through* a paradox, they were trying to *live out* a solution to an insoluble problem. These women traveled the strange loop of their contradictory role definition ceaselessly, always thinking that if they did *this* thing or *that* thing they would finally be able to rest, secure in their own sense of accomplishment and the approval of others.

It never happened.

What did happen was that, as time passed and more life events made paradoxical demands on these women, the strange loop began to obsess them. They worked harder and harder, faster and faster, and found themselves more trapped than ever in a double bind. When you simply try harder to solve a paradox, you can't break through it. You just increase the pressure and anxiety, as though someone put a gun to your head and screamed, "*I am lying! I AM LYING! If you don't believe I'm lying, I'm going to blow your brains out!!!*"

This kind of urgent, imperative double message is exactly what American culture is communicating (shouting, screaming, bellowing) to its women. Each move a woman takes toward fulfilling traditional requirements draws fire from those who favor the modern worldview. Each shift toward the modern ideal horrifies traditionalists. As the distance between traditional and modern structures in American society becomes greater, the conflict over how to define women's roles grows to more than an argument. A better term is *war*; out-and-out, no-holds-barred, take-no-prisoners, fight-to-the-death holy war. Which brings us to the next chapter.

CHAPTER FOUR

.⁺.

Refugees from the Holy War

W hen I first set out to interview women about their gender identity, I suffered an affliction that is very common among graduate students: I knew *exactly* what I was going to find. I had read all the
major books on American women's roles and talked to a lot of experts. I
could clearly see that there were only two ways a woman could go in
American society. She could either follow a traditional pattern, which
meant that she would essentially trade domestic labor for a share of a
man's income; or she could adhere to modern values by insisting on her
independence, earning her own money, and refusing to be treated as
anything other than a rational individual.

My plan was to take my interviews and divide the subjects into "traditional" and "modern" categories. Then I would count how many
women fell into each category, and analyze how the argument between
them was proceeding. I think I actually believed that I could find out
who was "winning" the argument over how women's roles should be defined in the United States. This was to be the first stage of my research,
the quick, initial sorting out of the data. It was going to be a breeze.
Really it was.

Yeah, right.

After conducting my first five or six interviews, I sat down with my notes
to divide the subjects into traditional and modern categories. I couldn't.
The subjects who had told me about their lives were not cooperating. A

woman who chose marriage and children over school and work talked like a die-hard feminist. A chemist who had just participated in a pro-choice rally told me she was giving up a research grant to care for her two-year-old child. A devout Catholic great-grandmother who had never been out of her home state described at length her political work on behalf of the ERA. In short, these people were not acting or talking the way I expected them to act and talk. I found this exceedingly frustrating. I had barely begun my research, and I already felt at sea.

As I was puzzling over my data, I read something that summed up exactly how I was feeling. In the 1940s, a group of psychologists designed the following experiment: they flashed playing cards at a group of volunteers, while the volunteers called out the name of each card—"two of diamonds," "jack of clubs," etc., etc. The tricky part was that some of the cards in the deck were anomalous. They had the design of one card suit combined with the color of another (as in a red ten of spades or black king of hearts).

When these cards were flashed quickly, the subjects didn't have any problem with them. When they were shown the anomalous cards, they wouldn't even pause. They'd just sing out a name that corresponded to *either* the color *or* the design—for example, they would say that a red ace of spades was the ace of hearts. The trouble began when the subjects were allowed to look at the cards for a longer period of time. Then they would stare at the anomalous cards, becoming more and more confused. One man, after gazing at an anomalous card for some time, exclaimed, "I can't make that suit out, whatever it is. It didn't even look like a card that time. I don't know what color it is now, or whether it's a spade or a heart. I'm not even sure what a spade looks like. My God!"[1]

This was how I felt as I shuffled through my interview notes, my "deck" of human "playing cards." And the more interviews I did, the worse it got. The women who were talking to me combined characteristics that, according to the rules I knew, weren't supposed to be combined. They mixed modern behaviors and ideologies with traditional ones, blithely ignoring the fact that these two ways of thinking contradicted each other. And in my "deck of cards," it was not the minority but the vast majority who were "anomalous."

It was always a relief to run across a woman who fit well into either the traditional or the modern category. It happened every now and again. There were churchgoing conservatives with six or seven children who thought women's lib was the work of Satan. There were career women with carefully planned families (or a carefully planned lack of family) who talked about traditional women's roles with the horror of people who had narrowly escaped being sent to a concentration camp. But these "pure" types were actually quite rare. As I continued to listen to women's life stories, I gradually came to see the reason for this. American society is so deeply rooted in *both* traditional and modern worldviews that sooner or later almost all of us find ourselves adopting a mixture of the two. This confused me enormously, because theoretically, modern and traditional attitudes don't mix. To work properly, *each system requires that everyone in the society be "purely" devoted to a single philosophy and lifestyle.*

I saw no way to make sense of these women's stories. I kept reexamining my notes, reshuffling my deck, rereading treatises on women's roles, and fussing in the way I generally do when life fails to meet my preconceptions.

THE TWO LANGUAGES OF AMERICAN WOMEN

One day it suddenly occurred to me that, in fact, the interviews I was collecting *could* be divided into two categories—they just weren't the modern versus traditional categories I had expected. The pattern appeared when I shifted from a visual way of thinking about my subjects to an auditory model: instead of *looking* for traditionalist and modern women by listing their behaviors, I realized that I was *hearing* two different voices in my interviews.

The first type of voice spoke the language of the pure traditional or modern values I had expected to see in all women. It was a language of clear dualities, of right and wrong, good and bad, black and white. And here was something odd: when I fished out the interviews of women who spoke in this voice, I found that this category contained *both* strongly traditional and strongly modern women. Women from the two sides said opposite things and supported contradictory policies. Each considered the other to be the worst thing since smallpox, and they were devoted to wiping each other out.

Only about 20 percent of my interviews fit into this category. That 20 percent was about evenly divided between traditionalists and modernists. The remaining 80 percent of my interview sample was composed of women who didn't match pure modern or pure traditional stereotypes, and who didn't talk like the first group at all. These women spoke a very cautious language, a language of red clubs and black diamonds, of unorthodox combinations, gray areas, and subjective judgments. Once I really began to listen to this voice, I suddenly realized something that should have been obvious to me all along. Most of the women I spoke to didn't belong in the traditional *or* the modern camp, and there was no way to put them on a spectrum running from one value system to the other. That would be like trying to create a spectrum running from hearts to spades in a deck of cards. A red ace of spades is neither a heart nor a spade. Nor is it somewhere between a heart and a spade. *It belongs in a different deck, and it renders the rules of familiar card games meaningless.*

WAR AND PEACE:
THE SOLDIERS AND THE CIVILIANS

Let me show you what I mean. Listen to the following two excerpts from my interviews. The first is from a middle-aged homemaker who fits beautifully into the purely traditional category.

Sarah, 53

If you ask me, it's just terrible how people's morals are being corrupted. Back when I was a child, men and women knew their places. You didn't have divorces and unwed mothers and women thinking they belonged where they don't belong. All these latchkey children are growing up to be criminals—if women would stay in the home, then we wouldn't have all this crime. I'm sorry, but I put a lot of our society's problems right square on those women who are getting out of their place.

. . . I just think it's insane, the way these young girls act today. How do they think they're ever going to get a man to look twice at them, the way they puff themselves up and put on airs? Men don't like women to be too smart, everyone knows that. I told all my daughters to be careful not to act too smart, and they all got married better than just about anyone else around this neighborhood. Half those working girls will probably *never* get husbands!

I trust that you now know where Sarah stands on issues related to women's roles. Now "listen" to Marielle, a college English teacher with equally strong modern values.

Marielle, 40

I can't believe how hypocritical these right-wingers are. Talking about "moral values"! How "moral" is it to force women to give themselves abortions with coat hangers? How "moral" is it to trap half the population in an inferior role? If we're ever going to achieve equality in this country, we've got a lot of work ahead of us. We're going to have to fight back against this so-called Moral Majority until we have a clear victory. . . . Women have got to get together on this. We've got to be united or we'll never win.

I really do believe that evil comes from men. Women will embrace it if they're around men too much . . . when was the last time a woman decided to bomb another country? Of course, some of these women are as bad as men. They play right into men's hands. I get so sick of my students talking about what their boyfriends think. We need an environment where women can be completely separated from men so that their minds won't be twisted.

Marielle sounds about as different from Sarah as possible, right? One is traditional, one is modern, each thinks the other is a traitor to women and to the moral order of our nation. But this kind of pure ideology was hard to come by in my interviews. Far more women talked like this:

Andrea, 48

What do I think about being a woman? You mean in general? Good grief, I don't know! I could tell you what *my* life is like, but I wouldn't want to put my experiences on somebody else. Everyone is so different, you know. . . .

Some things work for one woman, other things work for another woman. And things change as time goes by—what works for me today might not work next year, and that's all right. . . .

My life is about as different from my sister's as it could be, but that's what each of us wanted and needed. In a way, it has made us better friends. The differences make the world more interesting. We can enrich each other, if we're willing to accept each other's uniqueness.

Listen to the difference and similarities in the language used by Sarah, Marielle, and Andrea. Suddenly, you can see a lot of ways in which *both* purely modern and purely traditional ideologies are alike, and how they both differ from Andrea's thinking. Sarah and Marielle make a lot of

sweeping generalizations. They both maintain an air of righteous indignation. They are both angry at women who have ideas different from
theirs, or who act in ways that don't match their own moral system. They
have very clear ideas about what *every* woman "should" do and be. Andrea's language is completely different. She goes to great lengths to
point out that a woman's behavior may change according to her experience, "and that's all right." She is hesitant to say what all women
should do, preferring not to generalize beyond her own experience.
Sarah and Marielle talk as though they are in the midst of a great battle
of evil against good—although they disagree on what constitutes good
and evil. By contrast, Andrea's language is one of compromise and acceptance.

You could say that the two categories that appeared when I listened to
my interviews were "Those Who Divided Everybody into Two Categories," and "Those Who Didn't." Because the first group (the "pure"
modern or traditional thinkers) were so devoted to the idea of ideological battle, I came to think of them as soldiers in a holy war between the
two sides of the American value system. In contrast to the holy warriors,
most of my interview subjects were averse to the idea of wiping out dif-
fering viewpoints. They seemed to yearn for peace in the battle over
women's roles. They had never wanted to fight, and, as we will see later
in this chapter, when they got caught up in the holy war it came as an
unpleasant surprise. I decided to call this majority of women "civilians"
to distinguish them from the "warriors."

Once I had divided my interviews into these categories (holy warriors
and civilians), I began to understand the dynamics at work in Americans'
definitions of women's roles. If you read the papers or watch the news,
you will realize that wars over deep-seated values (like the religious wars
in the Middle East, Ireland, or anywhere else, for that matter) are some
of the most vicious, brutal wars ever fought. They call a great deal of attention to themselves, because the warring factions aren't interested only
in winning battles, but in spreading their philosophy as far as possible.
The war over women's social position in the United States isn't just
about who cares for the children and who wears the pants in American
families. It's a struggle to the death between two mutually exclusive
philosophies—both of which happen to be essential to the American way
of life. This war has created so much noise that it's easy to think all
women are caught up in it.

THE HOLY WAR AND PARADOX

Actually, I am convinced that the holy warriors constitute a small minority of American women. As I have already mentioned, only about 20 percent of the women I interviewed fell into the "holy warrior" category. My interview sample wasn't big enough to allow me to generalize this number to the United States population as a whole, but the work of other social scientists supports my belief that most American women speak the language I called "civilian."

For example, in a popular 1981 book entitled *In a Different Voice,* psychologist Carol Gilligan gave an intimate description of the "civilian" voice. Gilligan's book suggested that *all* women speak in this voice (particularistic, subjective, rejecting moral absolutes in favor of case-by-case decisions), because women have a pattern of moral development different from that of men.[2] Other researchers validated Gilligan's claims, finding the same "voice" among other samples of American women.

I'm not at all surprised that researchers have found that so many American women speak in the "civilian voice." On the other hand, I'm not convinced that this voice just comes automatically with a woman's two X chromosomes. For one thing, there are indeed women—the holy warriors—who speak in a voice Gilligan would call masculine (we will be hearing from some of these women in the next few pages). But the main reason I believe that most women adopt this civilian voice is that they are living out a paradoxical role definition.

All humans, male or female, are likely to adopt a subjective, cautious, nonjudgmental way of speaking if the social pressures placed on them are paradoxical. For example, in the 1930s sociologists who studied the modernization of "primitive" societies found that men who were "caught" between a traditional social role and a modern rationalist one began to think, talk, and see the world very much the way Carol Gilligan's female subjects did. They became introspective, rejected absolute judgments, and worried that their actions would be negatively judged by both the "old" and "new" values in their changing cultures. Women are routinely "supposed to be" two things, each of which negates the other. When you've lived with this kind of split role definition all your life, you don't have a ready answer to the question "What would you do if . . . ?" The best answer you can give is "Well, that depends on the situation."

My interview data corroborated other researchers' impression that most women speak this relativistic language. The women weren't at all prepared to make bold, universal statements about What All Women Should Do—or even about what they themselves might do in different circumstances. Having lived with paradox from birth, they were very careful to speak in the accepting, particular terms of the "civilian" language.

GRABBING THE LIMELIGHT: THE AMERICAN MEDIA AND THE HOLY WAR

When you realize how few American women speak the language of the holy war between traditional and modern values, it begins to seem downright odd that so much publicity goes to the warriors. The American media, from academic studies to advertising, highlight and celebrate the combative, divided message of the holy war. The different perspective brought to women's roles by civilians isn't nearly as easy to sum up in a headline, and so—even though most American women *are* civilians—the media tend to either ignore them or, like the volunteers looking at anomalous playing cards, to simply assign all civilians into one side or the other of our contradictory value systems.

Throughout most of this book I rely on the voices of women I interviewed to illustrate my ideas about American women. In the next few pages, however, I'm going to turn to the voices of women who are better known to American culture in general. I want to point out how the voices of holy warriors thunder through the American media, giving the impression of an entire nation of women at war.

There's an old Chinese saying that "when elephants fight, it's the grass that suffers." In the United States, the "elephants"—those powerful voices that dominate academic learning and the media—are hammering out their disagreements almost nonstop. Most grassroots women, who have to operate in the middle of this battle day and night, would rather not fight it. But all too often, these women find themselves in the path of the elephants. As American values go deeper and deeper into the strange loop of paradox, the voices of civilian women have been all but silenced by the escalating shrillness of the holy war.

THE HOLY WARRIORS AND FEMININE IDENTITY

The first thing that struck me about the holy warriors was this: when they are asked about women's roles or identity, they will immediately begin to talk about men. This is true of traditional and modern warriors.

All holy warriors are keenly aware that our society is male-dominated, and their ideas about feminine identity center on how women should react to the power exercised by men. They believe that the formation of female identity is basically dictated by male power. Along with this goes the belief that *for women to maximize their own well-being, they must first and foremost control men.*

Of course, there is dramatic disagreement between different holy warriors about how this should be done. Modern-thinking warriors believe that the balance of power in our society is a moral evil, and that enough power must be transferred from men to women to create equality. This will give women access to social goodies, like wealth and status, which men have historically kept for themselves. Traditionalist warriors, on the other hand, believe that the historical balance of power is right and proper. In their view, the relative powerlessness of women is part of a correct value system that obliges males to protect and support females. If traditional values are honored, they point out, women have access to goodies through their benevolent fathers and husbands. But whatever their differences, all holy warriors focus on male power as *the* essential issue women must address to assure their well-being.

FASCINATING WOMANHOOD: HOW TO CONTROL A MAN IN THE TRADITIONAL MANNER

The two camps of holy warriors obviously recommend different strategies for women who are setting out to control their own lives by controlling men. Naturally, traditionalists believe in laws and policies that require men to support their families. But they also tend to bank heavily on time-honored methods that women have always used to influence men in traditional cultures; methods like seductiveness, manipulation, and playing up to the male ego. The idea is to get a man, and then to lean on traditional obligations for all you're worth, to give that man the greatest possible motivation to protect and provide for you. Remember, the values of a pure traditional society *absolutely require* the powerful to protect and provide for the powerless. Therefore, traditional holy warriors believe that the best way for a woman to get the most out of life is to remain as dependent on men as possible, eliciting the highest possible levels of support and protection.

This viewpoint is thriving in the American media of the 1990s. It is a foundation stone for holy warriors like Rush Limbaugh—people whose voices clamor for attention on American airwaves, newsstands, and television programs. It is also big money. An obvious example is a 1996 bestseller entitled *The Rules: Time-Tested Secrets for Capturing the Heart of Mr. Right*. The authors of *The Rules*, Ellen Fein and Sherrie Schneider, are boldly unapologetic about their philosophy that capturing a man should be the central goal of their readers' lives. Women must be willing to obey a variety of strict "Rules" in order to lure Mr. Right into the vows of matrimony.

The Rules include things like always ending interactions first (giving a man the impression that you lead a busy, active life) and refusing to divulge all those unpleasant truths about your own thoughts, personality, or life history. These and the many other "Rules" create an image of traditional femininity, whether or not that is an accurate representation of the woman in question. Fein and Schneider repeat, often and explicitly, that a "Rules girl" will deliberately opt to remain in a traditionally subordinate position to a man, never "taking the lead," telling him what to do, or asking him to change any aspect of his behavior.

Make no mistake, though—Fein and Schneider are not suggesting this relinquishment of power to a man as an end in itself. Far from it. *The Rules* are behaviors designed to "train" men to do what women want them to. The authors are full of explicit directives to this effect. "If you call him," they say, "he won't get trained to ask you out,"[3] or "Men must be conditioned to feel that . . . they have to marry you."[4] Traditional gender roles, complete with an unequal balance of obvious power (in favor of men) and the use of manipulation (by women), are seen as desirable, and even inevitable, for the writers of *The Rules*.

The perspective of traditionalist holy warriors is clearly still with us. But rarely has the United States produced a more stunning example of this worldview than another book, *Fascinating Womanhood*, by one Helen Andelin. This guide to "proper" female behavior was first published in 1963—ironically (and not coincidentally), the same year as *The Feminine Mystique*. Several of my interview subjects, from Arizona to Iowa to Connecticut, told me that they had once considered *Fascinating Womanhood* to be *the* handbook for maximizing their feminine potential.

One of my interview subjects was a radio-talk-show host who interviewed Andelin on the air in 1964, shortly after her book came out.

Theodora, 65

That Helen Andelin, she was amazing. Let me tell you, she could get a man to eat out of the palm of her hand. She came into the studio with her husband—he was this little mouse of a man who would look at her first before he said anything. I think he was scared to death of her. She sure had him under control! When she said, "Jump," he said, "How high?" I ran right out and bought my daughter a copy of [Andelin's] book, because if a woman could learn how to twist a man around her little finger like that, she'd do pretty well for herself.

Since I can practically hear all you readers out there aching for information on how Mrs. Andelin worked her magic on Mr. Andelin, I will quote some passages from *Fascinating Womanhood*. Let us turn to the chapter entitled "Feminine Dependency," which starts out briskly with a Guide to Achieving Helplessness. I am not kidding. All the capital letters and italics in the following passage were put there by Andelin. Note that though the author advises women to become as helpless as possible, *this is a deliberate, carefully executed strategy for manipulating and controlling men, a way for women to maximize their own power and influence.*

(Helplessness)

The role of man . . . is to lead, protect and provide for a woman. Her need for his manly care is called feminine dependency. . . .

What happens when the average red-blooded man comes in contact with an obviously able, intellectual and competent woman . . . ? He simply doesn't feel like a man any longer. . . .

A MAN CANNOT DERIVE ANY JOY OR SATISFACTION FROM PROTECTING A WOMAN WHO CAN OBVIOUSLY DO VERY WELL WITHOUT HIM. HE ONLY DELIGHTS IN PROTECTING OR SHELTERING A WOMAN WHO NEEDS HIS MANLY CARE, OR AT LEAST APPEARS TO NEED IT. . . .

How Do We Acquire Feminine Dependency?

1. *Manner and Attitude.* You must dispense with any air of strength and ability, of competence and fearlessness and acquire instead an air of frail dependency upon a man to take care of you.

The author goes on at some length describing the childlike, coquettish mannerisms that work best to convince a man of a woman's complete ineptitude. She then instructs her readers to act confused and indecisive, whether they actually are or not. In case your man is not getting the message, Andelin suggests that you "PROVE your dependency" by refraining from "manly" duties and activities, thus becoming more and more proficient at helplessness.

There are, however, some notable exceptions. *Fascinating Womanhood* encourages female readers to "retain some of the lesser masculine duties and do them inefficiently to prove your dependency." The purpose of this exercise, which Andelin states quite overtly, is to give men maximum motivation to protect and provide for women. In Andelin's view, a show of helplessness and incompetence is a good way—indeed, the best way—a woman can take care of herself, *because it will make men do things for her.* Male power is the focus of her attention, and female "power" should be used, ironically, to appear as powerless as possible, thus eliciting care from men.

Andelin gives a few illustrations of how this should be done. One example is the inspiring story of a woman who deliberately mounted a paper cup dispenser upside down. "When her husband came home," Andelin tells us, "he said, 'Say, this isn't on right! Why did you mount it upside down?' Then she said, 'Oh, how do you tell which side is right side up?' He immediately took out the screwdriver and mounted it right."

Another of Andelin's heroines did a purposely shabby job building a planter box, sawing the boards crookedly in the best tradition of feminine helplessness. The woman's husband was drawn into the subterfuge like a bass biting a carefully crafted fly. "Was he ashamed of her inferior work?" Andelin asks (rhetorically, to be sure). "No! He was delighted, for it made him feel superior."

The ultimate testimonial is a story about a woman who lost her job and decided, out of fear and passivity, not to apply for another. According to Andelin, the woman's husband told the story to his boss, who then increased the employee's salary to cover the amount his wife earned in her previous job. Andelin cites this as "just one of the many solutions to problems when you make a man feel like one."[5] The object is for women to prosper, to gain access to power, wealth, and status. The method is to control male power. The ideology, obviously, is deeply traditional.

This book is the origin of "Domestic Goddess," a phrase the comedian Roseanne would use, a generation later, to make American audiences shriek with laughter. Things changed a lot in those decades. *Fascinating Womanhood* was published just as the women's movement of the 1960s was picking up speed. The book was lent to me by a woman I interviewed, who told me that she had received it from her mother-in-law with "the important parts" already underlined in red. Another woman told me that her entire Seventh-Day Adventist congregation had read the book at approximately the same time. "Suddenly, all these women were sprouting ruffles everywhere," she said. "I never read it, but it was clear there were a lot of ruffles involved. Everyone tried it." Andelin's advice was as welcome to the American women of the 1960s as *The Rules* were in the 1990s.

"LASHING BACK": THE MODERN APPROACH TO CONTROLLING MEN

Some thirty years after the publication of *Fascinating Womanhood*, when women's lib had long since become a household word, another book became a national best-seller. Susan Faludi's *Backlash: The Undeclared War Against American Women* was as modern in its stance as *Fascinating Womanhood* had been traditional. Helen Andelin would probably have recommended that American women burn Faludi's book and use the ashes as eyeliner. But strange as it may seem, there is an underlying similarity between *Backlash* and *Fascinating Womanhood*. The authors share certain crucial assumptions and ways of looking at women's identity.

Like Andelin, Faludi defined women's roles as being formed in response to men and male power. Her implicit argument was that since women's behavior is dominated by men, women must focus on male power in order to gain power of their own. *The same can be said of Andelin.* The difference is that where *Fascinating Womanhood* assumes that women must manipulate male social power to their own advantage, *Backlash* takes the position that women must *resist* that power, with an equal or superior force. Despite their differences, both authors see the struggle for full feminine identity as revolving around *how much control women achieve in relation to men.*

In the following passage from *Backlash*, Faludi describes American women's response to a society-wide modernization during the 1980s. But she depicts this solely as courageous female resistance to a male-engineered backlash. She rejects out of hand the idea that some women may have chosen traditional behavior because it contributed to the quality of their lives. She writes:

The backlash decade produced one long, painful, and unremitting campaign to thwart women's progress. And yet . . . women never really surrendered. . . . Women continued to postpone their wedding dates, limit their family size, and combine work with having children. . . . No matter how bruising and discouraging her collisions with the backlash wall, each woman in her own way persisted in pushing against it. This quiet female resistance was the uncelebrated counterpoint to the antifeminist campaign of the '80s, a common thread in the narrative of so many women's lives, no matter where they belonged in the ideological spectrum, no matter what their rung on the class ladder. . . .

The backlash did manage to infiltrate the thoughts of women, broadcasting on these private channels its sound waves of shame and reproach. But it never quite silenced . . . the whisper of self-determination that spurred on so many nearly defeated women. It was this voice, so long held in check, so desperate to be heard, that kept dispatcher Diane Joyce on the job, long after the mockery, threats, and ostracism from the men around her had become intolerable. It was this voice that finally provoked Beverly LaHay to shuck her housecoat and paralyzing timidity, to write her many books and deliver her many speeches. . . . It was this voice, barely audible but still unsquelched, that murmured even in the heart of Operation Rescue's goodwife Cindy Terry, who confessed to wanting "to make something of my life." . . .[6]

In the past, women have proven that they can resist in a meaningful way, when they have had a clear agenda that is unsanitized and unapologetic, a mobilized mass that is forceful and public, and a conviction that is uncompromising and relentless. . . .[7]

While many women in the backlash era have feared "offending men" with feminist demands, women in the '70s who were assertive and persistent discovered that they could begin to change men's views.[8]

Susan Faludi never even considers the possibility that some women may feel they are "making something of their lives" without "relentlessly" writing books, organizing campaigns, delaying childbirth, or working outside their homes. She seems to reject the very idea that the work women do in housecoats might actually be considered "something." The Enlightenment scholar's disregard for the traditional labor women have always performed is as clear in Faludi's voice as the assumption that women should do *nothing but* traditional labor is in Andelin's.

The generalized absolutist "language" of the holy war is clear in both

Fascinating Womanhood and *Backlash*. Seeing her own position as an absolute moral good, Faludi makes it very clear that *any traditional behavior whatsoever* is destructive to *all* American women. Andelin is her mirror image, assuming that any modern behavior undermines traditional values and puts *all* women at risk. Both Faludi and Andelin have very clear, though opposite, definitions of failure and success. Andelin says that women have "succeeded" when they completely control men through displays of helplessness. For her, women who stay in the workforce are definitely failures. For Faludi, women's successes must *always* be seen by *all* women as progress toward a purely rational individual role—for her, any woman who *doesn't* stay in the workforce is a failure. Their positions are opposite, but the language of black-and-white judgments and righteous anger is the same.

THE "CIVILIAN" APPROACH
TO FEMALE ROLE DEFINITION

Imagine that you are setting out to sculpt the form of a woman in clay. There are two ways you might proceed. One way is to get a mold and press the clay into it, mashing it in as tightly as the mold will allow, pressing your material against the limits of a restraining object. The other way is to make an armature (a sort of stick figure) out of wood or metal, and build up the clay around it to form the body.

If women's identity were a lump of clay, the holy warriors' way of defining its shape would be to press it against the limitations created by male dominance. The civilian way of looking at women's roles takes the armature approach. When they set out to define their identity, they first look for a core self, then build up their role around it. Masculine domination is only one of the factors that may interfere with their intended design, and they deal with it when they encounter it. Holy warriors are concerned with pushing the limits of an external power; civilians are preoccupied with a quest for the unique core of personal identity. The holy warrior method yields women who look almost exactly alike. The civilian method makes it very difficult to come up with exactly the same shape twice.

As I listened to women's voices, I noticed that the language of the civilians was a first-person language—these women spoke in terms of their own experience, rather than making generalized claims about all women's experience. They did not see the world in clear dualities (good/bad, right/wrong, black/white), but as an infinite variety of possible variations on themes. They regarded men, like women, as unique individuals, and sometimes commented that both men and women have a wide range of personality features. Some men and women, they noted, might be more like each other than like "all women" or "all men." Because of this, gender was not the absolute division for civilians that it was for holy warriors. Both men and women struggle with inward issues, as well as outward ones, to define their unique identities.

The next passage is from Gloria Steinem's 1993 book, *Revolution from Within*. According to Steinem, this book is her attempt to address the social problems of women by helping them enhance their self-esteem. It is written in classic civilian language. Notice the difference in tone, method of persuasion, and definition of identity between this passage and the quotations from *Fascinating Womanhood* and *Backlash*.

The more I talked to men as well as women, the more it seemed that inner feelings of incompleteness, emptiness, self-doubt, and self-hatred were the same, no matter who experienced them, and even if they were expressed in culturally opposite ways. I don't mean to gloss over the difficulties of equalizing power, even when there is the will to do so: to the overvalued and defensive, the urge to control and dominate may be as organic as a mollusk's shell; and to the undervalued and resentful, the power to destroy the self (and others who resemble the self) may be the only power there is. But at both extremes—as well as the more subtle areas in between, where most of us struggle every day—people seemed to stop punishing others or themselves only when they gained some faith in their own unique, intrinsic worth. Making male readers feel welcome, this book decided, was the least it could do.[9]

. . . I had retreated to researching and reporting because I doubted the reality of my inner voice. So I started over in a very different way. . . . I did write much more personally. My hope is that each time you come upon a story of mine, you will turn inward and listen to a story told by your own inner voice. These last three years have taught me that, like the spider spinning her web, we create much of the outer world from within ourselves. . . . I know, however, that each of us enters the spiral at a different place and should progress along its circles in the direction we have not been. For me . . . this meant traveling inward, but for others, it may mean the reverse.[10]

Because it is written in the language of civilians, *Revolution from Within* has been condemned by modern holy warriors as an example of "the most disturbing (and potentially influential) development in the feminist movement today," an attack on women's equality.[11] On the other hand, traditionalist holy warriors reject it as being written by a "feminazi," who is trying to destroy traditional values. And here we come to a key point: *Even though the civilian position focuses on acceptance and personal experience, it is seen by* both *sides of the holy war as an attack from the enemy.*

Books on "women's issues" that are written in a civilian voice generally don't get a lot of attention from the American media. They aren't as juicy as holy war books; and the warriors shoot them down almost immediately. The only ones that make it to the best-seller lists are those written by former holy warriors who have switched to civilian thinking. Such women are often condemned for "selling out," "degenerating," or in some other way losing their ideological purity.

THE IDEOLOGICAL "FILTER": WHY HOLY WARRIORS SEE CIVILIANS AS THE ENEMY

After I'd done a hundred interviews or so, and found that the vast majority of my subjects used civilian language, I started wondering why I had once been under such a strong impression that every American woman was fighting on one side of the holy war or the other. The reason, of course, is that the civilian voice leaves room for different points of view, including both traditional and modern ideas, while the holy warriors are intent on eradicating every voice that doesn't completely agree with them. The civilian position, focusing on the values of diversity and uniqueness, tends to see "pure" modern or traditional ideals as unattainable, perhaps even undesirable. They don't want to force *any* one code of conduct on *every* woman. As a result, *holy warriors are far more vocal than civilians, even though they are far less numerous.*

Another reason why the language of the holy war dominates our media is that warriors seem to see the world through an ideological lens that turns everyone who doesn't agree with them on *everything* into a member of the opposition. Traditionalist holy warriors are sure that every woman who wishes to be free from traditional roles is a "radical feminist." Modern-thinking warriors are positive that any woman who depends on her husband's salary is "antifeminist." Both sides of the war believe very strongly that "those who are not with us are against us."

This means that if you aren't a holy warrior yourself, *both sides of the holy war consider you to be the enemy.* Women who speak or write publicly about accepting different versions of female life can expect to be attacked by both the right and the left. At the end of this chapter, I'll discuss how this affected some of the civilian women I interviewed. But it's worthwhile to show how violently women are punished for speaking "civilian" language in the public media.

Naomi Wolf is a "second wave" feminist who became famous by criticizing the "beauty myth" that leads many American women to hate and abuse their bodies. In a recent book, *Fire with Fire*, Wolf came at women's issues from a civilian perspective. You can "hear" that voice in the following suggestions Wolf made to American feminists.

1) Avoid generalizations about men that imply that their maleness is the unchangeable source of the problem; 2) avoid generalizations about men that are totalizing, that is, that do not admit to exceptions; 3) never choose to widen the rift between the sexes when the option exists to narrow it, without censoring the truth; 4) never unreflectingly judge men in a way that we would consider sexist if men applied it to women . . . ; 5) distinguish between the men we love, who are on our side, and the male system of power, which we must resist. It is not "hating men" to fight sexism. But the fight against sexism must not lead to hating men.[12]

Feminist holy warriors who read Wolf's suggestions went through the ceiling. They had thought Wolf was "one of them," and now, by suggesting that women apply the Golden Rule to men, she was clearly selling out to the enemy. One feminist, Phyllis Chesler, called her "a Wolf in feminist clothing." She made the following comments about the passage I just quoted.

I think it's cowardly, and insulting, to appeal to men by saying that feminists *personally* love and adore men—all men, any men—and/or that feminism doesn't really threaten the status quo because feminist leaders love/adore their sons, fathers, brothers, husbands, or boyfriends.[13]

Isn't this a bit eerie? It's almost as if Chesler *can't see* all the careful qualifications in Wolf's language. Wolf never says that all feminists "love and adore . . . all men, any men." In fact, she goes to great pains pointing out that everybody's different, and that she doesn't want to generalize. But Chesler is looking through the magical filter of the holy war. To people who are wearing this filter, *every statement that isn't* absolutely *on one side of the war must be absolutely on the other.* And in the holy warrior's book of rules, this kind of opposition must be destroyed.

WAR-WORDS: HOW THE HOLY WARRIORS USE LANGUAGE TO DESTROY THE ENEMY

◆ *1. Blunt Instruments: Verbal Bullying* After *Fire with Fire* came out, Naomi Wolf got a barrage of criticism from her onetime allies. Another commentator on women's roles called Wolf "a parent-pleasing, teacher-pleasing little kiss-ass." [14] Lest you are mistakenly thinking that these sound like the words of a dim-witted, ignorant bully, let me hasten to correct you. They are, in fact, the words of an *extremely intelligent* and *highly educated* bully, a woman who has won the veneration of the American academic community with her stunning combination of brilliant scholarship and flat-out nastiness.

The use of bullying, punitive language is a favorite strategy for both sides of the holy war. In the conflict over American women's roles, as in all holy wars, propaganda is the most commonly used weapon, and words are the ammunition. We've already seen how Naomi Wolf was attacked by a couple of holy warriors from the modern camp. Here's an example of how traditionalist warriors have used the "war-words" to blacken the reputations of their "enemies."

In 1973 the National Organization for Women began lobbying for gender equality in television and radio stations. NOW members asked broadcasters to sign a contract in which they agreed to move toward more equal representation of women in both their hiring practices and their depictions of society. Their efforts came to the attention of a major leader in the traditionalist holy war, Phyllis Schlafly. In her monthly newsletter, Schlafly accused NOW of orchestrating a secret campaign to convince television and radio stations to give NOW authority over virtually every aspect of their existence:

> This extraordinary drive was operating in secret across the country until exposed by the alert members of STOP ERA and Happiness of

Women (HOW) in Detroit. . . . Tell your stations that NOW—whose official policy is to welcome lesbians into membership . . . is a way-out, fringe group which does not represent the women of your community.[15]

To a reader in the late 1990s, the media stations contract reads like a mild agreement to move in the direction of gender equality. Schlafly's war-words, however, transform it into a much more exciting, epic, military images; a secret army of malevolent lesbians slithering into the very living rooms of an unsuspecting public via the airwaves, washing blank the defenseless brains of media managers, then filling them with ideas that will destroy the Happiness of Women. Traditional values, Schlafly makes it clear, must be defended.

The rhetoric of the traditional holy warriors, like that of their left-wing antagonists, has only become more strident as the years go by. Here, for example, is the way a woman named Mary Pride described the American primary school curriculum. Her book *The Way Home*, published in 1985, is still in print and on bookstore shelves.

I sent away recently for an outline of the typical course of study followed by public schools from kindergarten through grade 12. Grade 10 Social Studies featured "The search for peace" and "Role of women in today's society." Grade 11 included . . . the "struggle for women's rights" and again, "the role of women in today's society." And once again, in twelfth grade, social studies featured the "role of women in today's society."

. . . Parents for the past 150 years have been expecting public schools to do the job of shaping children's values. Now the bitter fruit of this error is appearing. . . . Values clarification classes systematically destroy the Biblical concept of an absolute right and an absolute wrong. One-world government programs in Social Studies are meant to destroy patriotism, while the study of "women's roles in today's society" is a front for indoctrination in feminism. Economics courses teach socialism; English teachers assign pornography as required reading; even my high-school gym class featured instruction in occult yoga techniques.[16]

◆ *2. The Ultimate Weapon: Shaming Words* Because holy warriors operate on the belief that human identity is formed mainly by exterior force, they also think that people can be "pushed" into different value systems if only they are attacked with enough energy. The words holy warriors use are carefully chosen to exert the maximum pressure and control on other women, as well as on men. Both sides of the war rely on one of the most potent tools for controlling people in any society: *shame.* All people are devastated by public shame, and as children grow up, they learn to do a lot of things they may not want to do, from wearing a certain style of clothes to tormenting other children, in order to avoid the horror of being shamed. Holy warriors focus torrents of shaming words at their opponents' most vulnerable feelings. They rely heavily on popular negative stereotypes to reinforce the effect of their words.

Take, for example, the way Schlafly uses homophobia to attack the National Organization for Women. The NOW proposal for changes in broadcasting had absolutely nothing to do with lesbianism, but Schlafly used the word "lesbians" to bring all the power of homophobia to bear on the NOW organization. From Schlafly's perspective, the shame attached to homosexuality is so strong that the "taint" of lesbianism colors the purist's view of *all* NOW members. Her tone makes it clear that in her view all lesbians should be ashamed of themselves. The implicit threat is that if *you* side with NOW on any issue, you're probably a lesbian, and you should be ashamed of yourself as well.

This is a very popular theme with traditionalist holy warriors. Mary Pride also warns that "we [women] are being asked to kill our babies, endorse homosexuality (and perhaps become lesbians), nag our husbands to do our job so we can do theirs—under threat of divorce." She mentions a few pages later that "planned parenthood leads to abortion, homosexuality, careerism, 'chronic economic depression,' and all that smacks of anti-human ugliness."[17] Quite a river of shame to direct toward any woman who decides to space out her children, rather than acting out the strictest ideals of the traditionalist holy warriors.

Holy warrior attacks are often directed at women's sexuality, because in our culture there's a lot of shame attached to sexual issues. Holy warriors on the modern side are as likely as traditionalists to use this type of shame. For example, here's another selection from Phyllis Chesler's attack on Naomi Wolf.

Wolf describes herself as a practitioner of "radical heterosexual feminism." She writes, "Male sexual attention is the sun in which I bloom. The male body is ground and shelter to me, my lifelong destination. When it is maligned categorically, I feel as if my homeland is maligned." . . . Radical heterosexuality? Okay, I'm open. Persuade me that . . . my declaration that I can't do without sexual pleasure, is somehow equivalent to political analysis.[18]

Just as Schlafly did, Chesler is using a stereotype about women's sexuality to shame her "enemy." The stereotype she calls on isn't the "perverted homosexual," but the "airheaded bimbo," the sex-hungry idiot who pursues men blindly, thinking with her glands and her genitals rather than her brain. This image has been used to shame women since the Dark Ages. Chesler only needs a quick reference to it to shame Naomi Wolf.

◆ 3. *The Subtle Weapon: Disinformation* Another type of propaganda used by holy warriors (as by the combatants in most wars) is "disinformation." This is a polite, military sort of word that in practice can mean anything from "little white fibs" to "bald-faced lies." The holy warriors on both sides seem to be so sure that their mission is morally correct that the cause of defending it may obscure the way they see factual evidence. When civilians come across facts that conflict with their beliefs, they tend to change their beliefs in order to fit the evidence. Holy warriors, consciously or unconsciously, sometimes take the opposite approach, changing, overlooking, or distorting evidence to fit their beliefs.

When I read the texts of holy warriors, I am reminded of a day when one of my grade school teachers managed to convince our local district attorney to regale her students with stories about his high-profile career. He was a very charismatic man, who recounted several fascinating anecdotes about how he had convicted various ne'er-do-wells. During question-and-answer time, one of my classmates asked him, "What would you do if you were assigned to prosecute someone you thought was innocent?" The D.A. went into a series of different anecdotes, this time about instances in which he had won convictions on comparatively flimsy evidence. Another student restated the question: "But what if you really believed the defendant was innocent?" There was a general murmur of agreement. At this the D.A. gave a snort of frustration and said, "How can I explain this to you kids? I'm talking about *getting a conviction.* There might be hundreds of thousands of dollars at stake." And that was the end of that.

What we grade-schoolers did not understand was that in our judicial system the lawyer's first obligation is to fight to win the case, no matter what. Law schools teach prospective attorneys to highlight information that proves their point, and discount or ignore evidence that doesn't.

The highest moral ground is to serve the client, whether the client is a plaintiff or a defendant—not to come to an objective conclusion about the case. It is up to the jury and the judge to establish the truth. The lawyer's job is simply to win.

Holy warriors often seem to have a similar moral position. They accept the establishment of an ideologically "pure" society as the highest good. Whether they are traditional or modern, liberal or conservative, the triumph of their position—not an unbiased presentation of evidence—is the paramount goal. They therefore can perpetuate "disinformation," both indirectly, by doing it themselves, and directly, by telling other people to do it. For example, in *Fascinating Womanhood,* Helen Andelin is very clear about the virtue of lying for the cause of traditional gender roles. She repeatedly urges women to perpetrate deceptions upon the men in their lives, deliberately appearing far more helpless and passive than they really are. "Don't feel deceitful about doing this," she says. "Women are supposed to be inferior in the masculine duties."[19]

The authors of *The Rules* recommend similar behavior. Many of "The Rules" themselves rest on deception. For example, Fein and Schneider instruct readers to end phone calls by saying they have an important engagement elsewhere, and to have roommates or parents tell men they are not at home when they are.[20] They strongly prohibit any declaration of a woman's own thoughts and feelings. They insist that women must play by *The Rules* even after they get their men, leading to some rather frightening images of wives who consistently tell lies to, and keep secrets from, their own husbands. This is not really perceived as deceit, because it is understood that achieving traditional goals is well worth the occasional presentation of a false self. ("You may feel that you won't be able to be yourself," say *The Rules* authors, "but men will love it!")[21]

Some left-wing holy warriors seem similarly unperturbed by distortions of the truth. Take, for example, the students at the University of Maryland who in 1993 put out posters and flyers containing the names of several male students under the heading "Notice: These Men Are Potential Rapists." The women reportedly didn't even know the men on the list; the names had been selected at random from the college phone directory, on the grounds that *any* man is a potential rapist.[22]

For holy warriors, an even more common strategy than outright manipulation of the truth is the biased use of evidence. Traditionalist authors like Andelin, and the team of Fein and Schneider, seem fond of selecting isolated examples to "prove" their points about how "all men" and "all women" act. The two or three women of Andelin's acquaintance who manage to manipulate men successfully are taken as universal proofs of the ideals expressed in *Fascinating Womanhood*. *The Rules* authors cite similar stories of women managing to capture men successfully by using strategies such as pretending to be busier than they are, or refusing to answer the phone. Anyone who has had even the most rudimentary training in psychology, formal or informal, will agree that such small and selective samples aren't useful for making generalities about the human condition (even if you could prove that the women actually "caused" the men's behavior, which you can't). But holy warriors, as far as I can tell, often simply *don't see* evidence that contradicts their worldview.

Left-wing holy warriors, as well as conservatives, are likely to demonstrate this kind of bias. Susan Faludi's *Backlash*, for example, presents some one-sided views of facts, focusing on any data that support the author's agenda, overlooking items that contradict her perspective. To take one broad example, Faludi portrays the media of the 1980s as overwhelmingly negative toward feminism, overlooking the fact that thousands of articles *supporting* feminism were also published during this time period.

In addition to these generalized biases, *Backlash* reported inaccuracies about things such as whether older women were more likely to bear a child with certain birth defects, the number of single men versus single women in the U.S., changes in women's workforce participation, and American women's attitudes toward many aspects of their lives. For example, Faludi reported that in the 1990 Virginia Slims poll, women placed a desire to get married as a relatively unimportant priority (her point was that American women really want to remain single, and that the "backlash" is trying to *convince* them that getting married is a high priority). What Faludi failed to mention—or perhaps even to notice—was that 62 percent of the women in the sample were already married.[23]

Partly because of the popularity of *Backlash*, Faludi's evidence was closely scrutinized by other journalists, as well as by scholars. While all agreed that Faludi had done a great deal of solid research, many also pointed to errors in her reporting. One critic wrote:

Faludi's approach is that of a muckraking reporter bent on saving women by exposing the lies, half-truths, and deceits that the male-oriented media have created to demoralize women and keep them out of the workplace. Her readers might naturally assume that she herself has taken care to be truthful. However, not a few astonished reviewers discovered that *Backlash* relies for its impact on many untruths—some far more serious than any it exposes.[24]

Another scholar alleged that Faludi "skews data, misquotes primary sources, and makes serious errors of omission."[25] These authors seem to believe that any inaccuracies in *Backlash* were put there intentionally. But if she was like other holy warriors I interviewed, Faludi probably wasn't even aware that she was presenting biased facts. We have all had the experience of "zooming in" on information that has particular importance for us; it is quite likely that both traditional and modern holy warriors do this whenever they scan the newspaper or a library shelf. Perhaps Faludi was so swept up in her desire to prove the existence of a conspiracy against women's liberation that she literally didn't know she was misinterpreting some sources and leaving out information that didn't support her thesis.

In this respect, again, feminist holy warriors demonstrate an unwitting kinship with their sworn enemies, the women who recommend traditional ways of manipulating men. Both sides of the war will defend their "client cause" at the expense of objectivity. The social ideals the warriors have internalized seem so necessary to them, so *right*, that their goal (persuading other women to act the way they think *all* women should act) takes precedence over a balanced analysis.

DOUBLE JEOPARDY: LIVING IN THE WAR ZONE

Holy warriors from both sides of the American political divide aren't one bit shy about announcing what women are *supposed* to be. As we saw earlier in this chapter, the arguments for either modern or traditional values can make logical sense. Women really *do* suffer in societies where traditional values are mixed with modern ones, and *vice versa*. But in the frenzied attempt to impose their absolutes on all women, holy warriors tend to lose sight of women's actual experience. Their medium—shame, rigidity, absolutism, and judgment—becomes their message.

I don't know about you, but when I read or listen to holy warriors arguing over women's roles, I find myself in the same mood of thoughtful agreement I would feel if someone strapped me to a bench and hit me over the head with a two-by-four. A lot of the civilian women I interviewed seemed to share my feelings. They described themselves as being unnerved by both sides of the holy war, agreeing with some ideas from each side but rejecting the way the argument was being waged. They often told me that their reaction to the holy war was a desire to avoid it.

MUTING THE CIVILIAN VOICE

Now that we've seen how the battle of the elephants is going, I'd like to turn back to the experiences of the "ordinary women" I interviewed. As I've said, the vast majority of them did not want to fight in the holy war. They weren't comfortable with sweeping generalizations, dogmatic opinions, or the "us-against-them" mentality of the holy warriors. But, as so often happens in war, the militant minority had managed to make the peaceful majority live in constant fear of attack.

As one of my interview subjects, a local TV news producer, put it:

Grace, 39

I've been called a bimbo, I've been called a bitch, I've been called all kinds of things. Kinda makes you want to crawl into the woodwork, if you want to know the truth. If you're going to put your thoughts out there, you'd better be able to handle a lot of name-calling.

Most women have two-stage reactions to the antagonism they get from holy warriors. First, they become more and more cautious and subjective in their thinking and especially in their speech. They try constantly, sometimes desperately, to make it clear that they are not trying to attack modern *or* traditional values.

"Civilians" may also develop enormously conflicted feelings about the word "feminism." They may call themselves feminists—meaning that they believe women should be freed from their traditionally subordinate role—only to find that conservatives reject them out-of-hand for identifying themselves with the feminist cause, *and* that other feminists become blisteringly angry at them for not being the "right kind" of feminist, or not being feminist "enough." This is a problem both for "ordinary" women and for women who have devoted their whole lives to the issues of women's liberation.

Civilians say things like "Well, I can only speak for myself," and "I really don't judge what other women do—different strokes for different folks," and "This is right for *me*, right *now*, but it may be wrong for other people, and I may change my mind tomorrow," and "I agree with *some* of what each of you said."

This approach is designed to assure the holy warriors that the speaker is not against them. It doesn't work. Since warriors live by the ideal of making society "pure" and consistent, they hear the "different strokes for different folks" position as a declaration of calculated aggression. When civilian women realize this, they often turn to a second and final technique for staying out of the holy war:

Silence.

Once you have realized that "anything you say may be used against you" in the conflict over women's roles, your only chance of passing un-molested through the battling armies is to say nothing at all. Even women who never had any particular desire to join the debate learn that their tentative views on the subject of women's roles cannot be articulated without provoking attack. For this reason, women who are uncomfortable with the holy warriors' worldview tend to withdraw into a confused, apologetic silence about their opinions—and often become unsure, themselves, what those opinions are.

SILENCING WOMEN'S STORIES

Even after a woman has stopped voicing her opinions about women's roles, her very life might still draw fire from the holy war. If a woman's experience has taken her into situations where "pure" modern thinking or "pure" traditionalism doesn't seem to work, *that experience itself* is often condemned as a deliberate attack on both sides of the holy war. As upsetting as it is to have one's opinions shamed and condemned, it is much more disturbing to find that the everyday doings of a woman's life may be seen by holy warriors as an act of aggression.

Angelica, 18

Since I started college I worry every day about what to wear. I used to wear dresses that I thought looked pretty on me. They had a little lace here and there, and I thought my body looked nice in them. And I wore eye shadow. But a bunch of girls—excuse me, women—in my dorm told me I was giving our whole dorm a bad reputation by dressing to please men. They made me feel so bad I wanted to give up and go home. I cried for a whole day. Now I wear jeans and baggy sweaters, even though I don't like them.

Marlo, 50

I didn't think it would be any big deal when I got a business degree and started working part-time after my kids were all in school. I thought my friends would be happy for me. Instead, I hear them talking behind my back about how I've gone off the deep end and become a radical feminist. They expect my marriage to end every day. They act cold and disinterested when I talk about work, so I finally just stopped mentioning it. It hurts, you know? It really hurts.

Any action a woman performs, from choosing a hairstyle to falling in love, may be perceived as hostile to one holy war cause or the other—and often to both. This applies not only to what we do, but to what we know, suspect, and believe—even the physical sensations of our own bodies.

A couple of examples: When I was approaching puberty in my deeply conservative hometown, my girlfriends and I were all given a pamphlet that described the development of human sexuality. Drawing on a confused amalgamation of Freudian theory and the Cult of True Womanhood, the authors of this pamphlet assured us that only boys and men actually experience sexual urges. Women, the pamphlet informed us, are only interested in sex because of their deep-seated desire to have babies. It took decades of shame-bound silence before my friends and I admitted the truth to one another. In our early teens, we would rather have died than let anyone know we entertained sexual thoughts, sensations, and even fantasies, from which babies were entirely—in fact rather pointedly—absent. We didn't stop having sexual feelings because of the doctrines of the holy war. But we never talked about them.

Some years later, I was a doctoral candidate at Harvard studying the sociology of gender. I had long since discarded the conservatism of my hometown. I became pregnant with my first child fully expecting to disprove all the antifemale stereotypes about the fragility of expectant mothers. To my indignant surprise, my pregnancy brought on nausea so intense that I had to be intravenously rehydrated on a regular basis. One day, feeling particularly queasy, I complained about my morning sickness to my classmates from a seminar on gender. To my surprise, some of the women in the group found this extremely offensive. They told me that morning sickness did not exist; that it was a myth invented by men to keep women out of the workforce. Clearly, I had absorbed this myth to the point of creating psychosomatic nausea. A visiting scholar, a feminist whose work on gender in organizations I much admire, looked me dead in the eye and said, "I had a macho pregnancy, and so can you." Despite intense guilt at my lack of machismo and betrayal of the feminist cause, I kept throwing up. But I stopped talking about it.

Most of the American women I have interviewed could report similar experiences. When Deirdre got a job, her husband accused her of abandoning her responsibilities to her children, but when she gave up her job to stay at home full-time he made fun of her for "not doing anything." On a lark, Jessie stopped at a department-store cosmetics counter and let the saleswomen spritz her with perfume and "remake" her face. Her boyfriend was horrified, telling her she looked like a "complete slut." She found a rest room, washed her face, walked back into the mall, and heard two teenage boys speculating on whether or not, as a woman with no makeup, she was necessarily a "dyke." At a PTA meeting, Erin found herself being patronized by the local president as "one of you less educated women." When she responded that she had a master's degree, the vice president began to condemn women who were "intellectual snobs."

Labels like these are meant to hurt, and they do. They cripple women not only by creating negative stereotypes with which other people condemn them, but also by showing each woman a distorted social mirror, an image that has been passed through the filters of the holy war. In this mirror a woman appears, *to herself*, not as a person doing her best to negotiate a difficult world with integrity, but as a caricature, a monster, a thing at once deficient and grotesquely overendowed.

The silence that grows out of this experience is not calm, but suffocating. It is an effort to avoid social ostracism, but, ironically, its effect is to cut women off from social support. The links between one human being and another are forged when people tell their own stories to each other, without embarrassment or fear of condemnation. The violence, scale, and high profile of the holy war have made this experience rare for American women.

The holy war has wounded more noncombatants than soldiers. Warriors on both sides may feel oppressed and endangered, but at least they can see their way clear. For the majority of women, caught between two value systems which have never existed in their pure forms, walking out into American society can feel like a dangerous crossing. The fighting is fierce, everyone is a target, and the only road signs contradict one another.

Many of the "civilian" women I interviewed were convinced that if they could live their lives carefully enough, if they could listen to both sides respectfully and never speak about their own thoughts, feelings, or experiences, they would finally escape being injured by the holy war. They were wrong. Paradoxical role definitions leave no avenue for escape, no way to steer clear of the contradictions, no way to avoid doing something wrong. Instead of finding peace and safe harbor, women who tried to placate the holy warriors found themselves getting more and more double-bound by the strange loop of paradox. The loop became tighter and tighter over time, until finally, for some women, it trapped them in a place of absolute paralysis. The holy war, along with all the other contradictory social forces that may muzzle, disparage, weaken, and consume American women, had brought them to the breaking point.

PHASE ONE:
SOCIALIZATION

PHASE TWO:
ENCOUNTERING PARADOX

PHASE THREE:
REACHING THE BREAKING POINT

PHASE FOUR:
TRANSCENDENCE

PHASE FIVE:
RE-CREATION

PHASE THREE

Reaching the
Breaking Point

·✦·
.✦.

CHAPTER FIVE

Hitting the Breaking Point

A ll right, I admit it. In 1995, like most Americans, I watched my fair share of the O. J. Simpson murder trial. However, there is an important difference between me and the majority of O.J. watchers in that I, being a sociologist, could pretend that I was not glued to the tube just because of morbid interest in a sensational murder. I was doing Research on a Cultural Phenomenon, thank you very much.

I knew that I would be able to make this claim successfully on the day that I saw The Look appear on the face of Marcia Clark, the lead prosecutor.

And what, you may rightfully ask me, is The Look? Actually, I'm sure you have seen this look yourself, although you may not have put a specific name on it. I am talking about a look I saw on dozens of American women's faces during my interview research: an expression of utter paralysis, the look of a small herbivorous animal caught in the headlight of an oncoming train. If it contained slightly more anger, it would be outrage; if it were a little more frightened, it would be panic; if it were a bit sadder, it would be hopelessness. It contains hints of all three emotions, but it is frozen in the center where they all meet, so that none of them can create a clear impulse to act. It is the look of a woman reaching the breaking point.

The day The Look passed over the features of America's best-known female prosecutor had been a long and hard one for all the litigators in the Simpson trial. Both the defense and the prosecution had been battering away at an expert witness, apparently trying to get the poor man to confess to the killings himself just to get out of the witness box. Needless to say, the TV commentators had been praising the male lawyers for their merciless questioning style, while Marcia Clark had been criticized ("too aggressive," "not nice enough," etc., etc.) for acting just like them.[1] But Clark was probably used to that particular double bind. The problem that brought The Look to her face was much more personal.

Clark's ex-husband had just announced that he was planning to sue for custody of their sons, who were three and five, on the grounds that Marcia Clark was an unfit parent. His reasoning was that the Trial of the Century was obviously devouring a huge amount of Clark's energy, and a woman who spent that much time away from her children could not possibly be a fit mother. (Can you imagine a successful male attorney being attacked as an unfit father because he was involved in a high-pressure trial? For that matter, what about business tycoons, generals, presidents, and all the other famous men whose jobs take enormous time and attention? Children are expected to honor and revere fathers who become successful as "rational individuals," but a mother who does so is quite likely to be accused of inadequate parenting. Just another version of the ubiquitous double binds that lie in wait for American women.)

Apparently, this particular assault on her character really punched Marcia Clark's buttons. The prospect of either losing her sons or opting out of her prosecutorial role seemed to be much more unsettling for her than the old "be a man but act like a lady" paradox. On this particular day, when the court was about to recess, the defense team proposed that everyone involved in the trial stay late to resolve one of the approximately five zillion sidebar issues that had arisen during the afternoon. Ms. Clark said that she couldn't stay. The indefatigable Judge Lance Ito, apparently forgetting that Clark had explained her situation to him earlier, peered at her through his glasses and asked why not.

It was at that moment that I saw The Look in Marcia Clark's eyes. For a split second, her face was exactly like the faces of women I'd interviewed in all sorts of circumstances: in trailer parks and lovely estates, office buildings and nurseries, scientific laboratories and churches. When The Look comes over a woman's face, it's as though her soul has suddenly deserted her. Her eyes turn blank and unfocused, and though she may be looking straight at you, you know she doesn't see you at all. The muscles in her face go limp, allowing an immense weariness to show in the contours of her skin. She seems disoriented, lost, vulnerable. She may begin to send short, nervous glances around her, as though she is trying to find a way to escape. But she doesn't move. Watching her, you get the very clear impression that she *can't*. This is the look of a woman at the breaking point.

NOWHERE TO GO

A woman reaches the breaking point when she has done absolutely everything she can think of, spent all the energy she has and then some, to try to fulfill the paradoxical demands being made of her. The more she has given, trying with every ounce of endurance to satisfy the voices demanding that she be *more* of this and *more* of that, the louder and more condemnatory those voices have become. At a certain point, when she simply can't do any more, the woman's perception of the world around her fades into a blur of overwhelming pressure, pressure that seems to come from everywhere at once. When she tries to "snap herself out of it," nothing happens. As one subject told me, "It's like I press on the gas pedal and the car is dead. Absolutely dead. There's just nothing left to go on."

For Marcia Clark, this interlude didn't last very long. Judge Ito, seeing The Look on Clark's face, suddenly remembered what she had told him about her situation. He agreed that court should be recessed. Naturally, the defense team argued that Marcia Clark was using her personal life as a ploy to delay the trial (after all, any rational individual shouldn't have to worry about something so trivial as a child). She was ready for this argument, and launched a blistering verbal attack in defense of motherhood. Judge Ito concurred, and presto! No more breaking point. Marcia Clark would retain custody of her children. But during that one moment, the moment when she thought there might be no way out, I saw The Look on Clark's face so clearly that I considered writing off my time watching the Simpson trial as a professional expense.

Other women do not escape the breaking point so easily. Some may stay in this fragmented, paralyzed condition for hours, days, even years. Women in this state have become some of our culture's favorite scapegoats, the "carriers" for the destructive effects of contradictions that form the core of our society's value system. Men are negatively affected by these contradictions as well, but women are far more likely to be blamed for them—and pulled deeply into the strange loop of paradoxical expectations. The vast ramifications of institutions, laws, policies, and attitudes based on incompatible philosophies are manifested in the tormented lives of women who truly believe it is their job to fulfill these irreconcilable demands.

THE BREAKING POINT DEFINED

Virtually all Americans grow up venerating the contradictory value system that dominates our culture. Men, women, and children in this country are likely to champion mutually exclusive aspects of traditional and modern values without recognizing their incompatibility. This may be logically confusing, and may even cause rather distressing double binds for people who stop to think about it. But it is not impossible to *value* two opposite things at once. It may occur to you, for example, that the ideal of complete individual liberty doesn't work very well with traditional social obligations. But you can continue to value both, despite possible contradictions.

The breaking point occurs at the stage when values are being *acted out*, in real time, by someone who has deeply internalized paradoxical role definitions. In other words, a woman hits her breaking point when her deepest core values dictate that she must *do* two incompatible things at once. She is faced with a choice between "the devil and the deep blue sea"; if she does one thing she sees as absolutely necessary, another thing, which she also believes to be absolutely necessary, will go undone. What is merely bothersome in theory becomes impossible in practice, and the inevitable failure to *do* the impossible is beyond the woman's moral, emotional, and physical tolerance.

Marcia Clark's dilemma, on the day I saw The Look on her face, was a classic example. On one hand, the entire country was watching Clark's every professional move. She was criticized for incompetence by panels of legal experts for things like sighing deeply, let alone running off to care for children. She was being judged against a courtroomful of other attorneys who didn't have to worry about meeting the high domestic standards required of a "fit mother." On the other hand, Clark's husband was threatening her with another legal judgment, this time about her parenting choices, in a society where mothers are supposed to be the ultimate domestic caretakers. Losing custody of her children would have been not only an intense emotional loss, but a failure in the motherly role her society had set up for her. In the second that she thought she would have to make this choice—either failing to pick up her sons or walking out of the courtroom with court still in session—Marcia Clark hit the breaking point.

HOW IT LOOKS FROM THE INSIDE:
THE SYMPTOMS OF THE BREAKING POINT

Once you become familiar with The Look of the breaking point, it is easy to spot from the outside. One of its symptoms, however, is that when you're at it yourself, you often don't recognize it. The nature of paradox sets your mind in circular motion, spinning around a logical strange loop so dizzily that it is impossible to detach from it. In order to escape paradox, one must be able to see the problem *from a distance*. This is impossible for a woman at the breaking point, because she is not merely listening to contradictory advice from outside herself. The paradoxical directive—the double bind—comes from *within* her own value system, so that she cannot run from it. Wherever she goes, deadlock comes with her.

This is what differentiates the women in the previous chapter from those who are truly at the breaking point. A woman in this state is not just receiving contradictory commands from her society. *She herself* has taken over the role of taskmaster, insisting that she do incompatible things, punishing herself when she fails. It's not just that she has a great deal to do. Studies have shown that women tend to feel more stress than men with similar workloads, because of the intense value judgments they—and our society—place on women's activities. For example, when the average man goes off to work, leaving his children with a competent caretaker, he is likely to feel very little stress. When a woman does exactly the same thing, she is likely to feel guilty and anxious because she is abdicating the role of constant caretaker prescribed for her by her culture. The man's role may separate him from his children, but at least it's consistent: he is to be first and foremost a rational individual. A woman, on the other hand, has been socialized into a role where individual achievement *and* care of dependent children are both supposed to come first.

We have already seen how violently women may be attacked for simply trying to live life in a culture that defines female roles paradoxically. It is impossible for any American woman to do everything it would take to avoid criticism from one source or another. The woman at the breaking point internalizes this criticism, judging herself even for the very best choices she can make. If she succeeds in the traditional area of female roles, she will feel ashamed because she hasn't achieved enough as a rational individual. If she is tremendously successful in her career, she berates herself for failing on the traditional front. She may feel indignant or discounted if she is categorized with other women, but ashamed at her lack of femininity if she is categorized with men. She blames herself for everything that goes wrong in her own life, her home, or her workplace, because she (like her culture) believes that women are primarily responsible not only for their own individual success, but also for the physical and emotional well-being of the people around them.

Geraldine, 36

One day I started noticing how often I say "I'm sorry." I'm sorry that I got up too late. I'm sorry I had to get everyone else up too early. I'm sorry I didn't make more breakfast, and I'm sorry the breakfast I made isn't good enough. I'm sorry that eggs are high in cholesterol. I'm sorry it's raining. I say "I'm sorry" for everything that could possibly go wrong in the universe. My whole family looks at me whenever anything goes wrong, like, "Well? Aren't you sorry?" I've trained them to believe that everything that happens to any of them is my fault.

The more a woman tries to free herself from the negative judgments associated with one side of her paradoxical role, the more she finds herself suffering negative judgments associated with the other. Both sets of attitudes are like the sting of whips, driving her harder and harder in two directions at once. She may alternate back and forth between contradictory aspects of her role for a long time, getting more and more tired, deriving less and less joy from any of her activities. Eventually, she reaches a point at which the "whips" from both sides are cutting into her at the very same time. She literally cannot escape one by turning toward the other—nor can she run from them both, because she herself is one of the people wielding them. This is the moment when a woman's eyes go blank and her energy flickers out. She cannot think of anything to do except stand under the rain of blows, confused, aching, and exhausted. As a woman comes closer to this point, she may exhibit the following signs and symptoms.

SENSE OF ENTRAPMENT

Many of the women I interviewed who were at the breaking point mentioned images of being bound, suffocated, or trapped. Some described their internal experience as a sense of being locked in some kind of shrinking enclosure. Judy, a single mother, put it this way:

Judy, 40

It's like I'm in this tunnel, trying to get through to the light. I keep running and running, looking for the way out, but the tunnel gets narrower and darker the farther I run. And then, it finally gets so cramped I can't go on anymore, so I turn around to run back, but the walls have caved in behind me. I'm trapped.

An elementary school teacher named Virginia had a recurring dream in which she was trying to escape from a maze of mirrors. She kept seeing escape hatches, only to find that she had been fooled by multiple reflections and drawn deeper into the labyrinth. Mary, an art student whose role conflict had contributed to her recent divorce, showed me drawings of trapped or bound women that she drew almost obsessively during her nonexistent spare time. "I thought the trap was my marriage," Mary said. "But that was only part of it. Even without my ex-husband around, it's like I'm tied up inside my own mind."

This kind of image—of being "tied up in one's mind," trapped, or smothered—was a common theme in my interviews. It was as though the strange loop by which they defined their own roles was a tightening spiral, growing smaller and smaller until there was no room for these women to breathe.

DISMEMBERMENT

Another common metaphor women used to describe being at the breaking point was that of being torn to pieces. Samantha, a farm wife with five small children, told me that she kept remembering the way she had once seen vultures attack the carcass of a cow.

Samantha, 48

Sometimes I feel like that cow. It's like I can feel everything carving out chunks of me—pieces of my self. I tell people, "Yes, fine, I'll do all these things." And the person I'm talking to doesn't realize I've just given up another part of me. They just think I'm doing what I should—barely even that. There's not very much of me left.

Most women were not so graphic about their sense of being parceled out to others, but they used similar language, saying they felt "pulled in two," "torn," "split," or "divided." This was not only characteristic of women who were trying to combine career and family. Jenny, a physical therapist who has never married, felt the same way at her job.

Jenny, 35

I work with patients who are facing terrible losses—loss of motion or health—and it's like I can't do enough for them. I'm supposed to be the tough doctor, pushing them to do their exercises and their therapy, but because I'm the only woman there, I'm the one they look to for comfort as well. I feel like I'm pulled two ways all the time, like I'm coming apart.

Women who tried to describe the breaking point to me used contradictory images of being trapped *and* dismembered, "pushed" into a corner at the same time they were "pulled" to the point of brittle fragility. Often, the same individuals told me that they felt simultaneously fragmented and confined, "spread too thin" and claustrophobically restricted. These oxymoronic images are perfectly logical when you consider that the demands made of women are paradoxical. Both traditional and modern ideals place confining limitations on women, and each also requires full-time work to be properly fulfilled. Breaking points result when the combination of demands (which "pull") and constraints (which "push") reach a woman's own personal level of tolerance.

I interviewed a number of men as well as women during my research. On one occasion Tim, an aeronautical engineer, called me soon after I interviewed his wife, Julia. Tim wanted to talk to me because he was concerned about his wife, who had gone into a deep depression following the birth of the couple's fourth child.

Tim, 40

When you design a plane, you have to worry about making it strong enough to handle a lot of different sources of pressure—from the jets, from the interior, from gravity, from a number of different sources. . . . I came home one day, and Julia was just standing in the kitchen, with all the kids jumping up and down all around her. She looked like she was dead, she was standing there not moving at all. I thought, "Oh my God, she's exceeded her design capacity."

At some moment, depending on the individual woman's "design capacity," each woman may reach her limit and simply become unable to continue.

LOSS OF SELF-ESTEEM

The woman who is trying to fulfill contradictory demands experiences a steady erosion of self-esteem and self-trust. She repeatedly makes choices and takes actions designed to satisfy her own (and other people's) sense of what she *should* be, and every single time, those choices end up having negative repercussions. Though she may realize that her best-intentioned efforts are exactly the actions that land her in the most trouble, she rarely recognizes that she is trying to reconcile a paradox. Instead, she feels that she has somehow made a stupid choice, or that she is inordinately slow or weak.

Carma, 58

Everything I do goes wrong. I'll try so hard to make my husband happy, and all of a sudden my daughters are all upset with me. I try to make them happy, and my husband gets irritable. I want to be a good person. I've tried *so hard,* all my life, to do the right thing. But I never seem to get it. I just don't get it.

When they confront situations where contradictory pressures become intense, some women give in completely to their self-blame, steadily withdrawing from life rather than risking more "wrong" decisions. Others put up an epic struggle to do better, constantly discounting and accusing themselves for their imagined inadequacies. One woman told me that she borrowed the motto "I will work harder" from Boxer, the horse in the George Orwell novel *Animal Farm.* She commented wryly that Boxer ended up working himself almost to death, and was rewarded by being sent off to the knacker to be killed.

Apology and self-blame are constant features of such women's self-descriptions. Both types seem to lose faith in their ability to judge situations and plot their own course through life. "Every choice I made turned out to be the wrong one," said one of my subjects. But I had spoken to women who made the opposite choices, and I knew that many of them thought those, too, were the "wrong ones." Few American women seem to realize that, because their role definition is paradoxical, *every choice they make about their lives may be seen as the wrong one.*

THE INNER LIZARD

One thing that may account for the numbness that overtakes a woman at the breaking point is the structure and function of the brain. The following explanation is simplified, but it provides a basic explanation of what may be happening to women in this state.

The human brain can be divided into three layers. The deepest layer, the brain stem, controls autonomic functions like breathing, sleeping, and jerking a finger away from a hot stove. Some neurologists call this the "reptilian brain," because reptiles' brains stop here. (I suppose breathing and sleeping are about the most complex problems reptiles ever have to solve.) The next layer of the brain, the limbic system, is where mammals, including humans, store emotions and survival reactions. The outermost layer, the neocortex, is where reasoning and logic take place.

Most of the time, we humans are engaging our neocortex as we think our way through life: driving, cooking, filling out tax forms. However, when we are confronted by a threat that cannot be solved by logic, the neocortex stops directing our behavior. It defers to the less complex portions of the brain, which trigger fight-or-flight responses and other automatic reactions to danger. (This is why, if you've ever been in an accident, you may have responded automatically, without being conscious of any thoughts whatsoever. Time may also seem to stop at such moments, because the neocortex, which takes care of time sequencing, is "off duty.") One troublesome thing about being human nowadays is that we don't have to be facing a rock slide or a grizzly bear to feel deeply threatened. Getting up to speak in front of a roomful of people is enough to send our neocortex into deep freeze—and so, just when we need to think logically, our brains are gearing us up to run for our lives, sending messages through the body ("Heart rate *up*, mouth *dry*, sweat glands *active*, now *scream scream scream!*") that actually work against the tasks we're trying to perform.

Something similar may happen when a person is deeply engaged in a logical strange loop. Because of the nature of paradox, the reasoning brain *cannot solve the problem*. Depending on how intensely she feels about the choices she must make, a woman in this situation may feel so threatened, and her problem-solving skills be so baffled by paradox, that her logical neocortex defers to more primitive parts of the brain. My friend and colleague Karen Gerdes has observed this mental gear-shifting in poverty-stricken women who are trying to figure out how to feed and clothe themselves and their children. In situations of extreme pressure, when their problems seem insurmountable, these women temporarily move into a fight-or-flight response. They cannot process logical information that would be easy for them at other times. They may literally not hear such information, or record it in their memories. The Look comes over their faces. Their bodies may be sitting quite still in a welfare office, but their minds are a thousand miles away and still running. The limbic system and the "reptilian brain" (or, as I like to call it, the Inner Lizard) have taken control.[2]

FIGHT AND/OR FLIGHT: THE LIZARD DOES ITS STUFF

It is very important to protect one's Inner Lizard, for once a woman is so panicked or "paradoxed" that her reasoning mind shuts down, she has reached the breaking point in all its dismal glory. A woman in such a situation literally stops thinking clearly. She experiences intense anxiety, the feeling that she must "fight or flee," without any clear directives about *how* to fight, or *where* to flee. As a result, she may lash out in anger, or psychologically "run away," or both.

♦ *Fight: Free-Floating Anger*   There is rarely a clear target for the anger of a woman at the breaking point. Part of her problem is as vague and omnipresent as society itself. Another part lies within her own internalized value system. Both are elusive and difficult to see clearly. And so, in an instinctive effort to reduce the overwhelming number of should-do's in her life, she may hear herself shouting, crying, or snarling at anyone who approaches her with any request whatsoever—including herself. She will "fight" her children, her husband, her best friend, or some hapless driver who happens to stall in front of her at a traffic light. She is chronically short-tempered, always ready to flare into impatient shouts or tears.

Joanne, 29

I think I'm feeling fine, but lately my life feels so stressful that I fly right off the handle over nothing. I don't even know why I'm doing it. It's so easy for me to get to the end of my rope that I've decided I must have been born with a really short rope.

♦ *Flight: Dissociation*   Another woman at the breaking point may "flee" by involuntarily dissociating, mentally checking out. She may feel unable to keep her attention in the here-and-now. Because her mind is desperately running away, a woman in this situation has trouble focusing. She forgets things. She will start one task, only to drop it and rush to another, until her environment is crammed with unfinished projects. When people talk to her she answers them, but without seeming to hear. You could tell her that she has just been sold as a slave to work in the poppy fields of some tropical Third World country, harvesting heroin for drug lords, and she will simply get a worried furrow in her brow and promise that she'll get around to it as soon as she can. I heard many accounts like this one, from a homemaker with three teenagers:

Priscilla, 45

Sometimes when I'm coming home from shopping or something, I'll drive to my house and then go right past it. It's like if I can just stay in the car a little longer, where it's quiet and nobody's asking me for anything, I'll be able to pull myself together. It doesn't work, but sometimes I just can't get out of the car, can't go in the house, can't go back into my life again. The challenges are just too much.

PARALYSIS

In the middle of all the frenzied "action" of fight-or-flight responses, the woman at the breaking point feels utterly frozen. As the saying goes, her motivation to act, to get up and go, just got up and went. She can't remember why she once enjoyed things like going to the beach or a football game; such activities sound exhausting to her. She loses the ability to "play," to enjoy the simple fact of being alive. She stops laughing—except when laughing is proper etiquette, at which point she laughs in exactly the same way that she cleans her toilets: dutifully but without enthusiasm. She has trouble sleeping, even though she is always tired. Because everything she does seems to preclude something else she *should* be doing, she ends up feeling that she cannot do anything at all.

Caitlin, 26

I started my own company a year ago, right after I left my husband. The company is doing well, but I've had to put the profits right back into the business. I can't relax. It always feels as though I can't do enough to keep myself and my children secure. I'm always worried that they're not getting the kind of mothering they need. There never seems to be enough money to meet my payroll and still raise my kids, pay for day care, all the rest of it. There's never enough energy, never enough time, never enough *me*!

HELP FOR THE HELPER

Many women who had reached the breaking point told me they had consulted doctors about the problems of free-floating anger, dissociation, and their sense of paralysis. They were often diagnosed with depression and treated with psychoactive drugs (Prozac was the favorite) or psychotherapy. The interesting thing about these cases was the way that both the women themselves and the professional healers had approached the problem. Consider the following comment from Justine, a young homemaker whose husband was unemployed:

Justine, 25

I'm just not up to anything anymore. A lot of days I just sit and stare at the wall. A lot of it is because I had to go off my Prozac when I got pregnant. I'd been really tired and depressed before I went on the Prozac. It really helped. I could get a lot more done, so I didn't feel as guilty. I could work, so we had more money. Now I can't work, and I can't even take care of the kids. My doctor says that if I don't nurse, I can go back on the Prozac right after the baby's born. I'm just waiting to have the baby so I can get back on [the drug] and take care of everything again.

Here's another quote, from a woman who opted for therapy after her doctor diagnosed depression:

Elise, 30

I think the therapy has really helped me because now I have more to give to my family and my job. Before, you know, there wasn't a time that I just sat down and focused on myself, and now I get that once a week, and so I have a lot more to give.

Certainly, the doctors' diagnoses in these cases were correct. Both these women were depressed. The interesting thing about these cases, and many others like them, was that the women, their doctors, and their therapists almost always assumed that the problem they had to work on was with the individual woman's inability to cope with an enormous amount and variety of tasks—not the extraordinary demands themselves.

There seemed to be a consensus that a "good woman" in our culture *should* be able to cope with all these demands. If she can't, she must be sick, in need of medicine or therapy.

This is the way the women had "framed" their problems when they went to their doctors, and the doctors (who, after all, have been educated in a medical-school culture of superhuman achievement) had naturally responded from the same system of beliefs. Together, doctors and patients were using chemical assistance or therapy *as a way for women to fulfill paradoxical expectations, rather than questioning the validity of those expectations.* One unusual therapist, who had been through a version of the breaking point herself before becoming a psychologist, told me that when a woman was referred to her for depression, one of the first things she told her to do was hire a weekly housecleaner. "A lot of them feel better immediately," she said. "If they don't, *then* we start into their subconscious and the rest of it."

Women who told me about their experiences in therapy rarely encountered this kind of approach. When a woman at the breaking point sought counseling, both she and her therapist would usually set to work trying to "fix" women so that they could fulfill all the demands made on them—even though these demands were often contradictory. For example, Alma was taken to a therapist by her husband when she fell victim to the paralysis of the breaking point. In the therapist's office, Alma's husband brought out a list of the tasks he felt Alma should be able to accomplish. The list included earning enough to pay for an even 50 percent of the family's expenses, doing all the domestic work for herself, two children, her husband, and her husband's elderly mother (who lived with them), being "emotionally present" to comfort and soothe every other family member, buffering them from the slings and arrows of the cruel world, running all family errands and chauffeuring the children and mother-in-law on their daily rounds, and never complaining. Alma looked at the list, agreed that a "normal woman" should be able to do all these things, and then began to cry. Together, Alma, her husband, and the therapist went about the task of "fixing" Alma so that she wouldn't exhibit symptoms of depression in the face of a "normal" workload.

ILLEGAL LENGTHS

Women who sought professional help for the symptoms of the breaking point were far better off than some other women I interviewed. These were people who had turned to illegal drugs, or legal drugs in dangerous dosages, to cope with paradoxical expectations. One single mother told me:

Lenora, 46

I been on crystal meth [a cheap street amphetamine] ever since my divorce. My husband wasn't good for nothing. He took off, and I had a lot of work to do, trying to keep my trailer and raise the kids. I did odd jobs for money. I made the boys' clothes for school, so they looked good. I always repaired the trailer myself. When I'm on crystal, I don't have to sleep for three or four days at a time. You can get a lot done that way. I ain't proud of myself, but I got to get by. I can't just be sleeping all the time.

It wasn't only poor women who fell into the drug-abusing category. High-achieving women with perfect-looking homes and prestigious careers often told me they relied on over-the-counter uppers, from No-Doz to enormous amounts of caffeinated drinks, to help them answer a blizzard of different demands. A professor's wife, a veritable Mary Poppins of a woman who organized projects to feed the homeless while raising three children, told me:

Joyce, 55

I was getting very run down, and then one of the ladies from my monthly book club gave me this vitamin supplement. I started taking it every morning, and I've been getting a lot more things accomplished. But about a month ago there was a news report on the company that makes this supplement. Apparently, it has quite a few amphetamines in it. When they said they were going to take it off the market, I went and bought as much as I could find. I just can't keep going without it. I'm scared that when I run out, I'll go back to being a deadweight again, not doing anybody any good.

Illegal or over-the-counter drugs, like doctors' prescriptions and psychotherapy, all have the same purpose for the woman who is trying to fulfill a contradictory role definition. The treatments are supposed to extend the woman's personal resources, heighten her energy so that she can fulfill more and more demands. The idea is to avoid the breaking point, but the effect is only to forestall it. If a woman is in a situation that is truly paradoxical, the longer she holds out, the more intense the breaking point will be when she finally reaches it.

WHO HITS THE BREAKING POINT?

Anyone, regardless of sex or nationality, can be forced to the breaking point by paradoxical role expectations. While all the women I interviewed had been affected in one way or another by our society's paradoxical definition of women's roles, only about a third had actually reached what I would call the breaking point. Some had gone beyond it (as we will see in a later chapter); others had managed to push the wolf from the door, the way Marcia Clark did on the day she spoke to Judge Ito about needing to leave work on schedule. Some of my subjects, mostly very young women, had never come close to this state. The large majority of women in my sample were somewhere in between: they could see the potential for the breaking point but had so far managed to work hard enough to avoid becoming completely overwhelmed.

LIFE ACCIDENTS

As I've said, the breaking point is not just a paradoxical set of beliefs or attitudes; it happens when a woman encounters a truly irreconcilable situation. One of the ways I saw such situations emerging in the lives of women I interviewed was through what sociologists call "life accidents." In general, this term refers to any unexpected difficulty that falls outside what one would expect of a "normal" life (although the longer I live, the more I think our definition of "normal" is abnormally optimistic). Illness, injury, bankruptcy, crime, flood, fire, earthquake—anything that comes out of nowhere to alter the course of someone's existence may be called a "life accident." Because life accidents often create an intensified need for modern resources (like money) *and* for more reliance on traditional relationships, they are highly likely to push a woman to the breaking point.

Some life accidents can seem relatively minor from the outside. The factors that make a life accident into a breaking point have less to do with the severity of the "accident" than *the level of importance the individual woman attaches to various aspects of her role, and the extent to which the "accident" prevents her from fulfilling her own expectations.* Often, women who have been holding the breaking point at bay for years experience a relatively minor life accident as the straw that breaks the camel's back; the incident may not seem like much in itself, but on top of all the other pressures in their lives, it is more than they can endure.

For example, Kendra, an air traffic controller, was filling in for not one but two absent colleagues when her aging mother called to say she had slipped on a patch of ice outside her home. The older woman was worried that she might have broken a hip, and asked if her daughter would leave work and drive her to the hospital. For some people, this might not have created a breaking point, but for Kendra it did. She felt that she could not leave her job without endangering the lives of pilots and passengers, but she couldn't tolerate being away from her mother at a difficult time. She called a friend, who agreed to go help Kendra's mother while Kendra stayed on duty in the control tower. As she turned back to her work, Kendra became literally paralyzed.

Kendra, 44

I couldn't see the instruments. I forgot how to communicate with the pilots. I was like a statue. It was one of the most horrifying moments of my life.

. . . I asked my supervisor if I could go. I must have looked terrible, because he didn't even mention how understaffed we were. I started walking to my car. In the parking lot, I kept thinking about the people who might be in danger because there weren't enough controllers in the tower. It got worse the closer I got to my car. It was like I was being pulled in two directions by these very strong cords that I couldn't see. Finally I just stopped. I stood in that parking lot and felt like I was about to die.

Kendra stayed rooted in the airport parking lot for what seemed like a very long time, absolutely undecided, neither fulfilling her traditional obligations to her mother nor acting as a rational individual on the job. Shortly after this incident, Kendra quit work as an air traffic controller to spend her days helping her mother recuperate. When I spoke to her, she was running out of money, but could not face going back to work. A month after her first bout of "paralysis," Kendra still felt immobilized, trapped, and torn. She was still at the breaking point.

Other life accidents I heard about in my interviews were more obviously overwhelming. One of my first subjects was a young Mormon woman named Donna. Donna had been married just over a year, and had a three-week-old baby, when her husband, Garth (who, like Donna, was twenty-two years old), was diagnosed with a particularly aggressive form of cancer. Surgery and chemotherapy left Garth terribly ill, unable to work, and still not free from the disease. Donna took a job as an assistant in a medical laboratory to bring in a little money and, more important, provide medical benefits. She did not earn enough to completely cover Garth's medical bills, which were enormous even with the insurance, and her salary was barely enough to pay for baby-sitting and a little food. Still, the job gave Donna a sense that she could survive Garth's illness even if he did not; that she could support herself and her baby in the worst of circumstances.

It was at about this time that the president of the Mormon church gave a speech which strongly emphasized that mothers who work outside their homes are violating their divinely appointed role. Although the speech did leave room for exceptional circumstances, Donna and Garth were from extremely devout families who followed their religion's guidelines strictly.

Donna, 36

They—I mean we—honestly believed that God wouldn't heal Garth if I kept working. I felt like if I obeyed all the church's commandments to the letter, maybe God would give us a miracle. That's certainly what Garth's family believed. It got to where they were acting like I was responsible for the cancer; that if I hadn't gotten a job he would be better already.

Under intense pressure, especially from her mother-in-law, Donna quit her job at the hospital. During the next several months, Donna was, as she put it, "a mess." She was grieving, angry, and utterly stuck. Her one response to the prospect of early widowhood, poverty, and single parenthood—her job—had been stopped short by her religious culture's devotion to traditional values. Later she would tell me that during this period she "couldn't think straight," that she often didn't have the strength to get out of bed, that her small daughter sometimes cried for hours before Donna could make herself respond.

Part of this reaction was depression brought on by the sudden and terrible loss of her husband's health. But Donna had not "stopped moving" until she received a strong directive from her church and family to avoid working. Until then, Donna had at least been able to channel her fear into an activity she associated with survival. When that channel was blocked, she became paralyzed.

You've got to remember . . . not everyone in my church felt like me. All my friends worked. They couldn't believe I was being so strict.

They thought that in my case, of course God would make an exception and let me work. But I was desperate to make myself "perfect," so that God would heal Garth.

Whether Donna was "right" or "wrong" is not the point. The important thing is that she genuinely believed that if she chose to work, she would be violating her deepest values—and yet she also felt terribly guilty and vulnerable when she did *not* work.

Women who come from strongly traditional backgrounds, whether religious or ethnic, are likely to be more deeply engaged in a split modern/traditional value system than women without such ties. However, even nonreligious people are affected by value systems that are often grounded in, and similar to, religious faith. American society was founded by religious pilgrims who paradoxically combined their beliefs with a stern economic realism. Our national motto is "In God We Trust"—and in case you ever forget that, it's printed on our money, which always helps bolster one's faith if God doesn't seem to be responding appropriately. Values lie outside the scope of "rational" proof, so in a sense, anyone who has absorbed "American values" is relying on moral judgments as strong and directive as religious ones.

I saw this when I encountered a "life accident" of my own. At the time I was a second-year Ph.D. candidate, already well into my interview research, nearly six months pregnant with my second child. There had been some minor difficulty with the pregnancy, and in order to "put my mind at rest," the doctors at the Harvard Health Clinic suggested that I have an amniocentesis—a procedure in which fluid is taken from the mother's womb to check for birth defects in the fetus. Two weeks after the test, the nurse practitioner at the clinic called with the results. A chromosome count had revealed that my unborn son had trisomy 21, the condition commonly called Down syndrome or (in a more vivid descriptive vein) "mongoloid idiocy." All five obstetricians at University Health Services agreed that the best course of action would be a therapeutic abortion. I was advised that any other course of action would very probably ruin my life, my marriage, and the mental health of my two-year-old daughter. No one seemed to even consider allowing the pregnancy to continue.

For me, the decision was not so simple. It had been months since I had heard my son's heart beat for the first time, and felt the first fluttering sensations of tiny hands and feet exploring my own interior. During those months I had been daydreaming about the baby, thinking about what foods I should eat to keep him healthy, talking to him when no one was around to hear me and think I was off my rocker. The ultrasound screen that had been used during the amniocentesis showed a beautiful, fully formed little boy who yawned, stretched, and sucked his finger while I watched. My husband and I had already named him, and taken a picture of him home to show to his big sister. I knew that the abortion procedure at this stage would probably include injecting my uterus with a saline solution and waiting a day or so for the fetus to stop moving, after which I would undergo induced labor and deliver the tiny dead body. My immediate and continued reaction to this proposition was a protectiveness toward my unborn child that shocked me with its violence.

My decision not to end the pregnancy threw me squarely into the middle of the holy war between the traditional and modern definitions of women's roles. In the entire holy war, there is no issue that creates more intense ideological battles than abortion. It is the topic that is most likely to go beyond the bounds of debate and become literal war, complete with guns and explosives. Even knowing this, and after interviewing dozens of women (I would interview many more later) who had been pulled into the holy war when they thought they were innocent bystanders, I was stunned by the way people reacted to what I thought was a very private decision.

On one hand, I suddenly found myself being labeled a champion of the pro-life movement. People I barely knew called me on the phone, inviting me to speak at antiabortion gatherings or participate in political work against legalized abortion. All of them seemed to assume that I was as deeply devoted to this aspect of conservative traditional values as they were. They were wrong; I had never been particularly good at fitting the traditional female mold, and after experiencing the anguish of my own choice, the very last thing I wanted to do was take away another woman's right to make her own decision about her pregnancy. This came as a shock to people who assumed I would join in prolife activism, and I was roundly scolded for my "inconsistency" by traditional holy warriors.

On the other hand, many people in the Harvard community responded to my decision with equal horror. The "culture" that has developed at Harvard over the centuries is devoted to the worship of individual achievement in its most rational form. Although this value system is explicitly *non*religious, many of the people I knew at Harvard reacted to my choice to bear a retarded child as though I had violated their faith. Again, people who had very little to do with me suddenly became intensely interested in what I was doing. Some felt compelled to persuade me that I *must not* have the baby. A fellow student told me it was "every woman's duty to screen her pregnancies" and abort fetuses that would be "detrimental to society." A grim-faced Harvard doctor compared my choice against abortion to refusing to let him remove a cancerous tumor. A professor told my husband that neither of us would ever get our Ph.D.'s unless I consented to an abortion. In particular, some people told me frankly that my choice was "antifeminist," a blow against women's right to choose abortion and a willful curtailment of my own success as a rational individual. One acquaintance suggested that I was being terribly selfish to put my own feelings above the cause of women's liberation.

The pressure I received from both sides of the holy war struck me as exceedingly bizarre. In retrospect, I explain it to myself by suspecting that some people become violently opposed to abortion because they identify themselves with unwanted babies, taking out their angst, pain, and lack of self-worth on women who are already up to their ears in problems and very unlikely to defend themselves. On the other hand, many people associated with Harvard base their self-worth on achievement in the good old Enlightenment model, in which being successful means superiority in rational thought and complete freedom from traditional obligations. From this perspective, my decision to bear and raise a child with Down syndrome is incomprehensible; after all, I knew from the start that my son was most unlikely to be a rational high achiever, and my entire family took on a major traditional obligation by welcoming him. To the "modern" thinkers at Harvard, I was damaging my own happiness, the happiness of my husband and daughter, and especially the happiness of my son, by refusing to put the child out of his "misery."

There's no way for me to test whether my analysis is accurate or not, but in the end it satisfied my need to understand people's intense reactions to my "life accident." At any rate, I didn't come up with it quickly. At the time I had to make the choice to abort or continue my pregnancy, I merely felt battered and bewildered by the antagonistic passions of the holy warriors around me. I was not trying to make a political statement, one way or the other. I was devastated by the news that my son would never be "normal," terrified by the unknown, and very unsure where my life would go from that point. However, if I tried to talk about these feelings with the people around me, the response was likely to contain as much ideological oratory as comfort and support.

The day I hit the breaking point, I was sitting on the sofa in my apartment waiting for some friends who were planning to take my husband and me to lunch, by way of cheering us up. I had been fielding phone calls all morning, from people whose names I hardly remembered, but who had strong views to express about my situation and a strong desire to express them. At that point I was still naïvely concerned with what people thought of my decision, and so I had tried, with each conversation, to explain why my experience was not whatever the caller seemed sure it was. So far, I had found it impossible to avoid being categorized in ways that didn't fit.

Just before our friends arrived, a curious numbness descended over me, as though a thick fog had settled between the synapses in my brain. The doorbell rang, the door opened, and I heard our friends' voices speaking to John. I meant to get up and greet them, but I absolutely could not move. Although I was becoming accustomed to hearing judgments passed about my choice from virtually everyone who knew me, each encounter had left me feeling more misunderstood and less sure of myself, until I felt as though I were physically dissolving. I was too tired to keep up any defenses, but still terribly sensitive to every disapproving or misguided assumption directed at me. In the end I couldn't face anyone, not even good friends. I stayed home from the luncheon, sat on the couch, and spun around the strange loop of paradox, finding no resolution to the questions in my head.

Since that day, whenever I watch The Look come over a woman's face, I feel a stab of empathy. I didn't check a mirror, but I am absolutely sure that I wore The Look as I sat on the sofa and tried to force myself to move. Once you've been at the breaking point, you don't forget it easily. You know it when you see it.

And see it I did, during the next several years, as I interviewed more and more American women who had suffered "life accidents." There was the elementary school teacher whose inner-city students longed for her to be both their mother figure and their professional adviser, who was sued by a parent for "overinvolvement" in a ten-year-old's life at the same time that the child in question was begging for a closer relationship. There was the wife who unofficially ran more than half of her husband's business, but lost the business when he was killed in a small-plane crash because she had no documented title, no personal credit history, no salary—nothing, in fact, but a reputation as a devoted housewife. There was the student who was called home from business school because her little sister was dying, whose professors "would have liked to sympathized" but felt honor-bound to ignore her private life and judge her by the standards of a "rational individual"—a model which simply does not allow for attention to sick relatives. There was the research scientist who was encouraged by her mentors to develop her phenomenal mind and talent for her work. When she returned from completing a postdoctoral degree—brilliantly—those same scientists voted to give a job to a less qualified man because they "didn't want to discourage a woman from having children."

WHY EVERY BREAKING POINT IS A CRISIS, BUT NOT EVERY CRISIS IS A BREAKING POINT

When I first encountered women who had hit the breaking point following a "life accident," I assumed that the feelings they described to me were simply their natural responses to the kind of personal disasters all of us hope to avoid. After all, it's hardly surprising that a woman whose young husband is dying, or whose mother is ill, or who has lost a job, might feel anxious or paralyzed. As my research progressed, however, two facts began to emerge from the interviews to convince me that there was a difference between a straightforward reaction to crisis and a true breaking point.

First of all, not every woman who went through a life accident ended up at a breaking point. Most of the people I spoke to had experienced something sad or life-changing that intruded on their "normal" lives, but many had simply grieved, adjusted to the change, and carried on. The women who reached the breaking point were those whose culture, loved ones, and personal beliefs had turned their life accidents into insoluble double binds.

The second reason I came to see that breaking points and crises are not identical is that many women who did *not* report any life accidents seemed to be facing the breaking point anyway. In fact, these women were in the majority. Despite the fact that their lives appeared to be going along well enough, I spoke to many women who felt as spent, as trapped, and as torn as others who were in obvious crisis. In some ways, these women suffered more than others whose problems were more obvious. As one woman told me:

Judith, 39

I almost wish something terrible would happen to me, because then I'd have an excuse to feel bad. As it is, I have a nice home, beautiful children, a good husband—all these really good things. I tell my friends that I'm not happy, and they say, "Look at you! Look at how good your life is! What do *you* have to complain about?" And they're right. I know they're right, so I try not to complain. But I feel like I'm falling to pieces.

THE MARCH OF PROGRESS AND
THE MARCH OF TIME:
HOW "NORMAL LIFE" BLINDSIDES WOMEN

The fact is that American women no longer have to fall victim to freak accidents or go out seeking unusual experiences to find themselves at the breaking point. The more time passes, the more this condition is creeping into the most ordinary of lives. The reason for this is a combination of historical progress and the life cycle. Just thirty years ago, it was very rare for a woman to contribute a substantial percentage of a family's income: since then, both the opportunity and economic need to work have become major factors in the lives of the *majority* of American women. The sheer number of people affected by this change is astonishing. The role of women in our society has changed so dramatically, so fast that American mothers can hardly comprehend the different world into which they are sending their daughters, and the daughters find little in their mothers' histories to guide them through their present challenges.

The pace of modernization has become so rapid that its transformation of women's lives has been revolutionary, not evolutionary. It has happened in less than the span of a single lifetime. We have *watched* it happen, whether we were slugging it out in the trenches of feminism, campaigning against threats to traditional values, or just standing on the sidelines wondering what in the world was going on. Because the change has been so fast, it "caught" women at different stages of the life cycle.

The paradox of being female in the United States has the potential to bring women of every age to the breaking point, but depending on when we were born and how our lives have unfolded, it has affected us in different ways. It has crept into the definition of what we now call "normal" female life at all stages of the life cycle, but it looks different depending on where each woman is when it catches up with her. In the next chapter, we'll look at how paradoxical role definitions are creating breaking points in the lives of American women of all ages, why more and more women are encountering this dilemma all the time, and why the risk is still increasing for every woman in our society—whether she is standing in a courtroom with the eyes of the world watching The Look flash across her face, sitting at home adjusting the vertical hold on her TV screen, feeding her children, punching a time clock, shopping for groceries, or reading this book.

CHAPTER SIX

.✶.

The Age Factor

M y sister, Christina, and I grew up in different countries. Mind
you, from the moment I was born, when Christina was thirteen,
the two of us lived in the same house, ate at the same table, attended the
same schools, and hung around in the same neighborhood. We weren't
raised in different countries because of geography. In our case, the
thing that separated our nations was history. In the short space of time
between my sister's birth and my own, the social environment that defined what an American female should be changed so dramatically that as
we both look back on our childhood and adolescent experiences, the
culture I remember is quite different from the one in which my sister
grew up.

In the United States where Christina spent her childhood and adolescence, girls had only one career path: they were to be domestic caretakers. Their two social functions were set out clearly by the sociologists of
the day; one was to excite male sensibilities by looking and acting glamorous, the other was to take care of other people's needs in a matronly
manner.[1] Christina was gifted at almost everything she did, excelling in
academics and playing the flute at a professional level while still in her
teens. Later, when she had teenagers of her own, she would go back to
school, pick up two graduate degrees, and become first an English
teacher and then an attorney. But back in the 1950s and '60s, nobody
(including Christina) paid much attention to her improprietously "masculine" brain. The moment that I remember as her great adolescent success was her triumphant return from a beauty pageant, wearing a long

white satin dress and the winner's crown on her head. That crown meant that my sister didn't have to go with the matronly side of a woman's role; she could opt for glamour. In the country where Christina grew up, a woman could hardly ask for anything more.

The members of my family who grew up in Christina's country, the "prefeminist" United States, were seriously worried about me. From my infancy it was clear that I wasn't headed for the glamour role; I did not even faintly resemble Doris Day, Audrey Hepburn, or any other film star of the day (although my older siblings claimed that when they messed up my hair and got me to scowl, I did look just like Beethoven).

On the other hand, I was about as matronly as a tire iron. I learned to read early, and thereafter spent my days risking my life to reenact scenes from *Robin Hood* (I once impaled myself when I tripped while running with the point of an arrow in my mouth), *Tarzan* (I knocked myself out while swinging from the living-room drapes dressed only in training pants, which I referred to as "loincloths"), and *The Lord of the Rings* (I carried a sling and several rocks in case I was attacked by the monstrous Orcs). Every now and then a concerned relative would take me aside and warn me that I was going to have to be more feminine if I wanted to get along at all happily in their culture.

Fortunately, I never had to do this. By the time I hit adolescence, in the 1970s, I was living in a nation where feminism had cracked the narrow boundaries of female roles, and women were spilling into all sorts of formerly masculine domains. In the United States of my teenage years, it was becoming illegal to bar a girl from taking shop class or even trying out for the football team. The words "Title Nine," the name of a bill mandating gender equality in public education, floated around my junior high school like some sort of dimly understood divine decree. With those words, my girlfriends and I could put a serious dent in any policy that excluded us from doing anything boys could do. True, there were still hundreds of ways in which the citizens of my country discriminated against females, often without even realizing it, but by the time I was old enough to care, it was common practice to point out such unwitting prejudice and abolish it. Most of my teachers strongly supported the startling new idea of gender equity. The male teachers did so with a sense of apologetic fairness, the females with barely concealed jubilance. We were strong, we were invincible, we could do anything.

All of this amazed my sister Christina, who by this time had married and started a family (maintaining her glamour all the way, I might add). As I progressed through high school and on to college, Christina and

I had many conversations about how different my experience was from hers. When Christina was going through the same high school I attended, the administration did not push career counseling for girls. Nobody told her about academic competitions, scholarships, or prizes—she knew such things existed, but girls were never invited to find out about them in detail, any more than they were instructed in the proper use of jockstraps. Christina wouldn't have been accepted by Harvard, not because she wasn't qualified but because at the time she graduated from high school, Harvard did not admit women. Between my sister's adolescence and my own, our national culture had changed so much that the conditions and constraints on my life were completely different from the ones Christina had encountered only a dozen years before.

WHERE WERE YOU WHEN FEMINISM HAPPENED?

As we saw in previous chapters, the modernization of American women's roles has been going on since before the United States became a nation. However, the rate of change seems to have followed a sort of geometric curve, rising steadily but very slowly for almost two hundred years and then, in the course of a decade or two, swinging suddenly upward like a fighter jet heading for the outer limits of the atmosphere. The change in women's roles has progressed so quickly over the past few decades that it "caught" individuals almost like a single, stunning event. Most of us who were around in 1963 know where we were when John F. Kennedy was assassinated; American women (like my sister and me) tend to have similar conversations about "where we were" when women's liberation began its transformation of our society. We don't remember the spot where we were standing (the changes weren't quite *that* rapid), but we do remember *where we were in the life cycle.*

The life cycle refers to the typical pattern of life events that human beings experience as they go from infancy, to childhood, to adolescence, and so on to old age and death. Because the role of American women has changed so dramatically within less than a lifetime, women who were born at different times were at different stages in their life cycles when feminism caught up with them. One of the difficulties with theorizing about women in the United States is that it's hard to generalize about us; American women are as varied as any bunch of human beings you could rope together under one label. I have already mentioned how drastically American women of different races, classes, and ethnicities may differ from each other. In my research, another variable that dominated how women viewed themselves and their social role—no matter what their racial or ethnic origin—was *age*.

COHORTS

A cohort is a group of people that are moving through the same experience at the same point in time. For example, if you are a high school graduate, all the people who finished high school the same year you did are in your cohort of graduates. The famous Baby Boom is the cohort of Americans born from about 1946 to 1963. When a social trend occurs— say a rise in "heart-smart" eating patterns—it may be caused by an overall change in social attitudes (people of all ages are becoming more health conscious) or it could be just a cohort effect (a large cohort of people have reached the age where they worry about heart disease). Cohort effects, then, are trends that come about because a group of people are being affected by the same things at the same time.

After I had interviewed more than three hundred American women, I realized that I was seeing wave after wave of cohort effects. Depending on where a woman was in her life cycle during the dramatic changes of the late twentieth century, she is likely to have had very different life experiences, a different view of her own role as a woman, different problems, and a different way of coping with those problems. While all American women have become more and more vulnerable to the breaking point as time goes by and American society moves farther along the path of modernization, the *form* the breaking points take often depends on a woman's age.

I want to stress that the descriptions of age groups in the next few pages are *generalizations,* taken from loose, overall patterns I observed in my research. Needless to say, there are many exceptions, since every woman's experience is determined by countless factors besides her age. In addition, women may enter the same life phase (say, the childbearing years) at different ages but the same time.

For example, a forty-year-old woman having her first child will probably encounter some of the same paradoxical expectations as a new mother of twenty, while having less in common with a childless woman her own age. I was born in the 1960s, but because I married and had children a bit earlier than most of my age cohort, I tend to identify more with women born in the fifties. Some of the teenage mothers I interviewed behaved and spoke more like middle-aged women than other girls their age. But, in general, we human beings tend to follow fairly similar life courses, doing things at more or less the same time as others in our age cohort. So, while the following categories have a good deal of overlap, and women of similar ages may "see themselves" in different groups, most female readers will probably recognize some of their own experiences in one cohort or another.

COHORTS OF AMERICAN WOMEN

I. The Devalued
(Born before 1940, 57 years old and older in 1997)

II. The Betrayed
(Born between 1940 and 1949, 47 to 56 years old in 1997)

III. The Overwhelmed
(Born between 1950 and 1959, 37 to 46 years old in 1997)

IV. The Embattled
(Born between 1960 and 1969, 27 to 36 years old in 1997)

V. The Unsuspecting
(Born 1970 or later, 27 years old or younger in 1997)

I. THE DEVALUED

(Born before 1940, 57 years old and older in 1997)

In traditional cultures, grandmothers are a priceless resource. I first saw this for myself as a junior in college, when I went to Asia to "collect" folktales from elderly Chinese women for a thesis on female roles in traditional China. I am reminded of it again when I go to the Native American craft fairs that pass through my hometown of Phoenix every so often. I'm the worst kind of customer: I show up with very little money but lots and lots of questions. I'm always asking the long-suffering artisans things like "What does that design mean?" or "Where does that clay come from?" or "How do you use that pot?" The answers given by the unfailingly polite Native American craftmasters are often footnoted with the word "grandmother." "Well, my grandmother told me . . ." "My grandmother showed me where to find it . . ." "I don't know about that, I'll have to ask my grandmother . . ."

At first this surprised me. I'm not used to hearing grandmothers quoted as authorities, especially by highly skilled adults, both male and female. After all, I come from a modern society, and in modern societies grandmothers are respected mainly to the degree that they act like something else. One of the most profound effects of adopting the modern worldview of the European Enlightenment is an overall societal devaluation of older women.

MODERNIZATION AND THE DEVALUATION OF THE WISEWOMAN

There are very good reasons why elderly women are precious in traditional cultures. In most of those cultures, men do heavy labor associated with protecting the group and getting food and shelter, while women are responsible for turning raw materials into meals that can be eaten, clothes that can be worn, and dwellings that can be lived in. Women are the interface between people's physical and emotional needs and the cold, cruel world. Because humans are subtle and infinitely complex beings, taking care of their needs involves as much art as science, and the skill to do it well comes only with years of attentive practice.

The grandmothers, the Wisewomen, are the people who have had that practice. Older women are repositories of enormous stores of practical wisdom; the doctors, teachers, research scientists, business managers, restaurateurs, psychologists, fashion designers, and historians of traditional cultures. Even though these societies may be extremely male-dominated, there is no question that the grandmothers are crucial to the survival of the group.

Because women are considered responsible for taking care of society's traditional elements, we are much more likely than men to run up against the need for "grandmother wisdom." For example, the day after my first child was born, my mother flew to Boston to ease my transition into parenthood. I had read an enormous amount of literature about babies, including the most up-to-date medical journals. I knew that breast milk was the healthiest food for a baby—I had read all about colostrum and antibodies and so on—and I was determined to nurse.

At two o'clock in the morning, when my daughter started crying, my book-learning didn't do me much good. The baby kicked and screamed for half an hour as I tried awkwardly to feed her (I was still rather shocked by the concept of milk emerging from my own body, which to me seemed about as normal as pulling beef Wellington out of my knees). I was locked in a futile struggle with my shrieking daughter when my mother came sleepily into the room and with few words, in about five minutes, showed me what a book couldn't have described in a thousand pages: how a nursing mother cups her body around a newborn so that the two can meld into a balanced, comfortable symbiosis. Under my mother's guidance, the baby immediately relaxed, my milk began to flow, and one small life became more secure in the world.

I heard many similar stories from younger women who had at some point realized how valuable and irreplaceable "grandmother wisdom" is to any society. But as American culture continues along the course of modernization, this wisdom is receiving less and less credit. In a modern society, we value people who have learned their skills "by the book," the way Enlightenment scholars did. A thirty-five-year-old doctor fresh out of medical school can earn more money and respect than all but a very few other members of our culture; a sixty-year-old nurse who has spent thousands of hours learning the art of healing is likely to get much less respect and barely enough money to support herself. A grandmother who has done the same thing with no formal training at all will be near the lowest rungs of social prestige and earn nothing for her skill.

In fact, the closer our culture comes to realizing the perfect modern ideal, the less value is placed on the Wisewoman, the time-tempered artist who knows in her bones how to soothe a sick child or make a friend or comfort a broken heart. The women's movement of the 1960s was based on the idea that all women should be able to achieve as rational individuals, in that narrow frame of reference favored by Enlightenment scholars. The practice of caring, and the wisdom that comes from it, have become less and less respectable as women have fought innumerable battles to achieve rational status—and won many of them. This means that an American woman who was born before the 1940s will approach old age in a social environment completely different from that of her own grandmothers.

STRANGERS IN A STRANGE LAND

If my older sister and I feel as if we grew up in different countries, women who were raised in the United States of the teens, twenties, and thirties often feel as though they are now living on a different planet—and it is not a kind one to women of their age. They grew up in a culture where traditional thinking still defined the role of women, and few of them pursued the individualistic skills and advantages needed to thrive in a modern environment. The gains women reaped from the women's movement occurred when these Wisewomen were already middle-aged and deeply committed to raising families, and so these benefits were largely inaccessible to them. Most of the older women I interviewed said that by the time it was possible for a woman to achieve in modern ways, they didn't have the freedom, the health, or the ambition to go back to school or enter a new profession.

To women in this age group, it often seems that the world has gone crazy, that nothing is turning out the way they expected it to. Genevieve, a sixty-five-year-old widow with twenty grandchildren, told me:

Genevieve, 65

When I was young, I never even thought about doing anything but taking care of my family. I never wanted anything else. I loved raising my children and keeping a house nice. I loved being a wife. But in the old days, you could expect things to work the way they're supposed to.

You took care of your family, and when you were older, they took care of you. Nowadays nobody takes care of anybody, it's just everybody for themselves. It's terrible!

Modern life is especially "terrible" for women who have been left alone through divorce or widowhood. Many older women told me that once they had lost the protection and support they had gained from husbands (in classic traditional style), they found that their culture had changed in such a way that no one had much motivation to think about them. Even if they have good health, older women are often the very last candidates to be hired for jobs in the modern work world, and traditional ways of caring for the aging are becoming more difficult to sustain. All of these changes have left many older women in a no-win situation.

Because of this, the women I interviewed who were born before 1940 were almost universally frightened. For those who were reasonably well-off financially, and who had strong family ties, this fear took the form of a nagging uneasiness about the future. For others, it was the bewildered panic of someone who has just taken a confident step forward, only to have the ground disappear from under her feet. Women in this cohort had followed the rules of traditional society, in which care for the group is rewarded by care *from* the group, only to have the rules change just as they spent their last drams of energy on other people and began to require care themselves. In the words of Myra, a seventy-three-year-old homemaker:

Myra, 73

When did things change? I never really noticed until it was too late. If I had known, when I was younger, what the world was going to be like, I would have lived my life a completely different way. I would have saved more money for myself, spent more time on myself. I would have been more selfish. But I wasn't, and now I spend every night lying awake scared that my money will run out before I die, and I'll end up a bag lady on the street.

The bitterness of the situation is that most women born before the 1940s grew up restricted from activities that could have earned them money and social status—and, in practical terms, they are now being punished for not doing the very things they were forbidden to do. This double bind often leads to the breaking point for women whose health is failing, whose sources of financial and emotional support are disappearing, or who are simply too tired to start all over again. Others manage to keep going, but live in what one octogenarian called "the constant struggle to remain significant."

The themes of fear, scarcity, and loneliness in older women's stories were accompanied by the understanding that "I know young people are so busy these days." The people who traditionally care for older women are their children, especially (in our culture) adult daughters. The older women I interviewed often mentioned how tired and overworked their daughters were, and how bad they felt about needing attention from younger women who were already exhausted.

Mary Alice, 82

Things were different when I was a girl. Life was slower . . . there was a lot to do, but we didn't try to do so many *different* things at once. My daughter works all day at the office, then she comes home and there's dinner and the kids and the housecleaning . . . I don't know how she does it. I know how hard it is for her to find time to take care of an old lady. Nobody has time.

THE GOOD NEWS

Despite all the negatives, there was a bright side to the stories of women born before the 1940s. On one hand, some of these women were still able to rely on traditional attitudes and structures that encourage families to care for their aging caregivers. The paradox in women's roles had accelerated so rapidly that these women had managed to sail through the majority of their lives without confronting a breaking point, while their daughters and granddaughters ran headlong into problems that hadn't existed before.

On the other hand, a few women of exceptional energy had enthusiastically taken advantage of women's liberation to move into whole new lives during middle age. As one sixty-year-old told me, "I've been able to live twice; once as a woman raising a family, once as a 'man' starting a career. This is a great time to be alive." Most older women who had "lived twice" in this fashion had experienced a life accident, such as widowhood, while still in early middle age. They had passed through the breaking point and emerged ready to take advantage of the society they lived in. (But I'm getting ahead of myself. You can read more about these women in the following chapters.)

The other positive feature of older women's lives was a strong self-concept and confidence in their early choices, which I did not see in younger women. Because they had been raised in a culture where women's roles did not compete with rational pursuits, older women didn't see any shame in not having a college degree, an impressive résumé, or a job. Early in their lives, they had been well-supported in a traditional "female" role, and later they were still proud of their life decisions. They knew that society had devalued them, but they did not devalue themselves.

Harriet, 80

I remember watching my grandmother making pickles in the kitchen, telling me how to cut the cucumbers. Well, I just thought Grandma knew everything there was to know. She could teach me everything I needed to live a happy life. I thought about how someday I would teach my own granddaughter, and I had this sense of the balance of things, the way women pass on the spine of living, the core of things that keeps us all going. Now I look at my granddaughter, and she's doing chemical research at [a university]. I don't know anything about her life. I can't teach her what she wants to learn. That makes me so sad. It makes me wonder how she sees me, what she thinks I'm worth.

Although the older women I interviewed sometimes wondered what their social worth had become, most of them directed their frustration at the world around them, instead of berating themselves for not having learned to live in a modern way. They knew that their devaluation was a facet of cultural change, and they stubbornly refused to deny the value of the role Wisewomen must play in any society. After all, they had lived long enough to know that human life still relies on the subtle connections and skills we can learn only by caring for each other.

As long as human beings are flesh and blood, society will have things to learn from the grandmothers. But as the modernization of our culture has progressed, creating upheavals in the way we define human worth, as well as women's roles, the *recognized* and *rewarded* social value of the Wisewoman has been reduced almost to nothing.

II. THE BETRAYED

(Born between 1940 and 1949, 47 to 56 years old in 1997)

If women born before the 1940s reminded me of the grandmothers of traditional societies, women born in the forties reminded me of shell-shocked soldiers returning from an unpopular war. In our culture, the group that would fit this description best would be Vietnam veterans.

Why would I make such a comparison? Because both these soldiers and this particular group of women made enormous sacrifices to preserve their culture's values, only to find that while they were giving their all, their society switched course so suddenly and drastically that they were castigated and accused for the very sacrifices they had made out of hero-ism. The soldiers who went to Vietnam, enduring danger and misery for their nation, often came home to find themselves taunted as immoral warmongers. The pain of both their war experience and the rejection they faced at home is still devastating. In a less dramatic but still very de-structive way, the cohort of American women born in the 1940s are suf-fering the same kind of double-edged punishment.

This cohort came of age in the 1950s and early 1960s, in a United States where the ideal of True Womanhood was perhaps more extreme than at any time before or since. This was the time when the country had the prosperity, the mass media, and the war-weary need to create a fan-tasy female who combined glamorous sexuality with all-nurturing mater-nity. The United States of this time produced books like Helen Andelin's *Fascinating Womanhood* and TV role models like June Cleaver. It was a country where a woman with a strong personality, career aspirations, or an analytical mind was seen as a freakish, pathological aberration from the feminine ideal.

SACRIFICE WITHOUT HONOR

The vast majority of American women who were born in the 1940s made every effort to conform to the social expectations placed on women in the postwar era. They focused on keeping themselves "glamorous" enough to catch a man, and after they had done so they set out to realize an almost unattainable image of perfect wife-and-motherhood. In the attempt, many put their talents on a back burner, let go of passionate dreams, left educational or professional environments that thrilled them to focus on domestic chores that bored them. In a society that was already very "modernized," these women knew the value of the things they gave up—but keeping them didn't seem to be a choice. They simply couldn't hope for the kind of fulfillment, prestige, or freedom some men found in the world outside their homes. They were women. It was that simple.

Except, of course, that it wasn't. Just as most women born in the 1940s were settling into their traditional marriages, a small (but rapidly growing) minority were beginning to protest the limitations of their gender role. These women moved into the workforce, joined consciousness-raising groups, lobbied to change discriminatory laws. They were mad as hell, and they weren't going to take it anymore. Their anger was directed not only at men but also at women who accepted the traditional roles of glamour girl and career homemaker. The rejection of traditional female limitations was often accompanied by disdain for women who did not move into rational pursuits. Instead of being rewarded and esteemed for the sacrifices they had made to support their society's needs, women who had chosen a traditional female role were seen as weaklings, or worse, as traitors. They were attacked for helping to uphold archaic, chauvinistic ideals.

This bewildering switch, from the valuative position that celebrated the traditional woman to the one that honored only the modern, trapped women born in the forties in a massive double bind. Very few were able to avoid being wounded in the transition from "fascinating womanhood" to "liberated womanhood." The attacks on their lifestyles, their characters, their choices, seemed to come from every direction. Here are some typical selections from my interviews with women born in the 1940s:

Janice, 49

I quit college to marry my husband. It was what you did in those days. I had loved college, and he hated it. He used to complain about how much he hated school, and I'd think how I would give anything to have his problems. Then when the kids were teenagers, he started telling me that I wasn't interesting enough. He criticized me for not finishing college. He seems to have forgotten that *I gave it up for him*—and now he's the one beating up on me about it.

Barbra, 51

The other day, my daughter said to me that she couldn't look to me as an example because I'd never done anything with my life. I said, "Well, I raised you, didn't I?" She said, "Yeah, but you never did anything *real*." I had nothing to say to her, I just stared at her and felt like crying. I look back now and I wonder why I didn't do anything "real." It seems like back when I was her age, I didn't have a choice.

Shelley, 50

I've never been married, but even working flat-out it took me so much longer to climb the ladder than if I'd been a man. And the men could have families, children, a wife, while they were getting promoted. I gave that up for my career, and sometimes it really kills me. . . . Now I see younger women getting promoted to positions over me. They've got M.B.A.s, they have experience that I just wasn't allowed to get. I'm glad for younger women, but it still makes me angry that I had to give up so much, and I got so much less for it.

ANGER AND LOW SELF-ESTEEM

A powerful undercurrent of anger flowed through many of my interviews with women in this age cohort. They felt double-crossed, and rightly so. Just about every woman in this age group knew someone like Bernice Llewelyn, the woman in Chapter 3 whose husband left her after almost twenty years to start a relationship with a "liberated" younger woman. By going to great lengths to be "the right kind of woman" for a man in the fifties and early sixties, women in this cohort had become exactly "the wrong kind of woman" for a man in the seventies, eighties, and nineties. Many told me, with thinly veiled bitterness, that their husbands, friends, and children criticized them for being less well educated, "interesting," or "successful" than other women.

Olive, 48

My husband is well known on our local political scene. When I was younger and wanted to work, he wouldn't let me. He said it would ruin his image with the voters. Now I've got four teenagers to raise.

I'm tired out. And yet now he's telling me I have to get a job because the most successful men have successful wives. He used to want me to be Maria Von Trapp, and now all of a sudden he wants me to be Elizabeth Dole.

Women born in the 1940s see the contradictions in this kind of doublethink, but many have trouble separating their own self-concept from the judgments placed on them by their society. Part of them *believes* that they should somehow have "done more with their lives," even though they know they were doing their best all the time. Because of this, the intense anger they may feel at the way society has judged them is often directed partly at themselves.

LOW SELF-ESTEEM FACTOR 1:
WHAT WOULD MARILYN LOOK LIKE TODAY?

Women in this age cohort had the lowest self-esteem of any group I interviewed. To begin with, they tended to express a great deal of anxiety about their bodies. Remember the "glamour versus matron" division of women's roles in the 1950s? Well, the glamour ideal demanded that women possess a combination of sexuality and childishness that is best (if not only) achieved by the very young. Marilyn Monroe, with her little-girl voice, bedroom eyes—and early death—was the quintessential example of the glamour girl. (Meanwhile, male attractiveness, which focused more on power and success, could range from the "lean young athlete" look to the "distinguished graying executive," giving men a much longer time frame in which to be judged physically appealing.) By the time I started my research, in the late eighties, many women born during the forties were already beginning to panic about losing their looks.

This was especially pronounced in women who had considered themselves beautiful in their twenties and thirties. Women whose looks had never matched society's idea of the "perfect" female had suffered a great deal because of it, but also seemed to have found other foundations for their self-concept. But women who had become accustomed to thinking of their looks as their most important feminine virtue—and a powerful social advantage—were terrified of aging. They talked about liposuction, diets, plastic surgery, and health spas with a kind of desperate determination, but for many of these women the reality of physical aging took on the dimensions of a tragic destiny. It was not that they were afraid of dying—no, they were afraid of *living* without one of the most important things that had made them feel acceptable and valuable when they were younger: the ability to match certain narrow physical criteria designated as the feminine ideal. As this became harder for them, their self-esteem suffered tremendously.

LOW SELF-ESTEEM FACTOR 2:
HOW COME *I'M* NOT ON THE SUPREME COURT?

The fear that they weren't measuring up to the traditional female ideal was matched, in this age cohort, by the fear that they weren't living up to the image of the perfect modern career woman. Women born in the 1940s had a pronounced habit of comparing their own accomplishments to the feats of two other groups: a few exceptional women their age, who pioneered female participation in the "masculine" career world, and a slew of younger women who had arrived on the American scene when some barriers to female achievement were already dissolving. By contrasting their own track records to these other women, the majority of women born in the forties managed to cast themselves in the most negative possible light.

Heidi, 46

I see women younger than me becoming doctors, lawyers, orchestra conductors, all kinds of things that look so exciting, and I feel like my whole life is a waste. I'm too old to start any of those things now, but I'm young enough that I'll be hanging around for fifty years watching other people get the spotlight. Why didn't I start to become something when I had the chance?

What many women in this cohort didn't seem to realize was that if they had "started to become something" as adolescents and young adults, back in the 1950s and '60s, they would have faced almost insuperable obstacles—which would have made it difficult or impossible to obtain the things they actually *did* end up choosing. Women born during the forties who went into fast-track careers had just as many regrets as their homemaker sisters.

Gladys, 56

I know a lot of people think I've got it all together because I've been successful in my job. But I would have given it up in a heartbeat if I could have had children. Women who were having babies when I was

in graduate school say they envy me, and I just shake my head. They
have no idea what I *didn't* get. They take all that for granted.

The habit of comparing themselves to other women increased the
anger forties babies felt at being betrayed by their society's changing
feminine ideals. Some of the anger was directed at women who had
made choices different from theirs, but, again, women in this age group
saved their most vitriolic rage for themselves.

Val, 49

There's not a day that I don't kick myself for everything I didn't do. I
don't know how I got so stuck, but here I am. I know now my kids are
out of the house I should be making something of my life, but it feels
like I'm already so many years behind.

THE DEPENDENCY TRAP

Many women in this age cohort were frustrated by the fact that their
husbands participated in the double bind their society placed on them.
The majority were reasonably happy with their marriages, but some felt
judged by their husbands for not maintaining the ideal of youthful feminine beauty, raising perfect children, *and* bringing in money and prestige
through a high-profile career. The shift in social attitudes seems to have
made it more likely for men in this age range to pass judgment on
women. One theme I heard over and over from this cohort was frustration at being financially dependent on men who, following broad trends
in social attitudes, discounted their wives' life choices and personal
worth.

Lois, 50

My husband always seems very restrained, but he criticizes me so much
that it just cuts me in pieces. We'll be at a party where there are other
women who work in his firm, or other wives who have their own jobs,
and he'll say, "Well, my Lois never did anything, she just went bare-
foot and pregnant for a few years, and now she's retired. That's all
she was good for." Ha, ha. Very funny. I hate it! . . . But he pays for
my life, so I can't talk back. There have been a lot of nights that
I've stayed up trying to figure out how I could support myself and
the kids, but I can't think of a way. I have no degrees, no skills. I
always end up realizing that [my husband] is right about me. I'm not
good for anything.

A woman of Baby Boomer age recounted a little ditty her mother-in-law had taught her after the birth of her first child. It goes like this: "Clap hands, clap hands/'Cause Daddy is home/'Cause Daddy has money/And Mommy has none." To the younger woman, this was an appalling example of the explicit devaluing of women's lives and contribution; to the older woman, it was simply a cute description of reality, something to pass on to her grandson. Not all women in this age group are so blithe about the financial "worthlessness" imposed on them by their place in society and history. Many told me something like this:

Corinne, 48

I've got no voice in my marriage, because the bottom line is, he brings in the money. It's like I owe him thousands and thousands of dollars, and he's not getting his money's worth. I can never do enough, and I can't leave, because I have no way to support myself. He *owns* me.

STARTING OVER

Because women in this age cohort had rarely received extensive career training in young adulthood, they often lacked confidence in their ability to excel in nondomestic areas. This was especially difficult for women whose children were grown. The "empty nest" syndrome was accompanied by a sort of desperation as women felt their self-image of usefulness walking out the door with their grown children.

At this point, about half the women I interviewed who were born in the forties took their courage in both hands and went back to school, or picked up a job interest they had pursued earlier in their lives. Happily, the fear and shame many of these women felt at being "the oldest new kid in the class" usually dissipated when they found themselves enjoying their new activities—and doing very well at them. Although many said they had a harder time with memorization than when they were younger, they more than compensated for this with a very clear grasp of the logic and meaning behind the subjects they studied.

Abby, 49

I had my first accounting exam last week, and it was a breeze! I mean, I managed my household budget for twenty-eight years, I know the *reasons* for everything. I got the best score in the class!

Diana, 50

I'm by far the best in my office at organizing the files and information. The other office managers seem to get all confused. But you don't raise five kids without figuring out how to be organized.

The excitement these women felt was tempered by a sense of loss as they looked back on the years they had lived more restricted lives. A "junior" journalist told me:

Verna, 50

The thing that kills me is that I should have been doing this all along. I was born for this stuff. I'm loving it, but I should be so far ahead of where I am. I wasted all those years. Now I'm afraid that just as I begin to find out who I really am and what I can do, I'll be too old to really experience it.

A woman who had been a statistician for a life insurance company before marrying at thirty and raising four children put it this way:

Sylvia, 53

I thought I was just taking a little time off, I thought I'd be the same person when my kids were grown. Now I'm finding out I was wrong. I'm too old. It's too late. If you don't "make it" by the time you're in your forties, it's just too late.

Although not all women in this age cohort agreed that it was "too late" for them to start new lives or careers after their children were raised (and not all of them wanted to), most felt the frustration of being judged by a society which had reversed its ideals and blamed them for not measuring up to two contradictory sets of criteria. Those who did not want to move out of a traditional role felt that their contribution to society was belittled, that their sacrifices had earned them scorn rather than appreciation. Those who were moving into modern roles felt the disadvantage of their age in competing with men and with younger women, whose paths to individual achievement had never been interrupted. No matter what their choices had been, women born in the 1940s often felt defensive, regretful, and, above all, betrayed.

BORN TO BE A BRIDGE

This cohort of American women is a complex group, full of anger and pride, hope and despair, determination and discouragement. They are personifications of the contradictory pressures their culture imposed on them as it swung from the model of the perfect maternal sex goddess to the high-achieving professional woman. Jeanette, a mother of three who is just returning to her career as a stockbroker after twenty-five years as a homemaker, summed up her cohort's mixed bag of feelings and experiences articulately.

Jeanette, 50

My generation is the bridge that connects an ancient view of women with a completely different vision. We have our feet planted in the old-fashioned way of being female, and we're hanging on with our fingernails to this new way of looking at our lives, but most of our self-concept is out there twisting in the wind, hanging over this huge abyss. Aaaaagh! It's terrifying and difficult and painful, but we were the ones born to it.

I think women my age are glad that we created a path for other women to follow, but you know, it isn't easy being a bridge. You're always unsure of yourself and scared to death, and angry that you're the one who happened to end up connecting that gap, instead of being born on the other side of it.

III. THE OVERWHELMED

(Born between 1950 and 1959, 37 to 46 years old in 1997)

To begin with, the cohort of American women born in the 1950s is huge. The Baby Boom years extend from 1946 to 1963, meaning that most of the Boomers were children of the fifties. Between 1950 and 1959, over twenty million baby girls were born in the United States, about a million more than would be born in the 1960s (the next most fertile decade for Americans), and a whopping four and a half million more than had come on the scene in the 1940s.[2] Because of this, journalists, casual commentators, and, yes, even social scientists often make the mistake of thinking that the experiences and attitudes of this cohort represent *all* American women. I've been guilty of this myself, in this very book, simply because the Baby Boom generation is so large that, statistically, it can make Boomer characteristics look like the most common American life pattern. In fact, this is a classic example of the cohort effect: even though there are a lot of people in this age group, the Boomers' experience of being female in the United States is unique.

A GENERATION OF FEMINISTS

Women in this cohort were raised knowing the phrase "women's liberation" as something more than an obscure activist movement on the fringes of society. They were teenagers and young adults—a very idealistic age—when the feminist movement was transforming American society. Remember, this "first wave" of feminism tried to reconcile the paradoxical expectations placed on American women by proudly claiming that anybody worth her salt should be able to accomplish all the "trivial" traditional tasks women had always done, as well as successfully competing with men in modern professional settings. At about the same time, modernization was moving the U.S. economy away from heavy industry into service and information technologies, which require less physical strength. Scientists had finally developed a birth-control pill that gave women a reliable way to avoid unwanted pregnancy. Combine these events with a mandatory educational system that schooled girls as well as boys to value modern achievement, and the United States ended up seeing the most successful push toward the modernization of women's roles in history.

Because American attitudes about female roles were changing so rapidly, the cohort of women born in the 1950s planned their lives very differently from their mothers, or even their older sisters. They stayed in school longer, started not only jobs but genuine careers, and waited longer to marry and bear children. Many met intense opposition in the male-dominated professional worlds they entered. They also received criticism or cautionary advice from older women, who warned them against "unfeminine" behavior. Typically, they greeted this advice with disdain and irritation, feeling that benighted women, as well as men, were trying to lock them into an unwanted, subordinate traditional role. Joanne, a never-married clinical psychologist, told me:

Joanne, 40

My mother thinks that all my problems come from acting too "masculine"—too smart, too direct, too assertive. In her way of thinking, a woman hides her intelligence and uses it on the sly, to manipulate or control people without ever actually looking powerful. She tells me if I'd just act that way, I'd be married now. The idea that I don't *want* to be married is absolutely incomprehensible to her. After all, what else would a woman do with her life?

LIVING IN THE NEW WORLD

Like the counsel Joanne received from her mother, much of the advice fifties babies got from older women was based on social norms that had already vanished. Even when members of the fifties cohort tried to follow the example of their elders, the strategy often didn't work.

This often contributed to strained relationships between women born in the fifties and those born a generation earlier. As you might expect, this conflict was often played out between mothers and daughters. Peg, a freelance writer, told me:

Peg, 38

My roommates and I used to sit around in college and talk about what complete idiots our mothers were. They were always telling us to find nice guys, get married, settle down and have babies. It was like, Hello,

Mom? Knock knock, anybody home? Have you checked out the world lately, or have you just been in bed letting your curlers set?

Though the sarcastic tone of this comment reflects the modern disparagement of women who stay in traditional roles, the basic frustration Peg felt about her mother's advice was grounded in social reality. Few women born in the 1950s could confidently plan to spend their lives raising children while being fully supported by husbands. For this cohort, life had become much more open, and much less predictable. The changes that occurred as the fifties babies were reaching maturity created pressures that, in one sociologist's words, both "pushed" women out of traditional roles through need, and "pulled" them out through increased opportunity.[3]

OPPORTUNITY KNOCKS

As they emerged from the educational system in the 1970s and '80s, the young-adult women born during the 1950s faced a social landscape that had never existed before. The egalitarianism of American values was at long last being applied to them, as well as to their male classmates. The June Cleaver media ideal had been replaced by Mary Tyler Moore, the attractive single woman with the terrific career. Women were applying for positions as truck drivers, contractors, business managers, police officers, university professors, airplane pilots, and every other job under the sun. Sometimes they actually got them.

The growing niche for women in modern society promised all the benefits men had been receiving for years: money, freedom, power, status, excitement, self-respect. For many women in the fifties cohort, the pull of such opportunities was much stronger than the temptation to become a low-status, economically dependent, traditional homemaker.

Shirley, 39

After we graduated from high school my boyfriend wanted to get married, but it really freaked me out to think about being—you know—a *wife*. I went to live in Aspen for a while, to be a ski bum, basically. I had a little money I'd made waitressing, and I figured I could get another job at a restaurant in Aspen. I'd been there about two weeks when this guy (he's now my boss) saw me ski and offered me a job as a ski instructor. I thought, All right! It's about time someone thought about my performance, instead of just the fact that I was female. I told my boyfriend I wasn't ready to marry him yet. I felt like I wanted to live first.

Marjorie, 36

I applied for a job as a consultant at [a major firm] right out of college. I didn't really think they'd even look at a woman, but I thought it was worth applying. I was shocked when they offered me the job. I hadn't even told anyone about it. My fiancé threw a fit because I'd be making more money than he would. It was the first time I'd realized how he really felt about women. We broke up. I took the job. That was fifteen years ago. Now I'm up for a partnership.

Despite the expanding horizons for females in the American job market, women born in the fifties still faced a daunting array of discriminatory practices and attitudes. Compared to men, they were paid lower wages for the same work, evaluated more harshly, promoted less often, and generally given less support in their careers. But the attitude of the Baby Boom cohort was that women should scale the walls of traditional chauvinism and take the city by storm, rather than retreat in defeat.

This meant that as they emerged from the educational system, many women this age plunged directly into careers that were difficult to begin with, and were made more difficult because of sex discrimination. Often these jobs took every bit of energy, intelligence, courage, and endurance a woman could muster. Some studies showed that women are generally *more* productive at their jobs than men (they work more hours, and they produce more per hour). However, their work is judged, *not only by men but by the women themselves*, as being worth less money.[4]

Nina, 40

When I came out of law school in 1980, I had a lot of doors slammed in my face. Most firms didn't even want to interview a woman—although, of course, by then they knew better than to say so openly. When I did get a job, I had to work about fifty hours a day because they discredited everything I did. The first five years were hell. Come to think of it, the next five years weren't all that great, either.

Joy, 46

When I came in [to my job] as an assistant professor, they put me through a hazing process you wouldn't believe. It's hard to point to any one thing that made the job so difficult—it was a million tiny things, a million times my opinions were ignored, or I was given the least desirable teaching assignment, or my publication record was discounted, or my pay raises didn't keep up with the men's. I'd say it is still five or six times harder for a woman to get tenure at [the university where I work] than it is for a man. And let me tell you, that's a huge improvement over what it was when I started!

KEEPING THE WOLF FROM THE DOOR

While women with extensive training struggled against sexism in their chosen careers, other women born in the fifties were encountering circumstances that were sometimes literally life-threatening. Along with the pull of opportunity came the push of financial need, as the transformation in women's roles interacted with other changes throughout American social structures. In the "new world" of the late 1970s to the mid-1980s, the flood of women entering the job market made the dual-career couple commonplace. Because so many families were now bringing in two incomes, the value of the typical wage gradually declined relative to the cost of living. More and more, salaries were designed to fill *some* of a family's needs, not the full amount. It became increasingly difficult for a family to survive on a typical single income. The Baby Boomers became the first generation in American history to be less well off, in terms of real income, than their parents.

This put a tremendous strain on men—especially young men who weren't yet at higher-paying levels in their own careers—who were trying to support families without help from working wives.

Another social change that increased the economic pressure on this cohort was the abrupt rise in the divorce rate that began in the 1960s. The belief that women should be able to free themselves from unhappy relationships was inextricably linked to the acceptance of women in the workplace: an unhappy marriage was unlikely to last when the husband was no longer the wife's only source of income. As American laws changed to make divorce easier and the economy changed to provide jobs for more women, the United States saw a tremendous upsurge in divorce. The number of American divorces in 1988 was triple that of 1950. Divorce peaked at almost two-thirds of marriages in the late sixties, then settled at about 50 percent, where it has remained, with slight variations, ever since. By the beginning of the 1990s,[5] almost half of all marriages in the United States could be expected to end in divorce.

Demographers now estimate that of all married American women aged twenty to fifty-four, almost 40 percent will go through a divorce at some time in their lives.[6]

The combination of shrinking real wages, systematic discrimination against women in the workforce, and the traditional view that children should stay with their mothers was a disastrous mixture for many women born in the 1950s. The statistics cited in Chapter 2 about the feminization of poverty are easy to see in this cohort. Poverty is especially likely to follow divorce for mothers with young children—a profile that fits many American women in this age group. I heard stories from divorcées that seemed to come straight out of a Dickens novel: women who lived in one-room apartments without furniture, heat, or electricity; women who had been homeless with small children; women who went days without eating in order to leave the food for their children; women who worked two or three menial jobs to pay for food and rent while their children grew up with virtually no supervision.

Zoe, 42

You know, I can't handle much more of this. I got two jobs and two babies [one-year-old twins]. Two of everything. There's never enough money, you know? Never enough money, never enough money, never enough money. It's all I can think about every day. It's made me a rotten mama for my babies. I hardly see them, and when I do I'm too tired to even smile at them. I get sick all the time, and I can't afford a doctor.

TAKING ON THE DOUBLE BURDEN

While American mothers born in the fifties got less help raising children than any group before them, the standards of "good motherhood" were becoming higher and higher. The Baby Boomers had stellar ideals where child-rearing (and almost everything else) were concerned. Mothers in this cohort felt pressure to be constantly attentive but never short-tempered with their children, to discipline them very gently, and to "enrich" their environments with everything from classical music to daily reading-time to organically grown vegetables.

Gabrielle, 44

My mom just couldn't believe all the things people do for their kids these days. When she was raising us, we were just outside playing all day. I could be arrested for letting my kids wander around unsupervised! I spend hours and hours going around evaluating preschools and trying to get my children a chance at being enrolled. You have to qualify for good schools, you know. I can't just send my kids off to the local elementary school. You have to start planning their futures from the time they're born.

For single mothers who must also put bread on the table, this high standard of motherhood is truly overwhelming.

While single mothers of young children reported the most stressful lives of *any* group I interviewed, married women born in the 1950s weren't exactly floating along, either. The paradoxical value system of the United States is at its most destructive when the pressure to perform both modern and traditional labor is greatest. On the modern side of the equation, this typically occurs in a young adult's early career, when the time, energy, and money necessary to obtain credentials and experience must be subtracted from the time, energy, and opportunity to earn a living. On the traditional side, demands are greatest for a person who is responsible for supporting others who are too young, too old, or too sick to take care of themselves. Does this scenario ring any bells in your mind? If you were born in the 1950s, chances are it does. You may well be one of the millions of American women who, for the first time in history, tried to combine a full-fledged modern career with a full house of traditional responsibilities.

At the same time that Baby Boomer women shouldered this double burden, many began to hear the ticking of the infamous biological clock. Despite the protests of feminists who object to the implications of the biological clock concept, medical data consistently confirm that fertility declines, and the incidence of certain birth defects rises, as a woman ages. Many studies show rather sharp increases in both types of problems after the age of thirty-five.[7] As career women born in the 1950s began to approach this "magic age," many decided that it was time to start bearing the children they had always planned to have. On the other hand, as we've already seen, women who had married and had children rather than working were under increasing economic pressure to bring in money for their families—whether or not those families included employed husbands.

MAXIMUM PARADOX

The result of all these forces was that between the mid-1980s and the early 1990s an enormous cohort of young women undertook the task of fulfilling both modern and traditional roles *at their most difficult levels.*

The women's movement had popularized the idea that this should not be difficult, as well as the notion that men should share household and parenting chores. This seems to have led mainly to a rise in the amount of domestic work husbands *thought* they did, rather than the amount they actually performed. In most two-parent households where both spouses were employed, women still did a far greater share of the domestic work than men. As Annabelle, a salesclerk, put it:

Annabelle, 37

My husband changes one diaper a week, takes out the trash twice, and thinks he's doing 50 percent of the housework. He doesn't even know that things like toilets need to be cleaned. Plus, even though we have almost the same job, he gets paid more than I do, so I would have to work a lot more hours than him to earn the same. So he can still talk like he's the big breadwinner and it's still my job to take care of the house and kids.

American women of the 1950s birth cohort moved into adulthood bearing the double burden of domestic and professional work, with scarce help from men and even scarcer examples of women who had gone their way before. There were virtually no role models for how a woman might combine raising young children with participation in a workforce designed *by* men with wives, *for* men with wives. In a way, the media-created females on TV soap operas and situation comedies could be seen as role models; they seemed to juggle career and family with ease. For example, in the eighties, the immensely popular *Cosby Show* followed a father who was a physician, a mother who was a lawyer, five children who always found their parents ready to talk through their problems with them, and a house that was invariably spotless despite the fact that no one was ever observed actually cleaning it. This type of media image showed women what they "should" be. However, it did not tell them how to be it.

THE YOUNG AND THE SLEEPLESS

In 1995 a thirty-something editor with two small children wrote that "sleep has become the sex of the '90s. Sleep is replacing sex as that obscure object of desire that inhabits our daydreams—if we still have time for daydreams."[8] Over the course of my research, I interviewed several dozen working moms born in the 1950s. When I asked them about their lives, the majority told me stories that revolved around one thing: sleep deprivation. This is a simple enough phenomenon, but over a long period of time it can be enormously destructive to physical and mental health—not to mention intimate relationships, child-rearing skills, and everyday human activities. Here's a typical comment from a working mother born in the 1950s.

Molly, 38

I've forgotten what it's like not to be tired. I thought I had chronic fatigue syndrome, so I went to the doctor for a checkup. The doctor asked me about my lifestyle, so I told her that I work nine to six, commute two more hours, and try to keep the house clean, cook good dinners, help my kids with their schoolwork, and spend time with my husband in the evenings. After all that, I'm sometimes literally too tired to sleep. The doctor said, "Trust me, you haven't got any medical chronic fatigue syndrome. Your *life* is a chronic fatigue syndrome." She said she knew all about it, because she had a six-month-old baby herself. She looked exhausted!

The working women who reached their childbearing years in the exuberantly optimistic seventies and eighties, when women were supposed to be able to "have it all," were unprepared for the immensity and the internal contradictions of the task they had set out to accomplish. As one woman put it, "The truth is, you can't have it all. Not quite. You can have everything except sleep."

OPERATING ON OVERWHELM

In summary, the majority of American women born in the 1950s have been overwhelmed, at least since they reached adulthood, by the expectations our society (including the women themselves) places on them. Those who entered the male-dominated American workforce, boldly going where no woman had gone before, had to work in the context of stereotyping, underpayment, overwork, harassment, and ostracism by various "old boy" networks. Many women who were already struggling with this formidable task began having children at the same time, increasing the requirements on their time and energy to truly superhuman levels. Women who chose to marry and have children instead of going the "career" route often encountered economic circumstances that forced them to find jobs anyway. More than a third of the marriages would dissolve, often leaving mothers of small children without any financial support.

All of this occurred at a historical moment when American conventional wisdom decreed that women should have no problem raising children and succeeding in the workforce at the very same time, with no help from anyone. The cohort of women born in the 1950s was the first group to actually test this belief in the real world. Judging by the stories I heard in my interviews, they found a major infestation of bugs in the system.

IV. THE EMBATTLED

(Born between 1960 and 1969, 27 to 36 years old in 1997)

Women born in the early 1960s might identify more with the Baby Boom generation than women born in the later years of the decade. Those who got swept up in the massive Baby Boom cohort will have had a very different experience from those who did not. "Generation X," as the post–Baby Boomers are sometimes known, has a characteristic wariness and caution, born of observation. These women were watching as the Boomers enthusiastically embraced causes and demanded social change, often in ways that were more idealistic than practical. When things didn't work out as perfectly as the Baby Boomers expected, the next cohort of Americans suffered the consequences.

Bonnie, 27

When I was a kid we'd always go to the big Fourth of July parade downtown. I loved watching the rodeo stars and the mounted police go by on horseback. They were great—the horses were beautiful, and the riders sat up so high. But there was always this gap right after them, where these guys with shovels would run behind scooping up manure and dumping it in pushcarts. I think it's like that with Americans and the Baby Boom. All my life, I watch the people just older than me getting all this attention and all this glory. My generation has to walk behind them and shovel up the manure they left when they went by.

Liza, 29

My boyfriend is always talking about how people my age don't have the kind of passion he and his friends had in the sixties. I tell him, "Look what a lot of good your passion did *us*. You had a sexual revolution, we've got to worry about herpes and AIDS. You got great jobs, now there aren't any left for us. You got to let it all hang out when you were young, and you screwed things up so bad that now we've got to watch every step we take."

Changes in female roles were some of the most dramatic innovations in United States society during the young-adult years of the Baby Boom. The Boomers reached maturity at a time when women were just moving into new territory, postponing traditional families and fighting for equality in the workplace. Women born in the sixties, on the other hand, became young adults when the stress of the double burden was beginning to show pronounced negative effects on their older sisters. The cohort born in the sixties did not display the Baby Boomers' serene conviction that all the problems women face could be eradicated in a single, bold revolutionary act. They weren't convinced that getting a good job would catapult them into equal status with men—they had seen that resistance to gender equality in the workplace occurs in innumerable subtle and persistent ways. They didn't see divorce only as a way for women to liberate themselves from domineering husbands—they all knew divorced women whose lives were incredibly difficult. Nor did this cohort share the assumption that traditional "women's work" would *just happen*, invisibly and easily, while they were achieving in the modern work world. Generation X had seen all these things in practice, rather than just in theory, and from their perspective, things just didn't look as simple as the Baby Boomers had once assumed they would be.

INHERITING PARADOX

From the beginning, Americans have maintained the paradoxical value system that aspired to both perfect "modernity" and perfect "traditionalism." The Baby Boom generation was the first to actually *apply* this paradox to women's roles. The legacy inherited by the women of Generation X, then, is a paradoxical one. In some ways, it offers them enormous advantages. In other ways, *those very factors* can be seen as problems. For example, by the time females born in the sixties became adults, most American women were expected to work. This is a big step forward for women—*if* you're looking at life from a modern value system. If you're thinking about how to achieve traditional goals, however, the expectation that women should be employed creates intense stress for women who are trying to meet traditional obligations (such as mothering young children). The "advantage" of being expected to work can actually *diminish* their quality of life.

Other changes instigated by the Baby Boomers have similarly paradoxical consequences. Because the traditional aspects of our society have been in place all along, and because the first wave of feminism was based on the Enlightenment model of human equality, most of the transformations brought about by the Baby Boom look positive from a modern value system, and negative from a traditional one.

For example, the push for easier, no-fault divorce laws made American marriages much less durable: this is an advantage for women who might otherwise be trapped in bad relationships, but a disadvantage for women who depend—financially, logistically, or emotionally—on a stable marriage. The fact that laws and policies now sometimes allow women to compete with men in a "gender blind" workplace is a terrific step forward for women who are not bearing heavy traditional loads, but, again, it tips the scales against women who are raising young families or caring for aging parents while trying to climb the career ladder. Educational institutions are treating boys and girls more and more similarly, which is a terrific way to give young women the same kinds of motivation men have always felt, but doesn't prepare *either men or women* for the complexities of a life that includes traditional responsibilities (and you know which sex gets the raw end of that deal). These are only a few of the many paradoxes, large and small, that women born in the sixties have inherited from the generation that went before them.

NO-WIN DECISIONS

When I was conducting my research, women in this age group were in their twenties and early thirties, a period of life in which Americans typically make some of the most important decisions that will shape their lives. This is the age range when most women first choose husbands or life partners, consider becoming pregnant, decide on continued education, jobs, and careers. For women born before the 1950s, these choices were limited, or in some cases, nonexistent. For those born *in* the fifties, traditional life patterns were often postponed while women went to graduate or professional school, or started long-term jobs. Women born in the sixties watched the fifties babies do a double take, fretting about having postponed marriage, worrying about infertility, and complaining about the exhaustion that comes with the "double burden." As a result, Generation X-ers tend to approach their life choices carefully, dubiously, without the sense of enthusiastic certainty that characterized young-adult women of the previous cohort.

Karen, 30

I don't think things are as easy as they told me when I was a kid. I look at my friends who are a little older than me, and a lot of them seem to be having a really hard time. It's hard to combine career and kids, things like that. I don't say this to them, but I always think, well, it's not like someone forced you to do this. They went into everything with their eyes open. They just overestimated themselves, expected to be Supermom. That's just cockiness. I don't want to make the same mistakes.

Emma, 26

I'll tell you one thing, I'm not assuming anything about my future. In this day and age, you can't afford to assume things, like that you can depend on a man forever, or that you won't lose your job because of harassment or something. Life's a jungle; you have to be careful.

BORN ON THE BATTLEFIELD

This cohort, like all the age groups I studied, had its share of holy warriors, on both the modern and traditionalist sides. As in every cohort, "warriors" constituted a small minority of the women in this age group—but they were very vocal. Because women born in the sixties were cautious about making life decisions and were likely to see both sides of the paradoxical effects their choices had on their lives, they generally fit into the civilian category. Not surprisingly, agitators of all ages, on both sides of the holy war, were likely to condemn them as being insufficiently committed.

To "left-wing" holy warriors, women born in the sixties seemed shamefully reluctant to espouse egalitarianism. Sixties babies who were cautious about some of the ideals of the first wave of feminism were seen as part of the backlash designed to push American women into their traditional (read: stunted and subordinate) role. Women born in the sixties tend to be especially reluctant to put labels on themselves. If they are backed into a corner, they will say that they are "feminists, but . . ." The "but" may be followed by any number of caveats distancing the speaker from total acceptance of what holy warriors may see as feminism. The tone of these remarks tends to be somewhat defensive, as though the women in this cohort are used to being attacked for their opinions.

Brooke, 33

I'd say I'm a feminist. Yes, I'm definitely a feminist. But not the kind that hates men or thinks men are scum. I know that things used to be a lot worse, and women had to fight really hard for their rights. But I think a lot of what men do is just because that's what they've learned, and they're trying to learn more. I *like* men. Is that a problem?

Gwen, 35

You know, before I can even talk about being a feminist or not I think we need to define what feminism is. It seems to me feminism can be just about anything. I'm not a feminist who believes we should fight constantly. I think women need the space to prove themselves, but fighting can take away from that. So I'm a feminist, but I get to say what that means for me.

Jolene, 27

It really bothered me for a while because even though I'm a feminist, I want kids, and I want to stay home with them for the first few years. People will talk to me like I'm not even a feminist, but I am. I think you can have a traditional marriage, and kids, and still be a feminist.

As you'd expect, this sort of hesitant agreement with equal-rights ideology drives holy warriors crazy. They accuse Generation X women of having weak wills, treacherous tendencies, or even outright male-chauvinistic leanings. Because they are used to being accused of sedition, women in the Generation X cohort often seem unsure about declaring their own position on what it means to be female.

Naturally, holy warriors on the right, as well as those on the left, bewail the moral lassitude of the sixties cohort. Traditionalists claim that this age group's willingness to accept many feminist ideas is destroying privileges for all women. Contrary to the claims of feminist holy warriors, women born in the sixties are as cautious in their embrace of conservative ideals as they are of liberal ones. Many have mothers born in the forties (the cohort that was heavily pressured into a traditional female role, only to be abandoned by a society in which women's liberation had suddenly become a powerful force). I heard dozens of Generation X-ers describe the frustration they had seen in women of their mothers' generation. Many X-ers had been explicitly counseled by their mothers not to let themselves become too dependent on men, give up on dreams and goals, or fail to develop skills with which they could support themselves. Others had figured out these lessons just by watching what was happening to other women.

Because of this, American women born in the sixties are almost universally determined to achieve at least enough modern success to ensure that they can live independently. I did not speak to many women in this cohort who didn't intend to be prepared for some kind of career. Homemakers from the Baby Boomer age group, born ten years earlier, often *apologized* for not wanting jobs, as though this were an embarrassing sin of omission. But women born in the sixties simply never described their plans for living without throwing in at least some mention of a career possibility. Take Adrienne, a college student who had worked as a nanny since she was sixteen, and vastly preferred her job to school:

Adrienne, 18

I don't do very well in school. I'm just not interested. I love spending time with kids. . . . Sometimes I just want to drop out, but my mom keeps telling me if I don't get my degree, the time will come when I'll regret it. I know she's right. What I really want is to run a day-care center—well, what I really *really* want is to have my own babies. But of course I'll keep working. You can't take chances.

The holy warriors on the traditionalist side were appalled by the assumption that women should always have career skills. I interviewed one woman from the Generation X cohort after her mother, whom I had interviewed earlier, called and asked for an "appointment." Sociologists are both pleased and wary when subjects present themselves like this. It's an easy way to get an interview, but it often means that the subjects have an agenda. In this case, it turned out that the mother, who was a devoted traditionalist holy warrior, had mistaken my relative silence during her interview for agreement (as I mentioned in Chapter 4, holy warriors often make this assumption). When she scheduled her daughter's interview, it was with the expectation that I would talk the younger woman out of her plan to become a doctor.

I didn't. The daughter and I spent a pleasant hour as she described her wish to become a surgeon, and I nodded and took notes. After the interview, the mother called me back and gave me a thorough tongue-lashing. "I thought you were going to talk some sense into her!" she complained. "Who is going to get these ideas out of young people's heads? What they're doing is immoral! What *you're* doing is immoral!" I tried to stay in my neutral-sociologist mode, but the force of this woman's attack on modern thinking hit me like a blast furnace. This kind of pressure, from both the right and the left, is often leveled at the cautious, street-smart, thoughtful way women born in the 1960s define their own social role.

In short, women in the sixties cohort were born on the battlegrounds of the holy war. They grew up amid the ideological chaos of a paradoxical value system in full swing, and they show the wariness, practicality, distrust, and cynicism characteristic of all war children. I call them the "embattled" because, more than any generation that went before them, these women have had to defend every choice they make, *as well as* fighting the difficult logistical battles all American women are facing in the workplace and at home.

LIFE IN THE TRENCHES

In the mid-1990s, as I am writing this book, the women of Generation X are moving into the phase of the life cycle that overwhelmed the Baby Boomers a few years back. They are at the beginning of their careers, and also at the age when many people begin families. The conditions they encounter at work, at home, and in American society in general are still based on a set of values that glorifies *both* Enlightenment-style achievement *and* traditional family values. Even though women have been overwhelmed by the attempt to realize this paradox for some time now, Americans in general have not realized the basic contradiction in these two worldviews. Educational institutions, where most students are still able to approximate the lifestyle of an Enlightenment scholar, are coming closer and closer to gender equality. However, in the "real world" of work and family, women of Generation X still face contradictory demands, heavy burdens, and constant struggle.

At work, women born in the sixties continue to experience discrimination, lack of support from male professionals, and the common perception that their work is simply worth less than the same amount of labor by a man. Conditions and attitudes are often more hospitable than those encountered by women twenty years ago, but other factors make the workplace even more threatening to women born in the sixties than those born in the fifties. For instance, the huge demographic bulge of the Baby Boom flooded the economy with able-bodied workers. The Baby Boomers are still in their jobs, in an economy where reengineering, downsizing, and restructuring have become necessary for companies to survive. Women born in the sixties are entering a more competitive job market than the one Baby Boomer women faced a few years earlier. The Angry White Male is partly a product of this increased competition: some members of privileged groups, who are suffering economic pressure along with everybody else, blame new entrants to the job market (i.e., women and minorities) for taking "their" jobs. This has exacerbated the prejudice that labeled women "subrational" and unfit for participation in the job market. Members of Generation X have to fight both old- and new-fashioned forms of sexist attitudes.

On the home front, the fact that women are being forced to carry a double burden has been recognized, but not much has been done about it. This is not an easy problem to solve, because, as we've seen, *there are virtually no incentives for Americans of either gender to care for the traditional needs of the society.* Most men are in jobs that assume they will be supported by free domestic labor, and those jobs are the same ones women have fought so hard to earn. Such careers do not mesh well with traditional responsibilities or activities. The fact that women are the last line of defense against the dissolution of informal care structures has not changed just because it's been recognized. The only difference between the "double burden" taken on by fifties babies and those born in the sixties is that the former didn't expect it, while the latter have seen it coming.

Kat, 33

My mom and dad got divorced when I was a kid. I watched my mom try to take care of us while she worked. I decided right then that it wasn't going to happen to me. No, sir—I wanted the traditional family, the white picket fence, home baking cookies, the whole deal. Well, I got married, had my kids, and started baking. Except I didn't like it. I felt like a prisoner, and people looked down on me because I didn't work. So I got a job. Even though my marriage is still going, my life is just like my mother's. And I *tried* to get away from that!

Like Kat, many women born in the sixties are in conflict with themselves. As you probably learned in your high school English classes, this type of struggle is supposed to be the most interesting and meaningful kind of battle a character in a novel can fight. But it's a lot less fun to live than it is to read about. In response to both internal and external attacks on their character, the women of Generation X are grimly pragmatic, rather than airily idealistic. They also tend to mistrust the generalizations or sweeping ideological claims of others, leading them to a kind of personal isolationism. Ironically, even when they are alone, many of the women in this cohort aren't ready to relax. In the final analysis, they don't even trust themselves.

Rachel, 30

I know I'm not going to let anyone else make my decisions for me. I don't really think anyone understands my life as well as I do, and there aren't many people I see whose lives are so terrific that I'd want to imitate them. I know I want to make my own decisions. But then, sometimes that's pretty scary too. Sometimes it'll just hit me: "What if I'm doing totally the wrong thing?" I have these moments of panic.

For the women I interviewed in this cohort, "moments of panic" often expanded into long-term stress, when women who were making major life decisions contemplated the contradictory advice, crisis-ridden lives, or ideological absolutism of people around them. Women born in the sixties are well aware of the complexities of a society which is spinning around the strange loop of paradox; they are caught in it themselves. And while a great many people are blaming them for it, very few have even begun to show them a way out.

V. THE UNSUSPECTING

(Born 1970 or later, 27 years old or younger in 1997)

At the time I did my research, the cohort of women born in the 1970s or later were the youngest subjects who could be considered adults. Interviewing them is usually a cheering experience, because this cohort, unlike women ten years older, possess a sort of infectious optimism that is partly an attribute of youth and partly the experience of growing up in a culture where the ideal (if not the practice) of gender equality has been widely accepted. Women born in the seventies are well aware that female roles have changed dramatically over the past decades, but for many this is an intellectual awareness rather than an experiential one. In other words, they know about the days when American women were barred from most professions, treated as "subrational" creatures, and valued far less than men in terms of modern rewards. But they remember it the way I look back on women's struggle to get the vote—it's an interesting stage of history, but it was before their time. Women born in the seventies (with some exceptions, which I'll talk about in a minute) grew up in a far more egalitarian culture than the cohorts that went before them.

SCHOOL DAYS

When I say "egalitarian culture," I'm not referring to American society in general. True, our national culture is firmly committed to the ideal of individual equality—but as we have seen, it's also committed to traditional values based on hierarchy, rather than equality. The "culture" in which the cohort of women born in the seventies has grown up is much less conflicted. I'm talking about the norms, practices, and values of the American educational system.

As American society has modernized, two factors have emerged to make the educational system into a close facsimile of the rarefied world in which Enlightenment scholars came up with their model of equality.

First, our concept of "childhood" has stretched out to encompass all the years from birth to at least the late teen years, and even the early twenties. Different cultures have different ways of deciding when childhood ends and adult life begins. In many traditional cultures, the demarcation line is puberty. In ancient Britain, a boy was allowed to fight in battle as an adult when he could reach over his head with his right hand to touch his left ear. (This is probably easy for you, but check it out—small children have proportionately big heads and short arms.) The standard for assessing adulthood in our highly "modernized" society has less to do with physical maturity and more to do with moral reasoning, impulse control, and last but by no means least, the sacredness that childhood has taken on as children have become less and less economically useful to adults.

As a result, American adolescents are in the extraordinary position of being able to do almost anything an adult can do, from learning theoretical physics to planning and committing murder, while their parents are still legally required to provide for all their needs. This long childhood is necessary for adolescents to survive in a world where an immense amount of knowledge, rather than physical strength and basic survival skills, is necessary to prosper. Once upon a time in the United States, a fourteen-year-old boy was considered quite old enough to learn a trade, perhaps as an apprentice, and thereafter to support himself. But in today's society, where it takes a fair amount of education just to pay your taxes and a great deal more to be judged really successful, the intense, full-time learning that characterizes childhood may extend well past the first two decades of life.

Another major factor that shapes childhood and adolescence in the United States is mandatory education. Our culture allows young people to stay in a purely dependent role for a long time, but also makes it very clear that the central task of youth is mastering a large body of formal knowledge. Parents who keep a youngster home from school have to prove that the child is learning these standard skills at home.

Ideally, then, the educational system of the United States is a structure where people absorb intellectual skills and information, while their physical and financial needs are taken care of by other people. In other words, we have re-created for modern American children the conditions that only upper-class gentlemen scholars enjoyed during the European Enlightenment. We have provided a long period in which they inhabit a rarefied environment, protected and served by traditional social structures, but insulated from traditional obligations. In this kind of specialized environment, the contradictions between traditional and modern values simply aren't a problem. Someone Else is taking care of the traditional aspects of life.

STUDENT WOMEN: EXPECTING THE BEST

The cohort of American women born in the 1970s or later has a higher percentage of women in college than any previous cohort.[9] During the time I was doing my research, women born in the seventies were in their late teens and early twenties; and many of them were college students. The interviews with these women were quite different from those I conducted with nonstudents. I'll describe the student group first.

As a teacher, I have asked hundreds of college students (the vast majority of whom were born after 1970) about their plans for the future. I have never had one student who did not intend to have a successful modern career and a happy traditional family. When I interview women in this age category *and socioeconomic level*, it is clear that they don't anticipate much trouble "having it all." Here's an excerpt from a 1993 interview with Deborah and Kristen, college roommates who were both born in 1974. I went to their apartment to interview Kristen, and since Deborah happened to be there, she ended up participating in the discussion.

DEBORAH: I haven't quite decided what I want to do yet. For a career, I mean. I'm thinking of being a doctor, though. A researcher, instead of practicing. I figure research would give me more time to spend with my kids.

KRISTEN: Yes, and I think it's important to get a good husband— you know, somebody who will do his 50 percent.

QUESTION: Fifty percent?

KRISTEN: Of the housework, and taking care of the kids and everything. I'm thinking of going into politics, so I'll need a guy who does his share.

QUESTION: What kind of politics?

KRISTEN: Well [laughs], this is sort of embarrassing. . . . I'd like to run for office. Maybe be a senator.

Kristen said she wanted three children, and Deborah, who had grown up in a big family, was planning on four. Clearly, they had considered the problem of combining motherhood with career, but only to the extent that Deborah was inclined toward research, rather than medical practice, and each intended to find a husband who would do "at least 50 percent" of the parenting and domestic work. Like most women of their age and educational level, Deborah and Kristen believed, in a theoretical sort of way, that women can achieve high levels of success in the modern world, that they shouldn't have much trouble maintaining a traditional family at the same time, and that there is an ample supply of men who are willing and able to do half the domestic work necessary to maintain a traditional household.

Of those three assumptions, only the first has even begun to hold up under "real world" conditions. Women *are* capable of doing the kinds of jobs that have always brought men wealth and power. But in an American society steeped in traditional as well as modern values, women still face discrimination in the workplace. (Count the number of women in the Senate. You won't need all your fingers.) High-profile, high-paying jobs (including medical research) tend to assume that the jobholder has no traditional responsibilities elsewhere. Humans obstinately continue to have complex and inconvenient needs, and the environments in which we attain modern success are still the direct opposite of the conditions necessary to care for the sick, the young, the old, or the injured. Men have been taught to feel guiltier than before about not participating in traditional work, but on the average their jobs pay them less than their fathers earned in comparison with the cost of living, their employers still require a full commitment of their time and energy, and men are still far more positively reinforced for sticking with their careers than helping out at home. Divorce is holding steady at about one out of three American marriages, and research shows that even if a husband pays child support, divorced women, especially those with children, have a tough financial row to hoe.

In short, the ideals being taught in our educational system are designed to equalize men and women *and* preserve traditional values—and they're doing a great job of creating high expectations that this is possible, even probable. But until actual real-world conditions change, many of the expectations young people pick up in the educational system will continue to prove false. Here are a few more selections from interviews with college students.

Brenda, 20

I don't think discrimination is really a problem anymore. I haven't noticed it in my own life. I know in the old days, professors used to discriminate against women in the classroom, but I really haven't seen much of that. So I think the sexes are pretty much equal in America.

Lucille, 22

I think people really should give more time to their children. I was a latchkey kid, and there's no way I'm going to raise my children like that. I'm going to be home for them. I'm sure that once I get a job, my employer will understand that.

Sandy, 18

I think it used to be hard to "do it all," but now everybody just puts their kids in day care, so it's not a problem.

Denise, 25

I figure I'll just make enough money before I have kids so that by the time they're born, I'll basically be retired.

Theresa, 21

People should hold open jobs for women to come back to, if they want to take a few months or years off and then come back. I certainly would hope they would do that. They should.

THE HOLY WAR GOES TO COLLEGE

There were holy warriors among the women in this cohort, as in all the other age groups. Like the college students who saw "no problem" in realizing both modern and traditional ideals, these women spoke from a theoretical rather than experiential basis. As a result, they were some of the most intense and fiery warriors I interviewed, with a positively hyperbolic tendency toward bold and sweeping generalizations. They told me war stories, which often involved conflict with a professor over some behavior they found objectionable. Here's a sample from the right-wing side of the holy war:

April, 21

I had a professor who was a total feminist. She spoke at this rally in favor of abortion. It wasn't on campus, but it was in the news. I wrote a letter to [the president of the university] saying she should be fired. She didn't get tenure, and I like to think that was partly because of me. Somebody has to stand up for family values.

And another sample, this time from the political left:

Sheila, 21

I had an art history class where the professor showed slides. One day she showed pictures of three statues of nude women. I think they were Egyptian or something. I felt totally exploited. I mean, here I was with all these men in the room, looking at these pictures of women with bare breasts! All these male students are gawking, and I'm thinking, God, I thought this was the *nineties!* I told my mom, and she called the professor's department chairman and [the professor] got a reprimand. I think they should replace her.

College students, who had been educated to detect even the smallest ideological conflict, worried more about insults to their gender than other women their age who were not in college. This struck me as ironic, because life at a university was a privileged existence compared to the lifestyles of American women who were not in school. As one female attorney and college administrator recently wrote, "Young women getting out of college today have no idea how tough it's going to be for them ten years down the road."[10] Nothing threw this fact into sharper relief than the contrast between college women born in the seventies, and women of the same age range who, for one reason or another, had left the educational system, or who were trying to complete their education while also taking on traditional responsibilities.

LIFE IN THE "REAL WORLD"

After the angst and skepticism I encountered in older American women, the confidence exuded by college students born in the seventies was almost touching. But there were other women in this age group in whom only the battered remnants of that confidence still existed. This group included women who were not able to afford college, women who grew up in blue-collar families and never intended to gain higher degrees, women who had married and started families while in their teens and early twenties, and women who had been forced to drop out of school because of an unplanned pregnancy.

The experiences of these women presented me with grim evidence that the college students' optimistic expectations were based mainly on theory, rather than the actual existence of a happy synthesis between modern and traditional ideals. When women born in the seventies were still in the educational system, they believed more strongly than any older group in their ability to "have it all." But when they left the educational system, especially to have their own children, they immediately became locked in tighter and more desperate double binds than any other women I interviewed.

Like all paradoxical problems, the intensifying strange loop of women's role definition seems to be making things harder and harder for women, while teaching them to believe that things should be getting easier and easier. I saw evidence for this on many different levels.

For example, the cohort of women born in the seventies or later had almost no traditional expectations of men their age—and the men didn't seem to think much about it either. The days when a young man was considered an unspeakable cad if he failed to support his pregnant lover are long gone. However, the days when a young wife worked to put her husband through college and graduate school are not. In fact, now more than ever before, such women are expected to keep on bringing in the bacon right through the birth of their children. For the generation of women born in the seventies, the double burden of domestic and professional work is heavier than ever. Consider some thoughts from young women who, at the time I interviewed them, had moved on to the world of work and family outside the educational system.

Jacquée, 20

I tell you, I didn't know what was coming. If I did, I probably would have put my son up for adoption. He's four now, and I love him, but it's been damn hard. I been living with my mom since I got pregnant. I dropped out of [high] school. They said I could stay in a special program for unwed mothers, but my mom can't afford an extra mouth without me working too. It's hard, trying to take care of a baby and work. It's . . . [shaking her head] it's really hard. I just never knew how hard it would be.

Stacey, 19

I'm doing pretty good. I got my cosmetology license and I'm working in a real nice beauty salon now. I want to go back to school, but I haven't saved enough money yet. It makes me mad because I know that there are other salons where guys cut hair, same as me, only they get paid three times as much. There's something about a man that people will pay them more to cut their hair. That really burns me, but what am I supposed to do? So I just keep trying to save my money.

Tiffany, 22

I just had my second baby—a little boy. He's beautiful. Now I've got two under two years old. I have a good job—I'm an editorial assistant for a magazine—but it's been really hard to keep getting the work done since the baby was born. I'm going to quit work as soon as [my husband] gets a job. He's got good prospects. Of course, that's how it's been for the past three years, ever since we got married, but I'm sure something will come through soon. It better. I can't keep this up forever.

The women in this cohort who were not in college (or college-bound) sounded almost exactly like older women who were trying to fulfill our society's paradoxical expectations. The major difference was that these young women had been less prepared than previous generations for the conditions they would actually face outside of school. As Lena, a nineteen-year-old single mother, put it:

Lena, 19

I wasn't ready for this. Nobody told me what it would be like. Me and my friends used to talk all the time about what we'd do, how we'd have these great careers and everything. I wanted a family, too—that's why I kept this baby. I always wanted kids. But I never knew what it was like. I used to have all these hopes and dreams. Now I don't even let myself think about them, because then I hate my life and I just feel so *mad!* I do better if I just take it one day at a time.

Women like Lena had lost the optimism I saw in women who had never taken on traditional responsibilities, who were still their parents' children rather than their children's parents. In fact, they acted, thought, talked, and even looked more like Baby Boomers, who were twice as old as they were, than like college women their own age. Many of them mentioned the rapid emotional aging they had undergone when they assumed the double burden of modern and traditional responsibilities that American society has assigned to its women.

Tara, 22

I remember in my [junior high school] art class we got these boards
and painted signs on them. Then we did this thing called "antiquing."
We put this paint on them and rubbed it off so they looked stained,
and then we banged on them with hammers and things so they were all
dented up. We were supposed to make them look real old.

Well, since I got pregnant and had my daughter I feel like I've been
"antiqued." It's so intense, what happens to you. It makes you feel old
real fast. The other day my big sister was talking about what she's
going to do when she graduates, and I said, "Girl, you don't know
nothing about it." Oh, man, she was mad! She's older, you know, she
thinks she knows everything. But she hasn't been through what I have.
She doesn't know. It's like I'm the older one now, but she acts so superior because she's the one with the college education.

With all the emphasis on the importance of education in American society, Tara's judgment is still correct: our educational system, with its
earnest efforts to be egalitarian and its emphasis on the world as seen
from a scholar's lifestyle (not just a scholar's learning), does little to prepare women for the heavy and contradictory burdens the "real world"
will place on them.

GREAT EXPECTATIONS

Young American women have higher expectations than ever before, and
this has improved the quality of their lives by removing the strictures that
once limited the female role. However, the expectations our society is
placing on this generation of women are *also* higher than ever before, and
this is something that academic training, with its upper-class scholar's
view of the world, doesn't tell them. They find it out the hard way, when
the world they were taught to believe in collides with the world in which
women take on a paradoxical role definition. This collision comes as a
shock to some, and a catastrophe to others. Few women born after the
1970s have had a chance to brace themselves for the impact.

SUMMARY:
THE BREAKING POINT ACROSS THE GENERATIONS

Looking across the span of all age groups, it is clear that American
women of different cohorts share experiences that relate to the way the

rapid changes of the last few decades "caught" them. Some women only a few years apart in age, like my sister Christina and me, may have experienced their culture as though they were living in different countries. However, *all of the problems I have described in this chapter share the underlying dynamics of a paradoxical role definition.* The paradox of being female looks very different for women at different stages of the life cycle, but the feeling of being trapped, divided, and confused is common to all. Women in every generation have been brought to the breaking point, and as our society continues to modernize, all ages are more vulnerable to this painful condition.

From within the logic of our culture, the future does not look promising for women. As we've seen, there is no way to solve a paradoxical problem; when you're stuck in one, you just continue to circle the strange loop *ad infinitum*. Logically, it seems as though there is no way for women to solve the paradoxical problem our culture has handed us. It seems as though, for women of any age, there is no way to escape the breaking point. And yet, against all odds, American women have found one.

PHASE ONE:

SOCIALIZATION

PHASE TWO:

ENCOUNTERING PARADOX

PHASE THREE:

REACHING THE BREAKING POINT

PHASE FOUR:

TRANSCENDENCE

PHASE FIVE:

RE-CREATION

PHASE FOUR

Transcendence

✦

CHAPTER SEVEN

Meltdown

L et me be perfectly clear: there is no escape from the breaking point. If you are there now, rest assured that you will never get out. Don't misunderstand me—I'm not saying that *someone* won't emerge on the other side of your particular breaking point, into a place of possibility and freedom rather than straitjacketed confinement. *Someone* certainly can, and I sincerely hope she does. It's just that the *someone* won't be you—or, at any rate, not the person you were when you felt the enervating grip of this situation close around you. The journey by which women transcend the breaking point is not an expedition through space or time, but through the transformation of identity. It is neither displacement, nor exile, nor pilgrimage, nor evasion, but *metamorphosis*. You won't escape the breaking point any more than a caterpillar escapes from its cocoon. The caterpillar never gets out alive. The butterfly does.

DISSOLUTION

The similarity between a woman at the breaking point and a caterpillar in a chrysalis was suggested to me by one of the women I interviewed. Maxine is a highly intelligent, dynamic woman of fifty. She was a successful Wall Street banker in the early 1960s, when, as she told me, "most New York firms would have hired a chimpanzee before they hired a woman." When Maxine became pregnant with her first child, neither she nor her company even considered the idea that she might continue to work. Maxine handed in her resignation and spent the next twenty years raising three children and watching her husband develop a successful law practice. When her youngest child was a teenager, Maxine began to feel the restless, frustrated discontent that many women of her generation (born in the forties) experienced at midlife. A series of events both public and private, including the burgeoning impact of the women's movement, brought Maxine to the breaking point when she was about forty-five. Five years later, when I interviewed her, she brought up the image of metamorphosis to describe what she had been through.

Maxine, 50

Do you know what happens when a caterpillar changes into a butterfly? It's not like a tadpole growing into a frog, where you see its little legs popping out of its body and its eyes getting bigger, and the new thing clearly grows *from* the old thing. That's not how caterpillars do it. A caterpillar makes its little cocoon, goes inside, and then—*it dissolves!* For a while, it doesn't look like anything—it's just this puddle of gel, this mass of goo! I mean, caterpillars aren't all that impressive-looking to begin with, but once they get in that cocoon, let me tell you, it's straight downhill for a while. And then this lump, this blob, this thing that shows no promise whatsoever, reorganizes itself into the most amazing, magical creature: long legs, huge wings, brilliant colors, all the rest of it. And do you know what? *I know exactly how that feels.*

I checked out Maxine's butterfly lore with an entomologist who said that while her account isn't precisely accurate, it's "a pretty good metaphor for what actually happens." It's also a pretty good metaphor for what Maxine, and many other women, experience at some point after they reach the breaking point. Things go from bad to worse to truly impossible, and sooner or later, the woman begins to "dissolve." She enters the terrifying phase of the process that I call "meltdown."

YOUR OWN PRIVATE NUCLEAR MELTDOWN

The awful thing about a paradoxical role definition is that even though you can't solve it, you can't just walk away from it. The breaking point isn't a crossword puzzle or a Rubik's Cube that you can set aside for a month, or simply throw away in frustration when you have trouble solving it. The puzzle you're trying to solve is your own existence. Everything you do, say, think, or feel becomes a "move" in the game, bringing consequences and judgments down on you no matter how hard you try to stay out of the fray. Often, just when you feel that you can't go on, you are faced with the awful realization that you can't *not* go on. *There is no way out.* Audrey, a single mother trying to work and raise two sons while finishing college, put it this way:

Audrey, 29

My first baby was a posterior presentation—that means he was turned the wrong way, face down instead of face up. After I'd gone through the whole labor, I pushed for over four hours without getting any closer to delivering the baby. The doctor didn't want to anesthetize me much, because it would weaken the contractions. . . .

When you feel pain it's usually from something outside, something you could run away from if you had to. But during that delivery, it was my body—me, not something outside of me—that was creating the pain. There was this moment when I thought, "That's it. I'm quitting." But I couldn't quit. My body just went on pushing and hurting. I realized right then that women die from this, that sometimes *it just goes on*—and on, and on, and on—until you *die.*

There are times now when I feel that way, mentally. I want to just stop and go home, and then I realize—I *am* home. This is it, you know? There's no place I can live outside my own life.

Actually, the pain and pressure Audrey felt about her life as a single mother were in many ways *more* inescapable than the pain of childbirth. Physical pain has a specific location: the body. The pain of the breaking point can seem even more pervasive, because it's built into our consciousness, affecting every thought and experience we have. Women in our culture take in paradoxical expectations every day of their lives, so that eventually not only the image they have of themselves and the world around them, but also *the way they see* these things, becomes self-refuting. It is almost impossible for a woman to articulate the paradoxical aspects of her own worldview, for the same reason it's hard for her to observe the color of her own eyes. The last problem we are likely to see is a problem with our way of seeing.

LOST ILLUSIONS

While I was a student at Harvard, I worked as a teaching assistant in studio art, under the direction of William Reimann, a superbly talented artist and also one of the best teachers I have ever met. Every time Will gave a drawing assignment, he would carefully explain to his students that the *way they saw* was likely to interfere with their ability to draw accurate depictions of objects. Humans perceive many things in terms of their psychological importance. For example, practically every untrained artist will draw a human face with oversized eyes (eyes have enormous psychological significance to us) and an undersized skull (the back of the head doesn't matter much to us, so we minimize it when we draw). Other things, like floors, doorways, and tabletops, we perceive in terms of needing to move around them. The image that actually registers on your optic nerve when you look at a tabletop, for example, is a trapezoid. But the brain immediately translates the image into three dimensions, adjusts for perspective, and relays the message "rectangle" to your conscious mind.

All the art and architecture students in Will's class would nod and take notes while he explained these things to them. Then they would start drawing, and proceed to make exactly the mistakes he had just described, all the time remaining absolutely convinced that they were drawing exactly what they saw. When their drawings were finished, Will would sometimes have the students do "checking" exercises, like holding up a clear plastic screen and tracing the image of a tabletop on it, or outlining the reflections of their own heads on a mirror with a felt-tip pen. There was always a moment of shock when students compared the freehand drawings with the "checking" exercises, and realized that even given fair warning, they had drawn strange, distorted images—and actually *seen* these images as perfectly proportioned.

The point of this exercise was not to force students to draw "realistically," but to confront them with irrefutable evidence that the way they saw things, while very functional in most ways, didn't work when they were trying to represent objects in two dimensions. What they saw and what they *thought* they saw were two different things.

Will loved it when students finally "got" this concept. You could always tell when it happened. Most students would sit quite still for a while, staring incredulously at the difference between what they had thought was an accurate drawing and the images they had actually traced from life. Will never interfered with such a moment. Instead, he would stand back and grin.

"Look at them," he would say, beaming at the studio full of frustrated artists. "There they sit, in the shambles of their preconceptions."

In Will Reimann's eyes, sitting in the shambles of your preconceptions was a fine thing. He saw it as the foundation for future success; the best—perhaps the only—opportunity for a student to move into a new way of seeing. But for the students whose preconceptions were in shambles, it often felt like a baffling, nonsensical failure. Every year I taught with Will, I ended up spending extra hours in one-on-one discussions with perfectionist Harvard students who were so mortified by their "mistakes" that they wanted to throw in the artistic towel. Sometimes I could talk them into continuing, sometimes I couldn't. I didn't blame the ones that gave up. It is confusing, frustrating, and sometimes very frightening to allow the way you see—and by extension, the world as you see it—to fall apart.

THE END OF REALITY

Women who are entering the "meltdown" stage of the breaking point face the "shambles of their preconceptions" on a massive scale. We're not just talking about the functional biases that tell a person how to draw a tabletop on a piece of paper. We're talking about virtually everything that helps a woman know who she is, what she believes, how she interacts with other people, and what gives meaning to her life. Just to get up in the morning, we all need a sense of who we are and how we relate to the world around us. A woman who has reached the point of meltdown sees these most basic outlines of her worldview disintegrating, bit by bit. I interviewed Michelle, a homemaker, while she was in meltdown.

Michelle, 40

My husband says I've gone crazy, and I think he's right. I'm not joking. I can almost feel things breaking loose inside my head. I don't understand anything anymore. . . .

I look at other people doing things I used to think were important, and I find myself thinking, "Why in the world would you do a thing like that? What the heck are you doing? Why does it matter to you?" I don't understand my friends anymore, and they don't understand me. I used to see things the same way they did; one, two, three, four, good, bad, black, white. I knew what I wanted and where I was going. Now everything's gray. Nothing is certain. I used to be able to plan my life out from here until the day I died. Now I honestly can't say what I'll do or who I'll be tomorrow.

You might hear echoes in Michelle's account of Annie Leonard, the woman described in Chapter 1 who burst into tears at her husband's birthday celebration. Annie's uncontrollable weeping, her sense of purposelessness and even nonexistence, were all similar to Michelle's feelings. These experiences are typical of women at the meltdown stage.

As I mentioned in Chapter 5, I hit a major breaking point myself when I learned that my son, Adam, had Down syndrome, and had to make a choice as to whether or not I wanted a therapeutic abortion. For about five years after that event, I remained immensely confused about a variety of issues: what it meant for me to be a mother, what it meant to be successful, how to handle the conflicting obligations and desires that kept me in a perpetual strange loop. As I look back on it now, it is very obvious why I felt so divided. I was trying to achieve in two systems that were about as opposite each other, in terms of traditional versus modern values, as they could be.

On one hand, I was still a student at Harvard, very determined to finish a stressful and demanding Ph.D. program. On the other hand, after Adam's birth, John and I moved to Utah, where we had been raised and our families of origin still lived. Part of the reason for the move was that in the very traditional culture of Utah (which is dominated by religion like no other state in the Union), I knew my choice to bear a child with Down syndrome was not likely to be questioned—and I had no energy left to handle questions. However, as soon as I got back to the old Utah stomping grounds, I realized that other choices I had made—getting several academic degrees, working while my children were infants, using day care—were frowned upon by many in my community.

One semester, I finished my Harvard course work by commuting to Boston for a class in economic development. Using frequent-flier points John had racked up on his many business trips to Asia, I would board a plane in Salt Lake City every Tuesday night, arrive in Boston in the wee hours, take a taxi to the house of some good friends in Cambridge, stay up and study for the rest of the night, go to class in the morning, and then hustle back to the airport and arrive in Utah by evening. I felt like a secret operative for the CIA, living a double life as a graduate student while my neighbors thought I was single-mindedly devoted to homemaking and traditional motherhood. I was doing everything I could to exemplify the utmost extreme of traditional and modern versions of "what a woman should be." No wonder I began to "melt down."

I kept up my double life for several years, and even upped the stakes by having another baby and by adding teaching, as well as research and writing, to my work as an academic. The more energy I invested in my dual roles, the more people I tried to please, and the more accolades I raked in, the worse I felt. The modern, rationalist values I absorbed at Harvard hadn't fit with my own deepest feelings when it came to my decisions about my children. I had thought that maybe a shift to a more traditional area, with old-fashioned values, would be a healing alternative, but it wasn't. I didn't fit in any better in an extremely traditional environment than I had in an extremely modern one.

Mind you, at the time I didn't articulate it like this. I felt as though I were caught in a hurricane, but I didn't understand its source or its nature at all. I had already spent years interviewing women to see if I could learn from their stories, and had written my Harvard dissertation on what I found. But even when my Ph.D. was signed, sealed, and delivered, I didn't stop interviewing. I kept at it, because I knew there had to be some way to understand my own situation, and there must be some way to feel better than I felt. So I kept interviewing, all the time trapped at the breaking point, all the time melting down like a wax house afire.

For me, meltdown included all the feelings I've mentioned so far in this chapter, plus a variety of typical observable symptoms. I had trouble sleeping, lost weight uncontrollably, was almost always sick with something or other, and went through several surgeries to correct structural damage to my body. I cried a lot—I mean a *whole* lot. (John, who was the only person I allowed to actually see me cry, took to calling me "Puddles" during this period.) I went around in a daze of fatigue most of the time. Even though I would take on gargantuan tasks (so long as I thought they could buy me some approval), little things like calling the plumber to fix a stopped-up toilet, or the stress of a holiday party, seemed almost unmanageably difficult. I identified intensely with women like Michelle and Anne, who were in this phase of the breaking point themselves. I didn't understand other women I interviewed, who recalled being as torn as I felt but had moved beyond it. Clearly there was some way out of this muddled meltdown, but I couldn't see it.

WHY PROZAC WILL NOT "CURE" MELTDOWN

If you are familiar with the symptoms of clinical depression, you will have recognized that they overlap with the symptoms of the breaking point and meltdown. But meltdown is not simply depression. While a woman going through meltdown is almost certain to experience some depression, a woman who is depressed isn't necessarily in meltdown. Many women become depressed because of recognizable situations or events in their own lives: a bad marriage, for example, or the death of a loved one.

Others have a recognizable chemical imbalance. Women in meltdown often have no medical explanation for their depression, and they can't trace it to any single event in their lives. Everything bothers them, but nothing seems to be *the* problem, and when they try to pinpoint it, women end up contradicting themselves. Wendy, a kindergarten teacher, put it this way.

Wendy, 32

Sometimes when I get really to the end of my rope, I'll decide it's all because of one thing. Like, it's all about how my husband isn't home enough, he doesn't pitch in enough with the kids. So he'll tell me to take a weekend off and go stay with my sister while he takes care of the kids. But then I feel guilty and awful, like I'm not a good mother, so I tell him that's not a solution. He ends up saying, "What do you want?" I can see why he's frustrated. I don't understand it myself.

This self-contradiction—which is nothing more than a reflection of the incompatible aspects of women's social roles—is a sure sign that a woman is experiencing "meltdown depression," rather than depression over some other difficult situation. Women in meltdown are also different from people whose depression is physiological. I interviewed several women who had been depressed until they were treated with psychiatric drugs. If the depression was purely chemical in nature, it would lighten or disappear when the woman was given an appropriate antidepressant. For women at the breaking point, however, the process of meltdown continued even when their depression was being chemically treated.

Charlotte, 55

My doctor sent me to a psychiatrist, and he put me on Prozac. It's really helped. Before I had the Prozac, I'd walk around thinking, "God, what's happening to me? I don't know who I am or what I've done with my life or where I'm headed." Now I feel pretty cheerful. Oh, it's not like anything's all that different. I still don't know who I am or what I've done or where I'm headed. But now I feel like, oh, well, what the hell. It's like the difference between falling off a building drunk or sober. I still have this feeling I'm headed for catastrophe, but it doesn't bother me as much.

Irene, 50

For me, antidepressants gave me the help I needed to deal with the fact that everything around me was falling apart. It was so overwhelming to me that without the drugs I think I might have become suicidal. With them, I was able to face the fact that the way I had lived my whole life was not working anymore.

Women who had strong support (chemical or otherwise) to help them deal with the more frightening symptoms of a meltdown, often took longer to go through the process, but were less likely to have severe breakdowns and self-destructive thoughts along the way. The bottom line, however, was that no drug, no therapy, no help from a friend or comforting shoulder to cry on could stop the meltdown from proceeding. *It continued as long as a woman viewed herself in the paradoxical way she had learned from her culture.*

HOMEMADE REALITY

We've already seen how cultural norms and values are constructed and enforced by influential thinkers, style, and custom. Every individual does the same thing on a very small scale, *constructing* a personal vision of "reality" that is actually a kind of carefully selected and interpreted narrative about the world. Some mental illnesses, like schizophrenia, damage their victims' ability to censor information, rendering them helpless to do the things that are essential to social and physical survival. The rest of us learn to pay attention to some things while ignoring others, and to lump some phenomena together in categories. By this process we simplify the world enough to make sense out of it. *It is this simplified way of seeing the world, not the world itself, that we call "reality."*

As a child grows, then, her culture's "reality" is woven into the very fabric of her identity, including not only her observations of the things around her, but also the image she sees of herself and, at an even more basic level, *the way she sees it.* (Of course, in different cultures, the way things are categorized and evaluated may be quite dissimilar. When I lived in Singapore, my Malaysian friends ate their rice and fish with their fingers, which I had been taught to think of as unsanitary and uncouth. On the other hand, they were horrified to the point of nausea one day when they saw me pet a dog, since their culture considered dogs unclean. It was all they could do to forgive me, and I don't think they ever respected me as much after the dog incident.)

If you've ever experienced culture shock, you'll be able to think of your own examples of differences in people's worldviews. But despite all the localized disparities, the *process* of simplifying the world is a universal human survival skill; and, in fact, this mechanism seems to work especially strongly in teaching women what their social role should be—how they should live in the world and what they should think of themselves. Several studies[1] have indicated that women's perceptions tend to be more influenced by social pressure than men's.*

When a woman is at the breaking point, all of this—her worldview, the opinions of her friends and relatives, the values of her culture, her sense of herself—gradually stop making sense. Remember how the phrase "I am lying" creates a strange loop in which one aspect of the sentence keeps refuting the other part, which refutes the first part, which sends us back to the second part, etc., etc.? Because our culture's definition of "what a woman should be" is paradoxical, it creates the same logical dynamic in the way a woman views herself, and everything with which she interacts. In other words, *her whole personal reality can become engaged in a strange loop.*

Portia, 38

I'm not sure what people want of me anymore, or what I want of myself. Sometimes I think that all I want is freedom, to get away from all the obligations and all the people in my life, who need so many things from me. Then, I'll think that what I really want is to belong, to be with people and to have that security. I go around and around until it begins to seem meaningless.

Maxine, 50

For me, it was like everything came down, like there were walls and buildings all around me, and they all began to come down. As though a bomb had hit them. Everything was just leveled. I couldn't even re-

---

* Some people think this is because the female brain is wired differently from the male brain. That may be the case, but it is also true that only a tiny minority of women are as free to act for themselves as the vast majority of men. Our social structures still make women more likely than men to be dependent on others for survival, and put women in danger if others are antagonistic to them. For those reasons alone, it behooves a woman in our society to pay close attention to other people, and to maintain a sensitive responsiveness to others' thoughts, feelings, and actions. Whatever the cause, women frame their view of the world and their own identity in the context of powerful cultural pressures.

member what my life used to look like, or what it had felt like to be confident.

The reason that reality for a woman at the breaking point begins to deteriorate is that it negates itself. Her worldview provides countless instructions about how she should orient her behavior—and then contradicts every one of them. As a guide to action, such a worldview is useless. *When a woman is trapped in this state, her reality literally does not work anymore. This means that the world, as she has learned to understand the world, cannot continue.*

DEATH WITH A LITTLE "D"

Obviously, breaking points and meltdowns are not the exclusive domain of American women. People go through similar things whenever their worldviews are profoundly challenged. I remember sitting in on the first day of an introductory geology class when one of the eighteen-year-old students suddenly gasped, burst into tears, and ran for the exit. A teaching aide followed her to find out what was wrong. It turned out that the student had just read in her textbook that the Earth is approximately four billion years old. This contradicted her religious belief that God created the planet six thousand years ago. It completely disrupted her view of the cosmos, the role of humanity, and the meaning of her own life. In case you think this is a comment on the naïveté of religious people, I should say that I have seen scientists react just as violently when their own "orthodoxy," their image of reality, was contradicted by somebody else's discoveries. It is absolutely natural for all of us—at least initially—to resist information that undermines our worldview.

The difference between this kind of meltdown and the one that happens to a woman at the breaking point is that the geology student or the scientist is presented with (or, more accurately, confronted by) a new-and-improved set of truths, an alternative way to see the world. This is what happens when fresh information informs our ideas, whether that information comes from a scientific discovery, a creative insight, or an unfamiliar culture. *But in the case of a woman at the breaking point, the dissolution of the worldview doesn't come from some outside source. No new "truths" are being presented to her. Our culture's definition of female roles, being self-refuting, eventually collapses in on itself.* In effect, it self-destructs. This means that the woman experiencing meltdown isn't just dealing with a new set of facts. *No alternative to her former reality exists inside her culture's worldview. She is losing her self and the world as she has known it, and to the best of her knowledge she is moving forward into* nothing.

There's a punchy little word for this kind of thing. It's called death. Women in the meltdown phase have many of the feelings we associate with people approaching their own deaths. It is as though the part of the woman that has lived according to her cultural worldview anticipates its own annihilation; or as one of my subjects put it, "death with a little 'd.'" Several women told me that while in meltdown they had developed a strong conviction that they were literally about to die.

Jill, 50

I got a very prestigious promotion when I was about forty. It was something I'd always dreamed of, but it was also very demanding in terms of time and energy. I was determined to prove that I could do the job, so I worked harder than ever at the office. Also, my kids were teenagers, and I was knocking myself out trying to make their lives perfect—to be the kind of mother their friends had. I think I tried so hard at home because I felt guilty for working. My husband played on that guilt, too. He could get me to do anything, just by pulling those little guilt strings.

After a few months, I started feeling burnt out and crazy. I was so anxious I could hardly sleep, but at the same time I was exhausted. One night I told my husband I absolutely had to have some time alone. He took the kids out to McDonald's. When they'd gone and the house was quiet, I suddenly got this overwhelming sense that I was about to die. It was as strong as any feeling I've ever had—I was just sure of it. I went in and brushed my teeth and fixed my hair and makeup, so that I'd be presentable when they found me. I truly believed that when I lay down on my bed, I would die.

Faye, 38

About three years ago, I went through this crisis. . . . I couldn't figure out where my life was going, I couldn't seem to get myself in gear; I felt like I wasn't doing anything right. I felt terrible about myself. Around the same time, I started thinking I was going to die. Every time I got swollen glands from a cold, I'd be sure it was cancer. I was constantly sick, and every single time I got sick, I panicked.

Finally it got so bad that I went to a therapist. It's a good thing I did, too, because the next two years were crazy. I ended up changing everything in my life. I got a divorce, rethought all my family relationships, changed everything about my job, then quit and went back to school. One day right before I finished with therapy, I was reminiscing with my shrink about how I'd been obsessed with the fear of death. I was laughing at myself because there had been nothing to it. But my therapist said, "Now, wait a minute. You *did* die. The Faye that came into this office three years ago isn't around anymore. You are a different person with a different life."

As Faye's therapist pointed out, the meltdown of one's worldview is indeed a kind of death. Normal reactions to it include not only the unpleasant symptoms of the breaking point (confusion, inability to focus attention, low self-esteem, etc.) but also fear—sometimes intense fear. Women at this stage may think they're going crazy, because they feel extremely frightened without being able to see a logical reason why they should be afraid.

Michelle, 40

What is *wrong* with me? I can't understand it. Everybody thinks I have a perfect life. I have a beautiful house, great kids, a wonderful husband, all the bells and whistles. But at night I stare at the ceiling and feel as though I'm crumbling and I can't hold on to anything, and it *scares* me.

DISINTEGRATING LIFE PATTERNS

A woman who is experiencing meltdown comes to feel unsure of just about everything. She questions all the choices she has ever made, along with her upbringing, her religion, her career, her marriage, her daily routine, and the meaning of life. She "disconnects" from her usual work and many of her relationships, finding herself bored or frustrated by people and things she once enjoyed. She may develop a craving for solitude, which contrasts oddly with the fact that she is terribly lonely.

As meltdown continues, the patterns of behavior a woman has established in her life—the things she is used to doing, and the way she does them—begin to break down. She simply doesn't have the interest or the energy to keep up with activities that are losing their appeal. The people around such a woman can become very anxious as she begins to withdraw from her established life pattern. Husbands, coworkers, children, lovers, and friends may be even more alarmed than the woman herself by her changing interests, her uncertainty, her increasing need for introspection and solitude.

Sheri, 26

I know my parents and my fiancé don't understand what's going on with me right now. I don't really understand it myself. All I know is, I'm feeling like I have to peel away everything and find something new. It's a very intense feeling, like I'm being called from somewhere and I have to go. Sounds crazy, doesn't it? Everybody gets very nervous when I start talking like this. They don't like it at all. So usually I don't say anything.

Although women like Sheri don't want to upset the people around them, in the long run they are simply unable to continue in life patterns that have ceased to work for them, merely to alleviate other people's anxiety.

THE SENSE OF URGENCY

One thing I heard over and over from women at the breaking point was that they felt a strong inner need to search for a new way of making sense out of life. They had a sense of *urgency* that they could not quite pin down. They felt that there was something crucially important they needed to do, but they weren't quite sure what it was. During meltdown, this sense of urgency became almost compulsive. Several women told me that they had agreed to be interviewed because they thought I might be able to help them figure out the source of this intense but unfocused energy (I couldn't). Of the women I interviewed, about sixty (roughly 20 percent) mentioned this strong sense of urgency when they tried to describe how they defined their own identities. This is not a huge percentage, but it was large enough to amaze me because the sensations these women described to me were so odd, and so similar to those of the others. Here are two examples.

Carol, 57

My husband was killed in a car accident three years ago. I went through a terrible grieving period because of losing him, but on top of that I also hated to think that I was a "widow woman." That seemed like the loneliest, most pathetic thing I could be. On the other hand, what else was I? I didn't really know.

About six months after Dave died, I started having this feeling that a change was coming. I didn't know what it was, but it felt very big, very powerful. At first it scared me to death. I didn't like change. But on the other hand, at that point in my life I couldn't stand to *not* change.

. . . I felt like something terribly important was about to happen, and even though I was afraid of it, it drew me forward like a magnet. I started to feel discontent with my life, with myself—but it was a kind of excitement, a sense that I had to make something new, soon. I had to be *ready* for it. I started reading like crazy, finding out about everything I could. Instead of being terrified of change, I began to worry that I'd waited too long, that the changes I need to make may take longer than I have.

Marie, 27

I've always felt like there was something I was supposed to do, something important. I just don't know exactly what it is. Sometimes it's such a strong feeling it takes my breath away. . . .

I grew up in a family where my mother was divorced and I was the oldest girl, and sometimes things were real hard. It's still hard—it's like I'm still the mom to my brothers and sisters, and it's hard to remember who I am, outside of that. My mom had sort of like a nervous breakdown a couple of years ago, and that put a lot of pressure on me. . . . But the worse things get, the stronger I have this feeling that I need to do something. It's kept me going, but it also drives me crazy. I've learned to just accept it, to ride with it like the current in a river.

I'm still working toward my bachelor's degree. It's been so slow, but this feeling comes over me and I know I can't quit. I *can't* quit. It's not a matter of wanting to do something. It's more like being caught in a river that's carrying me along.

When I first started hearing this kind of story from women who didn't know each other, I was stunned by the similarity in their accounts. I took special precautions to ensure that I wasn't giving input that was eliciting these similar stories. (I actually stopped a couple of interviews that seemed to be headed in this direction, and brought in other social scientists to observe the interviews and make sure I wasn't unintentionally "guiding" the subjects.) At one point I spent months conferring with colleagues and plowing through sociological treatises, looking for something that would explain why a sizable minority of the women I interviewed might have this sense of urgency. I found some similarities in odd places: in accounts of societies that were under occupation by people from another culture; in descriptions of people in "primitive" societies who become shamans; in studies of people who, for one reason or another, were divided by loyalty to two different ways of life.

This was crucial in helping me see the process of meltdown and transcendence from a different perspective, but it didn't tell me what the sense of urgency was all about. I do have a couple of theories. It could be that since the women who felt this need to seek some new and important thing had found their gender identity unworkable, they might have been searching for *themselves* "in the shambles of their preconceptions." But most of the women who described the sense of urgency would disagree with this theory, and insist that there is more to their impulses than simple psychology. These women said that they anticipated an important change in the world around them, as well as in their own lives.

Another explanation might be that social conditions have created the kind of pressure on American women that has led to powerful innovations among other groups of people at other times. Historically, innovative ways of thinking and seeing tended to happen in "clusters." The ancient Greek philosophers who formed the foundation of Western society lived close to one another in time and geographic space. The European Renaissance saw another "cluster" of great thinkers. The French Impressionists had lunch together (as writer Julia Cameron says, "That's what they painted"). Different scientists discovered the structure of DNA at almost exactly the same time. Perhaps the sense of urgency, with its intimations of social change, is the energy leading many women, independently, toward a "clustered" cultural or artistic movement.

I have no way of knowing whether either theory holds any water. All I can do is report that women of different ages, from different backgrounds, who had never heard of one another, gave me eerily similar reports about feeling compelled to prepare for some momentous but undefined event.

MELTDOWN ROMANCE

Women in meltdown may become mildly (or very) introverted, turning away from many of their existing relationships. However, this is also a time when new relationships are likely to form—sometimes with heartstopping intensity. "Meltdown romance" is the term I use to describe the powerful attractions many women developed as their existing life patterns crumbled. I was amazed, looking back at women's accounts of their breaking-point experiences, to see how many of them had fallen in love—passionately in love—at precisely the time their reality was "melting down." About half the women I interviewed had been through the entire breaking-point process at least once. Of those, more than 80 percent said they had developed a strong love interest (sometimes consummated, more often not) during the meltdown stage of the process.

Most of these relationships reminded me of the love stories that develop during "action thriller" movies, where the hero and the heroine know nothing about each other, but manage to bond by sharing a series of traumatic and potentially lethal experiences. It seemed to me that one reason for meltdown romance was to provide an emotional haven for women during a period of intense change. Another was to allow the woman in transition to see herself through the eyes of someone altogether new, which actually encouraged her to move away from her "normal" way of defining herself. A common pattern was for a woman who had been at the breaking point for some time to find herself falling head over heels in love with someone who represented freedom, rest, and sometimes flat-out escape. The hurricane of feelings that went along with falling in love contributed to the meltdown of the woman's "normal" life.

The example of Mindy, a twenty-seven-year-old graduate student, comes to mind. When I interviewed her, Mindy had been engaged for two years to a man she described as her "perfect match." However, as she talked, it became clear that although Mindy loved her fiancé, she saw marriage as the end of her independence and was very ambivalent about it. She was a fine student with a bright future in her chosen field, and although in theory this did not seem to conflict with marriage, every time Mindy had gotten close to actually tying the knot, the conflict between the roles of "wife" and "career woman" had sent her spinning into the strange loop of paradoxical role definition. She simply couldn't imagine how to do both, but she didn't want to give up either aspect of her role. Mindy ended our conversation by telling me that she was, at long last, headed home to get married.

Mindy did in fact board a flight from Boston to her home in Los Angeles. However, she disappeared during a stopover in Chicago and never arrived home. Not long after, Mindy's friends and relations began to receive postcards from Florida, where Mindy was living with an extremely handsome surfer she had met in the Chicago airport.

This was the most extreme case of meltdown romance that I saw while doing my research. However, it wasn't unusual to find women going straight from a tormented breaking point to an intense new passion. Since I wasn't focusing on these relationships as my major area of study, I don't know how many of them lasted, or exactly what purpose they served. One likely explanation came from Roberta, a homemaker, who said of her own meltdown romance:

Roberta, 36

When I met him, everything in my life seemed to have fallen apart. I wasn't sure who I was anymore. [The man I fell in love with] wasn't somebody I actually wanted to live with. It was more as though he represented the part of me that I had never let myself know—the part that wasn't just trying to fit someone else's idea of who and what I should be. He didn't have those expectations. With him, I could be absolutely myself. When I met him, I didn't even know what my real self would look like—but you see, he did. It was as though I could see the reflection of who I really was in his eyes, and I had never seen that before.

As I mentioned earlier, most meltdown romances were not consummated, either sexually or in terms of establishing a firm romantic link. Many never got past the stage of a very intense "crush." However, by finding someone new to love, women managed to give themselves a powerful emotional grounding *outside their current life pattern*. This helped them find the courage to face the disintegration of their worldview, and the hope that something besides annihilation lay on the other side.

BURIED TREASURES

Women who did not have a meltdown romance with another person often developed a passion for certain activities or topics. Because they were often things that women had felt passionate about before, but had forgotten in the endless struggle to be "good women," I called these new interests "buried treasures." As the structures and attitudes that had defined their role began to crack and crumble, women in meltdown seemed to rediscover the core skills and interests they had always carried within them. This was because *the essential core self did not melt down along with the role definition a woman had learned from her society.* As her learned social identity dissolved, her innate ways of thinking, feeling, and doing were slowly revealed.

When I was in the meltdown phase I mentioned earlier, I had virtually no energy to put into the requirements of my job and family. However, I found myself spending hours doing two things that occupied most of my time as a child: reading novels and painting. In my view, both these activities were a colossal waste of time—time I should have been spending on something "important." I had given up reading for fun when I started college, and although I had toyed with the idea of becoming a professional artist, I'd decided years before that this idea was far too flaky to pursue. It seemed rather bizarre to me, then, that I could sit in an unheated room in my basement, inhaling turpentine fumes for hours at a time, without noticing much fatigue. Remember, this happened at a time when I was feeling too weak to open your average door. I chided myself severely for putting so much effort into two things that had nothing to do with being either the model of the ideal traditional mother or the modern professional sociologist. But I didn't stop. My ability to do what Seemed Right was melting away, leaving only my ability to pursue what Seemed Fun.

Olivia, a junior high school teacher, described the way this phenomenon occurred in her life:

Olivia, 32

I had one of those "battle fatigue" classes—a bunch of kids that couldn't handle regular school. They were mostly emotionally disturbed. Some had learning disorders. I was trying to teach them to make the grade in standard education, and they couldn't have cared less. They were angry and discouraged, and I knew they needed acceptance more than anything, but I also had to push them to do these things they hated.

Finally I started cracking up. I was totally exhausted, couldn't get out of bed in the morning. I'd teach and then come home and crawl right into bed again without even undressing. I couldn't remember why I should do anything.

Then this one day I woke up and I felt just fine. I got up and took a shower and got dressed, and I thought, "Well! What should I do today?" I decided to get my camera out and go take pictures, which was something I used to love, but I hadn't had the time for it since I got married and started teaching. I went out and had this great day. I kept thinking, "Why don't I do this more often?" When I got home there were like twelve messages on my answering machine saying, "Where the hell are you? Why aren't you at school?" I just stood there and thought, "Oh, my God. School!" I had totally forgotten about it. It was like I was so stressed trying to do and be everything for those kids, I just couldn't hold on to it anymore. I told them I'd been sick, and I figured that was true. I mean, my God! Photography! Is that *normal?*

Olivia's experience certainly *isn't* normal according to the way society defines a "good woman." But among women who had been through meltdown, Olivia had many empathetic allies. Toward the end of the meltdown stage, many women reach a point where they not only fail to fulfill the paradoxical expectations of the culture around them—or the expectations they have imposed on themselves—but they *stop caring* that they are failing. At this stage, you can throw any predictions about a woman's behavior out the window. Your dear old mom, who has cleaned and cooked all day for thirty years, may suddenly throw in the dust rag and begin to study Russian. Your overachieving sister, who has climbed the ranks of corporate success by working hundred-hour weeks, may take a leave of absence (as one such woman told me, laughing) "to watch more movies." Your predictable wallflower friend may elope with—well, with a surfer.

I heard all of these stories, and many more, from people whose cultural identity had trapped them in double binds, pushed them to the breaking point, and finally melted down. I spoke to women who had gone back to school, dredged up talents that were rusty with disuse, set out to protest logging in the Northwest, run for office, adopted babies, become certified chefs, or simply began to gather information about everything from managing their personal finances to fly-fishing. Meltdown is a curious time, when a woman feels intense sensations that are (of course) paradoxical. She is terrified and exhilarated, reluctant and eager, aching with grief to see the end of her old reality, and passionately engaged in freeing herself from it.

The stronger a woman is, the longer she is able to hold out under this storm of contradictory pressures from within and without. But as long as she maintains her culture's paradoxical way of defining her own identity, the pressure never stops. Eventually, even the strongest of women will reach the point where she cannot fight any longer. At this point, some women told me, they began to do unexpected things, without really feeling as though they were operating the controls of their own behavior. Ellen, a fifty-five-year-old real-estate agent, said that at this stage of her life, "it was almost as though someone besides myself was moving me around, like I was a puppet." Monica, a teacher, said, "It was like I was outside watching myself . . . I didn't have enough spirit left to resist." There is a sense of surrender in these accounts, a surrender to the limits of a woman's power to fulfill incompatible demands.

Plato wrote that we gain our first measure of intelligence on the same day that we admit to our own ignorance. By the end of meltdown, women have given up every sense of certainty and fully embraced their own ignorance. They may look and feel as though they have fallen apart—dissolved, as Maxine would put it, into "this blob of gel, this mass of goo." Their life patterns have disintegrated, to be replaced by behaviors that seem alarmingly strange to other people, and often to the women themselves. They have developed weird and apparently disconnected passions and goals. They have no idea who or what they are.

I was thinking about all these women when I called Arizona State University's Dr. Ronald Rustowski, my friendly local entomologist, to inquire about the truth or falsehood of Maxine's "caterpillar" analogy. This is what Dr. Rustowski told me.

> If you look into a chrysalis at an early stage of metamorphosis, it may seem completely disorganized, like an undifferentiated lump. But inside that tissue there are groups of cells—they're called imaginal discs—that begin to develop into the different parts of the mature butterfly, which is called the *imago*. The imaginal discs are there all along. No one knows exactly how or why they are able to reorganize the matter inside the chrysalis, but it happens without any input of energy from outside. The *imago* is created from within.

As I listened to Dr. Rustowski I thought of the women I had spoken to whose lives were melting down. No offense, but to all appearances, these poor people (and I certainly include myself) were basket cases. They had closed themselves off, ruptured their established life patterns, dissolved into disconnected, ill-defined remnants of the stalwart souls who had once striven so earnestly to fit their society's model of the "good woman." But inside these individuals, so odd and occasional that they would be easy to overlook, lay creative impulses that held in them the image of a creature with wings.

At the final stages of meltdown, when a woman feels most disoriented, fragmented, and lost, a curious transition begins to occur. This transition owes nothing to the social forces that have shaped a woman's reality. It does not come from the advice of friends and loved ones, the insights of science, the tried-and-true wisdom of tradition. A woman does not—*can not*—find a solution to the breaking point in any source outside herself.

The *imago* is created from within.

CHAPTER EIGHT

✦

Satori:
The Paradigm Shift

Sometime in my very first year of interview research, I began to notice that a certain number of the women I spoke to seemed . . . well,
frankly, a little loopy. These women were trying very hard to explain
something to me, something they had experienced that had affected
them profoundly, but something that made no sense to me at all. The
only reason I even noticed it was that, odd as these explanations always
sounded, they shared an underlying similarity. At the time, I didn't think
these women's descriptions of this peculiar event had anything to do
with gender roles. I noted them mainly as curiosities, like UFO accounts
or ghost stories. Here are a few examples to show you what I mean.

POPPING, BLIPPING, AND
STEPPING OUT OF THE BOX

Remember Jill, the executive described in the last chapter who sent her
husband and children off to McDonald's so that she could die in peace?
This is what happened to her on that fateful night.

Jill, 50

After I'd fixed myself up nicely for my own funeral, I lay down on my
bed. I really expected to die. I was a little afraid of it, but I was so tired,
and it seemed so inevitable, that I'd pretty much stopped caring. So I
lay down and just sort of let go. As soon as I did that, I felt this—uh,
it's hard to describe. It was this "pop." Almost a popping *sound.* As

though I'd popped into another world. And suddenly everything in my life looked completely different.

When Jill told me this story, I busily recorded it on my notepad, barely raising an eyebrow at the unusual nature of her experience. I figured that Jill had experienced some kind of psychological rupture because of the intense pressure she was feeling at the time. I filed the interview and forgot about it. The next week I interviewed Beth, a secretary who was recently divorced.

Beth, 37

My husband had moved in with another woman. I had no money, I was totally destroyed by the divorce, and my health was shot. When I went to sign the divorce papers I broke down and started crying. I was so humiliated. I remember thinking, "I can't get any lower than this." And then I seemed to pull away from myself, from the whole situation. I felt this burst of intense peace. It was almost like an explosion—a peace explosion. I looked around the room, and it looked totally different to me. I had felt like I was in this scary jungle, but at that moment I could see that no one in the room, nothing they did, could really hurt me. All of a sudden, for the first time, I knew I was in charge of my own life.

I nodded, made my favorite noncommittal "Mm-hm" noise, and jotted down Beth's "peace explosion" experience. Two days later, I interviewed a social worker named Anicka. She described why she had once taken a leave of absence from her job as a caseworker for abused children.

Anicka, 30

It's very common for people in my field to get burnt out. There are too many cases, not enough social workers, too much pain. You're supposed to be protecting the children, but also not interfering with the family, which is just plain impossible in many cases. You try to be nurturing, but you also represent justice, which is not always kind to everyone. I had begun to feel very torn apart, very stressed. I had become very doctrinaire about how to deal with things, and I didn't make room for alternative solutions. . . . Then, over a couple of weeks, I began to feel different. It's like I let go of all the old solutions that weren't working, and just let things take their course. One day I realized that I was approaching life totally differently, that I was like a different person. It was like "Oh! Things aren't the way I thought they were at all! Like the world flipped inside out. You know?"

I didn't know. I didn't have the vaguest idea what Anicka was talking about. But I did begin to notice that several women, like Jill and Beth, had already tried to explain events that seemed similar to Anicka's experience. I had assumed that this "popping," "exploding," "world-flipping" phenomenon was just another symptom of profound stress. But it seemed to be more than that. The women who described it saw the experience as a fundamental turning point, something that ultimately set them free. After it happened, their lives and worlds were different because they themselves had been transformed. They were describing a transition, not only in their way of understanding the world, but in their way of *being* in that world.

For instance, in each of the three examples above, this strange moment of transition was a watershed, a pivotal point which Jill, Beth, and Anicka would later come to see as the beginning of a new way of life. They did not experience an immediate or visible change in their life circumstances, like three Cinderellas suddenly finding themselves dressed to the nines and riding in their own coaches. Rather, each of these women told me that at this indescribable moment she moved into a sense of quiet accord with the management of her own life, which had once seemed so frighteningly, completely out of her control. After these experiences, Jill would go on to become much more self-assured in tending to her own need for solitude, uncluttered time, and physical rest. Beth would, for the first time, come to believe that she was a valuable person who deserved a relationship with a supportive spouse. Anicka developed a deep confidence that she was not the only source of compassion for the people whose lives she touched. From the outside, the experiences they described looked almost inconsequential. From the inside, they were tremendously powerful.

As I continued my research, I heard more versions of this same story—not from everyone, to be sure, but from a sizable and fascinating minority—about 25 percent of all the women I spoke to. For a long time, I didn't know what to call the experience that seemed to somehow push women "through" the sense of entrapment and confusion that came with meltdown. For a while, I referred to the phenomenon as "blipping out," but that gave an unwarranted impression of abnormality.

Then I borrowed the term "stepping out of the box" from one of my subjects, but that phrase was cumbersome and didn't capture the nuance of the thing.

There are some English words that address the idea of pushing past the breaking point into another way of seeing. The phrase "paradigm shift" probably comes closest. But that term doesn't do justice to the intense psychological and emotional elements of the passage through this phase. While I was puzzling over this issue, my husband and I took a research trip to Asia. There I learned that in Japanese, there is a precise term for the kind of experience by which women finally transcend this crisis. The word is *satori*.

THE PARADOX OF THE EMPTY MIRROR

The term *satori* (pronounced "sah-toe-ree") refers to an epiphanal moment when an individual transcends ordinary perception and enters a new level of awareness. We "modern" Westerners don't really have a place in our culture for *satori*. It exists in our founding myths, the hero sagas and epics on which our culture is based, but it is not something a typical American thinks much about today.

In Asian cultures, on the other hand, *satori* is a familiar theme. A classic Asian archetype is the world-weary pilgrim, discouraged by the suffering and injustice in the world, who retreats from society into the wilderness to seek enlightenment. This is usually done through various physical and mental disciplines, the most important of which is meditation. In Japanese Zen, the seeker of truth meditates on a *koan*, a phrase or thought that is designed to boggle the mind. You may have heard some of these phrases, like "What is reflected in two mirrors facing each other?" or "If a tree falls in the forest and no one is there to hear it, does it make a sound?" After concentrating on the *koan* for a long time—sometimes years—the seeker finally experiences a breakthrough to a different level of understanding, in which an entirely new perception of the universe is realized.

You may have noticed that the *koans* I just quoted are paradoxical questions. If you think about them for any length of time, you will find your mind going into a logical "strange loop." ("Let's see. If there are two mirrors facing each other, one will reflect the other, which is reflecting the first one, which is reflecting the second one, which is . . ." and so on, *ad infinitum*. "If a tree falls in the forest and nobody's there, does it make a sound? Well, I could check that out if I went and listened, but then I'd be there, so I wouldn't know, so I should go away, but then I couldn't check it out, so I'd have to go back and listen, which would mean . . ." You get the picture.) In other words, archetypal Asian pilgrims seek enlightenment by *deliberately creating paradoxical problems, and moving into those problems until paradox fills their consciousness.*

THE GIFT OF PARADOX

Seeking *satori* through paradox is not a task for the fainthearted. Asian cultures revere it as an act of great courage and discipline. In the process of meditating on the *koan,* the truth-seeker is deliberately attempting to reach the breaking point, where the mind is utterly baffled and the individual's whole reality "melts down." As you will know if you've been through it (or have read the last few chapters), this is not a pleasant experience. Because our sense of reality keeps us feeling safe in the world, we all naturally fear and resist having it dismantled. But those who stick with it, even when they are already surrounded by the shambles of their preconceptions, are rewarded with *satori,* the involuntary, indescribable shift to a new level of understanding the entire universe and their role within it.

From this perspective, then, the way American society defines women's roles may be seen as a kind of backhanded gift. Without even knowing it, American women are being forced to take the pilgrim's journey, to struggle with contradictory definitions of their own role, to move past the breaking point, to stay in the strange loop of a paradox that permeates everything women are supposed to do and be. As the tension between the two incompatible sides of our culture continues to place paradoxical pressure on women, more and more of us will find ourselves following this path all the way to *satori*—and without ever having to shave our heads, live on bamboo shoots, or retreat to caves in the mountains.

THE FINGER THAT POINTS TO THE MOON

Have I made the concept of *satori* perfectly clear? If so, there's something wrong with my explanation. Legend has it that when Siddhartha (the original Buddha) went through his own *satori* to achieve complete enlightenment, his first words were "This cannot be taught." The Japanese Zen masters said it this way: "The finger that points to the moon is not the moon." In other words, you can't read or listen to a mere description of *satori* and "get it." *Satori* must be experienced to be understood. If you have been through *satori*, you probably identified with the concept as soon as I described it—"Oh, *that's* what they call it!" If you haven't ever had such an experience, you may be wondering what all this Asian archetype business has to do with being an American woman. In order to give you more of a sense of *satori* (or to remind you what it feels like if you haven't been through it recently), I'd like to walk you through a couple of exercises that may help you experience it on a very small scale.

THIS IS NOT A DOG

I sometimes set up a *satori*-like experience for my students by bringing a photograph of something—say, a dog—to the classroom, tacking the picture up in front of them, and then telling them that I am about to make two true statements. I point to the picture and say the first statement: "This is not a dog." The second statement is "By the time you leave this classroom, you will all agree with me that it is not a dog." Then I just stand there and wait.

Typically, the students go into a barrage of suggestions: "Is it a really big cat?" "I know, it's a person *dressed up* as a dog." "It's some other species that looks just like a dog." "It's a hyena." "It's a dog skin—it's been stuffed." And so forth. Some of their ideas are really quite creative, but none of them is completely convincing. It usually takes five minutes or so before some bright young soul comes up with the perfectly obvious answer.

"Wait!" the student will shout. "Of course that's not a dog! It's just a piece of paper with ink on it!"

In a flash, the whole class gets it. You can almost hear the pop as an entire group of people suddenly sees the logic in an interpretation that had not occurred to them, even though it was right in front of their faces. This shift in perception is a minor form of *satori*. The class has left one paradigm, one habitual way of seeing, one *system of logic*, and moved into another.

BEYOND THE INESCAPABLE:
LOGICAL SYSTEMS, VALUES, AND PARADOX

A system of logic is any one of the realities we invent to simplify the world by categorizing and ranking information. We've already seen that this kind of reality is actually a shorthand, learned partly from our own experience and partly from people around us. The only reason I can confuse my students for even a few minutes with the "This is not a dog" trick is that their culture has taught them a *system of logic* in which a photograph of an object is understood as "being" the thing itself. I don't show a photograph to a friend and say, "This is a piece of chemically treated paper on which you can see a two-dimensional representation of my daughter Elizabeth." I say, "That's my Lizzie," and everyone understands. I may also add, "She has her father's eyes," without expecting my audience to gasp in horror; our system of logic allows children to "have" their parent's eyes without physical pain or visual impairment for the parent in question.

On the whole, our ability to simplify reality into manageable shorthand is helpful and necessary. But there are times when the inability to move out of a system of logic can trap us in problems and blind us to solutions. Here's another example. I call it the "nine dots" puzzle.

THE "NINE DOTS" PUZZLE

This is a very simple problem. Connect these nine dots by drawing four straight lines, without lifting your pencil from the paper or going back over any part of your drawing. Then turn the page for the solution. No peeking.

●　　●　　●

●　　●　　●

●　　●　　●

The solution appears on the top of page 260.

If you got this answer without being shown, you should pat yourself on the back. Most people can't solve the "nine dots" puzzle without a long period of frustration and perplexity—and a paradigm shift. It's not that the solution is difficult or complex. The reason it remains hidden to most people is that we have all received cultural training *not to see it*. As children, most of us made "dot-to-dot" pictures by connecting points to form the *outer* boundaries of an image—and I doubt there's a reader out there who hasn't been told, at one time or another, "No, no, dear, al-

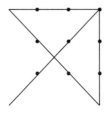

ways draw *inside* the lines."* In short, we often remain blind to the very simple solution for the "nine dots" puzzle, *because even though there is nothing mysterious or difficult about the solution, it lies outside the bounds of what we have been taught to think of as acceptable.*

BOUND UP IN THE VALUE CHAIN

Even though you were probably taught not to draw outside the lines, I doubt that you were deeply shocked by the solution to the "nine dots" puzzle. The *values* attached to staying inside the lines are mild ones; no one is going to be arrested for a stray crayon mark on a piece of paper. Even so, the idea that people should draw inside the lines is inculcated deeply enough to keep most of us wrestling with the "nine dots" puzzle for some time without arriving at the answer. The tendency to get "stuck" in one system of thinking is much stronger if we attach value to the issues involved. In fact, *the stronger the values attached to a logical system, the harder it is for us to see solutions outside that system.*

If you really want to get a rise out of somebody, try the "This is not a dog" trick with something that attacks your audience's *values*. For example, you might take a poster of the White House into a United States presidential convention and tell the crowd, "This is not the home of the president of the greatest nation on earth." Or present a photograph of the pope to a Catholic congregation and assert, "This is not a good man." Show slides of the president to a bunch of Marines and inform them, "That is not your commander in chief." There are all kinds of ways you can play this game, provided that you don't mind being severely beaten and left for dead. Even if you give away the answer: "It's just a piece of paper! It's just a photograph!" your audience is likely to feel resentful and resistant. *Where people's deepest values are concerned, they are*

---

* The exception to this, I have been told, are people raised in Inuit (Eskimo) or African societies, where there are very few right angles and the landscape appears limitless. People from these societies are much more likely to solve the puzzle immediately.

most unlikely to leave their current paradigm and see a solution—even though that solution may be right in front of them.

As we have already seen, the way women's roles are defined in the United States goes to the very heart of our culture's value system. If women rejected traditional values, the whole structure of American life, both public and private, would have to change. There would be no one left to care for the old, the young, the ill. Men would lose the support they need to maintain comfortable lives while working at jobs designed to demand all their energy. On the other hand, if women were to abandon modern values, they would feel no obligation to be self-sufficient. They would remain economically dependent, and men would be absolutely required to provide for all their needs. There is no basis in our philosophical heritage, our cultural paradigm, for considering women "less equal" than men. To do so would be to violate the principle of individual equality, another of our most treasured values.

In essence, then, American culture has taken a contradictory value system and "printed" the image of WOMAN on it like a photograph; something that appears to be a human female but is actually an imaginary composite of incompatible traits. All of this leads to the breaking point, in which women are presented with problems that seem to have no solution. And indeed, from within the value system our culture has created, no solution exists. Paradox does not go away if you try harder, do better, run faster. The more effort you put into solving it, the worse it gets. *There is only one way out of a paradox, and that is by leaving the system of logic in which the paradox was created.*

STEP OUTSIDE AND SEE THAT

The idea of leaving a logical system comes from mathematicians, who know that the only way to escape the circular reasoning of a mathematical paradox is to make a metastatement, a comment *about* the paradox, from a different logic base. You can tell when this happens—when you move from one logical system to another—because you can *feel* it. When you've been stuck in a problem like the "nine dots" puzzle, and then suddenly see the solution, you feel a sort of mental jolt, sometimes slightly embarrassing, but basically quite pleasant. It's as though the world has opened up a new angle in which all sorts of intriguing new possibilities seem possible. The "blipping," "popping," "stepping-out-of-the-box" phenomenon that some women tried to describe for me was the sensation they experienced when their *entire view of themselves moved outside the logical system they shared with their culture concerning what women should do and be.*

Here are some examples of women who have experienced this sensation. Each had deeply internalized a value system that prescribed a very specific—and contradictory—role for women. Each described one particular moment when, after struggling to stay in her prescribed role, she came to an absolute impasse. And each of these women left that absolute impasse behind as she moved into new ways of seeing and thinking about her own self-definition.

We've already covered some of Donna's story. She is the woman we met in Chapter 5 whose young husband was diagnosed with terminal cancer, and whose religion strongly discouraged her from working outside her home. This is what happened to her:

Donna, 36

After Garth got sick I worked for a while, to get insurance and make myself feel like I was doing something useful. It was a horrible time, but as long as I kept working I felt like at least I was hanging on to something. Then the church came out really clearly about how mothers shouldn't work, and my in-laws felt that I should quit my job. They told Garth and me that if we were willing to really live the best way, we would be blessed and maybe he would get better. . . . I was very desperate. I loved Garth so much. So I quit my job, and really believed that God would heal him and make sure we had plenty of money.

It didn't work out that way. The bills kept coming in, and Garth kept getting worse. I was trying to be a good mother and supportive wife, but I was so overloaded with everything that was happening . . . emotionally and every other way, it was a really hard time. There didn't seem to be anything I could do. I felt totally helpless. I lost my faith in God. The only thing I knew for sure was that Garth was going to die. Everything after that was just a big blank, like a drop off a cliff. I had never thought about what I would do if I wasn't a wife. I thought that's who I was—*all* I was.

One day it got so bad I couldn't take it anymore. I had just been to the pharmacy to pick up a prescription of pain medication for Garth. I had the bottle of pills in the car, and I was driving home. On the way I passed the liquor store—the only one in our town. I'd never been inside it. I'd never even tasted an alcoholic drink. But I'd worked in a medical lab, and I'd learned some things about drug interactions. I went into the liquor store and bought a bottle of something. I didn't even know what it was, I just got the highest percentage of alcohol I could find. They almost didn't give it to me, because they thought I was too young [Donna was twenty-two at the time], but I got the liquor.

Instead of going home, I drove to a lake near our house. You've got to understand that I truly didn't think anyone would miss me if I were to die—Garth would be gone soon anyway, and my mother-in-law had almost totally taken over caring for my daughter. I really didn't think I would be missed. I took the pills out of their package and opened the bottle of booze. This was not a "cry for help" situation. I was absolutely serious. I figured if I took at least half the pills and washed them down with at least a third of the alcohol, I'd die before I had time to even throw up.

Once I'd counted out the pills and opened the bottle, I felt this absolute peace come over me. I knew I was going to be dead soon, and all the requirements on me wouldn't matter anymore. It wouldn't matter what my parents thought, or my mother-in-law, or Garth, or anybody. I totally relaxed. I felt so free. In that moment, I could be anything I wanted to be, because no one could force me to be something *they* wanted.

After a couple of minutes, I thought, "Wait a minute. I feel *good!* I don't want to die! I just don't want to live like everybody wants me to live." I started to think, "What if I just *pretended* to die, and then I could go on and be whoever I wanted to?" And slowly I realized that I had already made that shift, in the car, as though I really had died. In fact, when I thought about my life, it was like I'd been somebody else all along. It was *her*—the person I had been—that wanted to die. Not me. So, I figured, if *she* wants to die, why not let her? Why not just bury her, and go on with my own life?

I went home feeling like a different person. When my mother-in-law would talk to me, I'd think, "You're not talking to me. You're talking to that other girl, and she's dead. I'm nothing like her. You've got no claim on me." I went back to work and started getting my feet on the ground financially.

After that, Garth and I connected in a totally new way. I don't think he ever would have let me be who I was if *he* hadn't been dying, too. Neither one of us had anything to lose, so it was like we could truly know each other, at least for that short time before he died. Our parents didn't understand our relationship after that. We both just dropped all the "man-does-this, woman-does-that" stuff and became ourselves. It was a terrible time, but it was also a gift. I could have lived with him for years and never really known him, or had him really know me.

Donna went on to become a registered nurse, and later earned a degree in hospital administration. She is respected among her colleagues as a competent professional who deals especially well with helping patients and families cope with terminal illness. All in all, this seems like a good alternative to suicide.

Sandra is another woman whose marriage brought her to the breaking point, though in a very different way:

Sandra, 41

When Craig and I got married, the minister gave a little speech to me and my husband. He told me all the standard stuff about being a good little obedient wife and mom and all that. Thinking about it now makes me angry, but at the time it went right along with my own beliefs. Then he told my husband, "Craig, always remember that the best thing you can do for your children is to take good care of their mother."

That phrase really stuck in my mind, because almost as soon as we were married my husband started acting abusive toward me. He was in the military, and we were living in Korea, where he was assigned. Craig would go into these rages where he would come into the apartment and start going through the rooms locking all the doors and windows, and screaming that he was going to lock me up. It was really scary. At first when I would cry it would sort of snap him out of it, and he would laugh and say it was a joke.

Then I got pregnant, and things got worse with Craig. Something about the idea of having a baby just sent him over the edge. He would lock me in the bedroom for hours, and when I tried to get the door open he would come in and threaten me. Over time he got more and more physical, until he was actually beating me up on a regular basis.

Like a lot of abused wives, I made excuses for him and kept the whole thing to myself. I wanted so bad for the marriage to work. But I was scared. I used to think constantly about what the minister had said: "Craig, the best thing you can do for your children is to take good care of their mother." I would rage inside about how badly I was being treated. I even thought about calling the minister and having him force Craig to stop abusing me. But I was a long way from home, and so I didn't actually talk to anyone about it. I'd also been trained to be "nice," especially to my own husband. And I had no way to support myself. I kept hoping every time Craig got violent was the last time, that something I could do would change him once and for all.

One day when I was about six months pregnant, Craig went into a real tizzy. He beat on me so bad I was scared I'd have a miscarriage. After he locked me in the bedroom I was on the bed crying, and I was worried about the baby. That same phrase came into my head. It was almost like a voice I could hear: "The best thing you can do for your children is to take good care of their mother." Only this time, for some reason, the voice was talking to *me.*

In that one second, it was like everything turned inside out. I started thinking, "Wait a minute! What am *I* doing for my child's mother? Am I taking care of her? Would I leave a pregnant woman with a man who beats her?" I guess I had never thought I could actually be the one who did things for myself. In the family I was raised in, women just didn't do that.

This was a totally new way for me to think. . . . I didn't feel stuck anymore. I knew that if I even for a second thought about what other people would think, I would feel totally helpless again. It was like, *the way I'd been taught to think about myself was the real trap.* From there, I couldn't see a way out. But if I didn't think about what other people thought, if I just hung on to that one idea that *I* could be the one to plan my own life, I would somehow find a way to get out. When Craig finally let me out of the bedroom I told him I was going to a prenatal class. I went out and called my parents collect from a phone booth, and they flew me back home. I spent two days in the hospital, and then filed for divorce by the end of that week.

Five years after this event, when I interviewed Sandra, she was one year into a new marriage and expecting a second child. According to Sandra, her new husband was a gentle and nurturing man, who considered her his best friend, had bonded very well with her two-year-old son (this was certainly the impression I got when I met them), and was ecstatic about her pregnancy. Now the mother of three, Sandra has returned to a youthful passion for songwriting and has seen some of her work recorded by well-known musicians.

Kathleen grew up with the intention of becoming a nun. Although she never entered an official order—and in fact, no longer considers herself Catholic—she has stayed fairly close to her original plan, choosing not to marry and spending her adult years working to "improve the quality of life for those who have been oppressed."

Kathleen, 38

This was at a very hard time in my life. I had been overseas, doing development work in different Third World countries, and I was disillusioned with my religion, my country, and especially myself. I had thought I could save the world single-handed, and after years of trying, I wasn't sure I'd had any positive effect at all. In the meantime, my own life had become more and more lonely. I felt lost, tired, alone, and afraid.

. . . Some friends recommended that I attend a seminar on self-esteem, and in desperation, I agreed to go. At the seminar we did a guided-imagery exercise. At first I listened to the facilitator's voice, but eventually I drifted into my own meditation.

After I had been meditating for several minutes, the most amazing thing happened. I had a very visual image of a light appearing, very bright, warm light. I was aware that this light contained the love of people who had cared about me—very specific personalities—and also people I had worried about and grieved for. I knew that in this light, all those people were safe. I also realized that in a way, the light was *me*, my real self. It was as though I stepped through a dark screen into a place where I could know who I really was, apart from everything I had ever been taught about myself. It was like going back to the moment of my own birth, where I had no set ideas about what I *should be*, and I could simply experience the person I truly *was*.

By this time I was crying uncontrollably, and other people in the seminar were wondering if I was losing my mind. But it was more like getting it back. I realized that I had spent my life running from myself, trying not to know who I was, not to be who I was. I had learned from my family, from my church, from the media, from *everywhere*, that a woman was such-and-such a thing, and I didn't want to be that thing. I had been afraid to look for the person I really was, because I was afraid that if I did, I would find out that "the person I really was" would be the kind of person everyone told me a woman should be. I didn't want to be "that person." Ever since that day I've stopped being so afraid. I know that I am nobody's stereotype. I'm absolutely unique, and that's just the way I like it.

Kathleen is now the director of the undergraduate program in a university school of social work. Although her days of doing charitable work in the world's worst ghettos are over, she is helping hundreds of fledgling social workers increase their ability to help the poor and disenfranchised. She says that whenever she begins to fall into the interpersonal and political conflicts that erupt in her department (as they do in all academic settings), she can return to the basic sense of the world she discovered during the experience of *satori*. "It keeps me grounded," she says. "It keeps my focus where it always should have been, on making the world a better place and having a joyful life."

Satori is not a once-in-a-lifetime event. It can happen in small ways, like realizing that you can draw outside the lines, every day of your life. But going "outside the lines" in the way you define your own identity is a dramatic, life-changing experience. Donna, Sandra, and Kathleen all remembered the exact moment when they first experienced this transformation. Other women I spoke with referred to a similar change in perspective that occurred in more subtle ways, over longer periods of time. Nevertheless, there was generally some moment of "awakening" which stuck in their minds.

Alice, 42

I'm not sure I can pinpoint the day it happened. But I *can* pinpoint the day I looked around me and realized, "Hey, wait a minute! I'm not the same person I used to be, not at all!" It was Christmas Eve, 1992. It had been a wild year, with a lot of things falling apart and a lot of new learning on my part. And I just realized that day that I was in a totally different place, because *I* was totally different.

I've been describing my own most difficult experience with the breaking point and meltdown as I've explained the way I see the process, so it seems fitting to recount my moment of *satori* as well. When this incident occurred, I was in the last year of my graduate school program. I had three children, including two who couldn't walk and weren't toilet trained. I was teaching at a university in Utah, communicating by E-mail and telephone with my advisers at Harvard, and writing my dissertation. In my typically pigheaded and insecure way, I was trying to be perfect at incompatible aspects of women's roles. I was exhausted, confused, and unhappy, and yet I hung on to the belief that if I just achieved *enough* at both the modern and traditional games, I would have inner peace and an enjoyable life.

I kept getting sick during this whole time. My immune system must have felt like one of those suitcases in the Samsonite luggage ads, with gorillas dancing on it and throwing it against metal bars—and I was the head gorilla. One day I went to the hospital for some minor surgery. I had a suspicious-looking lump, and the doctors wanted to make sure it was nothing serious. Even though it turned out to be an insignificant cyst, they put me under general anesthesia in case exploratory surgery revealed something that would require more intensive intervention. This was nothing new to me: I'd had an average of one surgery every six months for the previous five years. I was frustrated at being sick—again—and a bit worried, but it wasn't that big a deal.

At some point during the surgery, I became completely conscious. I don't mean that I "woke up." I wasn't aware of any pain, but I felt quite alert and could see the whole room—which surprised me, because I knew my eyes were closed. I watched the medical personnel operate for a minute or so, and heard them saying that the problem was just a cyst, but that it was bleeding profusely, and other, similar comments. Then I lost interest in the operation and began to look above my head at the surgical lights. Suddenly, in the middle of those very bright lamps, appeared—yep, you guessed it—a small globe of brilliant white light, much brighter than anything else in the room.

As I watched it, the light began to grow outward in all directions. For the most tiny fraction of a second I thought, "Gee whiz, I get a white light, and I'm not even dying!" Then I stopped thinking, because the light touched me. When it did, I felt the most unimaginably warm and comforting feeling, a feeling of absolute and limitless acceptance. It was the most wonderful thing I have ever felt in my life.

I began to cry (which, after all, was pretty much a full-time occupation for me by this time). Tears of utter joy and relief rolled out of my eyes and fell backward onto that stupid little paper hat you always get when you go into surgery. The doctors noticed this and became very agitated.

"Why is she crying?" I heard the surgeon say sharply to the anesthesiologist. "Is she in pain?"

The anesthesiologist, a man with a silver beard and a kindly manner, looked at my face for a second and then said, "I think she's happy."

That was as much attention as I wanted to pay to the doctors. I was swimming in an ocean of emotional and physical bliss. I don't know how long the light stayed there. It didn't take me on a tour of the universe or command me to lead the French army to victory or tell me what really happened to the dinosaurs. Instead, it created in me two distinct and dramatic changes: one, an experiential knowledge of what it felt like to be loved for myself, rather than for my achievements; and two, a sense that no matter what changes I made in the outside world, the only change that would make me happy was a change in the way I saw myself and my life.

When I came to in the recovery room, I was still crying like a leaky faucet. The nurses were very concerned, and bustled around me trying to help me feel better. Let me tell you, there was no way I could have felt better than I did right then. If there was a drug that could re-create that feeling, I'd be on it now.

So anyway, I kept asking the nurses if this was a normal reaction to surgery. They said yes, surgery was a very traumatic experience, and a lot of people cried.

"No," I sobbed, "I mean, do they cry because they're *happy?*"

They looked at me uneasily and asked if I wanted to talk to the doctor. I said yes, I would—specifically, the anesthesiologist. When the silver-bearded gentleman came in, I grilled him in a groggy sort of way about what drugs he had given me and what their effects might be. After a few minutes, he stopped me.

"I knew something unusual was happening in there," he said. "What was it?"

I didn't exactly tell him about the white light, because it was like a wonderful present I wasn't yet willing to share, but I hinted around a little. Then he told me that when I started to cry during the surgery, something very powerful and definite had told him that I was simply happy, not in pain, and that he didn't need to mess up my system with any more knockout potion. A few weeks after the surgery, he sent me a letter thanking me for letting him in on my experience. I still have the letter.

Now, I don't make any claim to know what that white light was. Certainly, it's not a particularly unusual phenomenon—Gallup polls suggest that as many as one out of twenty Americans report having had experiences similar to this at some time in their lives.[1] Some people theorize that "white lights" are products of a stressed-out brain, or hallucinations to protect the mind at a time of intense crisis. Others think that they are angels, or even manifestations of God. I don't pretend to know, and in the final analysis it doesn't change the way that experience affected me. Whether I was "seeing" a manifestation of my own personality, an illusion created by massive circuit-firing in my brain, or some spiritual being, the outcome was that I abruptly shifted my search for fulfillment away from achieving society's goals, and toward any activity that felt anything at all like that light had made me feel.

I once read a study designed to prove that worms can learn. The worms were put in a little maze, where they were positioned at the bottom of a T-shaped runway. Then the researchers put some wormfood, which sounds really delicious, at both ends of the top crossbar of the T. The worms would mosey on up the T, headed for the food. If they turned one way, they got their food without any problem. If they turned the other way, they'd get an electric shock. And sure enough, the worms eventually learned never to turn in the direction of the shock. This is kind of how I see myself since that moment of *satori* in the operating room. I still bumble dim-wittedly along, making decisions that hurt my body and sometimes my heart as well. But ever since my *satori*, I know what it feels like to get an incredibly powerful dose of the very thing I'm seeking—love and acceptance—without lurching through a wall of pain to get there.

In making sense of all this, it helped that I had years' worth of interview experience with women who had described a similar change in their own thinking. As we'll see in a few pages, many of them did describe *satori* in spiritual or metaphysical terms—but that was by no means the majority. What they (and now I) all had in common was the memory of a moment when they had stepped away from their society's definition of them into an appreciation of themselves as unique and innately lovable beings.

HOW *SATORI* CHANGES WOMEN

I continued my research, both by conducting new interviews and revisiting interviews I had already done. It soon became apparent that however they described it, the *satori* women experienced after the breaking point and meltdown had similar effects in completely different women; women of different ages, races, religious beliefs, ethnic backgrounds, education, and socioeconomic groups. They seemed to be universal features of the world such diverse women created for themselves beyond the crisis.

1. SELF-DISCOVERY

I've gone on at length in this book about how important other people are in establishing a woman's sense of self. Whether by nature or by nurture, women tend to be very highly attuned to the signals and definitions sent out by the people around them. Most women draw their self-concept—from self-esteem all the way to self-hatred—from their social environment. The fact that this environment is making paradoxical demands on American women is the reason so many of us get to the breaking point in the first place. When a woman cannot live up to this paradoxical value system, and experiences *satori* as a result, she gains a sense of herself as existing apart from all social context. She simply steps away from all the social conditioning that defined who she was.

Whether the woman has a spiritual belief or not, this is a tremendous leap of faith. By daring to see herself as wholly independent, a woman risks losing the approval and support of the society around her. To understand how drastically this may affect her, try to imagine what you would do if you lost *all* your deeply learned social instructions about how to act, and simply followed your animal instincts for a single day. What would you do? Probably not comb your hair or brush your teeth. You wouldn't use utensils to eat if it was more convenient to use your fingers, and you might decide to simply chomp food right off the plate— if you bothered with a plate—with your teeth. If you were out walking and felt the need to relieve yourself, you wouldn't go searching for a lavatory—you'd just do the natural thing wherever you happened to be standing. This would be easy if it happened to be a hot day, because you'd probably be naked. I doubt very much that you'd show up at the office to work for your nasty, demanding boss, and if you met that boss on the street you'd probably bite him or her on the arm.

Why don't we all live this way? Because if we did, by failing to keep our part of the social contract—the implicit agreement we all share about how we should behave—we would give up our claim to exist in society. We'd probably be locked up in a prison or mental hospital where "normal" people wouldn't have to deal with us. We all have a subconscious alarm system set up in our brains that constantly reminds us what we must do, and what we must avoid, to remain socially acceptable. The thought of violating that set of guidelines is simply horrifying to most of us, and it is very hard to "reprogram." For example, speaking of Japan (and I was, just a few pages ago), when my husband, John, lived there for several years, he absorbed the Japanese abhorrence for wearing shoes in the house to the extent that he had terrible nightmares about walking into houses in the United States with his shoes on. Once we human beings internalize the dos and don'ts of a particular culture, we develop powerful conscious and subconscious restrictions against breaking the rules.

Women who experience a *satori*-like redefinition of self break away from virtually *all* the social instructions that tell them what a person of their gender should do and be. They don't revert to truly animalistic behavior, but they do detach themselves from rules that say (to give just a few examples) what words a woman should use, how and when she should smile, how she should dress, how much passion she should feel, what or whom should be the object of that passion, how she should style her hair, how she should position her body, how she should respond to men, how she should talk to other women, how she should deal with children, how to earn money, how to spend money, what to eat, how much to eat, whom to eat with, where to sleep, how much to sleep, whom to sleep with—in short, all the countless small and large ways in which each female acts out the role of WOMAN.

The paradoxical role definition that prescribes all these things in our culture can force a woman to the breaking point at any level, from the most insignificant mannerisms to the most important life choices. When she leaves her culture's system of logic, the woman "lets go" of *all* these defining instructions. She no longer sees herself as WOMAN, but simply as *self*—an intelligent being with a unique set of likes and dislikes, dreams and ideas, joys and sorrows.

Satori *occurs when the pain of being trapped in a role definition that is impossible to fulfill becomes stronger than the fear of being rejected, isolated, or punished for breaking the "social contract."*

Women seem to have different "pain thresholds" in this regard. Some can sustain years of contradictory demands and punishments, while others find themselves "popping" out of their role definition under relatively light pressure. (I have often thought that the reason it took a fairly dramatic event to push me out of my preconceptions is that I clung to them with the tenacity of a mentally impaired bulldog.) Some women told me they experienced meltdowns, in series, without experiencing *satori,* until the repetitive strain of facing more than one meltdown became truly untenable. Whether it comes with great difficulty or relative ease, *satori* is not a once-in-a-lifetime event.

Even after they have experienced their first view of the world beyond the breaking point, women remain vulnerable to the social forces around them—that is simply one of the risks of being human. Under the heavy and constant pressure of a paradoxical social role, a woman who has experienced *satori* may still lose sight of her *self* and attempt to fill other people's definitions of WOMAN. I certainly do. All it takes is a couple of contradictory obligations to put me in a minor tizzy—but at least I know that an alternative to this torn, trapped sensation exists. I can start fumbling around for it like a worm in a T-maze. Before I had my own *satori,* I didn't even know that such options were available.

Each of the people I interviewed who had been through *satori* told me something like this:

Kathleen, 38

Since I had that one pivotal experience, I've gone back and forth a lot. Sometimes I forget the things I learned in that moment, the moment when I saw who I really was. Then I start caving in to the problems around me, to the demands people make of me. I start feeling almost as crazy and anxious as I did before that experience. But now I recognize the feeling. Sooner or later, I stick its proper label on it and say, "Oh, that's happening to me again." Then I know I need to get back to my center, where I knew who and what I was and nobody else's opinion really mattered. Sometimes it's hard to find that place again— but never as hard as finding it for the first time.

Candice, a vigorous great-grandmother with clear brown eyes and a thoughtful manner, put it like this:

Candice, 75

It goes in cycles; learning, forgetting, and learning again. Every time I go through it, I understand better how to put away all those voices in my head and find room for myself. Every time around, you learn something new. But the first time is definitely the hardest. It gets easier with each repetition.

However many times it happens, the *satori* that follows the breaking point always entails the discovery (or rediscovery) of a woman's "true self," the self that has been pushed out of sight to make way for the version of WOMAN preferred by her family, her friends, and her society in general.

2. THE MYSTIC'S MIRROR

In Asia, the pilgrim who experiences *satori* is thought to have seen beyond physical reality and into the *meta*physical. The word "metaphysical" literally means something that is "apart from" or "other than" the mundane world of physical existence. Without being precisely religious, *satori* is seen by Asian philosophy as a deeply spiritual, mystical experience.

For women at the breaking point—women who have been trained from birth to pay attention only to others' definitions of what they should be—meeting the *self*, apart from and other than the definition created for them by their society, is a truly metaphysical event. Many people who had been through it described it to me in explicitly spiritual terms. I am more than happy to entertain spiritual interpretations of *satori* (including my own and others' "white light" experiences), although I claim no certainty in these matters. My experience did change the way I looked at my research in one key way. Before that fateful surgery, when a woman described something in spiritual terms, I had always ignored the information, seeing it as unrelated to social issues. Afterward, I realized that by editing out the spiritual events that women reported, I was imposing the beliefs of modern science on my data, rather than considering that everything women said was important to them in determining their own identity.

After my own *satori*, then, I had a great deal more respect for information like Kathleen's report of "a very visual image of a light appearing" and Sandra's experience of "almost a voice . . . talking to me." I heard similar reports several times during my research, sometimes less dramatic than these, and sometimes much more. Predictably, women were more likely to describe *satori* in mystical terms if they were actively religious, but even those who belonged to no church often told me that the realization of their unique identity could best be described as a spiritual event.

Paula, 28

Before this change occurred, I never believed in the soul. I wasn't religious, and the idea of the soul was just another fairy tale to me. Well, I'm still not religious, but the fact is, I now feel that there is some basic part of me, apart from my body, that would continue to be *me* even if I were brain-damaged or in a coma. Without believing in God or anything else, I'd have to say that I would call that part of myself my soul.

Other women were not nearly as reserved as Paula when it came to assigning spiritual dimensions to the experience of *satori*. Some described it to me as a moment of communion with God, and/or their own divine nature. After going through it, they seemed to be more open to the idea of spirituality in general. June, an artist with a wry sense of humor, told me that after an emotional meltdown and a sudden experience of *satori*:

June, 45

I opened my eyes and it seemed to me that there were angels in the room. Several of them, maybe eight or nine, all around me. I decided they were my guardian angels, who had protected me all the times when I couldn't protect myself because I didn't know myself. I thought, "Wow! I actually have guardian angels!" So now I drive like I always wanted to.

3. REDEFINING THE POSSIBLE

Like June, women I interviewed who had been through *satori* ended up doing a lot of things "like they always wanted to." These women made many of the same decisions, lived much the same lives, as they had before *satori*. But the range of possibilities from which they made those choices had become wider, and their ability to cope with the demands on their lives became much stronger.

For example: Casey, an entrepreneur who sells sporting goods, had a "shift in consciousness" while watching a tennis match. After this "shift" she went on selling sporting goods, but told me, "I'm coming from a different place now. I know who I am and I know that's what I was supposed to be." She attributed her financial success to this inner security, which has allowed her to take business risks she would never have ventured before.

Belinda, an African-American taxi driver, had a near-death experience during an accident on a snowy road. She believes she was visited by the spirit of her deceased mother, who assured her (among other things) that driving a cab was a fine thing for a woman to do. After the accident, she lived much the same way—except that she bought her own cab, something she had never even thought of before. She now has much more freedom to set her own hours and earn as much as she can. Belinda says that since her *satori*, she is "much more content to be myself, much more secure as a woman."

Ellen, a mother of two who works for a brokerage firm, was at the end of her emotional rope after dealing for two years with a demanding, arbitrary bureaucratic system and her children's needs. After a gentle *satori* that occurred when she took her first real vacation in five years, she returned to her job and her life with the sense that "no matter how crazy the system around me may get, I can hold it at bay. It's not inside me anymore. And I can bring solutions to the table that I never would have thought of before. I'm more creative."

When I show my students the solution to the "nine dots" puzzle, one or two of them always exclaim, in a wounded tone, "Well, you didn't *tell* us we could draw outside the lines!" Of course, that's exactly the point.

If I were to give them a set of instructions about how to move out of a certain paradigm, they would not experience the solution as a conceptual shift. They wouldn't know what it felt like to go *beyond* the rules in their minds—only to follow a new set. Seeing beyond the implicit and explicit rules our society has created for WOMAN is the challenge that takes individual women to the breaking point, and finally to *satori*. Once a woman learns the basic truth that solutions exist beyond her current way of understanding life, and that she is free to "think outside the lines," the whole definition of the possible—of what we "can" and "can't" do—begins to change.

One of the women I interviewed suggested that we should all be attached to buzzers that would go off every time we used words like "have to" or "can't" when they aren't literally true. For example:

Can't Number One

"I've only been working at my job for six months. I hate it, but I can't quit so soon."

BZZZZZ! Why not? Are you mute, illiterate, and incapable of miming the concept "I quit"? Does some irresistible instinctive force drive you into the office every morning the way a lemming is driven to the ocean? Would you be restrained by armed guards if you attempted to leave your workplace? Is your life dependent on staying in your hated job for a certain length of time? Or do you really mean that it's against your internal rules and social norms to quit a job after only six months?

Can't Number Two

"I desperately need to get away, and my husband has invited me to go with him to Hawaii, but I can't leave my kids for a whole weekend!"

BZZZZZ! Sure, you can. Technically speaking, you could just hide in the attic for forty-eight hours, starting Friday night—the kids would probably never find you. Of course, going to Hawaii would probably be more fun. You'd also probably want to arrange baby-sitting and make sure the children are well provided for. Given all these logistical problems, you may decide it's not worth it to go. But the bottom line is, leaving your children for a weekend is almost certainly within the scope of your physical capabilities.

Can't Number Two (again)
"No, wait! You don't understand! One of my children has a disability! He needs constant care! I can't leave him!"

BZZZZZ! This used to be one of my own favorite can'ts. In the end, though, it doesn't stand up to solid scrutiny. Reread the response above. You can train a caregiver, and maybe get state or federal "respite care" to help.

Can't Number Three
"My boss keeps piling responsibilities on me because no one else at the office can really get things done. I've tried to say no, but the work really does have to get done, and I can't just walk away from it. I'd probably get fired if I did!"

BZZZZZ! I've heard this can't over and over from women whose jobs are wearing them out. I've also heard the stories of women who become seriously ill, not once but repeatedly, because they are working beyond their physical and psychological limits. As one woman who had been through this told me, "I started to wonder why I was afraid to be fired from a job when the alternative was to literally work myself to death. I started setting my real limits at work. It was scary at first, but it was well within my power." If you need a capper on this story, I wish you could hear still more women's stories about working themselves into exhaustion and burnout—and then being fired anyway, for their "incompetence." The fact is that you *can* say no, and if you won't say it consciously, with your own voice, your mind and body may end up saying it for you.

Can't Number Four
"Bob the Slob just spent over a hundred dollars on our first date! I can't just say no to him when he asks me out again—I have to go out with him."

BZZZZZ! Do we even need to go into this one?

Can't Number Five

"One of the guys I work with has asked me if I want to go into an entrepreneurial business with him and a couple of other partners. I'd love to do it, but I just can't see myself trying anything that daring!"

BZZZZZ! I have heard scores of women say that they can't pursue a dream, especially if it's a professional one. I teach at a graduate school of business, and some of my brightest students are women who are aiming for jobs far below the level of their ability and credentials. When I push them to tell me why they can't imagine a more adventurous goal, they often think for a while and then begin to laugh, realizing for the first time that there is nothing in the world to prevent them from aspiring to the dreams that really excite them. Many of these students go on to achieve their goals—goals they once thought they couldn't even imagine.

Can't Number Two (yet again)

"I forgot to mention that I'm physically attached to my children with cords of kryptonite, an indestructible substance formed on Superman's home planet. I can't get away for the weekend!"

DING DING DING! Okay! This may actually be a real can't! Dan, tell the contestant what we have for her . . .

The point of all this is that many of the things people feel they *cannot* do are not really impossible—they're just violations of social norms and internalized rules. At the moment of *satori*, when women first see themselves as separate from their culture, they also abandon many of the rules that have always governed them, and a whole host of "can'ts" simply disappear. Suddenly, they are "thinking outside the lines," and things which were impossible for them in their former mind-set are suddenly very possible—often even easy.

Some studies have shown that chronically depressed women can lighten their depression a significant amount simply by being careful to use words like "I choose not to" or "I don't want to," instead of words like "can't," when that is the literal truth. Females in our society are taught that there are almost infinite things a girl or woman "can't" do—and women are already doing most of them. But each individual faces the challenge of redefining what is possible for her. Until she does, she will be a prisoner of her own beliefs. She literally won't be able to see different ways of acting, any more than most people can see the solution to the "nine dots" puzzle before it is shown to them.

Before the transforming moment of *satori*, Donna *couldn't* disobey her parents and in-laws by continuing to work when her husband was dying of cancer. Before her *satori*, Sandra *couldn't* walk away from her abusive husband. *Satori* was the shift in consciousness that allowed Kathleen to rest easy in the knowledge that she had made a contribution to the world. Before that, she simply *couldn't* see it. I know what this feels like: before my *satori*, even with the stories of hundreds of women to guide me, I *couldn't* see my way out of a driven attempt to obtain "high-achiever" status in contradictory value systems.

From the outside, in hindsight, it is easy to see that, as Sandra said, "the way [women at the breaking point] had been taught to think about [themselves] was the real trap." The way out of the trap is always right under our noses, but we are usually unable to imagine solutions, no matter how obvious, that we have been trained *not* to imagine.

As we will see in the next chapter, women who have gone through *satori* become extremely creative problem-solvers. It is true that they risk being seen as strange or downright bizarre because they "think outside the lines" in a way that doesn't conform to social rules. The other people in a woman's life may respond to her "post-breaking-point" personality with anything from fussiness to outrage. However, this exterior flak causes no more damage than the criticism women suffer, every day, from a society that expects them to fulfill a paradoxical role definition. It is more than compensated for by the internal sense of peace, balance, and wholeness women report feeling during and after *satori*.

4. TRANSFERRING THE INSANITY

In some ways, *satori* is the most isolating experience a woman can ever have. In releasing her culture's accepted definitions of her, she stands utterly alone. And yet, women experience this as a reunion with the one person who is most important to them—their own unique self. In yet another paradox, women told me they felt desperately lonely when they were succeeding best at filling the cultural definition of WOMAN, and recovered a sense of belonging only when they abandoned other people's expectations and "found themselves." One of the key ingredients of this process consisted of *articulating the insanity of the demands being made on them.* By clearly seeing and defining the craziness of their paradoxical roles, women effectively "transferred" that insanity from themselves to the surrounding culture.

First, let me point out quite clearly that paradoxical systems are crazy. It is crazy to demand that one person do or be two mutually exclusive things at the same time. However, most paradoxical systems also do a good job of convincing people that, when they can't answer to incompatible demands, *they* are the crazy ones.

Over and over during my interview work, I heard women apologize, demean themselves, sometimes practically cower in shame, over their inability to be and do two incompatible things. When Brenda's husband demanded that she contribute to the family finances by helping with his business, but then criticized her for falling behind in the housework, guess who apologized for being inadequate? When Ashley studied as hard as she could and ended up first in her class in business school, guess who believed that she had made the "mistake" of putting off potential marriage partners with her success (or is that failure)? When Stephanie had her first child a month early, guess who took a scolding and a cut in salary for not paying enough attention to "the important things in life" at her job? After a few years of listening to women accuse and punish themselves in this way (especially after I had figured out the basic paradox at the heart of women's role definition), it became harder and harder for me to restrain myself from jumping up in a most unsociological fashion and shouting, "YOU'RE NOT THE CRAZY ONE IN THIS PICTURE!!!"

It is some consolation to me to realize that even if I had told them what I thought, none of these women could really have heard me until her own experience had brought her to the point where her preconceptions were in shambles and she finally reached *satori*. Even women who are very good at seeing the injustice in the demands on other people often continue to blame themselves, far beyond all reason, when they cannot be all things to all people in a paradoxical system. No matter how well this is explained, no matter how intelligent or perceptive the woman, her feelings of guilt, inadequacy, self-hatred, and confusion will persist until she steps free of a lifetime's subconscious messages into the indefinable, indescribable moment of *satori*.

The word "comedy" originally meant a story with a happy ending, whether or not the story was funny. The woman who goes through *satori* moves into a story that is both comic, in this sense of the word, and tragic. The story "ends" happily, because the woman finally realizes that she is not crazy. It ends sadly because she must accept the fact that the culture around her *is* crazy. Beverly, a student and single mother, gave me a good example of how this may happen on a very small scale.

Beverly, 27

I come from a very mixed-up family. My mother drank a lot, and she used to ask me to do all these things I couldn't do. I don't mean like they were too hard for me, I mean I *couldn't* do them. Like she would want me to say mean things about my dad, but then she'd punish me for criticizing him. She was like, "Come over here close to me," and then she'd slap me and say, "I told you never to get too close to me." She was hard to live with.

When I was fourteen I ran away from home. I got caught and sent to Juvenile Detention, and then placed with a foster family. They didn't treat me too good either, because mainly they couldn't understand me. They'd ask me to do something and I was like "Yeah, okay, that's what you're saying, but what do you really mean?" I didn't trust anyone.

. . . I got sent to court again for vandalism, and they put me in therapy. I didn't trust the therapist at first, either. But then we got to the point where I was talking about my mother, and the therapist says to me, "Boy, your mom was one crazy lady, wasn't she?" And right then I felt this total change, like I understood. It was like, "Oh, God, I'm really happy! I'm not crazy and I never was!" But at the same time, I started crying and crying because I had to admit that my mom really had been acting crazy. I felt like a little kid whose world just fell totally apart.

When a woman at the breaking point finally acknowledges that her culture, and not she, is the source of much of the craziness in her life, she must grieve the tragedy of the lost "mother," the idea of a surrounding society that will wisely support and nurture her. This is almost unbearably sad for many women—especially since the paradoxical demands often come from people who are close to them. In order to embrace their new vision of the world—the world in which they are not crazy—they may have to resist intense (but crazy) pressure from the people around them: lovers, coworkers, friends, children, business partners, husbands, bosses, mothers, and everybody else. The saving grace of *satori* is that it reveals the actual tragedy—the insanity of paradoxical demands—and offers women the opportunity to work out their own "happy endings" from a position of wholeness, sanity, and above all, compassion toward the self.

PHASE ONE:

SOCIALIZATION

PHASE TWO:

ENCOUNTERING PARADOX

PHASE THREE:

REACHING THE BREAKING POINT

PHASE FOUR:

TRANSCENDENCE

PHASE FIVE:

RE-CREATION

PHASE FIVE

Re-creation

✦

CHAPTER NINE

Caring for the True Self

Pretend for a minute that you and I are sitting in a darkened theater, watching a movie. The picture is called *Flight of the U.S.S.* Society. It is the story of a massive spaceship hurtling through the universe on a journey so long that no one remembers when it began. All the people now on board were born there, and no one ever questions that they must go along with the *Society*, wherever it is headed.

Not far into the movie, we begin to see that something is wrong with the *Society*. There is an error in the navigation system. Long ago, the designers of the ship put contradictory instructions into the guidance program, directing the *Society* toward two different planets at the same time. As long as these planets were fairly far away, the U.S.S. *Society* moved toward their sector of the galaxy without any trouble. But recently the ship has drawn quite near to both its objectives. The closer it gets, the more the *Society* begins to yaw back and forth, to creak and groan, to misbehave as it attempts to head off in different directions. Right now, it is lurching more and more violently from side to side as it proceeds toward a spot midway between the two planets. When it gets there, it will stop—hitting its breaking point—and completely disintegrate.

Obviously, things are not good for the passengers on the *Society*. They can see that the spacecraft is breaking down, and they are terrified. Everyone wants to blame somebody. Women blame men. Men blame women. Old people blame the young and young people blame their elders. All their anger is based on *fear*—for human beings are dependent on the *Society*. It is the only world they know, their whole reality. Everyone on the ship is aware that they can't survive in the frozen nothingness beyond the *Society*'s walls.

You and I are still sitting in the audience, munching popcorn and speculating on whether anyone in this mess is going to get out intact. It's hard to see a way. Certainly, the people on the *Society* can't think of one. They're all panicking, threatening mutiny, trying to patch up the holes and cracks that keep appearing wherever they look. Then, just when our pulses are pounding and we don't see how the heroes are going to save that ship, one of the characters looks straight into the camera. Close up. She speaks, and what she says is this:

"You know, this is a really stupid script. All this fussing and fighting and sweating and shaking is giving me a migraine. And, besides, I like happy endings. Y'all can keep going or y'all can come with me, but I'm going backstage to rewrite my part."

She walks over to the side of the spacecraft, the fragile shell of the *Society* that protects humanity from certain death, and carefully moves aside one of the wall panels. Behind it we can see some construction and lighting equipment, a few director's chairs, a spare tripod. She sits down in one of the chairs, loosens the collar of her space suit, and begins to jot notes to herself on a pad. "Let's see," she murmurs. "I've always wanted my character to do *this*. . . ."

We in the audience are taken aback. Isn't that woman breaking the rules? She can't *do* that, can she? It seems very strange, but I guess it's not illegal or anything . . . it *is* only a movie, after all. . . .

We look back over at the other passengers on the *Society*, and suddenly realize a very creepy thing. *Most of the actors in this movie don't know they are acting.* They can't comprehend that they could simply rewrite their parts any time they agreed to do so. They really think they can't exist apart from the *Society*, which is still heaving awkwardly on toward destruction. The passengers struggle to find hope. The woman with the pencil waves at them cheerfully from outside the spacecraft. Most of them don't even notice her, and those who do think she's crazy.

I don't know about you, but to me, she looks like one of the sanest people the *Society* ever produced.

RE-CREATING THE WORLD

This is almost exactly what I saw, over and over again, as I conducted my interviews with American women. I heard stories of concern, fear, and anger from virtually everyone I interviewed, but every so often, I'd run across a woman who had decided to junk society's versions of what she should be, and write her own script. When I began to see the pattern of the breaking-point process, I realized that these women had already gone through the entire procedure, usually many times. People who were still in the early phases were sure that they had no alternative but to go along with society, despite the fact that it was headed in contradictory directions and falling apart. In the stage I call "transcendence," women were shoved outside society—literally forced to realize that they could exist apart from it. In the final phase of the process, "re-creation," these women began to "rewrite" their social "roles" in a way that made sense to them.

After going through this whole painful ordeal several times, women became less and less likely to play the role society had written for them, and more and more likely to create their own lives according to their own needs. Because they were operating from a paradigm outside the one they shared with their society, their behavior was often seen as strange or erratic by the people around them. But they knew exactly what they were doing.

RE-CREATING LIFE IN THE HERE AND NOW

This book has mentioned a few statistical facts about the problems American women are facing; problems like poverty, overwork, lack of resources to help with child care, and discrimination in the workforce. Such facts are very useful, because they reveal trends and patterns in the population at large. But as one sociologist who studies the "feminization of poverty" has said, "statistics are people with the tears washed off."[1] Statistics make us think in terms of broad policy changes, collective movements, long-term goals for the whole society. But when you sit for many hours, as I have done, listening to the individual stories of individual women, you see them with the tears still on. This makes "big," long-term solutions to women's problems seem necessary but insufficient. For many women, the "big" solutions will be far too long in coming.

Here is how Maggie, a Native American divorcée with three small children, put it:

Maggie, 25
I'm always reading in the newspaper about how they're going after deadbeat dads to pay their child support, how people are pushing for good day care that doesn't cost too much for people like me, how

they're trying to make it so a nonwhite person can earn as much as an Anglo, and a woman can get as good a job as a man, and all those things. A lot of talk. Blah blah blah.

But you know, my back is against the wall. I've got to have somebody watch my kids so I can get work, and I've got to have enough money for rent and food. If I got sick right now, or if one of the kids got sick, I don't have enough money to go to the doctor. It would be nice to think that the whole country is going to work things out in a couple years. But the fact is, I can't wait that long. I have to find a way to survive right here, right now.

Whether the paradox comes in the form of "modern Caucasian worker" versus "traditional Native American mother," as it does for Maggie, or in any other guise, each woman in the United States today has to negotiate the contradictory attitudes and structures of her society *now*, before things get "fixed." She has to choose how she will divide *today's* time and energy between the infinite things she is "supposed" to do. She has to figure out *today* how to deal with the criticism and pressure that will inevitably come her way for failing to achieve the impossible. And she will face the same problems again tomorrow. "Re-creation" is the stage of the process where women devise strategies to cope with the craziness of their culture's paradoxical demands. The first step is rarely writing to a congressperson, running for office, or joining an equal-rights march. Usually it has to do with the re-creation of a woman's personal life, the way she thinks of herself and interacts with the people closest to her.

MEETING THE TRUE SELF

"Re-creation" really begins in the moment of *satori*, when a woman first steps back from the social definitions of her role and sees herself as a separate and complete being, rather than a social stereotype. In *satori*, the "space traveler" finally "walks away" from the U.S.S. *Society*, temporarily dropping *all* social roles. Before the stage of transcendence, women identify themselves by comparison with cultural constructions of the perfect WOMAN. They put all their energy into playing their role as their culture "writes" it for them. In doing so, they create false selves, which conform (more or less) to arbitrary social ideas, rather than springing from a woman's unique personality and experience. The nonsocial identity that women sense when they experience *satori*—the self-discovered soul that has nothing to do with society's "shoulds" and "ought tos"—is what I call the true self.

When a woman is reunited with her true self, perhaps for the first time since very early childhood, she feels an overwhelming sense of coming home. She has long believed that she can experience a sense of belonging, of self-worth, of sufficiency, only if she succeeds at the impossible effort of conforming to outlandish and contradictory stereotypes. She gives up that effort only under excruciating duress, expecting to be annihilated—and discovers that all along, the fulfillment she has been seeking lies in moving away from the demands of her society and into the company of her own true self. When women do this, their psychic wounds and illnesses (and, many told me, their physical ones) begin to heal. Encountering the true self after a prolonged exile is like coming out of a blasting storm into the warmth of a snug bed, like swallowing a glass of cool water when your throat is parched, like relaxing into a loving embrace after years of loneliness.

When a woman enters the re-creation phase, *the task before her is to modify her life in such a way that her true self is never again stifled, tortured, lost, or abandoned.* She must "rewrite" her social role to *care for* that self. As we will see in the next chapter, caring for the true self has led some women to create long-term, broad-scale social change. But the woman who has barely found her true self does not want—cannot bear—to put that self in cold storage again until her entire society is transformed into an ideal environment. She sets out, right away, to restructure her own behavior and her immediate social environment to fulfill the needs and dreams of the true self.

THE RULES OF RE-CREATION

While conducting my interviews, I noticed that women who had been through the whole breaking-point process remained unusually calm, confident, and "centered" even when they were dealing with situations that would have devastated most people. I went back to many of these women to ask them specific questions about how they managed to remain so serenely comfortable in their own skins and their own lives (of course, I had two reasons for this: research, and a desperate need for clues about how I could resolve my own problems). No two answers were exactly the same, but a common thread was that each woman had learned to follow at least two basic "rules" that helped her care for her true self. The first rule was to be consistently—almost breathtakingly—

honest about her feelings and perceptions. The second was to maintain an attitude of compassion and acceptance toward the true self, and to defend it against insult or injury, no matter what other people thought of it.

Neither of these rules is easy to keep. Society trains every girl, almost from the moment she is born, to abandon her true self, to stunt its growth, to lose it, let it die, or even deliberately kill it, so that her false selves (the ones created to fit social stereotypes) will be free to serve the needs of other people and institutions.* The pressure to abandon or destroy the true self only intensifies as women go through the life cycle. Daughters, wives, mothers, female employees, and every other type of woman are expected to be sensitively "tuned in" to the needs of their parents, spouses, children, and colleagues. Where men tend to be given more latitude to ignore other people's needs and pay attention to their own, women are trained to be so attentive to other people's "selves" that we often become fuzzy about our own identities.

THE WAY OF HONESTY:
RE-RE-RE-RE-REDISCOVERING THE TRUE SELF

As we've seen, abandoning and rediscovering the true self is a cycle that may occur over and over again throughout a woman's life. Women are constantly at risk of losing their connection to the true self amid the demands of relatives, friends, bosses, and coworkers, the shouting of holy warriors, and the media images that prescribe what WOMAN should be. The intensity of these messages is so overwhelming that many of the women I interviewed said they had trouble even identifying their personal needs, desires, and feelings. Those who had been through meltdown and finally transcended the breaking point kept in touch with their true selves by developing an unsparingly honest way of looking at their own lives. As Julie, a retired high school teacher, told me, "If you want to lose yourself, just lie to yourself. If you want to find yourself again, just tell yourself the truth."

Julie's comment, along with dozens of similar assertions I heard from other women, suggests that *at the core of all pressures to abandon the self is*

---

* The loss of the true self is not exclusive to women. Men also receive pressure to abandon their true selves, and this is every bit as painful for them as it is for women. However, since men generally have more social power, a man who rediscovers his true self and sets out to care for it is likely to meet less opposition than a woman in the same situation.

the temptation to lie about what we really think, feel, and believe. The reason this is tempting is that "polite" lying buys us social approval. Listed below are some favorite lies women are taught to tell. Of course, all these phrases can be used honestly—but they are "acceptable" even when (come to think of it, *especially* when) they *aren't* true.

Popular Lies for Women
"I'm feeling fine, thank you."
"Oh no, I don't mind."
"Of course I'm not angry."
"I don't need anything."
"I'd love to."
"It was great for me, too."
"I'd be glad to do that for you."
"I don't want anything."
"It doesn't bother me."
"Sure, go right ahead."

If I haven't included your most preferred lie in this list, you can pencil it in yourself—but only if you're willing to be honest about the fact that you haven't been honest. In our society, women, even more than men, are emphatically warned that if they can't say anything nice, they mustn't say anything at all. But saying something nice often requires blatant deception, and there are times when silence is a lie.

Gloria, a homemaker, learned this lesson the hard way. Gloria was at the breaking point for several years in an emotionally empty marriage and a country-club social circle that offered little nourishment for her true self. The odd thing was that Gloria really thought she had an ideal life, although she knew she had a tendency to become somewhat "nervous and depressed" from time to time. Then, one fateful day, after years of trying and failing, Gloria quit smoking—or, as she prefers to put it, "became a nonsmoker." When she gave up the cigarettes that had been her constant companions throughout her adult life, Gloria went straight into meltdown.

Gloria, 40
What I realized was that I had been miserable for a long time. I couldn't stand many of my "friends." I disagreed with them on basically everything that mattered. I was unbelievably angry and I felt as though I had been wasting a good part of my life. But smoking was

"my" vice; the perfect painkiller that helped me stay in a place I hated. I smoked the way other people drink or do drugs; to block out the things I didn't want, and the things I did want, but didn't think I should have. Whenever I disagreed with someone, whenever I began to get angry, whenever I was hurt, I would light up a cigarette and hide behind the smoke. That was how I kept the truth at bay.

One day I was visiting some friends who were having a sort of family reunion. There was one man in the family who was quite famous and had a very prestigious job. I went back to one of the bedrooms looking for my coat, and I walked in on this man molesting the family's little daughter. He backed off when I came in, and I went running back to the other room and told my friends about it. . . . The upshot of the whole thing was that everyone decided to ignore it, because, after all, this man was a very important member of the family. *And I let it happen*. I joined in the silence because I was following their twisted rules.

When I became a nonsmoker, all of this stuff came back and hit me right in the face. My whole world fell apart, because so much of it was based on "proper" lies. I went back to people and confronted them— the people who had been at that party and all the others I'd listened to for all those years without ever saying (or even really knowing) what I really thought and felt. Inside a year, I lost just about every "friend" I had. Honesty seems like a harsh thing, when you've been living with lies. But by that point in my life I knew that I was either going to tell the truth or kill myself.

Suzanne told me another dramatic story about the need for honesty in discovering and staying with the true self. Like Gloria, Suzanne had been deadlocked for years before she went through the crisis that finally pushed her to transcendence. The most difficult double binds in Suzanne's life came from her husband, Sam, who, unbeknownst to Suzanne, had a habit of hiring prostitutes during his frequent business trips. Sam was an angry, hostile man. He demanded that Suzanne be a "perfect wife" in at least a dozen contradictory ways, and was prone to bouts of violent anger when she could not live up to those demands. Suzanne's world began to melt down when Sam was diagnosed with AIDS. Suddenly, Suzanne (who, by sheer luck, is HIV-negative) began to realize that the harsh judgments she had been hearing from Sam and others might be *their* problem, not hers. She found her true self only after peeling away layer upon layer of polite dishonesty.

Suzanne, 45

Before this happened I had a lot of secrets—not so much secrets from other people as secrets from *myself*. As long as I could keep up a facade and pretend that we were this perfect happy family, I somehow kept myself from admitting how painful our marriage had really been for me and how angry I was. Because I was so interested in keeping up appearances—and because I was hiding so much behind them—I didn't talk openly to anyone or even let myself think my real thoughts. I know it sounds strange, but that's the way it was. I just kept telling myself that I was "a very private person." What I really meant was that I wanted to keep up the facade.

When Sam was diagnosed, the whole facade was ripped away at once. I'd get calls from "well-meaning" friends who would say things like "Do you know everybody in the neighborhood is speculating about your sex life?" It was the most traumatic thing that could have happened to me. I still wanted to keep up the facade, and so did Sam. He was still lying about most of his life; about having been promiscuous, about the way he had treated me and our children.

As Sam's health got worse, I finally realized that I was sick and tired of all the lies. I started to think through our entire marriage, my entire life, with a kind of coldness, almost like a surgeon cutting away damaged tissue. It hurt, but it was better than putting a Band-Aid over a wound that was already infected.

I became more and more honest with myself, and I started to get in touch with my real feelings and ideas. I found a person who had been in unbelievable pain for years. She was hurt and she was angry—but you know what? She was a terrific person. A kind, creative, talented person. When I buried all my pain so I wouldn't have to see it and feel it, I also buried all the good things.

. . . I became much more sensitive to whether other people were telling the truth. I realized that even facing death, Sam still lied most of the time. I told him that if he wanted to be honest with me, I'd be there for him. If he wanted to keep lying, he'd have to find another caretaker. Over several months, he gradually became more honest. It was a complete transformation. Before he got sick he was a distant, cruel person, full of rage and constantly hurting people who loved him. In the last few months he has become the sweet guy I married, a loving father, a jewel of a person.

I realized that lying had turned us both into people we really weren't. When we weren't being honest I didn't like Sam, and I didn't like myself. No matter how much it hurts, you have to tell the truth, the whole truth, and nothing but the truth if you want to stay in touch with who you really are.

My own experience in this process bears out the belief that honesty is crucial to caring for the true self. After careful self-scrutiny, I found that one of the most powerful negative behaviors in my repertoire was polite lying, and one of the most powerful positives was telling the absolute truth. So I got honest.

There are many people (most of them related to me) who will tell you that this is the point at which I went completely crazy. For years, I had been busting a gut trying to please and impress everyone around me. I'd felt lousy the whole time, but nobody knew that. Now, suddenly, I started telling the truth about how I felt. To me this was an incredible liberation, but (to put it very mildly) it did not please everyone I knew. Here's one reason why. Suppose I'd been invited to do something useful and proper, like helping to organize a PTA meeting. Here's how I would respond before my *satori* experience, and after it:

BEFORE: Oh, gee, of course I'd love to participate, it's just that I do have to—well, let's see, maybe if I stayed up all night getting this other thing done—okay, I think maybe—and then, if I can get a baby-sitter—of course, I've had this fever, but—yes, sure, I'd be happy to do it. No, really, it's no trouble at all. See you there.

AFTER: Nope. Don't want to. 'Bye.

I wouldn't even apologize. I wasn't particularly practiced at telling the truth in this social sense, so I offended a lot of people during that first year or so. Moreover, I had always gravitated toward friends and associates who fit in well with my pattern of high achievement and polite dishonesty. They were the very people most likely to be alienated by my new behavior. During the first year or so after my *satori*, most of the people I felt closest to either cut off our relationship or drifted away. It wasn't that they were bad or condemnatory; they simply weren't comfortable with me anymore. We didn't connect.

I grieved at the loss of these relationships, but I was simply incapable of going back to the horrible experience of never voicing—never even really letting myself know—what I genuinely felt, thought, and hoped. Even the sadness of losing many key people in my life was nothing compared to the pain of being stretched out between two antagonistic worldviews and absent from my true self.]

STAYING THE COURSE

Other women who had been through similar experiences told me that the more they developed a habit of being consistently honest with themselves about their own beliefs, doubts, emotions, opinions, and experiences, the less likely they were to lose touch with their true selves. I have no doubt that many women never get as mired in "courteous" dishonesty as I did, but for those who had been used to dissembling about their real feelings, emotional honesty seemed to grow with experience. Often, women who had been through the breaking-point process only once fell back into old patterns of behavior, became involved in new relationships that mirrored old patterns, or reacted to a new stage of the life cycle by trying to fill new versions of the same old paradoxical roles. Eventually, these women tended to find themselves back in the same confusing, sickening spin they had felt when they hit the breaking point the first time.

Daisy, 45

I was very caught up in my career for several years. I went through a kind of transition when I realized that I really did want children, and that it would mean I couldn't do the seven-full-days-per-week in the office I was used to. It was incredibly painful for me to break away from that identification of myself with my job, but in the process I discovered a whole new way of living and thinking.

The problem was, I got just as dogmatic about my new perspective as I had been about the old one. Here I was, a first-time mom at forty, and I was preaching the gospel of motherhood like I'd never thought of doing anything else. I got as rigid and obsessive about being a "good mother" as I had been about my job. I went through pretty much the same process as I had with work, where I realized that I wasn't a stereotypical mom any more than I was a stereotypical executive.

Eileen, 36

[After going through the breaking point process] I made friends with a woman who had been through something similar. I thought she was wonderful because she understood me. She seemed very wise—I just thought she had all the answers. I tried to do everything she thought was important. About six months after we became friends, I realized I was in almost the same place I'd started, only now, instead of trying to please my parents and my husband, I was trying to please my friend.

The second time through the breaking point was almost as traumatic as the first—sometimes more so, because the women concerned now began to realize that they might find *no* exterior force in society that was capable of fully protecting and nourishing their true selves. Women described this revelation as being both frightening and empowering:

Amelia, 33

It's a pretty scary thing when you realize that there are no perfect "grown-ups" somewhere out there who are making sure that everything works out for you. I finally had to sit down and say, "I'm the only grown-up who really knows enough about my life to make it a good one." In a way, it was a good feeling, because I realized that I actually do have a grown-up's power to make things better for myself.

Eventually, all these women began to realize that until they were willing to consistently tell themselves nothing but the truth, they would continue to risk hitting the breaking point.

HARD TRUTHS

As women who have been through this process develop the habit of honesty, they discover all kinds of interesting and useful (though socially inappropriate) information about themselves. I, for example, learned that many of the academic goals I had once aspired to (because they sounded impressive) were actually things I didn't care about at all. They would look great on a *curriculum vitae*, but they bored me. I wanted to read novels a lot more than I wanted to read most scholarly monographs. Here are some other examples of startling truths I heard in my interview research:

Helen, a homemaker and mother of three preschoolers, used to lock herself in the bathroom and cry when her children's demands pushed her past her physical and emotional limits. She had no idea what was wrong, because according to the criteria she had learned growing up, her life was perfect. In Helen's family, it was understood that *all* women loved *all* children, and wanted nothing more than to care for a passel of little ones

24 hours a day, 365 days a year. Helen was genuinely surprised when she realized that, while she loved each of her children as a person, she didn't particularly enjoy the company of children in general. In fact, she was sick of it. She didn't want any more babies, and she could hardly wait until her children went off to school and gave her some free time during the days.

Georgia was a high-powered management consultant. She arrived at the office by six o'clock every morning and did not leave until 10:00 P.M. at the earliest. She was one of the firm's best managers. The experienced consultants at her firm looked up to her, and the young interns idolized her. One summer, for no obvious reason, Georgia began to feel exhausted and unhappy at work. She secretly scheduled a medical checkup and a psychiatric examination, which failed to pinpoint what was wrong. It took Georgia several months to admit that even though she loved her job, she was carrying an inner loneliness that had come close to consuming her. When Georgia finally acknowledged this, she found out more "shocking" things about herself. For example, she thrilled to the idea of having a man in her life. She liked cooking. She loved babies. She yearned to putter around in a garden. In short, Georgia, the star consultant, was also a closet homemaker.

Carrie had just joined the marketing department at a Fortune 500 firm. She was ecstatic about getting the job, but after a few weeks, she found herself waking up with a sick feeling in her stomach. "I loved the work," she told me. "I couldn't figure out why I was so stressed." It took a few more weeks, and some honest digging into her own thoughts and feelings, before Carrie realized what was wrong. Although she was new at the company, she understood how it operated far better than the manager of her department. "I had dreamed that this man would be my mentor," she said. "I felt much safer thinking that he was much more competent than I was, but the plain truth was that I understood the work better." Once she had identified the problem, Carrie developed a good relationship with her boss, and he quickly recognized her as a star player. When he was transferred to another department a year later, he recommended Carrie as his replacement.

And so it went, life story after life story. When it came down to the bedrock truth, Lana realized that her boss's subtle but constant sexual innuendos had made her office a frightening place for her. Connie acknowledged that she had been suicidally depressed at her wedding because she was deeply in love—not with the bridegroom, but with the maid of honor. Roxanne admitted to herself that she felt underpaid and overworked in her job in the graphics department of an advertising firm.

Antonia found that she was sick and tired of caring for her aging father, who had Alzheimer's disease, with no help from her three brothers.

The reason all these women had lost track of their true selves was that those selves were somehow unacceptable to the important people in these women's lives, and to their society in general. It is a very frightening thing to embrace a self whom others may reject. Since the paradox of female role definition ensures that some aspect of a woman's true self will always be socially unacceptable, embracing that self in the context of our culture *invariably* requires a great deal of courage.

The women I spoke with who had been through the process repeatedly had courage to spare—much more than I did. Many of their stories left me in awe. They were not nearly as impressed by their own bravery as I was. These women invariably told me, "I just did what I had to do." One woman of fifty-seven, who had been widowed with five teenage children at the age of forty-two and gone on to get a Ph.D. and become a successful entrepreneur in not one but two professional fields, said of her own achievements, "What else was I supposed to do?" I could think of plenty of alternatives, including a complete nervous breakdown, but she couldn't. "I have to be true to who I am," she told me. "Even if there had been an 'easier' way, I don't think I could have done it without damaging my self-concept."

Women who had been through the breaking point were often so open to "hard truths" that they could scare the beejeebies out of other people. These were the women who saw right through everyone's facade, including mine ("You say you're doing research on women's roles, but really you're just trying to figure out what the hell is happening to you, right?"). Often, these people's friends and family saw such truth-telling as scandalous, or at the very least unnecessarily harsh. But the reason these women had developed the habit of telling the truth had nothing to do with harshness. They refused to operate through false selves partly because they had found that a woman in this society *can't* fulfill all the "false self" requirements, but mostly because they had learned that acting in synchrony with the true self was the only way for them to give or receive genuine compassion.

THE WAY OF COMPASSION:
NOURISHING THE TRUE SELF

The women I spoke to who had found their true selves through the exercise of laser-like honesty had also learned that the only environment in which the true self can thrive is a very gentle one. A universal human be-lief, spanning the differences among culture, gender, race, and all other forms of diversity, is the conviction that love is the natural environment of the true self—*anyone's* true self. Honesty cuts a clear path to the true self, but if that self finds itself in a cruel or condemnatory environment, it will disappear again. The process of "re-creation" is all about construct-ing a life in which the true self can thrive. To do that, a woman has to disown all the negative judgments her true self receives from society and stay firmly grounded in a position of acceptance and compassion toward that self.

This is an enormously difficult challenge, because (as this entire book should have made clear) social institutions, from the family to the nation, usually adopt an antagonistic and manipulative position toward women's true selves. Take something as simple as the shape of a woman's body. We are all born with different sets of genes, which, according to innu-merable studies, are the primary factor in establishing our physical char-acteristics. But at every point in history, society has created an image of the "ideal" female body, which is always rather unusual, and is often something that does not occur in nature at all.

When I was doing research for my undergraduate thesis on Chinese women, I met a few old ladies whose feet had been bound in the tradi-tional Chinese way, breaking and twisting the foot bones, causing untold anguish, crippling the women—but making them look the way their so-ciety said they were "supposed" to. We've already seen how nineteenth-century American and European women forced themselves into organ-squashing corsets. Do these body-altering practices seem strange to you? Most American women would say so—and yet virtually every women's magazine you can find on the rack at your local supermarket contains instructions about how *you* can achieve a body image just as un-usual and rigid. In our culture, of course, the main idea is that women should be thin, thin, thin. This comes naturally to a very small minority. Even when American women are thin, the vast bulk of them (and I do *not* mean that literally) believe they are too fat. It's like a bunch of Saint Bernard dogs insisting that they should look like greyhounds. Rochelle, who seemed plenty thin to me, had some interesting insights on this issue.

Rochelle, 30

After I had my first child, I had trouble losing weight. I'm five foot eight and I weigh about 150. I didn't like to be over 135. I feel better at this weight, and I'm a lot stronger and healthier, but I don't look model-thin.

So anyway, I kept trying to lose the weight, but I wanted to nurse my baby, and every time I'd start dieting, I would stop producing milk. Then the baby would get hungry, and she'd cry and fuss. I felt so terrible, really guilty, for not having enough milk. I couldn't stand the thought of my daughter going hungry.

Then one day it hit me. What was the difference between her going hungry and me going hungry? Was there going to be some magic day when all of a sudden my little girl would be old enough to start going hungry all the time? I would never starve someone I loved, or stop loving them because of how much they weighed. Why was I doing those things to myself?

Of course, the "role" our culture "writes" for females doesn't stop at prescribing exactly how a woman should look. It goes on to detail just about everything she should do, say, and believe. Try to go through a single day with your focus on caring for the true self, rather than filling these social requirements. If you get through even a couple of hours, you will realize why women who have done it told me that the "habit" of compassion toward the true self was even harder to develop than the habit of honesty. A woman who is consistently loving toward her own true self risks being castigated as a heretic, an outlaw, a traitor to both sides of the holy war, and a threat to civilization as we know it. For example, consider what happened when the women I mentioned in the past few pages decided to "re-create" their lives in a way that nourished their true selves. Gloria, without the cigarettes that had calmed her for so long, rebelled against the norms of her very wealthy, very "proper" neighborhood.

Gloria, 40

I started thinking about a lot of things, like . . . that little girl who was molested [at the party I attended.] I thought about the way everyone I knew ignored the fact that people were suffering, that maybe they could do something to help. I started talking about it to my friends, and they all started avoiding me. One day I got so angry I just couldn't take it anymore. I got a ladder, climbed up on my roof, and stood there screaming, "I've had it! I'm angry! I'm so f——ing angry!"

After this incident, Gloria stopped blandly agreeing with her friends at the country club. Because she could not bear to play her role as her social circle had "written" it, she soon earned a reputation as an "unstable, mentally ill, and dangerous person."

Suzanne cared for her AIDS-stricken husband until his death, after which she immediately started dating and fell madly in love with a man who had admired her from afar for years. Sam's family was scandalized, saying that it "didn't look right" for Suzanne to become involved so soon after Sam's death. Suzanne, having learned to stand firm in the face of social pressure, didn't pay the slightest attention to them. She is now happily remarried.

Lana filed a complaint against her sexually harassing boss. He fired her, and she filed a lawsuit. At that, four more women stepped forward with similar stories about the same man. The case has not yet gone to trial, but the boss in question will think twice before making sexual overtures to another female employee. Lana went back to business school and is now in a much better job. Connie found that she could not force herself to consummate her marriage. She finally confessed to her new husband that while she loved him as a friend, she was romantically and sexually attracted to women. The marriage was annulled, and Connie felt free to acknowledge her real feelings for the first time in her life. Roxanne quit her job at the advertising firm and became a successful graphics consultant for several companies—including the one she had just left. Antonia drove her father to her older brother's house, told her brother she'd be back for Dad in a week, and took off for a much-needed vacation.

My own story, again, is similar. During my years at the breaking point, I had set up a huge number of life structures that felt antagonistic and damaging to my true self. I thought I was being heroic and self-sacrificing—and deep down, I always expected some kind of reward for being so "good." Actually, I did get a lot of rewards: honors, friendships, jobs, titles. The only problem was that they weren't the rewards my true self really wanted. After my *satori* experience, I began to realize that forcing myself to work slavishly in the pursuit of things I didn't really want wasn't heroism at all. It was, to put it bluntly, stupidity.

After my *satori* experience, I could see that in order to really care for my true self, I was going to have to make some changes. My professional and personal obligations were overwhelming me, partly because I would run roughshod over my real desires in order to fulfill them. My husband and I, both in our late twenties, were in tenure-track positions at the university where both our fathers had worked. We were just a few months of hard work away from lifetime security in these comfortable jobs.

The only problem was that neither John nor I enjoyed academia. I love learning sociological theories, and I love applying them, but when I tried to teach them I always found myself veering off the subject and into a discussion of my students' actual lives. John has a passion for Asian cultures and languages—but for diving right into them, not for teaching them to non-Asians in tidy little classrooms. However, we both found teaching an absolute joy compared to dealing with the petty disagreements that are so typical of faculty politics in universities everywhere. Shortly after my *satori* experience, John and I started discussing how we really felt about the prospect of staying in our current jobs *for the rest of our lives*. It was a frightening thought. Although everything looked peachy on the surface, we both felt that our true selves were slowly dying in our work environment. We tried to adjust, but it just made us more miserable. In the end, we both decided to quit our jobs.

People at the university assumed that this was some kind of ploy we were acting out to get better salaries or more nifty-sounding titles or something along those lines. They assumed we had no intention of actually leaving; several of them told me so to my face. I don't think they even imagined how absolutely wonderful it felt for me to stop fighting my true self and leave the university. I literally felt as though I'd been trapped in a suit of plate armor that began to fall away, piece by piece, the day I decided to resign. I slept better than I had in years.

Of course, there were some rather sticky issues to deal with, like, for example, the fact that John and I did not have alternative jobs waiting for us. In fact, we weren't even looking, right at first. We decided to figure out what we wanted to do (an idea that had never occurred to us during our headlong rush for achievement) and then see if we could somehow make some money at it. The upshot was that I started turning out articles and books (like this one) meant for a nonacademic audience. It was similar to the writing I'd done in graduate school, but shorter on terms like phenomenological ethnography and epistemological relativism. For his part, John got heavily involved in helping to rebuild war-torn Cambodia. I've got to tell you, these are not the career choices you want to make if you're looking to pull in a fortune over the short term. For several long months John and I both worked flat-out doing work we loved, with no reliable income. We were both terrified by the uncertainty of it all, but that didn't stop us from having a great time. It was kind of like bungee jumping, only it lasted a whole lot longer.

Naturally, almost everyone we knew was horrified by our lack of responsible behavior. Friends and relatives appealed to our sense of shame.

They pointed out the fickle and bohemian nature of our decision, be-moaned the destruction we were bringing down on the heads of our in-nocent children, stressed the abnormality of the life we were leading, and, above all, told us that *this was simply not the way things were done.*

From what I've learned in interviews, I'd say that this is pretty much what any woman can expect, should she begin to change her life out of compassion for her true self. To go back to the examples given earlier in this chapter:

Gloria, the woman whose country-club friends had urged her not to report their child-molesting relative, found herself living among enemies when she went ahead and turned him in. Suzanne's in-laws berated and then rejected her for marrying another man after her husband Sam died of AIDS. Lana's boss, who had harassed her at work, accused her of cre-ating a "conspiracy" to destroy him. Virtually everyone in Connie's life labeled her a pervert, and both her parents and her ex-husband's family denounced her for "messing up their lives." (Interestingly, the man who was briefly Connie's husband, and who genuinely loved her, didn't join in the name-calling. He and Connie are still close friends.) Antonia's brothers and their wives called each other in a flurry of disapproval when she "abandoned" her elderly father for a week and "imposed" on her brothers to help with his care.

I must tell you that where the re-creation of women's lives is con-cerned, this is par for the course. After seeing what other women have gone through, I count myself very, very, very lucky to have had my hus-band as my ally in caring for my true self. Such allies are hard to find. The simplest attempt a woman may make to care for her true self is likely to be seen by those around her as a deliberate attack on other people's happiness. If you ever set out to "re-create" your own life, prepare to be labeled willful, mean, pushy, demanding, and, above all, selfish.

Selfishness is the cardinal sin a woman can commit in our society. "Selflessness" is the ideal we are supposed to strive for. Often, this trans-lates into an injunction for women to continue to abandon, stifle, dis-tort, belittle, or destroy their true selves. The veterans of various breaking points I spoke to saw this type of "selflessness" as worse than useless. Every one of them had made sincere efforts—often Herculean ones—to serve social systems by extinguishing the needs of their true selves. These efforts not only had robbed them of the opportunity to simply *be*, but also had robbed everybody else of their genuine presence. Women who are antagonistic to their true selves are angry, anguished, and unable to connect with others except as their obsequious slaves or their brutal overseers (and where you see one of these extremes, the other is always somewhere close by). When a woman begins to extend compassion toward her true self, she is able to perceive and genuinely nourish the true selves of others.

Celeste, who had just graduated from high school when I interviewed her, had already figured this out.

Celeste, 18

I remember the first time I went on an airplane and they gave the emergency instructions. The flight attendant was talking about using the oxygen masks, and she started to say, "Anybody who is traveling with small children . . ." I was sure they were going to say that mothers should take care of their families first. But it was exactly the opposite. They said for the moms to put on their own masks first. I was surprised. It's like, "Wait a minute! The mom *never* comes first!" But then, when you think about it, it's totally obvious. How can you take care of somebody else if you can't breathe yourself?

By the same token, a woman who has lost or savaged her own true self has very little ability to protect and care for the true selves of others. Beneath her polite smile and ingratiating manner, others will feel the woman's desperate need for honesty and compassion, her anger at the systems that have denied her access to her true self, and her grief at the long deprivation she has already suffered.

THE INTERSECTION OF HONESTY AND COMPASSION

When I speak to groups about the necessity of honesty and compassion in caring for the true self, I always get the same question: "What if you're in a situation where you can't be loving and honest at the same time?" The answer that comes from the experiences of women I interviewed is that the true self exists and operates at a line of intersection where honesty and compassion are identical. In fact, *when you find that you can't be honest and compassionate at the same time, it's a good clue that you may be operating from a "false" self.*

Alexandra, 52

My mother used to tell me that it wasn't nice to say things that hurt other people's feelings. It took me a long time to learn that in the end, the truth is always kinder than an untruth. I've been hurt much more by people being "nice" than by people telling me the truth. You don't have to be cruel to be truthful, but lying is always cruel in the end.

I heard stories about people who used the badge of "honesty" to be overtly vicious. For example, Rhonda's mother continually reminded her that she was unattractive and stupid, claiming that she was only trying to help Rhonda live her life "realistically." Rosalie's husband filled out "performance reviews" that minutely detailed every conceivable imperfection in his wife's housekeeping skills. Brittany, a high school student, had a group of friends who made it their personal mission to inform certain other girls that they would never be "popular." A group of male professors at the college where Karen worked decided that it was their obligation to "help" female faculty members by being especially harsh and critical of their teaching methods. Like these examples, a good deal of the criticism that is aimed at women rides under the banner of "honesty."

The difference between this kind of criticism and the honesty that liberates the true self must be felt to be understood. Compassionate truth, even when it is critical, always creates a sense of relief, openness, and hope ("Oh, now I see what's wrong, and I can change that!"). Cruelty creates pain, causes people to close up in order to protect themselves, and leads straight to despair. Many women I spoke to had consciously learned to discount the destructive attacks people made on them, even when those attacks were said to be "honest."

Even more common were stories about women who were taught to be "loving" by stifling their desire to claim the truth. Women who decided to be honest about their husband's philandering, their children's drug addiction, their subordinate's poor performance on the job, or their boss's embezzling were instantly attacked for failing to be "nicer" and "kinder." But women who had finally been reunited with their true selves believed that lying to protect the false selves of others isn't "nice" at all. It merely allows those others to become more and more separate from their own true selves—a condition these women recognized as exquisitely painful.

Though women who cared for their true selves were often accused of trying to ruin other people's lives, in the long run their honesty and compassion toward their own true selves also benefited the true selves of others. You can feel this when you talk to women who have learned to live on the common ground where honesty and compassion meet. You can tell that the thousand facades human beings are taught to wear, the strict social roles we are taught to play, are unnecessary and rather silly to such women. On the other hand, when you're around people who have learned to be honest and compassionate to their own unique true selves, you can feel in your bones that your own true self has reached a safe haven. You know that, should you care to allow your self out of its holding cell and into the light of day, women like these will accept and welcome it.

CARING FOR THE TRUE SELF:
THE FOUR-STEP WALTZ

I found that each woman had her own set of techniques for "rewriting" her social role when the pressures of society began to push her away from her true self. She used these techniques whenever they began to feel even the slightest hint of the lost, confused, exhausted sensation that accompanies a double bind. All these techniques shared four central steps, a sort of waltz-step pattern of moving away from social settings, articulating the pressures to create "false selves," identifying the needs of the true self, and then stepping back into society. None of the steps will work in the absence of the "basic rules" of honesty and compassion, but for women who had decided to lovingly face the truth, they are extremely useful. Here is how some women described this gentle "dance."

1. GETTING AWAY FROM IT ALL

When social pressures begin to push a woman toward the breaking point, she usually doesn't feel it happening. Without really knowing how, she finds herself doing things that her true self doesn't like at all. "I went in to ask for a raise," one woman tells me, "and I ended up letting my boss saddle me with another project—one I don't have time for." "I called my sister to talk because I was feeling really exhausted," another woman says, "and all of a sudden I realized that I'd agreed to baby-sit all her children for ten days." A third woman muses, "I never wanted to work in a big company, but once I got to business school it just seemed like everyone was doing it, and I was afraid that if I started my own company instead, everyone would think I was a failure."

The reason women may end up playing roles they don't want and don't like is that social drama has enormous power to draw us in. We know our parts very well, and when we hear our "cues," it's almost a reflexive reaction to get right into character.

Monica, 40

I'm a very tough, realistic employee. . . . I do performance appraisals and design training programs, and I'm damn good at it. But for some reason, when I'm talking with people who are higher up than me in the firm, I get completely tongue-tied and insecure. I'll have these great ideas about how things have to change, but when I'm talking to the higher-ups I start to stutter like an idiot and forget what I was going to say. I have this overwhelming need to please them, and it drowns out everything else. It drives me crazy!

We are all conditioned to be sensitive to other people's approval, to "forget what we were going to say" when social circumstances are hostile to our true selves. Psychologists have performed experiments in which human beings prove to be highly susceptible to social pressures—to the point of distorting their own perceptions to match the perceptions of the group.[2] Sociologists use the phrase "social contagion" to describe the phenomenon that makes people panic when they're in a room full of frightened people, or cry when they see someone else in pain. It's hard for anyone, male or female, to stay calm when everyone on board the U.S.S. *Society* is half-hysterical with fear and anxiety. Women, who (either by nature or training) tend to be especially attuned to others, may find other people's moods seeping into their own experience until the boundaries between their feelings and the needs and demands of others become blurred and elusive.

A useful first step to rediscovering the true self, then, is to get away from social pressure by literally putting geographic distance between yourself and other people—*all* other people. When your socially constructed "role" begins to feel like reality, it's very useful to get away from your usual scenery and the "actors" around you who don't know they are acting. Every time I interviewed a woman who had learned to care for her true self, I heard another strategy for getting away from it all. Some women found sanctuary in their cars, driving for hours just to enjoy the freedom and solitude of the road. Others went for long walks, took frequent vacations, or hired a sitter to take their children to the park so that they could be alone in their own houses.

Polly, 80

When my boys were small we had a farm—nothing fancy, just a few cows and chickens, and a field of corn. In the summer the cornstalks would grow so tall that you could walk between them and no one would even know you were there.

By the time I was twenty-two, I had four children. Being a farm wife is hard work. I did all the cooking and cleaning and caring for the children myself, plus milking the cows, taking care of the vegetable garden and about a thousand other chores. Sometimes all that work would get to be too much for me. Those times, I would leave the children in a safe place and run out into the cornfield. After a while I'd hear them calling, but they never did find me. I would stay under the corn until I could remember who I was. The one piece of advice I have for every woman is: find yourself a "cornfield," whether it's the top of a tree or a corner of your bedroom or an island in the Caribbean. Have someplace you can go to remember who you are.

For some women, going off by themselves wasn't enough. Even when they were alone, they could hear the voices of other "actors" in their social drama—parents, partners, friends, and enemies—clamoring in their heads. These voices constantly harped on them to remain "socially acceptable," no matter what the cost to the true self.

TIME OFF WORK

Getting away from it all can be particularly necessary—and difficult—in the modern work environment. Any employee who brings up "personal" issues, like her need to spend time with her children or her desire to care for an ailing relative, is likely to be looked upon as "unprofessional." Bosses and colleagues present tasks as absolute requirements, and many women are afraid that if they suggest time- or labor-saving alternatives, they will lose credibility.

Iris, 30

I spend about 50 percent of my time at work writing memos and reports that go straight to my boss. She's the only one who ever sees them, and most of the time she doesn't have time to read them. She'll call me into her office, we'll sit down with one of my reports on her desk between us, and she'll say, "Tell me what's in this thing." It's *so stupid* to keep putting all this time into writing the reports. I've sort of hinted that maybe we could just have the debriefing meetings and skip the written reports, but she won't hear of it. This is the way it's "supposed" to be done, and that's that. It just kills me to think of all the things I could be doing with that wasted time.

At the business school where I teach, I hear stories like this often, from both men and women. Redundant or inefficient work procedures are fine if you have all the time in the world, but most employees (contrary to modern theory) have actual lives outside of the office, and they would like some time to live them. Women with small children or other time-consuming personal obligations are often amazingly creative at finding ways to accomplish necessary work with more efficient procedures, saving some precious time:

Cora, 35

I take the concept of "quality time" very seriously, and I think if it applies at home, it should apply at work. . . . When I started out [in the advertising business] I used to find ways to simplify processes by using phones and faxes instead of sitting in endless meetings . . . [but] I found that when they saw I had free time, my employers would just ask more of me. So I kept my output just about level with everyone else's. . . . When I was first put in as a department manager I brought all my subordinates together and told them that we were going to rethink operations to be more efficient, and that if their work was satisfactory, *any time they saved was their own.* Our department has the best performance in the company. And the women are best at making operations more efficient. They have to be. They don't have time to fool around.

In order to work intensely and well, the employed women I spoke to placed even more emphasis than unemployed women on the need to get away from the obligations and demands of their everyday lives. "You have to leave work sometime," said one mother, who worked at an architectural firm. "And you must remember that for a woman, being at home is not the opposite of being at work. It's just another workplace. You have to make time to get away from it all—and I mean get away from it *all.*"

Ironically, women told me that when they become unshakably committed to taking regular vacations, simplifying work procedures, finding help with child care, and refusing to fret about housework, they tend to perform better, not worse, than when they tried to run as fast as they could, twenty-four hours a day, seven days a week.

Laura Ann, 45

I'm telling you, hon, I tried it both ways. You can't sprint life; it's a long run, and you want to stay in it as long as you can. You do better going slow and steady and stopping when you're tired. You got to get away from all those voices saying, You gotta do this, You gotta do that. You have to find some peace.

It took some time for women to still the "voices" that constantly reminded them of their obligations. Even when they weren't at work, women worried about tasks still unfinished. Even when their children were sleeping, they were racked with guilt that they might not be doing enough as mothers. The nagging voice had become a part of them, even when no one else was talking.

Because of this, aside from physically moving away from pressure situations, some of the women I interviewed had devised mental images to help them separate themselves from society's demands.

Cheryl, 46

I pretend that I have a remote control that can stop time, like the "pause" button on my VCR. I imagine myself pointing the control at my whole life and stopping everything, while I sit and figure out what to do.

Sue, 35

I have a Tupperware shelf in my mind. I can take something that's bothering me and imagine myself putting it in the dish, covering it up, putting it in the cupboard, and walking away.

Donna, the woman in Chapter 8 whose husband died of cancer, held on to the feeling she had experienced when she decided she was "already dead":

Donna, 36

To this day, I remind myself that if I were dead, other people would still find a way to live their lives. Their happiness doesn't depend on me doing whatever they say. I am free to feel whatever I'm really feeling, and do what I need to take care of myself.

All of these strategies have the same objective: to make space for a return to the moment of *satori*, when a woman encounters her true self apart from the pressures of society. Polly's "cornfield" is the equivalent of the pilgrim's mountain retreat; a place of stillness, where the demands of society are hushed and a woman can look steadily at the truth. Women I spoke to who had been through enough breaking points to have learned ways of avoiding them said that whatever her strategy, each woman *must* have a place, physically and psychologically, where she is free to simply be. From this place, she can move to the next step: identifying and articulating the forces that have begun to push her toward the breaking point.

2. ARTICULATING THE ISSUES

As we have seen, the only way to resolve a paradox is to step away from the whole system of logic that created it. Getting away from social pressures buys a woman a little space and time to do that, but the real movement away from the paradox of female role definition occurs when a woman *articulates* what is happening to her.

Because most women share the value system that creates women's roles, we're often unable to articulate the double binds it imposes on us. We may know that something is bothering us, that we feel confused, tired, inadequate, and off-center, but we are at a loss to say exactly why. At best, we may be able to spot the general area from which the problem is coming: the thought of going to work fills us with leaden unwillingness, or the baby's cries have our nerves stretched thin and raw, or our partner's sulky moods fill us with a vague sense of guilt. The dynamics of the situation, because they are socialized into us so deeply, may not be clear to us. All we know is that we don't like the "script" we're acting out, but we can't think how to improve on it.

The woman who articulates the paradoxical pressures she is facing "moves" the problem from inside her own skin to the world around her. "I'm not the problem," she states clearly. "This is a *ridiculous script*." Women whose work situations were unbearable often told me that once they stopped thinking *they* were the problem, it became suddenly clear that they had been trying to do contradictory things.

Elisabeth, 38

I was getting very anxious, waking up at night feeling as though I were suffocating. . . . I especially hated work, and that was strange, because usually I love my job. . . . I realized that I'd committed to two projects that were supposed to take place at the same time, in two different geographic locations. I'd felt a little uneasy when I accepted the assignments, but I hadn't really consciously realized that it was *impossible* for me to do both these things. Consciously, I'd been thinking, "Boy, I'm really going to have to work hard," but, subconsciously, I think I knew that the two jobs were totally incompatible.

Chelsea, 50

I was trying very hard to be a "better wife," and I was taking all my cues from [my husband]. I had to realize that he wasn't making reasonable demands before I could feel better about myself, and stand up to him. Our relationship actually improved a lot once I got that straight.

A woman who looks objectively at the contradictory roles she is being asked to play can see that her biggest mistake has been internalizing these pressures and forcing them on herself. Once that issue has been articulated, the woman can feel free to stop using discipline, deadlines, or drugs to enhance her energy or muffle her discontent. She'll realize that *although she does not have the power to fulfill society's paradoxical expectations, she does have the power to stop trying.*

Whitney, 43

When I start to feel crazy, I go into my basement and paint for a while. It's quiet down there and nobody really bothers me. I'll let the problems just float around in my head for a while, not really trying to solve them. Then, when I'm relaxed, I'll take out a piece of paper and write down all the problems, all the things I think I should be doing, all the things other people think I should be doing. Once it's all on paper, I can see that nobody could be expected to do it all. On a piece of paper, the problems look smaller. I can walk away from them for a while, and come back again when I can make sense of them.

Other women told me that their problems shrank to manageable size when they went out rowing, talked to a good friend or wise relative, or spent time in nature. The idea of tracing the source of the pain through writing was particularly useful to women who were "double-bound" by paradoxical demands. Double binds are immensely confusing, and "catching" them on paper is one of the most effective ways to escape their baffling effects.

Lydia, 51

I was very depressed for a while. I was convinced I was a terrible wife and that my husband was going to leave me. My therapist had me write down the things I thought a good wife did. Then we went over the list together, and she pointed things out: "Do you see how if you did *this*, there is no way you could also do *that*?" At the end of the hour I was crying, I was so relieved. I held up the paper and told her, "I'm not crazy after all. *This* is crazy!"

Articulating paradox always brings this sense of relief, whether it is done on paper, in conversation, or through careful thought (although I'm warning you, it's extremely hard to simply think through a double bind without being caught up in it).

REASSIGNING RESPONSIBILITY

When women step away from double binds by articulating them, they often notice something peculiar. Almost universally, they realize they have assumed responsibility for things they *cannot* control, while rejecting responsibility for things they *can* control. Society trains women to do this and applauds them for it. Almost every culture on earth contains assumptions that women are responsible for a wide variety of social "problems" over which they have no control. This is obvious in American popular culture. For example, *The Rules* (the best-selling how-to guide for women I quoted in Chapter 4) comments:

> Of course, the playboy type who falls in love with you because you did *The Rules* will automatically mend his ways. He will want to be monogamous . . . Do *The Rules* and even the biggest playboy can be all yours! [3]

The implicit message here is that if a man isn't monogamous, it's because the woman in his life did something wrong. Rather than being responsible for his own behavior, the man is controlled by "his" woman. Fein and Schneider comment that every woman should take it for granted that a man will want sex as soon and as often as possible. "It's your job to slow them down," they declare. [4] I interviewed more than one rape victim who had seen her rapist go free on the basis of *that* bit of homespun folk wisdom.

Unfortunately, popular culture is not the only source of American norms that tends to focus on what women do to "create" male behavior. Studies of abused wives, for example, focused for years on figuring out the psychological problems of the women—while no one thought of wondering what was wrong with the abusive husbands. And research on everything from criminal activity to homosexuality has dwelt almost obsessively on what people's *mothers* "did wrong."

On the other hand, it is generally accepted in our society that women have no options when it comes to charting their own course in life against the expectations of the people around them. "You *can't* stay home from the family reunion," women are told. "It would kill Mother!" Actually, you *can* stay home from the family reunion without any difficulty whatsoever, and if killing Mother were that easy, she'd be dead by now. "I have to make the boss happy," we tell ourselves, oblivious to the fact that we don't have the ability to single-handedly ensure the boss's happiness, and that we don't even have to try if we don't want to.

There may be consequences attached to "re-creating" the script for one's own life, but the consequences of caring for the true self are always better than the consequences of abandoning it. Women who have gone beyond the breaking point are very clear about taking responsibility for the things they can control, and rejecting responsibility for things they cannot.

LaShawn, 38

You gotta be real clear where the problems are coming from. I mean, you gotta see it clear as crystal. Sometimes it's your problem, sometimes it's somebody else's; and if it's somebody else's you can try till you die to fix it, and it ain't gonna work. If it's your problem, you can nag all your life to have someone else fix it for you, and that won't work either.

By reassembling the components of control and responsibility so that they correspond with each other, women free themselves to fully comprehend the insanity of the demands being made on them, without internalizing it. They can face the rather terrifying fact that their society is crazy, because they themselves attain an inner sense of sanity and stability. They do not "own" the paradoxical demands that have deadlocked them, but they do "own" the capability of walking away, rejecting other people's negative judgments of them, and inventing for themselves a social role that makes sense. They are ready to find the pattern for re-creating their lives by consulting the true self.

3. LISTENING FOR THE TRUE SELF

Once you've "walked away" from the U.S.S. *Society* and concluded that you don't like the way your part is "written," what comes next? This is a sticky problem for many people who are trying to improve the quality of American women's lives. A lot of activism is devoted to criticizing exist-ing social systems. That process is useful and necessary. It's also easy. Coming up with a useful alternative—now, that's a challenge. Since our society doesn't have an existing model of a balanced, fulfilling "role" for women, the only place women at the breaking point can go for ideas is the creative, unique, and unorthodox territory of the true self.

Women who had been through the whole process often spoke in terms of "listening" for their true selves. Some talked about "feeling for" their innermost thoughts and sensations. A few said they went "looking for" them. But "listen" was far and away the favorite word women used to describe accessing their true selves.

One of the primary objectives of exploitative social systems, including the holy war over women's roles, is to drown out the voices of true selves so that people will do whatever is necessary to preserve the system. The true self has a gentle voice. When a woman is involved in the turmoil of social contagion, she may not even know it's there. But once she has found a quiet space and hushed the voices in her mind, she may begin to hear a mental "sound" that is at once utterly familiar and completely original. It speaks very clearly, but very softly. It whispers to the woman things she has always known, but has been afraid to know she knows. It tells her which things in her life are destroying her, bit by bit; it sings to her about dreams she thought were dead and buried. It is the sweetest sound she has ever heard, as seductive, and as dangerous, as the kiss of a forbidden lover.

Claudia, 25

I was engaged to a boy from my high school. We'd been dating since we were about twelve, and everyone knew we'd get married as soon as we could. He was crazy about me, and I guess I just accepted what he and everybody else thought I should do.

One night about a week before we were going to get married, I couldn't sleep. I felt really strange, like I wanted to cry but I didn't know why. I got up and drove my parents' car out of the city to a place where I could see the stars. Then I got out and sat on the roof of the car and just sort of let go of everything. I sat there for hours. I cried a lot. I started to realize that I had just been going along with what people wanted from me. Just before the sun came up, I finally admitted that I didn't want to get married. I realized I *never had* wanted to marry Jeff. I decided that I would just call the wedding off.

I can't describe how happy I felt at that moment. It was like this tremendous burden disappeared. I almost felt like I was drunk; I was laughing and crying at the same time. I felt like I could fly.

The relief, the joy, and the comfort Claudia felt are typical of people who manage to detach from other people's demands enough to hear the voice of the true self. When the "space" traveler walks away from the *Society* and sits down to write her own script, her universe expands dramatically. A tremendous sense of freedom comes with this action, and also a level of emotional, psychological, physical, and spiritual comfort that women who have abandoned their true selves may never have felt. Where the breaking point is characterized by a no-win combination of suffocation and loneliness, identifying with the true self creates a no-lose mixture of openness and connection.

Of course, this lasts only if a woman is brave enough to complete the fourth step to caring for her true self: returning to society with the rock-solid intention of protecting and nourishing the core identity she has finally found.

4. TAKING THE TRUE SELF HOME

The only reason we desert our true selves in the first place is to please other people. When a woman listens for the voice of her true self, then, she is almost guaranteed to hear something that will *not* please others. The true self pulls no punches. It has no manners whatsoever, and very little concern for what People In General will think of you if you start to take care of it. It will tell you flat-out that your marriage isn't working, that you want to quit business school and become a karate instructor, that you resent caring for a sick relative, that you hate your roommate's dog and quite possibly your roommate as well. Women, who are trained to please people above all else, often turn pale at the very thought of acting on these "improper" feelings.

For example, consider the task that confronted Claudia after that night when she sat on top of her parents' car, looked at the stars, and listened to her true self's voice at last.

Claudia, 25

Once I knew I didn't want to get married, *and that I didn't have to*, I felt like I was being reborn. But then the sun came up, and I thought about going back and telling everybody that I was calling off the wedding. I mean, my mother was living for this wedding. My friends had all made bridesmaid dresses. And poor Jeff! I couldn't stand the thought of telling him. I almost got in the car and drove to Canada to start a new life rather than face all that.

When the true self delivers such inconvenient messages, many women rush to muzzle it, intending to continue to live through false selves, rather than risk other people's negative reactions.

For example, Annette, a managerial trainer for a large electronics firm, hated her job. She was her department's token woman, and she ended up with all the extra work (committee meetings, special projects, customer relations) and all the extra pressure ("We're watching you to see if a woman can really do this job!") that tokenism often entails.

Annette was worn out. She was also having trouble with some of her subordinates, who felt that she was ambivalent about many aspects of her job. As Annette freely admitted to me, they were right. Whenever Annette got away from her job and began to listen for her true self, she could see that she was worn out and miserable. This was especially troubling to Annette because of the fact that a few years earlier, she had suffered from a serious form of cancer. The disease had gone into remission, but Annette was terrified that the heavy pressure of her job situation would lower her immunities and result in the cancer's return.

Every time she got away and figured this out, Annette planned to return to her job, express her concerns to a superior, and ask for a lighter workload. But she never carried through on her intentions. All it took was a comment from a coworker about the latest power struggle in the office, or a conversation with a friend who told her she'd better prove herself or the company would think twice about hiring women in the future, and Annette would be right back where she started. The instant she heard her "cue," she would go straight back to playing the role that had caused her so much pain. The last time I saw her, she was still overworked, anxious about her health, and discontented with her job.

The same kinds of pressures confront all of us as we attempt to be our true selves, to write our own roles in the context of a U.S.S. *Society* that seems to be coming apart. Everything in society pushes women, and pushes them hard, toward the false selves that serve to sustain the *Society*'s momentum and course. But women who have been to the breaking point know that the *Society* is going off in two contradictory directions, and that they will help no one by continuing to go along with it until it tears them apart. Once they have stepped away from society, disowned the demands of others, and listened for the voice of the true self, they prepare to move back into society with a set of objectives different from those of most people around them. This requires attention, skill, and bravery.

Augusta, 70

It's a hard thing, to find your center and hold it *no matter what*. People will do what they can to get you off course. You mustn't be vicious, of course, but you must hold firm. It has taken me a long lifetime to learn to hold firm to my center.

For women like Augusta, who have transcended the breaking point so many times that they know the process by heart, charting a course through the tangled, crowded, and dangerous melee we call society becomes their way of life. They know how to listen for the true self, and they know that no good can come of abandoning it or allowing it to be hurt.

As they set out to re-create a life that cares for their true selves, women eventually begin to see something more: that not a single one of us can live honestly and compassionately without profoundly affecting everything around us. The traveler who takes the course her true self desires generates a ripple in society that spreads far, far beyond her immediate environment. It will take her into places she never imagined. It will bring others to the point where they, too, may have to re-think and re-create their lives. In the end, no matter how insignificant a woman believes herself to be, caring for her own true self will change the world.

CHAPTER TEN

Changing the Rules of the Game

Joanie Stanwick is sitting across from me in her living room, plotting revolution.

"The people at my church don't hardly think an old widow like me is worth a wooden nickel," she says. "They think I'm used up and wore out. Well, I'm not."

Joanie is eighty years old. She has a tidy white bun on the top of her head and an expression of firm resolve in her bright black eyes.

She also has a plan.

"I'll tell you what I'm going to do," says Joanie, leaning forward and dropping her voice to a rough whisper, so that I find myself leaning toward her as well.

"I'm going to be . . . the Bingo caller!" She sits back and raises her head defiantly. "I'm going to be the first woman Bingo caller in our congregation."

Joanie beams at me, displaying false teeth as white and regular as the keys of a piano.

"Everyone looks up to the Bingo caller," she goes on. "And there's no reason a woman can't do it. I've already asked Albert to let me call the games, and I'm just gonna keep nagging him 'til he does. I can call Bingo as good as the next person."

I nod. Everything about Joanie communicates that she means business. There is no doubt in my mind that Albert, whoever he is, will either have to permit her to call the next Bingo game, or change his identity and leave the country.

Years ago, when I started my research, I would not have thought that this plan of Joanie Stanwick's meant much to anyone but her. Now I know better. Now I believe that Joanie, and millions of American women more or less like her, are in the process of quietly transforming the way Americans think, act, and perceive the universe. They are accomplishing this enormous task not *in spite* of our culture's tendency to trap women at the breaking point, but *because* of it. Having been torn, twisted, and suffocated by the contradictory ways our society tells them they must behave, these women know that they have been caught up in a game that is impossible to win. And so, in a countless variety of ways—small and large, simple and complex, public and private—they are setting out to change the rules. In short, they are "re-creating" American society.

GAMES WITHIN GAMES:
THE NATURE OF SOCIETY

Joanie Stanwick happens to have decided that she will make her particular mark in the area of her church's Bingo matches—something we all recognize as a game. But women who have been through the breaking-point process come to see that almost all social interactions are "games" of a sort. I don't mean this negatively. Games are not necessarily bad things; at their best they are one of the joys of life. I'm referring to the fact that all social systems depend on the same two elements necessary to create a game: an established goal, which everyone agrees is the object of the game, and a set of rules that limits the way one can achieve the goal.

For example, in American football, everyone agrees that a certain patch of turf is the goal for one team, and another patch is the goal for the opposite team. To score, each team must move a piece of inflated animal skin onto their patch of turf, while the other team tries to stop them. But getting to the goal counts only if you do it a certain way. For example, if one team took out an assortment of automatic weapons and killed everyone on the opposing team, they would almost certainly get the ball into their end zone, but most Americans (I hope) would not consider this great football.

Using guns in a football game sounds ridiculous, but the truth is that there are other "games" in which guns are allowed. War, for example, is not unlike football in that opposing teams are trying to move onto various patches of turf by incapacitating each other, and here, too, the players are supposed to follow the rules. A soldier who shoots an enemy soldier in the head is playing by the rules. A soldier who shoots a civilian is breaking them. Even though in both cases someone ends up dead, the first soldier might get a medal, while the second goes to jail.

There may come a moment when an individual soldier looks straight into the eyes of some other young man or woman who is "playing" for the opposing "team." Both soldiers may realize that neither of them has any reason to hate the other, that under different circumstances they might well have been friends. Nonetheless, they are expected to do their best to kill each other, because those are the Rules of the Game. If the soldiers happen to be tired of fighting, or have never really understood what the war is about, or simply don't want to kill, they may experience a kind of *satori*, a mental detachment in which they realize that they have an awareness, a consciousness, an identity outside of the society that set up the goals and designed the rules of this "game." This true self may balk at killing another human being for someone else's purposes—may, in fact, find the entire premise of a "fair war" to be tragically absurd.

Almost every aspect of society has the elements of a game, and almost every social game has its absurdities. In all areas of human life, from motherhood to medicine to marketing, people agree on the object of the game and the rules for achieving the goals. We have uniforms for these games, and we are expected to stay in uniform while we're playing. (A doctor or executive who showed up for work dressed in toe shoes and a tutu, for example, would be violating the understood "rules" to the point where she might forfeit her game entirely.) You probably participate in dozens of social games every day. I'm not saying that you're being disingenuous or trying to mess with people's minds; it's just that in order to function cooperatively, human beings *must* share common goals and common rules. Most of the games we play are set up to help us live together harmoniously, and by and large they work pretty well.

THE PILGRIM PLAYS THE GAME

In Asian legends, the pilgrim who goes to the mountain to seek *satori* does not necessarily live in isolation thereafter. The image of the lone hermit, sitting forever on the mountaintop, interacting only with the occasional acolyte who hikes through the thin air to hear words of wisdom, is the exception. More commonly, the enlightened pilgrim returns to society to live productively and cooperatively with others. However, after *satori* the pilgrim sees life differently. Having embraced the true self that exists apart from all social context, the pilgrim participates in social systems, but is aware of doing so *as a participant in a game,* rather than someone whose whole existence is invested in succeeding at one game or another. After finding the true self, the pilgrim follows Plato's injunction that "life must be lived as play."

This is one of the reasons I call the last phase of the breaking-point process "re-creation." It is a re-creation in the sense of constructing a new version of a person's identity and worldview, but it is also *recreation,* in the sense that those who reach this stage show the same kind of intense involvement and joyfulness that children do when they play.

THE AMERICAN PLAY ETHIC (OR LACK THEREOF)

Playing is vastly underrated by American culture. In our Puritan-founded society, having fun is considered unproductive, lazy, and trivial. (H. L. Mencken once defined Puritanism as "the haunting fear that somebody, somewhere, might be happy.") In actuality, playing can be very productive, wonderfully dynamic, and extremely important. Most of the women I interviewed who had become outstanding at something, from growing roses to teaching physics, had great fun doing their "work." They were almost ashamed to admit this, because in our culture, you're not supposed to be playing when you're working. Doing both at the same time is considered reprehensible if not impossible. But the truth is that people who are brilliant at what they do are usually having fun.

I've seen this principle affirmed many times while teaching at a business school, both by doing research on the psychology of "successful" people and by observing my students. My own most memorable lesson, however, came when I was studying Japanese. I had already spent several grueling years in Chinese classes, which filled me with anxiety and made my brain hurt very badly. Japanese is in a separate language family from either English *or* Chinese, so I set out to learn it with the kind of resignation a reconvicted felon must feel on the way back to the Big House. However, instead of learning Japanese in a classroom, I hired a tutor to come to our house in Tokyo, where we were living for the summer.

At the time, my fifteen-month-old daughter was in the "language explosion" stage of her development. She spent most of her days picking up language—any language. I watched the way she went about it. She sang nursery rhymes, lip-synched endless repetitions of the same *Sesame Street* videos, and babbled a lot, not minding that her pronunciation and syntax weren't exactly right. I decided to imitate this "play" method of language learning. Although my tutor, the inimitable Habuto-san, spent much of her summer laughing openly at me in a most un-Japanese fashion while I mangled jingles from Japanese advertising ("Eat Tanaka-brand eels! Yummy yummy yum!!"), I learned enough Japanese in six weeks to test into the third-year language course when I returned to Harvard—and my brain didn't hurt a bit.

All of this may explain why women who have been through the breaking point and begun to care for their true selves generally become more successful at their "work," whatever that may be. They have a clear conception of themselves as valid individuals outside of any social context, so that when they join in some activity, they tend to approach it in a loose, relaxed way that is often highly effective. They are also likely to pick the "games" that please or interest their true selves, instead of somebody else's version of an important or prestigious or serious way of life. The result is that they genuinely enjoy what they are doing, and tend to be very good at it.

Women who have reached the stage of "re-creating" their lives often use the word "play" when they talk about their daily activities. Bonnie told me she loved her job as a stockbroker, "because it's so fun to *play* the market." Natalie got a license to operate a day care center in her home when her own children were old enough for school, "because I missed *playing* with babies." Clarissa is an administrator of a university department, and loves "*playing* with the resources—scheduling, timing, personalities." Gabrielle operates a franchise for a national restaurant chain not because she needs the money (she got past that point years ago) but because "it's like *playing* a game or solving a puzzle; there are problems and you have to work out creative solutions—it's terrific fun."

What all these women have in common is not only a love for their work, but *the clear recognition that they are operating in the context of social "games," and that these games do not constitute absolute reality.* They work toward the goals and keep the rules of their various vocations, but they do so with the sort of detachment you see in some great athletes. "Well," they think, "I'm probably going to win some and I'm probably going to lose some, but, after all, it's just a game." The true self will remain every bit as lovable and valuable no matter what the outcome.

MISTAKING THE GAME FOR ABSOLUTE REALITY

In every game, there are many people who fall into the illusion that the game they are playing is absolute reality. The game of football is sufficiently "real" to many young men that they take steroids, risking heart attacks, deformation, sterility, and early death to do well on the field. To these players, achieving the goals of football—getting that piece of pigskin onto that patch of turf—takes precedence over the goal of keeping themselves safe and healthy. Back up a step and consider the "game" of cheerleading. The goal here is ostensibly for the cheerleader to help the team win, but an even more central goal is for the cheerleader to be acknowledged as a performer, one of society's Beautiful People. This "game" was sufficiently real for a woman in Texas to arrange the murder of another woman. The idea was that the dead woman's daughter would be too upset to make the cheerleading squad, ensuring a spot for the daughter of the murderer.

Society is made up of games within games within games, like those little Russian dolls that pop open to show a series of smaller dolls inside. At early levels, both cheerleading and football require their players to be reasonably successful at another game, the Education Game. The goal of this game is to get certain pieces of paper, known as diplomas or degrees. In order to win these prizes, students have to show up at the classroom and perform a large number of tasks, from doing long division to memorizing poetry. Some of these skills are useful to them in other games besides the Education Game, but many of them never will be. Nevertheless, learning to do them is a rule of the Education Game. I have known students who took this game so seriously that they threatened to kill themselves if they couldn't get the diploma of their choice. Frequently, the students themselves didn't care as much about the diploma as did their parents, who had mistaken the Education Game for absolute reality, giving or withholding support for their children depending on whether or not the students were succeeding in school.

This is understandable when you realize that a diploma can be enormously helpful for a player in the Career Game—and just about everybody plays the Career Game. It has many different versions. You can play the Corporate Executive Game, where the principal goals are money and prestige. You will have to do some actual work, but also a lot of jockeying with personalities in your company, to achieve these goals. Or you could play the Academic Game. This game is really fascinating because, while it can be very hard to play, it often has virtually no relationship to anything most people would call "real life." For example, I once met a professor who had just spent an entire year doing research on how one Chinese artist, who had been dead for some five hundred years, pronounced his name. For this effort he had won many prizes: a lifetime job, respect, and admiration from other people in his game.

Many people in the Academic Game think of that game as absolute reality. I've already mentioned how strongly my associates at Harvard encouraged me to get rid of my son, Adam, in one way or another. Once I'd decided against an abortion, they suggested everything from institutionalizing him to putting him up for adoption. This struck me as strange, especially after he was born—he was an absolutely delightful baby and has become an absolutely delightful child. But to a lot of people at Harvard, succeeding in the Academic Game seems like absolute success, and failing at it means absolute failure. I think they simply couldn't imagine that my son's life was worth living (much less taking *my* time and effort away from the Academic Game) if he couldn't play by the rules and achieve the goals of the game they had chosen.

Adam himself isn't interested in treating any social games as absolute reality. He loves school and works hard there, but he does his "work" as play, for the joy and fun of the activity and the thrill of learning, rather than for a diploma. He wouldn't know a diploma if it bit him on the leg. Large sums of money mean absolutely nothing to Adam. Positions and titles do not impress him. The thought of acting cruelly, either toward other people or toward himself, is anathema to him no matter what he might "win" for it. If you told Adam that he should put on a uniform and kill someone who had never done him any harm, he would think you were crazy. (Well, all right, he'd probably like the uniform—but the killing part is definitely out.) Since Adam was born—about eight years ago at this writing—the only goals I have seen him pursue are to care for his true self and the true selves of others. The only rules I have seen him follow are the rules of honesty and compassion.

REAL GOALS, REAL RULES

People who take social games like the Academic Game to be absolute reality will always consider my son, Adam, to be a loser, a lesser being. But women who have been through the whole breaking-point process, and reached the stage of re-creating their lives, know exactly where Adam is coming from. Whether they are fashion designers or stay-at-home moms or rocket scientists, these women "play" their roles with the same mixture of intense involvement and ebullient joy I see in Adam. They are willing to work within the rules of various social "games," and they are pleased when they achieve the goals of those games. But their real goal, like Adam's, is to care for the true self, and their real rules are honesty and compassion.

I thought about these women when I read an interview with Greg Louganis, the great American diver who won two gold medals in the Olympics even after he was diagnosed with AIDS. Greg's adoptive father, like many American men, had absorbed the belief that doing well at sports was necessary in absolute reality, rather than merely being the goal of a game. In the interview I read, Greg mentioned that as a child he was constantly trying (and failing) to please his father, who would insist that Greg continue to practice even when he was shivering and exhausted. On the other hand, years later, after his parents had divorced, Greg said he knew that no matter how well or badly he performed, "my mother would still love me." It sounded to me as though Greg's father had not reached the stage beyond the breaking point, where the real goals and rules have to do with caring for the true self. Years later, Greg's mother had. She was pleased when her son did well at diving, but that goal never eclipsed her compassion for Greg's true self. Ironically, people who adopt this type of detachment from society's games often perform better at them than people who treat one particular game as a life-and-death struggle.

DEALING WITH SOCIAL GAMES
DURING RE-CREATION

Women who have been through the breaking point and emerged, transformed, on the other side return to society ready to play its "games" with skill and enthusiasm. However, they are also well aware that not all of these games will allow them to care for the true self (which I will call their Real Goal), and that many of the games have rules that are contrary to compassion and honesty (the Real Rules). As a woman "re-creates" her life, there are four possible ways she may deal with the "games" society has created. (1) She can play a game because her involvement in that game nourishes her true self. (2) She can join a game that indirectly supports or enhances her ability to care for her self. (3) She can refuse to play a certain game. Or finally (4) she can set out to change the rules. I talked to women, each of whom had taken one of these options.

• *Option 1: Choosing a Game That Supports Real Goals*   In the first stages of re-creation, when a woman seeks out her true self and becomes sensitive to its needs and desires, she may discover that there are social "games" that meet those needs and desires admirably. Kristina was one of those rare people who know from childhood which game will nourish her true self. In Kristina's case, the "game" was professional dancing.

Kristina, 29

I asked my parents for ballet lessons when I was about six. They weren't really into the arts, or into pushing their kids, so at first they didn't pay any attention. I must have asked every day for three years. I knew, I just *knew*, that I wanted to dance. They finally signed me up for lessons when I was nine, and from there I just took off.

Kristina left home to live in New York City when she was sixteen and danced professionally in New York and San Francisco before a back injury ended her professional career. However, Kristina knows what it feels like to find a "game" that nourishes her true self. She married and had two children for the same reason she took up ballet: because she felt in her bones that it was what she wanted at the time. As a result, she seems calmer and happier than women who have planned their lives according to other people's rules and goals.

Women like Kristina, who join social "games" that directly nourish their true selves, are like people who have married for love in a society where almost every marriage is arranged. They can hardly wait to get up in the morning. They smile easily. They have a lot of energy. Once they start to work (or should I say "play"?) they forget what time it is. They are having so much fun that you can almost feel fun radiating from them. When they achieve the goals of their "game," whatever that game may be, they may look up and nod—but then they plunge right back into doing what they love: "What? I won a Nobel Prize? Oh, that's nice. Just put it over there. . . . Now, where was I?"

Though they were often unusually proficient at what they did, women in the re-creation phase were no more gifted than anyone else. When they tried to do something that was "off target" for their true selves, they found it hard, even when it should have been easy.

Carla, 44

I was a psychology major in college, and all my friends say I'm the best therapist they've ever met. People are always telling me I should be a professional psychologist. At one point I got the application papers to get a master's degree in counseling. The more I looked through those papers, the more confused I got. I'm usually a very clear thinker, but I felt as though I couldn't even put the meaning of the words together.

Finally I realized that I wasn't being stupid. I was just trying to send myself a message. I didn't really want to be a therapist. Yes, I am a good "analyst" for my friends—but that's because they're my friends. They're people I like and care for. The thought of a stranger paying me to act the same way toward *them* gives me the creeps. I guess for me, being a therapist is like having sex; I'll do it for love, but not for money.

Jade, 50

When something is hard for me, when it sticks in my throat and I can't seem to get going with it, that's a big red flag that it's not the right thing for me to do.

DIFFERENT STROKES:
THE DIVERSITY OF TRUE SELVES

One thing I found interesting was the wide variety of games that served different women's true selves. I listened in amazement as one woman rhapsodized about the pleasure of getting the bugs out of her computer programs, another raved about the joy of running a wilderness program for juvenile delinquents, another about the thrill of inventing new recipes for her family, and still another about her job grooming horses. None of these things sounded even remotely appealing to me—but, then, I doubt that any of these women would have stayed up all night reading sociology, as I was wont to do. Every individual's true self has its own preferences.

To people who have mistaken a social "game" for absolute reality, this kind of diversity is incomprehensible. They don't think of social systems as games, and therefore can't understand that others may have different definitions of "winning." They will rank another woman depending on whether or not she has achieved the goals of *their* favorite "game," whether or not she is even interested in playing it. I interviewed an aerobics instructor who sneered openly at "physically unfit" people, as though percentage of body fat were the universal measure of a woman's worth. I spoke with a politician's wife who considered that very same aerobics instructor a "failure" because "her husband isn't anybody in the community." I watched rich women scorn "lower class" acquaintances because they couldn't keep up in the social game of displaying wealth. I used to imagine these women in a room together, every single person considering herself a winner, and each of the others a loser, simply because they were all playing different games.

Women who are re-creating their lives around the needs of the true self don't have this kind of narrow outlook. To them, the differences between individual skills and desires are wonderful, especially when women are playing diverse games as a way of nourishing their true selves. I have seen such women "connect" with each other instantly, even when they are of different ages, ethnicities, and backgrounds. Even though they may not be playing the same "game," they all share the Real Goal of caring for the true self. They talk about dealing with difficult situations according to the Real Rules of honesty and compassion, and find themselves on common ground even though their specific interests may be completely different. Women who have reached the re-creation stage are not scornful but congratulatory when a friend achieves a goal in her own game. Having observed the uniqueness of every individual's tastes and proclivities, they don't worry that another's gain will mean their loss. In their view, there are infinite ways of caring for the true self. There is room for everybody.

◆ *Option 2: Playing a Social Game as a Means to an End* Even the social games we most enjoy often have elements of drudgery in them. The professional artist who lives for her work may not enjoy cleaning her brushes. The most devoted mother may not be thrilled about diapers. A teacher who adores interacting with students (trust me on this one) may loathe grading papers. Furthermore, even if we find a way to spend most of our time doing things the true self loves, there are many games we have to play simply to live in society. These things may not be rewarding in and of themselves, but they do not violate the Real Rules of honesty and compassion, and in the end they serve the true self by avoiding even more unpleasant alternatives. Finishing a meaningless assignment for a boring class may not serve the true self directly, but it can "win" a diploma that will help the student get a job the true self loves. Explaining something politely to a coworker whom you'd love to whack on the head will create a much better environment for the true self in the long run. So will paying your taxes or stopping at a red light. A little tedium may avoid a great deal of unpleasantness, or purchase a great deal of enjoyment.

Many women who are in the process of re-creating their lives join in social games that serve the true self indirectly, as a means to an end. Josie, a freelance writer, took a job as a travel agent because "I don't mind the work, and it supports my writing." Leah is an actress who decided to go to design school between acting jobs. "It's not what I love most," she told me, "but I enjoy it. It's creative, I'm good at it, and it gives me skills to earn a dependable living, where acting is always uncertain."

I spoke to many women who had taken time away from the Career Game because their true selves wanted the experience of motherhood as much as, or more than, a professional position. They made this decision consciously, like players who have decided to spend some time playing a different game, rather than being forced off the field by injury or accident. Jane thrived on her job as a curator at the Metropolitan Museum in New York. She also had fond memories of growing up in a large family. After she and her long-term boyfriend got married, Jane had three sons within four years—and a complete change of lifestyle.

Jane, 36

My life is crazy right now. I've got these little guys underfoot all the time: "Mommy! Mommy! Mommy!" My friends are all getting rich and famous at one thing or another, and here I am—every three seconds somebody's screaming "Mommy!" at me. It can be pretty frazzling.

I'm glad that I wanted my children so much, because I definitely did lose status in society's eyes when I left the workforce and got pregnant—and got pregnant, and got pregnant. But even on the worst days, when the kids are sick and I'm dying to get out by myself, I'm very much aware that my decisions feel *right* to me. I chose my family the same way I chose my job. All of those decisions came from somewhere very deep in my core. When something is right for me, I have a sense of absolute calm about it, even when people disagree with my choices. It's a kind of inner quietness.

Jane's combination of "frazzling" demands and "inner quietness" is characteristic of women who are working through the less pleasant portions of a task in order to obtain something the true self desires. I spoke to many who were willing to tolerate enormous amounts of drudgery and difficulty—so long as it contributed to the end goal of caring for the true self. However, since caring for the self requires honesty and compassion, a woman cannot achieve this while also playing a game that requires dishonesty or cruelty—and there are many such games in our society. When she comes up against a game that violates her Real Rules and leads away from her Real Goal, a woman cannot simply go along with it unless she abandons herself. Women who have been to the breaking point repeatedly know that in the long run, this isn't worth it. When they encounter a game that is hostile to the true self, they have two options left.

✦ *Option 3: Refusing to Play the Game* American women receive tremendous pressure to play social games where the goal is to win social approval, rather than to care for the true self. Frequently, women believe that if they could only play these games well enough, they would at last feel completely content. If I could only be thin enough, they think, or rich enough, or smart enough, or powerful enough, or famous enough . . . But there is no such thing as "enough" in games that lead away from the true self. Women whose daily lives work toward the care of their true selves seem happy right where they are, doing exactly what they are doing; women who are endlessly pursuing "enough" of someone else's goals only end up closer to the breaking point. They frequently wreak havoc on their true selves, hating and abusing their bodies and minds for never being "enough."

Often, the women I interviewed who had been through the whole agonizing process of meltdown told me that other people envied them most just when they felt most miserable. This was certainly true of me when I was being Harvard Supermom on the outside while busily coming apart at the seams when no one was looking. I heard the same kind of thing from Cora, a wealthy socialite with a huge house, two minks, a Mercedes, and a perfect-looking family.

Cora, 55

There was a point when my marriage was on the rocks, my kids hated me, I had no friends, and I wanted to kill myself. In the middle of this, the people I knew were telling me that I had a perfect life and they wished they could be so lucky. I would just stare at them and say I wished so, too.

We see despair in the lives of many people who win big at society's games, and it always leaves us shaking our heads in wonder. Why on earth would a woman as famous and beautiful as Marilyn Monroe kill herself? Why would someone as talented and dynamic as Tina Turner put up with years of abuse from her husband? Why would Betty Ford—the country's First Lady, for crying out loud—have a problem with substance abuse?

If these famous personalities are anything like the women I interviewed, the reason is that, while all of them were "winning" according to the rules and goals of certain social games, they had lost their true selves along the way. They had been caught in the middle of games that required them to discount their deepest needs and feelings, to act without compassion toward themselves, and to put up a deceptively happy front whether they really felt happy or not.

When women observe this kind of social game from the perspective of the true self, the goals appear meaningless and the rules destructive. The whole game looks absurd. At this point, many women simply decide to walk away; to put the Real Rules of honesty and compassion above the demands of the system. In doing so, they will assuredly break the rules of the social game—and other players are likely to be upset by this.

Sabrina, 30

I was raised a good Catholic girl—and I mean strict Catholic. When I decided to leave my husband, my mother threw a fit. She'd rail at me about how divorce was evil and I was breaking up a family and would go to hell for it. I'd say, "Mom, this marriage already is hell." I told her what Susan B. Anthony said, that "resistance to tyranny is obedience to God." She didn't believe it, but I guess the important thing was that I did.

Women who walk away from social games are mysterious and alarming to the game players around them. Whatever game you decide to leave, there are always people who take that particular game for absolute reality, and to them, walking away from the game is like blasting off for outer space with no destination. People certainly reacted this way to me when I quit my university job as a sociology professor. It seemed almost incomprehensible to many people at the college that I was actually leaving. As I mentioned earlier, many of my colleagues theorized that I was simply looking to "win" the game more decisively, by jockeying for a better salary or favorable tenure consideration. Even when I explained to them, as clearly as I could, that I wanted to play some other kind of game, they didn't seem to hear me. It was as if their university were the only playing field they could imagine.

Women who withdraw from social games often elicit this sort of amazed response even from their nearest and dearest. For example, Erica and her husband, Trevor, argued constantly. Over several years, they had developed a pattern of bickering that gradually became their entire relationship. After going through the whole breaking-point process when her mother died, Erica decided that the "game" of constant disagreement she played with Trevor was meaningless. She had spent years telling Trevor to stop being so argumentative. Now she decided to change her tactics. She would simply refuse to enter the duet of disagreement and complaint that had become her marital routine. When she and Trevor got into an argument, she would listen to his position and then walk away to think about her response. Trevor's reaction to this behavior was startling.

Erica, 38

He went to pieces. It scared him to death that I wouldn't fight. He couldn't understand what I was doing; it was like I'd just mutated into an alien right before his eyes. He would follow me around, yelling worse and worse insults, almost begging me to fight with him. After a week, he said that I obviously didn't love him anymore! Once he realized that I wasn't going to fight him, it meant that he had to change the way he acted. I guess that scared him.

It is always interesting to watch how people who having mistaken a social game for absolute reality interact with a woman who has decided to care for her true self. Imagine how much chaos it would cause if, for example, you had a football game in which in order to reach a different goal, one player was playing by rules different from everybody else's. Suppose that single player was on the field with no other goal than to burn as many calories as possible. He would be running around like crazy, even during huddles, and wouldn't particularly care what was happening to the ball. Or suppose the player was interested only in keeping his uniform spotless, or making friends, or taking care of the grass. Each of these goals would lead to different behaviors, all of which would look mighty strange to the folks who were there to see that ball get into the end zone. Women who put the care of the true self above the rules of social systems appear "strange" in just this way.

Arlene, 20

I grew up poor, and no one thought I would make it to college. No one else in my family ever had. But I really loved school, and I got good grades because of that, even though my parents thought it would be better for me to take vocational classes so I could get a job right out of high school. I'm in college because I want to learn. I take classes I love, and I read anything the teacher recommends. It's like this incredible banquet for me, for my mind.

Last semester one of my professors called me in and said, "You can stop brownnosing; you've already got an A." I just looked at him for a minute, because I couldn't figure out what he was talking about. It turns out, he thinks I read the optional assignments because I'm trying to impress him. God, I couldn't care less about impressing him—what a dweeb! But I couldn't convince him of that. He was still sure I was grubbing for a grade.

Caring for the true self causes this type of misunderstanding regularly. It is upsetting enough to the players of various social games when a woman simply refuses to participate. When she stays on the field but plays by her Real Goals and Real Rules instead of the goals and rules of the game, things can get really wild. This is the type of behavior that creates the maximum pressure to *change the game*—and to the players who have built their entire life strategies around the game *as it is*, that is the very worst kind of threat.

◆ *Option 4: Changing the Rules* Every now and then a woman finds herself in the middle of a social game that is hostile to her true self, yet important enough to her that she doesn't want to quit. In the past, for example, virtually every Career Game in the United States had a rule (unspoken, but universally understood) that women were not allowed to participate. During the women's movement, feminists began to insist that the "no women allowed" rule be changed. They pointed out that the rule was illogical, hurtful, and arbitrary (why on earth should *gender* be the deciding factor in determining who dictates a memo, and who types it?).

This assault on the "no women allowed" rule has been going on for years now, and that rule is still fighting to hang on. The women who set out to change it are still condemned and vilified, though perhaps not as violently or as successfully as those who went before them. The rules of social games can be incredibly resilient, surviving every attempt to destroy them by logic or entreaty. This is because every single game that hopes to pass for absolute reality has one cardinal rule, an all-important rule beside which all the others pale to insignificance:

THOU SHALT NOT QUESTION THE RULES

All players must keep this commandment. They can fail at virtually every aspect of the game, but they will still be accepted by the other players as long as they never openly question its basic premises.

If you want to find out whether or not the game you are playing is supportive of the true self, here's a way to do so. In the presence of the other players, just rear up on your hind legs and ask the question "Why are we doing this?" If the people around you are caring for their true selves, they will have an immediate answer: "Because it makes the world a better place." "Because it makes me feel good!" "Because it's so much fun!" However, if the game you are playing has no relationship to caring for the true self, you will find that the other players fall silent, then begin to attack you. They will be shocked and offended by your question. In fact, the more destructive a game is to their true selves, the more violently they will defend the rules. It is as if, having deserted their own true selves and suffered the pain that separation brings, they have a huge investment in believing that their game is absolute reality, and that everybody must keep to the rules. Otherwise, they would have to admit that their own anguish has been pointless, and their "achievements" empty.

This is the only explanation I can think of for stories like the one I heard from Lisa. Lisa had always wanted to be a doctor. She had a passion for medicine that went far beyond her schoolmates' desire for a prestigious position and a good salary. She loved healing people for its own sake. Lisa breezed through medical school and entered her internship, working as an emergency-room physician in one of the poorest, most crime-ridden areas of a large northeastern city. Typically, Lisa would work alternating twenty-four-hour shifts: one day on, one day off. During the "days on" there was no time for sleep and no tolerance for fatigue. Occasionally, one of the other physicians would ask Lisa to "cover" a shift, meaning that she would work forty-eight hours at a stretch. One of the primary rules of our medical training system is that young doctors must work these long shifts, learning to ignore the needs of their own bodies while they care for the bodies of others.

Lisa, 39

There's no logic to the system. They've done experiments where they shortened the doctors' shifts to eight hours, and the care the patients got was much, much better. But it's like this hazing mentality in the medical profession; you know, "I had to work forty-eight-hour shifts when I was in training, and so you have to do the same."

Lisa was well known for volunteering to do extra shifts. She told me that the worst thing about the twenty-four-hours-on, twenty-four-hours-off schedule was that "you miss half the good cases." When the paramedics brought in a hysterical gunshot victim, a drug addict having seizures, a baby who had fallen from a third-story window, they would look for Lisa. Nothing seemed too much for her. If there was ever an enthusiastic player of the Physician-in-Training Game, Lisa was it. However, as time went by, Lisa's body began to protest the horrendous stress she was putting on it. She began to feel more and more exhausted. On her days off, she would slip into a sleep that was almost comatose, having no energy to eat or change her bloodstained clothes. Finally the inevitable happened. Lisa hit her limit.

It was the end of a forty-eight-hour shift. There had been a steady flow of cases during those two days, mostly gunshot wounds and other crime-related injuries—knife wounds, people who had been cut with broken bottles, people who had been driven over by cars. I was coming down with the flu, I was fifteen pounds underweight, and the whole thing just began to seem surreal. My hands were shaking so hard I couldn't hold a cup of coffee. If I had seen a patient who was in my condition, I would have admitted them to the hospital.

Just before my shift ended, the resident came over and said, "Lisa, scrub up. I've got a chest wound for you." I looked at him and thought, "Why is he asking me to do surgery? He knows I'm hammered. Why doesn't he wait five minutes for the next shift?" I had never argued with an assignment before, but I knew I couldn't do this. I said, "I can't do a chest wound right now, I'm dead beat." He said, "No, it's your job, go do it." I said, "That's crazy! Why not get someone who's rested?" He didn't say why. He just gave me this dirty look and said, "If you ever want to be a physician, you'll get into the goddamned O.R. and do that chest wound."

I put on a new set of greens [sterile uniforms] and scrubbed for surgery. I could hardly stand up. Everything was swimming in front of my eyes. I walked into the O.R. The guy was already anesthetized—middle-aged guy, about forty-five, with a bullet in his chest. I walked over to the table and picked up the scalpel. I couldn't stop my hand from shaking. I knew if I opened this man's chest, I would end up killing him.

I couldn't do it. I froze. I was thinking, "This is insane! This is just completely and absolutely insane! I'm about to kill a human being to save my career, and it's all totally pointless! What kind of a doctor lets her patient be cut open by a sick person who hasn't slept in days? What am I doing?"

Lisa had reached the breaking point, and she proceeded directly to meltdown. She backed away from the operating table and began to sob. The next day she left her internship. In the ensuing months she began to question almost everything about the Physician-in-Training Game. Lisa has not yet returned to medicine, but when she does, it will be with the intention of changing the rules—not because she hates her profession, but because she loves it.

Women who have been through the process often begin to question the unspoken rules of social games just as Lisa did. As they go into meltdown, step away from their established roles, and observe society from the perspective of the true self, they begin to act like the child in the fable who shouted, right out loud, that the emperor had no clothes. These women become expert at pointing out absurdities in social games and suggesting new ways of functioning that might make better sense to their own and others' true selves. (Lisa's idea of creating briefer shifts for medical interns is one example.)

Typically, society's game players respond with shock and horror to these suggestions. Rather than changing the rules, they will immediately attack the woman who "threatens" them with a better idea. They will insult everything about her, from her intelligence to her hairstyle. They will say she failed, dropped out because she didn't have the right stuff. They will effectively block themselves and other willing players from seeing any validity in a different way of playing the game.

PLAYING BY DIFFERENT RULES

The thing that interested me most about women who had decided to change the rules was that they were not working on any established political model. They didn't have an organized agenda or platform; they were listening to the voice of the true self, not to any exterior source. Nor did they focus on shifting the balance of power in existing systems so much as totally re-creating those systems from a different perspective. Sometimes the changes they made didn't create a huge social change. Joanie Stanwick's ambition of being a Bingo caller is one example. I doubt Joanie received much opposition from popes and presidents. But when they could not care for their true selves without requiring commensurate changes in the people around them, women re-created their worlds anyway.

Sometimes the major impact of a woman's "changing the rules" was felt by her family. For example, a homemaker named Marsha went through the whole breaking-point process when she was about forty. As she moved into the "re-creation" phase, she thought hard about the fact that she had been tired for twenty years because her husband, a well-known writer, liked to work at night. He often slept in short "catnaps," jumping up to write down an idea and then drowsing off again. This worked well for him, but Marsha's body clock was designed to sleep eight straight hours, from 9:00 P.M. to 5:00 A.M. When she realized that her health and happiness had been severely depleted by her interrupted sleep patterns, Marsha decided to care for her true self by asking her two sons to share a bedroom, and taking over the free bedroom herself.

At first Marsha's husband was extremely anxious about this decision. After all, the unofficial "rules" of the Marriage Game in our culture dictate that spouses should share both bed and bedroom. Did his wife's new sleeping arrangement mean that she didn't love him? That she found him sexually unappealing? That their marriage was doomed? It took him only a few weeks to see that his fears were groundless. Moving into her own bedroom meant only that Marsha's energy, health, and *joie de vivre* returned to the levels she remembered from her adolescence. Marsha, her husband, their children, and their marriage all benefited from her actions.

Bridget's job as a trainer for a large telecommunications firm was closely defined by an unspoken set of quasi-political "rules." Most of the energy Bridget expended at the office went into figuring out which factions were developing in the corporation, and how to align herself with the most likely "winners." There was an enormous amount of hostility among employees in the firm, and, as Bridget put it, "the turf battles never, ever stopped." When she first joined the company, Bridget thought she must have stumbled into a particularly volatile moment in its history. In fact, that's what she was told by the various personnel who took her aside to advise her about how she should "position" herself to get pay hikes, promotions, and corporate power.

Bridget, 42

The culture of the firm was incredibly powerful. It sucked you right in like a whirlpool, and once you started spinning around in it you could never stop. Some people seemed to love it, but it made me sick. I mean literally sick. I started developing stomach trouble about a month after I took the job, and it got worse over the next few years, until everything hit the fan.

"Everything hit the fan" around Bridget's thirty-ninth birthday. She had recently been given a managerial position that carried considerable power—at least on paper. In fact, Bridget knew that her *real* job description consisted mostly of remaining politically loyal to the person who had given her the promotion.

The surface story was that I had complete control over my department, including budgeting decisions. The real story was that [my immediate superior] had given me the position because he assumed that I wouldn't do anything without his direct approval. I was supposed to be completely independent, but really that was a front I was expected to keep up so that the company would look democratic while the top few guys called all the real shots.

Unbeknownst to the leading executives in the firm, Bridget was getting sick and tired of following the unofficial organizational rule book. She was aching for a change. When she turned thirty-nine, Bridget went into what she described as a "midlife crisis." Over the course of a few weeks, she went into meltdown, and then took a step that would dramatically change the way she did her job.

I asked for time to complete a training course for managers, and I selected the most unusual program I could find—a river-rafting trip where executives were supposed to learn leadership skills. My boss was very uncomfortable when I said I actually wanted to use the time and money I had been given for management training (nobody was actually supposed to use that money), but because it was an official rule, he had to let me go.

The rafting trip took Bridget completely away from her office culture, mentally as well as geographically, for the first time in years. From a distance, in the context of a completely different activity, she began to see her company in new ways.

The thing about the wilderness, about water and rocks and trees, is that they don't pretend to be anything they aren't. When you're fighting to get through a patch of white water without drowning, there's no time to sit and brood about which person in your raft is siding with which other people, or who gets to sit in the front of the boat, or whether you're jealous of somebody who saves the whole group by pushing off a huge rock. You have to work together. You have to find out what works, and who can do it. There's no excuse for b.s., and everybody is important.

When she went back to work, Bridget was a different woman. She had been given official autonomy over her department, although she was never expected to act autonomously. Now she decided to push her job as far in the direction of "dealing with the real world" as it could possibly go.

I began to hold meetings with my staff where I would call people—including me—on the little games we were all playing. I talked about the way the company culture had pulled me in, and how I didn't want to go that way anymore. I said we were going to run the department by focusing on the market and on customers, not on company politics. I challenged people openly, in a way they were *not* used to. Some of my people loved it—they treated me like a hero. And some of them, unfortunately, smiled in my face and then tried to stab me in the back. But that was pretty much what I expected, given how the company operated.

Before long, Bridget's superiors received private reports from people in her department who were shocked by her complete abandonment of the company's usual norms.

[My boss] called me in and said, "You're making a huge mistake. You've got to play by the rules in this company. Maybe you don't belong here." I could tell he was just afraid his own feet would be in the fire once the whole firm realized how differently I was running my department. All I said was "Give me a year. If I'm not helping the company, I'll leave." I was really ready to go—if I couldn't work in a way that felt "real" to me, I would have gotten major ulcers and had to leave the job anyway. I felt I had nothing to lose.

When the year had passed, Bridget's department was adding more to the company's revenues than it ever had under other leadership. Two years later, when I interviewed her, the department was performing so well that the CEO had recommended she train other managers to adopt her style. She was dubious about the possibility of doing so.

> They have no idea how different my people really are. We don't beat around the bush. We don't lie. When there's conflict, it's handled out in the open, not behind closed doors the way it is in the rest of the company. Once you learn to operate like that, it is incredibly effective and freeing. But it breaks every one of the rules these guys are living by. It breaks every single rule.

JUST THE SAME, BUT COMPLETELY DIFFERENT

Not all women who change the rules of their particular life "games" make drastic changes in their lifestyles, their jobs, or anything else that is easily apparent from the outside. For example, I now lead a life that is basically the same as my life before a major breaking point, meltdown, and *satori*. I am raising the same three children, spend my mornings typing at the same computer, and teach groups of students quite similar to the ones I taught in my old sociology department. My husband, too, is still a professor, business consultant, and passionate Asia lover. On the surface, not much has changed in my life since my most recent trip through the breaking point. But from my perspective, everything is different.

Many of the changes I made in my own life were inspired by the examples of the women I've interviewed. For example, when I saw that resourceful women relied on networks of friends to help with the stress of child care, I deliberately began to recruit a network of friends and loved ones who explicitly agree to exchange physical and emotional support with me. This has enriched my life enormously and made me a much calmer and happier mother. I also noticed that women past the breaking point tend toward creative projects, and this gave me the incentive to stop writing academic articles (which I find excruciatingly dull) and start writing things I enjoy. When I turn on my computer nowadays, I feel as if I'm sitting down for a chat with a few good friends; I can hardly wait to get to it, and it leaves me in a very jolly mood. I teach as an adjunct professor (not a tenure-track faculty member) at a graduate school of business (not social science). I love teaching business because it is gritty and practical and constantly applies social-science theories to people's real lives. And what, exactly, do I teach? A course the administration kindly allowed me to design myself, which allows me to learn about students' lives and help them create careers that suit their individual needs. Sometimes in the middle of a class session, I find myself wanting to crow, "I LOVE THIS STUFF!" Sometimes I actually do.

All in all, *my life looks almost exactly the way it did before I went through my most recent version of the breaking-point process. But it feels completely different.*

I heard this same comment from many other women who had weathered the crisis of the breaking point. The transformation that occurred in their inner lives sometimes created drastic changes on the outside, but this was not typical. Not everyone comes out on the other side of a breaking point burning incense, making macramé, and reading New Age literature. Most of the women I met who had been through the process over and over didn't seem particularly remarkable—until I got to know them. They were from all walks of life, all races, all ages, all religious and political persuasions. Each one fit into not one but many social systems, including families, corporations, schools, clubs, service organizations, and friendships. These dissimilar exteriors are actually a product of the things these women all have in common: a clear understanding of what they really need and want, compassionate self-acceptance, piercing honesty, and a perception of difference as enriching rather than threatening.

Sometimes, however, these very ordinary (and yet extraordinary) women find themselves running into social systems, or aspects of social systems, that do not support honesty and compassion. Not because they thrive on conflict or want attention or have great ambitions, but because they have decided never again to buy into a system that cannot work, these women may end up making changes that extend much farther than they had ever anticipated. Sometimes the rules of a social game are so restrictive that even to give the true self the most elementary respect, a woman ends up taking actions that send shock waves through her whole society.

REVOLUTION: WHEN CARING
FOR THE TRUE SELF MEANS CHANGING THE WORLD

One day in 1955, a tired American woman got on the bus at the end of a hard day. She wanted to sit down, and so she did; a simple act of basic self-care. Except that this woman, Rosa Parks, was African-American, and the rules of her society dictated that she was not supposed to sit in the nearest open seat. That seat was reserved for white people. Why? What sense did that rule make? In a culture that celebrated individual equality, what justification could there be for barring a weary traveler from sitting in an available seat just because of the color of her skin? When she sat down at the front of that bus, Rosa Parks pushed all these questions into the minds of people who were busily enforcing the rules while refusing to think about the injustice and illogic that underlay them. By caring for her true self in such a minor thing as sitting down on a bus seat, Rosa Parks helped fuel the civil rights movement.

Another hero of mine is a woman named Rachel Carson, who quietly broke all kinds of social rules throughout her life. She never married (which, in itself, goes against our culture's norms). She obtained a Ph.D. in biology when women were not considered capable of such a thing—and the rules wouldn't allow most of them to try. This was in the period of history right after World War II, when the United States had pulled ahead of all other nations as the most powerful country on earth, and American technology, bravado, and "progressive" attitude were about to solve all the world's problems. For one thing, our agricultural industry had come up with a wonderful new insecticide called DDT. Scientists were immensely proud of this chemical, and conducted demonstrations to show how safe it was, such as spraying it all over a table where groups of picnickers were having their lunch.

Rachel Carson, a nature lover who enjoyed taking long walks in the woods and marshes near her home, began to notice that in the areas where DDT was used, she no longer heard birdsong. She saw changes in the whole landscape of such places, and they worried her. She began to do some research. Over several years, Carson gathered an immense amount of data that proved something very frightening: the chemical poisons human beings were spraying all over the United States were destroying whole natural ecosystems.

Carson combined all this research into a book called *Silent Spring*, a masterpiece of both science and literature. The book, and Carson herself, were immediately and violently attacked by industry, agriculture, the government—just about anyone who had any stake in continuing to use toxic chemicals. Rachel Carson was publicly mocked as a bitter, dried-up old maid, a hysterical female who obviously couldn't have anything to teach the veritable armies of respectable gentlemen allied against her.

Rachel Carson died of cancer just two years after her book was published. But the voice of her true self, speaking from the pages of *Silent Spring*, proved to be so powerful that a new generation of scientists (who had not yet fully absorbed the rules of the Biologist Game) were drawn to it and convinced by it. Carson's book is usually credited with beginning the social trend we now call environmentalism. In her day, scientists raged at her for even mentioning the "preposterous" idea that human beings are part of the earth's biological system, rather than its absolute masters. Now, of course, that idea seems self-evident. When Rachel Carson questioned the rules about how we interact with our physical environment, she created a massive paradigm shift in the way Americans see their relationship to the earth. In doing so, she may well have saved us from ourselves.

THE QUIET REVOLUTIONARIES

It may seem odd to you to put Joanie Stanwick and her plan to become a Bingo caller in the same category with Rosa Parks and Rachel Carson. But even though they did very different things, the pattern of their actions was the same. It is a pattern they share with all the women I interviewed who had gone beyond the breaking point: they identified some aspect of a social game that was restricting or impinging on the well-being of their true selves, and they decided not to play by the rules. They put whatever energy, training, skill, or influence they had into changing the rules, so that their true selves could be better off.

Women who go beyond such personal crises learn, over time, that the phase of societal re-creation will take longer than one lifetime. Most seemed to think that it is essentially an endless process, by which humanity must always adjust to changing conditions. But although they shared their approach to life and understood each other's motivations, these women did not need to preach their beliefs. They were similar in their conviction that it was all right for them to be *dis*similar. They did not form a recognizable political wing or preach any set of ideological "musts." They did not adhere strictly to either the traditional or modern versions of what a woman should be. Whether they were wearing business suits, aprons, uniforms, or work shirts, they were simply themselves. To them, the very idea that a woman should be anything but herself, her simple and clear true self, was absurd.

These women, whom I take as my role models, knew from harsh experience that a woman who sets out to play the game by our society's rules can never win. The rules are inadequate, and they're paradoxical. When women set out to live by them, they end up losing the fight to improve the quality of their lives.

Joanie Stanwick knows this. Once she finishes telling me exactly how she is going to prevail upon Albert to let her call the Bingo game at her church, she says something that reveals her revolutionary nature.

Joanie, 80

I'll tell you something. If there's one thing you should say to women it's this: Figure out just one thing that would make your life better, and then you go out and you make it happen. Once that's done, then go ahead figure out the next thing, and do that, too.

These are the words of a world-changer. As I spoke to women who had decided to change "just one thing" that would make their lives better, I became convinced that caring for the true self is the most revolutionary position a human being can take. Military revolutions, political upsets, open warfare; all threaten the balance of power in a given system—*but they never threaten the system itself.* Their object is to win the game, not to walk away from it or change the rules.

There's a poetic little saying that describes the worldview behind these violent revolutions: "When you've got 'em by the balls, their hearts and minds will follow." A great many attempts at social change have adopted this philosophy. Unfortunately for them, it is fundamentally incorrect. The truth is that when you've got people by—uh—some tender part of their anatomy, they may do what you force them to do, but they will hate you with all their minds and all their hearts. In the end, it's the quiet revolutions, the ones that appeal to the true self, that attract people's hearts and minds. And once that has happened, once people know their true selves are safe and respected, those people will come with you, various tender body parts and all.

In the end, then, the revolution that appeals to the heart and mind is the most dangerous kind of threat to the many games that our society has established. This is why revolutionaries like Jesus, Gandhi, and Martin Luther King, Jr., were all killed; not for trying to win the games of force and domination, but for refusing to play them, and for telling other people that they didn't have to play them either. When human beings step back from their social context and begin to listen to their true selves, the games of their society—and the people who have given up their true selves to win those games—are shaken to their very cores.

The majority of the women I've described in this chapter decided to follow this course of action entirely on their own. Few of them knew each other. Most of them thought that they were isolated, almost freakish, in their decision not to play society's games. The acts of re-creation they performed were certainly not meant to be coordinated with each other. Each woman was just trying to carve out enough space in her daily life to allow her true self room to breathe. For one woman, re-creation meant pushing for policy changes in her company. For another, it meant taking time for a daily walk by herself. Some women filed for divorce, and others got married. Some got jobs, some quit jobs. Some had children, some decided not to. Many came up with creative approaches to problems like making money, caring for their children, improving their relationships. The commonality between them was not any single course of action, but *the firm intention to create a better environment for the true self, and a commitment to honesty and compassion.*

THE BEGINNING OF A NEW BEGINNING

I often wonder what our society would look like if every American woman took Joanie Stanwick's advice and made just one change, and then one more and one more, to make the world safer for her true self. I know what any devoted game player would say: that if women all did this, they would create anarchy.

I don't think so.

The biographer of the artist Käthe Kollwitz wrote, "What would happen if one woman told the truth about her life? The world would split open." [1] To some, this is a frightening prospect. But as we have seen, our society will eventually "split open" anyway, because it is built on a divided system of values. *The frightening things are happening already.* After listening for hundreds of hours while American women "told the truth about their lives," I am convinced that they are not destroying society's games, but creating a new way for human beings to live harmoniously and well.

In the aggregate stories of all the women I interviewed, I saw the fuzzy outlines of a pattern beginning to emerge. While that pattern was not chaotic or anarchic, I'll admit that it was *different*—different from the value system of either the traditional or the modern worldviews, different from the paradox that has shaped American society since its founding.

It is still a bit early to know what this new way of thinking and living will be, once our entire culture has been pushed to the breaking point and beyond by the paradoxes inherent in our current value system. It is too early to predict whether or not our society as a whole will even be able to transcend these paradoxes. But in my optimistic moments, I believe that the women I interviewed are the forefront of a quiet revolution that will result in a collective *satori*, a transition to a worldview that is more useful for our time and place in history. The next chapter will consider where that revolution—which I believe has already begun—may be taking American society.

✦

CHAPTER ELEVEN

The "Emergent" Society of the United States: A World Beyond the Breaking Point

I spent my junior year of college in Singapore, learning Mandarin Chinese and sweating a lot. Singapore is a hot, humid island that lies just one degree north of the equator. Before it was peopled, it was your classic tropical rain forest. The temperature varies between about seventy and eighty-five degrees Fahrenheit all year long.

One day during that year my friend Ling, who spoke little English and had never been out of Singapore, asked me some questions about life in the United States. To compensate for the many flaws in my Mandarin, I found my collection of snapshots and fished out a couple that I thought might interest Ling. She was very taken by a photograph of the Rocky Mountains in winter; jagged slabs of stone rising twelve thousand feet into the sky, covered with ice and snow.

"Oh!" said Ling, looking at the photograph. "I've always wanted to go somewhere like that. It looks so cool and refreshing."

I smiled. "Ling," I said, "let me assure you that winter weather conditions in the Rockies go far beyond cool."

Ling looked puzzled. Perhaps this was because, with my pronunciation, I had actually said something like "I am renting my face to a Korean lizard." (As I've already mentioned, Chinese was a struggle for me. I once read a story for my Modern Chinese Literature class about a man who was hired to carry a sandwich board for a Taiwanese merchant—except that throughout the entire story and the ensuing class discussion, I was under the firm impression that the sandwich board was the man's daughter. No one else in the class could figure out why I found the story so moving.)

Intent on making Ling understand how frigid Rocky Mountain winters really are, I picked up the photograph and tried the simple approach.

"Cold," I said. (If I focused on one word at a time, I did all right.)

Ling smiled and nodded. "Yes, refreshing," she said.

"No." I shook my head. "*Cold.* Very extremely much cold."

She looked at me kindly, the way you look at a demented child. "Yes, very extremely much refreshing," she said.

It began to come clear to me. What Ling and I were dealing with was not merely a language barrier. Ling had lived on a steaming tropical island her whole life. She had literally *never* been cold. Even the times when she had been *cool* were few and far between, and she remembered them fondly. The concept of cold simply wasn't in her range of experience. It was impossible for her to understand what it feels like to be so cold your face goes numb and your eyelashes freeze together. I could tell her about it, but until she'd been through it, she would never really understand.

WHY WOMEN ARE TRANSFORMING AMERICAN CULTURE

If you were looking for someone to design winter wear for your next ski trip, I doubt that you would go to my friend Ling. You'd be much better off talking to someone who had lived in the cold since birth, who knew what frostbite and snow blindness and windchill factors can do to a body. If you *really* wanted your designer to turn out a good set of winter clothes, you'd tell her that she'd have to wear her own creation into the Rockies in January. Experience and necessity, combined, make for the most effective possible design.

This is true of social systems as well as winter clothes. The people who have suffered the most from a social problem are in the best possible position to design a useful way of dealing with that problem. Other people can try, but there's really no substitute for experience. One of my favorite professors at Harvard, Orlando Patterson, is an expert on slavery (among many other things). Dr. Patterson has written about the history of slavery across many times and places, and pointed out something I find fascinating: *our concept of freedom was first and most clearly articulated in societies where slavery was practiced.* "Before slavery," Dr. Patterson writes, "people simply could not have conceived of the thing we call freedom." [1] Freedom is a clear concept for slaves for the same reason that body warmth is for Eskimos—because they know what it is like to be deprived of it. Since slaves know the pain of captivity, they can articulate what it takes to make a captive free.

It is not fair to say that the oppressed should be responsible for creating a world in which they can live happily. It is not fair that people who have been hurt by a social system should have to figure out a workable alternative. It is not fair, but it is practical. It is, in fact, the *only* practical way to come up with really useful strategies for solving social problems. Turning for solutions to the free, the comfortable, the privileged members of a society is like turning to my friend Ling for advice on winter clothing. She may be ready and willing to help out in the construction or the purchase of such clothing, but she wouldn't know what to do without some input from people who understand "cold" well enough to create a useful design.

TAKING U.S. CULTURE BEYOND THE BREAKING POINT

The paradoxical value system of our culture affects all Americans in one way or another. But women, having been designated as *the* repositories of blame and responsibility for this huge paradox, are the most likely people to be "frozen" by exposure to the elements. The true selves of women have been pushed into a very cold place, where discrimination, poverty, overwork, and divisive obligations are the order of the day. Because of this, the adult female population of the United States has been forced to push forward, beyond the breaking point, faster than the culture as a whole. In my years of interviewing American women, I have seen the beginnings of a transformation in social forms and institutions. I have watched individual women, one by one, struggle to articulate and express a perspective on life that does not match either the traditional or the modern worldview, and in doing so, create innovative life structures and processes to care for their true selves and the true selves of others.

CHALLENGES TO THE TRUE SELF

I'm always fascinated by the way Americans romanticize the rigid domination of the rational individual and the traditional group member over the true self. Some of the things we do in pursuit of this ideal aren't rational at all. For example, if you look over the magazines by the checkout counter on your next trip to the grocery store, I can almost guarantee that you'll find half a dozen articles which tell you that being above average weight—even a little bit—is bad for you and will take years off your life expectancy. But I'd be stunned if you could find even one article citing the equally well-tested fact that being *under* average weight is also unhealthy, and also decreases your statistical chances at a long life.

By the same token, we celebrate athletes who stay on their feet long enough to be beaten to a pulp, or who force themselves to play on injured limbs—even when this results in permanent damage. We do *not* congratulate the athlete who wisely pulls out of a competition in order to remain strong and healthy.

Why are Americans so enthusiastic about self-destruction? I think that as a culture we are in love with our Puritan forebears' belief that denying or overworking the true self is the way to succeed, and that, conversely, filling the true self's needs will ruin everything. The person who succeeds is the one who works harder, eats less, takes more punishment.

One of the sad commentaries on the progress of our ideals is the emergence of the "Inner Child" as a buzzword in American culture. Not that I think there's anything wrong with the Inner Child concept, mind you—as far as it goes, I'm all for it. What strikes me as strange is the fact that so many Americans have to think in pop psychology terms before they can allow themselves to do anything relaxing or entertaining or just plain silly. I heard the Inner Child theme from many women I interviewed: "My therapist told me I should take my Inner Child on an outing, so I went to a ball game for the first time in ten years." "I got my Inner Child some frozen yogurt." "I need to be alone for a while so my Inner Child can relax." The implication is that a true adult never goes to ball games, enjoys frozen yogurt, or relaxes. These things seem to be seen by many women as *therapeutic* activities—anyone who does them is not a robust, fully functioning grown-up.

This type of mentality affects all sorts of people; not just American women but people of both genders, from an enormous number of different cultures. Because I teach at an international business school, I have students from all over the world: Eastern and Western Europe, Asia, Africa, South America, the Middle East, Southeast Asia, the West Indies. Each of these places has its version of traditional culture, and each has been affected by the image of the rational individual created during the European Enlightenment. Through colonialism, conquest, trade, and other cross-cultural interactions, the paradox of modernization has crept into the whole developed—and developing—world. I have yet to run across a student, male or female, from anywhere on earth, who doesn't know what it is like to feel pushed and pulled and strained and confused by some aspect of this paradox. But of all these people, Americans have pushed the modern ideal to its furthest extent, and American women are the ones "freezing" in the full blast of incredibly exaggerated, contradictory stereotypes. Because of this, they are designing ways to live, raise families, and put food on the table that are suited to the world beyond the breaking point. It sounds bold, but I honestly believe that these women are acting as the "icebreakers" for a new way of thinking about human life.

Literal icebreakers are small boats that force their way through inaccessible, frozen waterways. Ocean liners and aircraft carriers can follow, carrying huge numbers of people with them, but the icebreakers have to brave the most difficult conditions. American women are not merely charting a course that members of their sex have never traveled. They are charting a course that *no one* has ever traveled. Having suffered the most from the paradoxes in our value system, they are in a position to design the most effective solutions. They are pushing forward through apparently impossible situations, finding ways more imposing and powerful social groups have failed to discover.

A NEW RECIPE FOR SOCIETY

American women's emerging worldview is neither an attack on traditional values nor a betrayal of modern ones. It is simply an attempt to combine the best aspects of both these value systems in a way that is not self-refuting. Our present society is an uneasy patchwork of traditional and modern values, a blend of opposites that are constantly at odds with one another. Despite the conflict, Americans have hung on to both sets of values because each is incomplete: *neither the traditional nor the modern value system is adequate to support all the necessary and desirable aspects of human beings' true selves.*

The traditional worldview depends on inequality, which invites discontent and abuse of power. The modern view sees human beings as having no irrational components, like the need to care for others and be cared for by them. We need both value systems because each of them covers for the deficiencies of the other. If it were possible to strike an enduring balance between them, Americans would have done so long ago. Instead, we have collectively decided to walk an unsteady tightrope between them—and blame women for the bulk of the problems this strategy creates.

The challenge women are taking on as they begin to transform our culture is not simply a conflict between men and women, in which one sex's gain is always the other's loss. Men as well as women have suffered from the way Americans define gender. American men's roles have become so constricted, and the range of activities considered acceptable for a "modern" male so narrow, that many men feel as trapped by their culture as women do. *What we need is not to give women what men now have, but to fundamentally change our entire cultural conception of what it means to be human.*

This is what I saw women do as they went beyond the breaking point into a new way of viewing themselves and their culture. As the writers of their own social scripts, these women stood back from traditional and modern value systems, carefully disaggregated the most basic elements of those systems, and then recombined the elements to make an altogether different worldview. The difference between this approach and the one taken by most legal and political solutions is the depth with which cultural concepts are questioned, stripped down to their most basic components, and then recombined.

Say, for example, you had two types of food—let's take bread and butter. The bread is made by combining flour, yeast, sugar, and water. You mix them up, put them in a warm place to rise, then stick the whole thing in a hot oven until it cooks. The butter is made by taking cream, mixing it with a little salt, and churning it until it congeals. You can use bread and butter together, but they are still recognizably different types of food.

Suppose you decided to look at the basic ingredients of bread and butter, and combine some of those ingredients in different proportions, under different conditions. You'd go back to a stage when the ingredients (flour, water, cream) didn't look like bread or butter at all. Once you'd done that, you'd be free to create some very different recipes. You might decide to eliminate some ingredients that didn't agree with you, and recombine others to form brand-new types of food. For instance, if you were allergic to wheat flour, but wanted to make something interesting out of the remaining ingredients for bread-and-butter, you could take water (an ingredient of bread), freeze it, and combine it with salt (an ingredient of butter). Then you could mix some cream (butter ingredient) with some sugar (bread ingredient), put the bowl in a bucket full of the salt-ice mixture, and stir it for a while. If the conditions were right, you'd end up with ice cream. Is ice cream bread? No. Is it butter? No. Is it bread-and-butter? I wish someone would convince my children that the two are the same, but they aren't. Ice cream and bread-and-butter, though they share some basic elements, are fundamentally different things.

The traditional and modern social systems I've referred to throughout this book are chock-full of perfectly good ingredients—ideas like the importance of caring and equality, of freedom and belonging. Other ingredients (like the traditional idea that some people are literally more important and valuable than others) have proved to have unpleasant and undesirable effects, but that is no reason to throw out every value or rule we have inherited from the traditional and modern systems. What we must realize is that the specific recipes that combined these values and rules in certain proportions, and under certain conditions, were created to fill needs that are different from the ones Americans now face. Women who become deadlocked by the contradictions are forced to examine each ingredient of both traditional and modern belief systems, and carefully recombine the best of them in proportions and conditions that yield something altogether new.

THE "HISTORICAL MOMENT" FOR CHANGE

In the last chapter, I mentioned a few world-changers, people like Rosa Parks, Rachel Carson, Jesus, Gandhi, and Martin Luther King, Jr. Each of these people set out to make the world a safer place for his or her true self. The depth of these heroes' actions came from their personal integrity and courage. But the breadth their impact had on their societies stemmed not only from their actions per se, but from the fact that *each lived at a place and time—a historical moment—when widespread social pressures were stressing the existing value systems of their cultures.*

The historical moment is the social equivalent of the conditions needed to make a collection of ingredients into a finished food. It is the heat that bakes the bread, the cold that thickens ice cream. The right ingredients must be present to make a dish, but so must the right environmental conditions. When certain human actions occur at certain historical moments, the combination shatters social barriers and creates new visions of society.

Rosa Parks's quietly heroic act of self-care happened to come at the perfect historical moment to help push the absurdity of racism into the

American consciousness. On the day when she sat down in that "whites only" seat, the United States was boiling with controversy over civil rights for African-Americans, and the excuses for treating black people as inferior beings were wearing very thin indeed. If Ms. Parks had sat down in a "whites only" area a century earlier, the action would have been at least as brave and self-affirming, but definitely less world-changing. Racism was too well accepted by white Americans in the nineteenth century to be rocked by the courageous resistance of a single African-American. At that point in history, a black woman who sat in a forbidden area would probably have been severely punished, and her impulse toward freedom kept from "spreading" to other African-Americans.

However, the mid-nineteenth century *was* a historical moment when another action, by another woman, could fuel abolitionist passion, the Civil War, and ultimately the Emancipation. That woman was Harriet Beecher Stowe and, in her historical moment, writing and publishing *Uncle Tom's Cabin* was an action that dramatically changed American society. Stowe spent years living just north of the Mason-Dixon line, listening to her highly religious family discuss the horrors of slavery, and once helping a slave escape north to freedom. When the U.S. Congress passed a rule requiring that all escaped slaves be returned to their masters, Stowe was so angry she wrote her vivid, emotional novel attacking the institution of slavery. It became the first genuine runaway best-seller (pun intended) in American history. Abraham Lincoln would later call Harriet Beecher Stowe "the little lady who started this big war." Of course this was not literally true; the northern and southern United States had been becoming less united, and more hostile toward each other, for years before *Uncle Tom's Cabin* was published. But Harriet Beecher Stowe's literary act of conscience set the spark that helped ignite antislavery tensions and ultimately led to the Emancipation Proclamation.

Vast numbers of women suffer from the contradictions in American society. They feel its paradoxical directives every moment of their lives. The oddly inconsistent facts I mentioned in the first few pages of this book will only grow odder and more inconsistent as our culture continues on its present course. American women will keep getting richer and poorer, more and less privileged, freer and more confined, than ever. Each woman in this country walks into a maelstrom of contradictions every time she opens her front door—either to go out of her home or to go into it. More and more of us are aware that eventually the breaking point is inevitable, and the time is ripe for it.

Erma, 80

The changes that have happened in my lifetime—well, I can only say I never thought I'd live to see them. There is so much fear, so much violence, so much unhappiness, so much danger. When I was young, it seems to me that folks took care of each other. Now, no one even knows how to take care of themselves. Things can't go on like this much longer.

Cecelia, 51

Women are having too hard a time. In the sixties I really believed that we were going to make everything perfect, and it didn't work out. As a feminist, I kept fighting to make things better, but it was all about making things better in American society as it is. Now, after all these years, I'm sensing something different. I don't know exactly what it is, but I feel a great change coming.

I mentioned in Chapter 8 that many of the women I spoke to—like Cecelia—said that they felt some profound transition, some "great change," rising up around them like a tide. Women who mentioned this feeling clearly thought that it had a close relationship to women's experiences and perspectives.

Vanya, 23

My father died when I was twelve, and I took it all on myself to make everything work. I never behaved like a child at all—never really got the chance. My mother says that I was old when I was young. . . .

But it's always been okay. I've been able to take anything life handed me, because I felt that it was necessary for me to understand the way things work for women. . . . Because the world is going to change for women, or maybe women are going to change the world. I've known that ever since I can remember, like it was hardwired into my head. It gets stronger all the time. I don't know where the feeling comes from, but I have always felt that if I could learn from everything that happens to me, I will be part of a positive change.

Kay, 68

In many ways I've had an average life. Privileged, I think, compared to most people in the world. But for some reason I was always driven to go slightly beyond what I had to do. I felt that it was important for me to learn and do certain things, because there was something important and new developing, and I needed to be part of it. It seems to me that women are at the forefront of it. And I was not raised to think this way.

I heard this same odd story from women who had never met each other, who seemed utterly different from each other, who came from different places, races, religions, educational levels, and socioeconomic groups. As I've said, I don't know what the strange confluence of such women's feelings might mean. But perhaps the reason they all felt "a great change coming" was that they sensed that American society is nearing a "historical moment" when deep-seated changes are inevitable. Perhaps, as American society moves closer and closer to the breaking point, our whole culture is groping for a worldview that will not contradict itself and damage so many lives.

NEW GROUND: COMPARING TRADITIONAL, MODERN, AND EMERGENT VALUES

The women I interviewed who had gone through the breaking point and learned to chart the territory beyond it were "re-creating" a worldview that seemed to keep them out of the contradictions and double binds inherent in a traditional-and-modern society. When I looked at the exterior measures of these women's lives (income levels, employment status, etc.), I didn't see any clear commonalities. As I've said before, the surface details of these women's lives didn't look any different from other women's. Their jobs, their marriages, their interactions with others, were all quite ordinary-looking. But when I listened for the core values that came through in these women's discussions of their own lives, I heard a lot of similarities. They shared a value system—a "recipe" of norms and beliefs—that differed from the rest of American society.

On the following page you'll find a chart that compares some of the elements of this new, "emergent" value system with the traditional and modern systems. To clarify the differences between them, it may be helpful to briefly discuss some of the elements on the chart.

◆ *Cultural Element 1: Image of God* Sociologists recognize a culture's image of God (or lack of God) as one of the most powerful influences on human behavior. Because this factor is so basic to social behavior, I've listed it first among the elements of the emergent society.

	"TRADITIONAL" WORLDVIEW	"MODERN" WORLDVIEW	"EMERGENT" WORLDVIEW
IMAGE OF GOD	External Authority Figure	Human Rationality	Interconnected Spirituality: the "Ecological Web"
VIEW OF NATURAL UNIVERSE	Magical	Mechanistic	Organic
BASIC LIFE APPROACH	Insularity and Hierarchy	Universality and Conformity	Uniqueness and Diversity
SOCIAL IDEALS	Reliance on Existing Ideas	Problem-solving	Creativity
GUIDELINES FOR BEHAVIOR	Obedience to Authority	Competition and Achievement	Being and Self-expression
RESPONSE TO CHALLENGE	Avoidance or Aggression	Domination and Conquest	Creative Engagement and Compromise
DEFINITION OF "SUCCESS"	Rising in the Hierarchy	Maximizing Personal Resources	Caring for the True Self
RELATION-SHIPS	Dependent or Authoritarian	Completely Independent	Interdependent
IDEAL STATE OF BEING	Acceptance	Satisfaction	Joy
ATTITUDE TOWARD CHANGE	Hostility and Rejection	Skepticism and Defensiveness	Openness and Fluidity

Only about 40 percent of the women I interviewed spoke specifically about God. Those who did had a view of God that differed from both traditional and modern worldviews.

Most traditional cultures had gods who were similar to humans, but with supernatural powers. Many societies believed in whole pantheons of gods, who bickered and feuded and grew dangerously annoyed if humans did not perform the right rituals. The Western tradition focuses on an all-powerful father figure, a God who loves and protects but also judges and punishes human beings for their behavior. The modern worldview did away with God altogether, putting rationality at the center of all truth sources. In effect, for the creators of the modern value system, reason took the place of God. For many people who chose rationality as a rejection of the traditional gods, atheism became—paradoxically—an article of faith. True believers in the modern worldview are as offended by the idea of a God as traditional thinkers are by the suggestion that God may not exist.

By contrast with these two models, here is the way three of the women I interviewed described their view of God:

Rosie, 37

I go to church regularly and my religion is very important to me. I believe that God is very interested in people learning to love each other without many conditions, that there is some of God in each of us and our job is to find that, in ourselves and other people. That's the way I interpret my religion. Others in my church may not always agree with my interpretation, but that's okay, too. We can all learn from each other.

Jo, 48

There is a connection between each of us, between us and everything. We are interlinked, like an ecological web; all things, all people, all souls. There are things science hasn't yet been able to perceive, but I don't think that means they don't exist. I think, with all our advances in knowledge, we still only understand the tiniest, littlest slice of reality . . . there's so much more to know. . . .

I believe we *feel* things we don't know how to perceive. We can feel them with our souls. It's very subtle; it's like looking for a butterfly with your eyes closed, feeling for the breeze the butterfly's wings make against your cheek.

Cathy, 50

I believe that everything has a spirit. My grandmother was Apache, and she taught me that the earth has a spirit, the rocks have a spirit, and all the beings that have ever lived or ever will live have a spirit . . . all of that together is the Great Spirit. You are part of the Great Spirit, and so am I, and so is that tree or that river. All of it is God.

Of these three examples, only Cathy was not a member of an existing religion; Rosie is an active Methodist and Jo is a faithful Catholic. And yet, within their own religious traditions, they expressed a very similar concept of God—one that might have sounded quite unusual in their churches not so many years ago. Cathy's reference to Native American religion was not uncommon among women who talked with me about their religious beliefs—whether or not they share in the Native American gene pool. Right now, the New Age trend in United States culture celebrates Indian lore and ideas, partly because the idea of a universal Great Spirit appeals to people who have found the idea of a humanlike Father or an atheistic universe unappealing.

The idea of a God who is "in all things, about all things, and through all things" has existed in many forms and many philosophical and religious systems, from Chinese Taoism to some interpretations of Christianity to mystical Judaism. The emerging value system I saw among American women apparently included this kind of God-image because it preserved the idea of a spiritual universe without the "only one way" philosophy of many organized religions. Even those who did belong to organized religions tended toward this model, as did people who had never thought much about religion in the first place. Bette is one of the latter.

Bette, 30

I do believe in God, I guess. I like the idea that God is love. But when people say that God only loves people who live a certain way, I can't accept that. I have so many friends who are different from each other, and I love them all. How could God not love different people exactly how they are, if I can do it?

Another popular way women articulated their view of God was the terminology of the so-called recovery movement. This movement puts God "as we understand God" at the center of the quest for a moral and spiritually satisfying life. If you're not familiar with the recovery movement, wander into any bookstore and ask where the recovery section is. There will be dozens of selections, offering self-help approaches to everything from overeating to compulsive gambling. Some feminists are appalled by the way the women's movement seems to have "blended" with the recovery movement in the United States, arguing that it celebrates women's victimology and dilutes the feminist agenda.[2]

From my interviews, it seemed that women were drawn to the recovery movement not because they wanted to think of themselves as victims, but because they had found the traditional and modern ways of thinking about spirituality to be contradictory, troubling, or inadequate to support a consistent moral system as they went through the breaking point. In the experience of *satori*, when they stepped back from their cultures, they had found ways to feel connected to some Divine source that did not depend on any social context. The "God as we understand God" spiritual approach of the recovery movement gave them a way to conceptualize a Divine power without requiring them to fit that power within a narrow or predetermined pattern.

The many women who didn't mention religion still seemed to follow a form of moral reasoning that was more casual than, but still similar to, that of the religious women. Most of my subjects weren't raiding the recovery sections of bookstores or attending lectures on Creating Your Own Reality with Crystals. They simply went about the business of living, with a vague notion in the backs of their minds that the "rules" of compassion and honesty constituted a robust guideline for their ethical choices. Their moral framework (which, in the very loosest sense, may be considered a concept of God) was one of a compassionate force linking human beings together, even if they never formally linked this moral framework with a Divine being.

◆ *Cultural Element 2: View of the Natural Universe* Traditional societies tend to see the universe as a place where things happen by "magic." People get sick because a witch has cursed them, droughts are punishments from angry spirits, mental illness is caused by possession, etc. The modern worldview is mechanistic, rejecting the "magical" claims of traditional cultures and portraying the universe as a huge machine, a sort of incredibly complex clockwork.

Few of the women I interviewed talked about this sort of cosmological perspective. But a "view of the natural universe" still came through in their words. They seemed to see the universe as neither magical nor mechanistic, but organic; a thing that lives and grows in a way that is partly predictable, but ordered from within by rules human beings are unable to fully know or manipulate. In the traditional worldview, humans have virtually no control over nature. In the modern view, they have virtually absolute control. The "emergent" view of the universe does not separate human understanding from nature itself, and the control human beings have is seen as being tempered by the need to respect the unknowable. Maureen, a foster mother and avid gardener, put it this way:

Maureen, 58

The more I see, the more I believe that anything you do is like growing a flower. You learn as much as you can about it, and you can create the perfect conditions so far as possible. You can give the flower everything you know it needs. But in the end, you have to stand back and watch it grow. It becomes what it was meant to be, and there is no way to control that.

. . . Medicine can try to extend our lives and make us into different beings, but I feel in my bones that when it is time for me to die, there will be no way to control it, and that will be as it should. . . .

Children—they're the same way. Some parents put their little ones in the best schools and get their teeth straightened and take them to psychologists and push them to achieve. Other parents abuse them and ignore them. And what the parent does makes a whale of a difference. But either way, there is something in each child that will remain as it is, that will not be snuffed out. Children are themselves, each one different and unique, and they will always be themselves. To see that and to treasure that is to love the child.

There is room in this worldview for the scientific, and there is room for the miraculous, although neither takes exactly the same form they do in the traditional and modern worldviews. In the emergent value system, there is a deep respect for both concrete knowledge and the operation of a universe that is beyond our absolute understanding.

◆ *Cultural Element 3: Basic Life Approach*   A culture's ideas of God and the natural universe come through in its members' approach to life. The traditional approach, as we saw in Chapter 1, is to rely on existing authority, whether that consists of scripture, the work of a few accepted scholars, or time-tested traditional custom. Modern thinkers, seeing the universe as a machine, set about life as you would set about solving a math equation or fixing an electronic device: one analyzes the machine, and then one can get it to do what one wants.

The emergent value system shares the modern belief that existing knowledge is infinitesimal, compared to what there is to be known. On the other hand, it doesn't square with the modern idea that every life problem can be solved like an equation. Women who had an emergent value system focused on taking a creative approach to the unique combination of controllable and uncontrollable elements in every situation.

This was a natural outgrowth of women's paradoxical role, which had ensured that any given woman never knew exactly what combinations of demands might be made on her at any given time—and that many of the problems she faced, being paradoxical, *couldn't be solved from within one logical system*. Such women had learned what it felt like to go through *satori*, to have a paradigm shift. They knew that the process was different from logical problem-solving, and they knew that it would happen to them again and again—if they let it. In short, they knew that there was much they didn't know. They had grown to accept and even delight in that fact as one facet of a creative approach to life.

Yvonne, 27

It's so amazing. No matter how hard I try to see what I'm not seeing, I don't see a thing! And then, just when I'm convinced I'm seeing all there is, a whole new world will open up—just come up out of the blue, from some place I didn't know was there. That's how the solutions to all my biggest problems have come—from places I didn't know were there. They all blindside me.

The flip side of that is, I now don't believe that there's anything that *can't* work. There are just narrow ways of looking at things, ways that don't allow you to be creative enough. . . . To solve a lot of our problems, we're going to have to put everything we know off to the side, and let ourselves see what we haven't been seeing.

◆ *Cultural Element 4: Social Ideals*   The traditional worldview, which was designed to help human beings survive at a time when survival was exceedingly difficult, is very hierarchical. The strong must care for the weak, and the weak must obey the strong. Leadership—and "followership"—are crucial in dangerous situations. In the modern value system, on the other hand, equality and universality are key. In the modern view, you don't put people in "inside" and "outside" groups. All individuals are to be treated *uniformly*, to avoid any inequality. This becomes a sticky issue when people (men and women, for example) are different from each other. Because of this, one whole branch of feminist thinking argues that men and women really *aren't* different, that all their supposed differences, from arm strength to aggressiveness, are the product of social conditioning.

The emergent value system doesn't rely on establishing uniform treatment for everyone. Nor does it support the traditional idea that all people should live in hierarchical systems, guarded from "outsiders." The women I spoke to had absorbed the basic individualism of modern social ideals, combined it with the pragmatism of the traditional arrangement, and cooked up something new. They valued equality, but equality *as judged by a person's subjective experience.*

For example, from the perspective of the emergent value system, if one woman wants to have two children, another wants six, and a third doesn't want children at all, then it wouldn't be "equal" to expect each of the three women to bear the same number of children. If a wife wants to stay home caring for her baby while her husband earns money in the traditional arrangement, it isn't fair or equal to force her to take a job that's similar to his, just to support the modern idea of women's rights. On the other hand, if a woman does want to work, or if a father wants to stay home with the children while his wife earns the money, emergent values would never force the couple to live by traditional arrangements. The social ideals here are practicality, diversity, and personal preferences.

Emily described this to me very clearly. She was an advertising executive; her husband, Doug, cared for their two preschoolers and restored antique furniture at home while Emily was at the office.

Emily, 35

It's not about how things have "always been done," and it's not about me trying to liberate myself in any ideological way. It's about who Doug is, and who I am. I love what I do, he loves what he does. It just makes sense for us to arrange it this way for now. We may change the whole thing in a few years.

It all depends on what fulfills us most as individuals. People get so into stereotypes they stop even thinking about how they feel. They convince themselves that if they've got the corner office or the big house or a traditional marriage or a job, that they'll automatically be happy. They make those things the goal. To me, they are not the goal. To me, the goal is to find what makes you happy and to do it. If we could all do that, every single person's life would be different from everybody else's, but we would all be much less angry at each other.

Not many of my interview subjects lived exactly like Doug and Emily, but women who had been through the breaking point all put the same emphasis on the value of uniqueness, diversity, and the individual's right to establish personal objectives, and evaluate his or her own happiness.

◆ *Cultural Element 5: The "Right Thing to Do"* Traditional societies are governed by one central rule: obedience to authority. God is at the top of the social hierarchy, human leaders are appointed by divine providence, and refusing to obey the commandments of any of these authorities is to undermine the legitimacy of the whole system. Modern societies, on the other hand, are meritocratic; you're not born into a position of prominence, you have to *earn* it by being better at certain things than other people. In modern values, the Right Thing to Do is to become very good at competitive achievement.

The emergent value system defines the Right Thing to Do from a very different perspective. Within the limitations of honesty and compassion, the behaviors women told me they valued were ways of revealing the inner nature of a unique personality, and expressing that uniqueness in a way that enriched others.

Patricia, 25

In the long run I hope we can all get away from that sense that everything we do has to be approved by someone bigger or better, or that we have to beat each other out in some kind of contest. Who can be bigger and better at being me than I can? If someone is really being themselves, how can I beat them at that? Why would I want to? I don't want to beat other people, or judge them. I just want to *know* them.

Helene, 40

Every person is like an artist who paints the world a little differently. Every time I see something from another person's perspective, I have a fuller life. You know, we can only have depth perception because we have two eyes, that compare how things look from slightly different angles. Life is about seeing as many ways, through as many different "eyes," as possible. Every time someone communicates their vision to me, my life becomes deeper.

By now you should be getting a feel for the emergent value system I saw in many of my interview subjects. This list of "cultural elements" could go on forever, because this value system is different in an infinite variety of ways from the contradictory values of traditional and modern societies.

THE WORLDVIEW THAT IS "EMERGING" EVERYWHERE

I know that many of my academic colleagues will recognize the paradigm I am calling the "emergent value system." They've already been writing about it for several years. Scholars in almost every field of the arts and sciences began running into the paradoxical consequences of a divided worldview decades ago. Physicists are busy investigating the "patterned disorder" of a realm beyond the magical and mechanical worlds of either the traditional or the modern scientific imagination. Philosophers and literary critics would say that the emergent value system is a version of postmodernism, a paradigm that favors diversity and subjectivity rather than hierarchy or uniformity. Social scientists have been pointing out the need to use postmodern ideas to analyze the life experiences of people who differ from one another.

Whatever you call it, this new way of thinking is "emerging" all over the place. But what many academics may not realize is that the way of seeing they reach by esoteric learning is already being put into practice by millions of women who couldn't care less about terms such as "postmodernism." The people who first put the emergent value system into practice aren't necessarily ivory-tower intellectuals. They aren't the administrators who have been running our society's prestigious institutions. They are exactly the people we have been conditioned *not* to look to for leadership: "ordinary" American women.

These women are designing a new way of living the way a frostbitten explorer designs winter gloves, the way a slave designs freedom. They are creating something to replace a paradoxical worldview that has failed to protect them, that instead has damaged them, and then blamed them for the damage.

I've said several times that this is not merely because of biological gender, but because of the way women's roles have developed over time. *Anyone* in our society who doesn't share the life experience of an Enlightenment scholar is likely to hit the breaking point and re-create a value system close to the emergent worldview. My friend Jesse has had to live with contradictory expectations, and has come to share emergent values, because he is a black man in a white man's society. Another friend, Norm, is Caucasian, male, brilliant, and highly educated. Nevertheless, he has arrived at his own eloquent version of emergent values, partly because he happens to have cerebral palsy.

EMERGING STRUCTURES

The structures and institutions of the United States, like our value system, are still grounded mainly in the traditional and modern worldviews. American laws and policies are still in the pendular swing that has always dominated women's issues. A law will be passed to equalize conditions for women from a modern perspective, but before long, people will begin to recognize that the consequences of the law are detrimental to traditional institutions like the family. Then new laws are put in place to protect traditional institutions—but it isn't long before people see that this is creating inequality. The pendulum goes on swinging, and women's lives are battered from two different directions.

Sometimes social change comes from the top down: laws and policies are designed and imposed by The Authorities to create a desired result. This has been tried (and tried, and tried) in policies that relate to women's roles in the United States. But because The Authorities in this country share our culture's paradoxical ideas of what women should be, the laws and policies they create tend to have unanticipated negative results. In the end, they deepen and widen the contradictory aspects of female roles. The sets of inconsistent facts listed in the Introduction to this book have all come from the inherent paradoxes in the top-down approach to designing women's lives.

When the top-down approach to making effective policy doesn't work, the real, lasting structural changes in a society often begin to come from the ground up—in other words, laws and institutions are changed to *match* what has already become common practice. That is the case with the norms American women are establishing in both public and private domains. I have spent thousands of hours listening to women describe the solutions they have devised to meet the challenge of living in a paradoxical social environment. Each had found her own way to create a social network that could sustain and support her, and to access the resources she needed to nurture herself and others.

◆ *Emergent Alternatives to Traditional Social Structures: Redefining the Family*   Just about any newspaper you pick up in the United States today will tell you that the traditional family is in trouble. Divorce is rampant, many children go unfathered in all but the strictest biological sense, and economic pressures are forcing many couples to spend all their time working, so that even children from homes that are not broken end up with less parental guidance than may be ideal.

American women are the favorite scapegoats for all these problems. If women just stayed in their place, the traditional argument goes, families would be as stable and secure as they were in the Good Old Days. What traditionalist advocates don't mention is that the Good Old Days weren't so good for women. In Chapter 2, I mentioned that for a man, establishing a traditional family means living the life of a European gentleman—while for his wife, it means assuming a rank similar to that of a peasant in the Dark Ages. If you think that a traditional marriage is the definition of paradise, go to your local battered women's shelter and listen to the stories of women who have been victims of spousal abuse. Many people who would lock up a man for attacking a woman he didn't know will shrug off such an attack—sometimes even find it amusing—when it comes from the woman's husband or boyfriend. Attempts to free women from the injustices of traditional systems have indeed contributed to the dissolution of many marriages. But in many cases, those families would have been broken even if they had all stayed together in the same house.

American women, faced with the problem of maintaining a nurturing environment for themselves and their loved ones while still enjoying personal freedom, are re-creating the definition of family. In the 1980s, sociologists noted that American society was turning from individualism and community-wide cohesion, and beginning to rely instead on "friendship enclaves."[3] These enclaves were clusters of people who shared common interests and outlooks, who loved and needed each other. Sometimes these people were related, sometimes not. Most of the women I spoke to did not refer to their friendship enclaves as their families. However, these close-knit networks of mutually supportive people served the purpose of family for people whose traditional families had been disrupted by divorce, job-related relocation, abuse, or simple lack of common goals.

Darcy, 26

I was at a craft store the other day, and while I was waiting in line at the cash register I saw these signs they had on display. The signs all said things about family, like "Your family are the people who love and accept you no matter what," or "Your family is where you go to recover from the rest of the world." I started to get pretty bitter, because my family is nothing like that. My parents are divorced. I've met my father once. My mom's an alcoholic, and my brother sexually abused me when I was a kid. I stood there and looked at those signs and got really angry. I started feeling pretty sorry for myself.

And then, all of a sudden, it was like I saw those signs the other way around. I thought, "Wait. If a family is really where people love and accept you, then the people I'm related to aren't my family, because they don't act that way at all." It's like maybe, instead of forcing myself to believe that my biological relatives are kind and loving, I should just decide that the people who are kind and loving to me are my family. I have really good friends. I have people who love me. I have a *real* family—it's just that I don't happen to be related to any of them.

American society is not structured in a way that publicly recognizes this type of family, but I saw many women who operated in such groups. One of the main reasons women built up friendship families is that they found it impossible to meet the demands of the American economy and the needs of their children at the same time. Women have had to team up, either with extended biological families or with friendship groups, to raise their children in a culture that is nearing the breaking point.

Jamie, 33

I always thought I'd have what my mom had—a little house in the suburbs, a husband with a good job, a couple of kids. Instead, I've had to work my whole life, and my first marriage broke up. At first my mom helped with the kids. Then I married my present husband, moved away from my mom—and I was supposed to take care of his little boy, as well as my own children. At first it just swamped me. Then I started to realize that other women at [my workplace] had the same problem. We started talking, and we came up with a plan to hire baby-sitters for all our kids. That way each of us pays less, the baby-sitter gets more, and we can fill in for each other when the sitter is sick. It's sort of like day care, but it feels like family.

Carmelita, 30

I came to this country from El Salvador, so I miss my family very much. But I think that in the United States, people will step in where families are gone. I have one friend who is older—she's like my children's grandmother. I have friends who call me, or I call them, almost every day. I think this is something that women do in every different country, but in the U.S. I have to rely on it more.

As modernization disrupts traditional family ties, women all over this country are creating families of choice in order to keep their heads above water financially and emotionally. I must repeat that this is still only an emerging structural pattern, not the mainstream practice of American society. The women I spoke to who were close to the breaking point typically didn't have strong support networks. The social groups they did belong to were often unresponsive or antagonistic to their true selves. But women who had been forced to learn the territory beyond the breaking point formed family groups consciously and carefully.

Opal, 44

As an army wife, part of my survival strategy is to set about making friends as soon as I get to a new location. It's not something I can just wait around for. I did that for years—and they were hard, lonely years. Our world is so mobile now. You don't grow up and live in one community all your life. There are a lot of things that tear people apart. I've learned to pay a lot of attention to bringing people together. It's the only way a woman can survive, nowadays, and the only way our children are going to grow up around people who nourish their spirits.

Glenne, 32

I've noticed that my [inner city] high school students have a very loose way of defining family. It's as though they have learned to accept just about any loving, cohesive group as a family. When I ask them about their lives, I start to understand why. Some of "my" kids have the traditional mom, dad, brother, sister arrangement. But a lot live with one parent, or one parent and two grandparents, or an aunt and uncle, or a foster family. I have one student who says her family consists of three divorced women, four children, and a cat.

Whether such an arrangement is ideal depends on your perspective, but for many American women, that point is moot. The contradictory structures of our society have already put them in situations where they have had to redefine the family to care for their true selves and the true selves of their loved ones. These women's creativity, resourcefulness, and willingness to stretch familial love beyond its usual boundaries (note that Glenne calls her students "my kids") are creating islands of affection and support in a society where those things are sorely needed.

◆ *Emergent Alternatives to Modern Social Structures: Redefining the American Career* As we've seen, the typical American job was designed for a man with a full-time wife. Since women have never been freed from their traditional responsibilities—much less given full-time domestic support—women have always had to be creative about participating in the American workforce. They work part-time, arrange time-sharing with other workers, run their own businesses, and find ways to earn money without leaving home. The fact that our economy is now based on information, and that new technologies are constantly making information transfer easier, has helped some women develop innovative ways of earning a living.

Rhona, 39

My partners and I run a catering business. We've been pretty successful, so that now most of my time goes into management, and we hire people to do most of the hands-on work. All of the partners in the company have kids, and there are whole weeks when we don't even see each other. I'll be calling Shirley from my cell phone while I'm taking my son to the dentist, and she'll fax me a contract or a menu, and then we'll both have a conference call with Linda to make corrections. Ten years ago we couldn't have begun to run a business. Women have a lot to gain from the new technology, if we can be smart about it.

The technologies that enabled Rhona to become a partner in an entrepreneurial venture have also accompanied a trend toward unorthodox job patterns in American business as a whole. Downsizing, pressure from globalization, and the increasing efficiency of information systems are changing the way both men's and women's jobs are structured.

The business structures of the United States are moving toward what one author, John Kotter, calls the "New Rules" of success. These rules include things like the need to be open to varied career paths, as opposed to the standard organization man career in which an individual climbs the ranks of a large corporation. Small companies and entrepreneurialism are becoming increasingly important, and professional management is giving way to consulting and other service industries. Businesspeople who want to succeed in the emerging marketplace will need strong, internalized standards and a high degree of openness to change.[4] Another analyst of the American workplace, Sally Helgesen, writes that "the twenty-first-century economy is fluid, technology-driven, based on creativity and relationships."[5] Helgesen's book, *The Web of Inclusion*, describes a workplace where "people at every level [have] the opportunity to exercise both autonomy and self-expression."[6]

Both these authors, as well as many others, predict a future in which American business will come to share the same values I saw emerging among the women I interviewed. American women have been following these "new" rules for decades. Since they've always carried the burden of paradoxical social pressures, women tend to have varied career paths. They gravitate toward service and information-based industries, rely on internal motivation and standards, and are flexible in their approach to work. American women are also increasingly entrepreneurial. The number of U.S. businesses owned by women grew from six million in 1992 to eight million in 1994. Women now employ more workers in this country than the Fortune 500.[7]

Ironically, most of the employed women I interviewed saw their innovative solutions to problems of the nineteenth-century job model as stopgap measures. They spoke about them apologetically, as though the nine-to-five corporate job were the respected Right Way, and their own arrangements were somehow inferior. Blanche, for example, works for a travel agency.

Blanche, 39

I still work at home three days a week. I expected that I'd be back at the office full-time when my baby was six months old, but the stress and the expense got to be too much. I realized that even when I'm in the office, the vast, vast majority of my work is over the phone or a modem. I get as much work done as I would at the office, but I worry about how long they'll put up with me not being there.

Veronica is a newspaper columnist. One of her children was born with serious health problems. Veronica knew that she needed her job for medical benefits, so she stayed with her career while her husband worked from home and tended the children.

Veronica, 35

The paper has been really good to me. I have a crazy schedule, between visits to the hospital, being with the children when Pete has to go somewhere, and the normal pressure that's always on you to meet your deadlines. I'm really grateful for how understanding my bosses have been.

What Blanche and Veronica didn't articulate is that they had no reason to be any more apologetic or grateful to their bosses than if they had *lived* at the office. The bottom line was that they both did all the work they were assigned (and then some), they both pleased customers, and they were both assets to their respective employers. The nature of their work and the nature of the on-the-spot job simply aren't linked. The normal job that the American economy is now leaving behind was based on an industrial factory system, in which workers had to be in one place, assembling physical things in tandem with other workers or overseeing their work. In our postindustrial, information-based economy, many jobs can be much more flexible and still remain just as effective—often more so—than a nine-to-five arrangement.

Many Americans, including many employers, don't see this. Going on the sheer momentum of our existing social norms, they still consider women's innovative job designs as makeshift strategies created by people who can't quite manage to live according to proper employment rules. But as the pressures of modernization increase the stress on both individual lives and American business as a whole, the fluid, inclusive, creative job structures designed by women who have lived through the breaking point will probably prove more robust than the rigid roles Americans inherited from traditional and modern worldviews.

THE REAL EXPERTS

Expert social commentators on both sides of the holy war—politicians, activists, media bigwigs—are deeply distressed by the emergent value system and the structures that are being built around it. They have their own visions of what women should be, and to them the idea of an emergent society is a clear threat. Going to these experts for answers to women's problems is like going to a Singaporean to design clothes for an Arctic expedition.

"We're cold," women tell the experts.

"Yes," the experts reply, "we know how refreshed you must feel."

"No," women entreat. "*Cold. Extremely cold!*"

"Yes," the experts repeat in a patronizing tone. "*Extremely refreshed!*" And they go on instituting social structures that force women to the breaking point.

The problem is that to be considered an expert on *anything* in the society of the United States, you still have to live the life of an upper-class gentleman. Women are only beginning to move into positions that will enable them to re-create this country's policies and institutions—and many of those who manage it have had many of the privileges of Enlightenment gentlemen: comfortable backgrounds, high education levels, and the money to hire Somebody Else to do some of their traditional chores while they achieved in the modern world. These experts have been protected from some of the contradictions that beset people who can't match the upper-class gentleman's lifestyle. Of course, female senators and judges and CEOs are participating in the transformation of American values. But the deepest, broadest change is coming from the grass roots, from ordinary homemakers and part-time office workers and the woman who rings up your groceries at the supermarket. These are the individuals who have had their lives disrupted, their hearts broken, their health strained by the paradoxical aspects of our current values. These are the Americans who know how to set the captives free.

Afterword:
Telling Women's Stories

This book has been devoted to communicating what hundreds of women told me over a period of several years. Before I conclude, there is something I want to say to those women, and to any other readers, in return.

The principal reason I was able to get the attention of a publisher and sell this book is that I have a Ph.D. in sociology. Having come from an academic family, I decided to play the Education Game, which felt relatively comfortable and familiar to me. I jumped through all the hoops and performed the diverse tasks (many of them quite meaningless) to win a piece of paper that, in the Career Game, gives a person some measure of credibility.

However, the principal reasons I could *write* the book have little to do with the Education Game. Two major ones come to mind. The first, of course, is that I have struggled through my own sleepless nights and daunting days trying to fulfill a paradoxical social role. The second—and more important—reason is that I have been privileged to *hear the stories* of so many women's lives.

I hope I am not alone in this. I know I am not the only listener who could benefit from the insights other women have developed through years of struggle, opportunity, challenge, and invention. So what I have to ask is this:

I want you to tell your story.

Tell your story—the *true* story, with all the details you've always thought you must keep to yourself—whenever and wherever it would hurt or diminish you to remain silent. Tell this story to your friends, and if it feels right, tell it to your enemies as well. Tell it to your family, even if some of them are horrified by your honesty. Tell your story to your lover, your partner, your spouse. Tell it to the ten o'clock news. Tell it in the most intimate circumstance, and the most public—*when and if you want to.* The true self knows when to speak and when to remain silent, and it expresses itself as desire. If you are afraid to tell your story, *and you don't want to,* by all means keep it to yourself. But if only fear is fighting your longing to be heard, take a deep breath and speak out. You may catch some flak, but you will find out that in the long run this is by far the safest passage through the war surrounding women's roles. In the end, a forced silence cannot protect you from anything. It will only push you closer to the breaking point.

As a general rule, women who have been through the process I've described in this book are hesitant to call attention to themselves. The detachment and tolerance for diversity that characterize their emergent value system lead such women to listen to others without "fighting back" by articulating their own position. It is the strident, argumentative voices of holy warriors and ideologues that speak most loudly about female roles in the United States.

When women do tell their stories in terms of their real experiences, insights, and strategies, they are often discounted or ignored. Remember, in order to publish the stories I've included here, I signed a contract in which I am "referred to as the author and designated by the masculine singular pronoun." The date on that contract is 1996. As we approach the twenty-first century, American culture still doesn't know quite how to handle women's ideas, told in women's voices. The stories of American women are still stifled, muted, and distorted by paradox.

This is tragic in at least two ways. First, it creates the illusion that the woman who is struggling in the grip of multiple double binds, who has reached the breaking point, or who has transcended her culture's worldview is unusual, freakish, and alone. Second, in silencing such women's voices, American society is robbing itself of the very information it needs to resolve some of its thorniest dilemmas, now and in the future.

There is a single remedy for both these ailments. It is for ordinary women, in whatever position they may be, to discard the shame and hesitancy they have been taught to feel about their identities and their choices, and simply talk about their lives.

Almost every woman I interviewed who had gone through a breaking point felt that she was probably the only person ever to experience such a thing. Ironically, women with the emergent value system almost universally shared a sense of being unique in the most negative sense. They all said things like this:

Tess, 42

I'm probably not the right person for you to be talking to, if you want to know what women in general are thinking. I'm really different from most women. I think I'm a feminist, but I think a lot of feminists would criticize me—I know they would, they do! But I'm definitely not your typical old-fashioned girl. I'm just . . . well, I guess I'm just weird.

Anita, 45

I really don't think there's anyone who sees things the way I do. It seems as though there's so much anger and antagonism out there. I just want us all to find some way to live reasonably happy lives. I'm not too particular about toeing any political lines. So I'm not really representative.

Both Tess and Anita actually *were* representative of most of the women I interviewed. But there is no collective movement to tell women like these that they are not alone, that they are holding a good course, that other people have reached the breaking point and transcended it very much as they are doing. So far, the women's movement has helped female Americans confront the contradictions in our value system—but it has only brought us *to* the breaking point, not *through* it.

This makes life more difficult than it has to be for women whose worldview is crumbling in on itself, who are experiencing the frightening, wrenching "death" of meltdowns and the indescribable insights of *satori* in isolated synchrony, as though they were singing the same song in unison but without being able to hear one another's voices. It also makes life harder for any American who is being swept along in our society's progress toward its own breaking point—and that means all of us, male and female, old and young, whatever our income, our educational level, or the shade of our skin. Every day, more and more Americans are finding themselves trapped in double binds, forced to puzzle through impossible problems and challenges as the strange loop of our paradoxical worldview tightens around us.

As you read this, millions of American women are hitting the breaking point. Millions more are emerging, re-created, into a new way of thinking and being. In turn, those women are re-creating every aspect of their social world, from its most abstract concepts to its most pragmatic institutions. Their stories—your stories—are maps of a territory our culture does not understand, but toward which we are all inexorably headed. To guide American society through the frightening, exhilarating metamorphosis that will allow us to thrive in this territory, we desperately need the wisdom that unremarkable, inconspicuous American women have bought with both suffering and joy. When the ordinary stories of these ordinary women begin to be told, heard, taken seriously, and used as a model for our culture's ideas and social structures, the whole society of the United States will be ready to move into a world beyond the breaking point.

Notes

CHAPTER ONE

Some History: The Foundation of a House Divided

1. Quoted by Simone de Beauvoir in "Women as 'Other,'" in *Issues in Feminism: A First Course in Women's Studies*, ed. Sheila Ruth (New York: Houghton Mifflin, 1980), p. 146.

CHAPTER TWO

Lurching Through Herstory

1. Wollstonecraft was especially disdainful of the philosopher Jean-Jacques Rousseau, who was convinced that women were placed on earth to entertain men. Rousseau's ideas about women seem rather dubious when you consider that his idea of a gratifying heterosexual encounter was to leap out in front of groups of women, drop his pants, and beg them to spank him. And you thought philosophers were boring.
2. Schmittroth, Linda, and Mary R. McCall. *Women's Almanac* (New York: Newspaper Enterprise Association, 1977), p. 541.
3. Wollstonecraft finally tied the knot with Godwin when she became pregnant a second time, but died from complications of the birth. The baby survived, was named after her mother, grew up, married Percy Bysshe Shelley, and wrote *Frankenstein*. This has very little to do with gender roles, but isn't it interesting?
4. Foner, Philip S. *Women and the American Labor Movement: From Colonial Times to the Eve of World War I* (New York: Free Press, 1979), p. 136.
5. A "busk" was the piece of steel or whalebone that stiffened the front of a woman's corset.
6. Douglas, Susan J. *Where the Girls Are: Growing Up Female with the Mass Media* (New York: Times Books, 1994), p. 128.

7. Friedan, Betty. *The Feminine Mystique* (New York: W. W. Norton & Company, 1963), p. 342.
8. Hochschild, Arlie, and Ann Machung. *The Second Shift* (New York: Avon Books, 1989), p. i.
9. Berg, Barbara J. *The Crisis of the Working Mother: Resolving the Conflict Between Family and Work* (New York: Summit Books, 1986), p. 20.
10. Wallis, Claudia. "Onward, Women!" *Time* 134:80 (Dec. 4, 1989), p. 82.
11. Weitzman, Lenore J. *The Divorce Revolution: The Unexpected Social and Economic Consequences for Women and Children in America* (New York: The Free Press, 1985).

CHAPTER THREE
Strange Loops and Double Binds: The Nature of Paradox

1. Mann, Judy. *The Difference: Growing Up Female in America* (New York: Warner Books, 1994).
2. Weitzman, Lenore J. et al. "Sex-Role Socialization in Picture Books for Pre-School Children," *American Journal of Sociology* 77 (1972), pp. 1125–1150.
3. Sadker, M., and D. Sadker, "Sexism in the Schoolroom of the '80s," *Psychology Today* (March 1985), pp. 54–57.
4. Broverman, I. K. et al. "Sex Role Stereotypes and Clinical Judgments of Mental Health," *Journal of Clinical and Consulting Psychology* 34:1 (1970), pp. 1–7.
5. Horner, Matina. "A Bright Woman Is in a Double Bind." *Issues in Feminism: A First Course in Women's Studies*, ed. Sheila Ruth (New York: Houghton Mifflin, 1980), pp. 170–173.

CHAPTER FOUR
Refugees from the Holy War

1. Gleick, James. *Chaos: Making a New Science* (New York: Penguin Books, 1987), p. 35.
2. Gilligan, Carol. *In a Different Voice: Psychological Theory and Women's Development* (Cambridge, Massachusetts: Harvard University Press, 1982).
3. Fein, Ellen, and Sherrie Schneider. *The Rules: Time-tested Secrets for Capturing the Heart of Mr. Right* (New York: Warner Books, 1996), p. 43.
4. Ibid., p. 75.
5. Andelin, Helen B. *Fascinating Womanhood* (Fresno, California: American Publishing Co., 1963), pp. 133–137.
6. Faludi, Susan. *Backlash: The Undeclared War Against American Women* (New York: Crown, 1991), pp. 454–455.
7. Ibid., p. 456.
8. Ibid., p. 457.
9. Steinem, Gloria. *Revolution from Within: A Book of Self-Esteem* (Boston: Little, Brown & Co., 1993), pp. 4–5.
10. Ibid., p. 8.
11. Kaminer, Wendy. "Feminism's Identity Crisis," *The Atlantic Monthly* (October 1993), p. 66.

12. Wolf, Naomi. *Fire with Fire: The New Female Power and How It Will Change the 21st Century* (New York: Random House, 1993), pp. 316–317.

13. Chesler, Phyllis. *Patriarchy: Notes of an Expert Witness* (Monroe, Maine: Common Courage Press, 1994), p. 61.

14. Olive, David. *Genderbabble: The Dumbest Things Men Ever Said About Women* (New York: Perigee Books, 1983), p. 77.

15. Schlafly, Phyllis. "Women's Lib Suppresses Freedom of the Press," *The Phyllis Schlafly Report* (vol. 7, no. 1, section 2: October, 1973), p. 1.

16. Pride, Mary. *The Way Home: Beyond Feminism and Back to Reality* (Westchester, Illinois: Crossway Books, 1985), pp 91–92.

17. Ibid., pp. 3, 11.

18. Chesler, pp. 58–59.

19. Andelin, p. 135.

20. Fein and Schneider, pp. 48–49.

21. Ibid., p. 20.

22. Reported in the *Washington Times*, May 7, 1993.

23. *Working Woman*, April 1992, p. 104.

24. Sommers, Christina Hoff. *Who Stole Feminism?* (New York: Simon & Schuster, 1994), p. 234.

25. Barbara Lovenheim, letter to *The New York Times Book Review*, February 9, 1992.

CHAPTER FIVE

Hitting the Breaking Point

1. Throughout the trial, the press also reported breathlessly on Marcia Clark's styles of hair and dress. Not once did I hear them say, "I think Barry Scheck is parting his hair on the opposite side today! And take a look at Johnnie Cochran's tie—a little wide, wouldn't you say?" Clark was measured against the scales of judgment used to "rate" both male professionals and female beauty-pageant contestants. In *Beyond the Double Bind*, Kathleen Jamieson relates the story of a judge who threw a female lawyer out of his courtroom for wearing slacks. "Next time you come in here," he said, "I'll expect you to dress like a lawyer!" The fact that the attorney in question was in fact dressed *exactly* like the male lawyers in the room did not, apparently, seem paradoxical to this particular judge.

2. Gerdes, Karen E. "'Making Safe': Reducing Threat and Increasing Security in the Administration of AFDC" (1996). Unpublished manuscript.

CHAPTER SIX

The Age Factor

1. Parsons, Talcott. "The Social Structure of the Family," in *The Family: Its Function and Destiny*, ed. Anshen (New York: Harper and Row, 1949), p. 267.

2. Kurian, George T. *Datapedia of the United States: America Year by Year* (Lanham, Maryland: Bernan Press, 1994), p. 37.

3. Gerson, Kathleen. *Hard Choices: How Women Decide about Work, Career, and Motherhood* (Berkeley and Los Angeles: University of California Press, 1985).

4. Bielby, Denise D., and William T. Bielby. "She Works Hard for the Money: Household Responsibilities and the Allocation of Work Effort," *American Journal of Sociology* 5:9 (March 1988), pp. 1055–1056.

5. Mintz, Steven, and Susan M. Kellogg. *Domestic Revolutions: A Social History of American Family Life* (New York: The Free Press, 1988), pp. 203–205.

6. DiMona, Lisa, and Constance Herndon, eds. *The 1995 Women's Sourcebook* (New York: Houghton Mifflin, 1994), p. 367.

7. Maranto, Gina. "Delayed Childbearing: How a Woman's Fertility Declines with Age," *The Atlantic Monthly* 6:275 (June 1995), p. 55.

8. Rapoport, Betsy. "The Story of Z," *The New York Times Magazine* (Sunday, January 13, 1995), p. 52.

9. Reis and Stone, eds. *The American Woman 1992–93: A Status Report* (New York: W. W. Norton & Co., 1992), p. 277.

10. Hedlund, Karen. Quoted in *The Radcliffe College Annual Report, 1994–95*, p. 37.

CHAPTER SEVEN

Meltdown

1. For example, Asch, Solomon, "Effects of Group Pressure upon the Modification and Distortion of Judgments," *Groups, Leadership, and Men* (Pittsburgh: Carnegie Press, 1951).

CHAPTER EIGHT

Satori: The Paradigm Shift

1. Moody, Raymond A., Jr. *The Light Beyond* (New York: Bantam Books, 1988), p. 5.

CHAPTER NINE

Caring for the True Self

1. Sidel, Ruth. *Women and Children Last: The Plight of Poor Women in Affluent America* (New York: Penguin Books, 1986), p. xvi.

2. Asch, Solomon, "Effects of Group Pressure Upon the Modification and Distortion of Judgments," *Groups, Leadership, and Men* (Pittsburgh: Carnegie Press, 1951).

3. Fein and Schneider, pp. 91–92.

4. Ibid., p. 78.

CHAPTER TEN

Changing the Rules of the Game

1. Rukeyser, Muriel, in "Käthe Kollwitz." Quoted in Bass and Davis, *The Courage to Heal* (New York: Harper & Row, 1989), p. 92.

CHAPTER ELEVEN

The "Emergent" Society of the United States: A World Beyond the Breaking Point

1. Patterson, Orlando. *Slavery and Social Death: A Comparative Study* (Cambridge, Massachusetts: Harvard University Press, 1982), p. 340.
2. Kaminer, Wendy. *I'm Dysfunctional, You're Dysfunctional: The Recovery Movement and Other Self-Help Fashions* (Reading, Massachusetts: Addison Wesley, 1992), pp. 89, 154.
3. Bellah, Robert N., et al. *Habits of the Heart* (New York: Harper & Row, 1985).
4. Kotter, John P. *The New Rules: How to Succeed in Today's Post-Corporate World* (New York: The Free Press, 1995).
5. Helgesen, Sally. *The Web of Inclusion* (New York: Doubleday, 1995), cover leaf.
6. Ibid., p. 276.
7. Based on census data. Reported in *Reuters, Limited*. January 6, 1996.

Bibliography

Andelin, Helen B. *Fascinating Womanhood* (Fresno, California: American Publishing Co., 1963).

Anshen, Ruth, ed. *The Family: Its Function and Destiny* (New York: Harper and Row, 1949).

Bellah, Robert N., Richard Madson, William M. Sullivan, Ann Swidler, and Steven M. Tipton. *Habits of the Heart* (New York: Harper & Row, 1985).

Berg, Barbara J. *The Crisis of the Working Mother: Resolving the Conflict Between Family and Work* (New York: Summit Books, 1986).

Boldt, Laurence G. *Zen and the Art of Making a Living* (New York: Arkana, 1992).

Chesler, Phyllis. *Patriarchy: Notes of an Expert Witness* (Monroe, Maine: Common Courage Press, 1994).

DiMona, Lisa, and Constance Herndon, eds. *The 1995 Information Please Women's Sourcebook* (New York: Houghton Mifflin, 1994).

Douglas, Susan J. *Where the Girls Are: Growing Up Female with the Mass Media* (New York: Times Books, 1994).

Faludi, Susan. *Backlash: The Undeclared War Against American Women* (New York: Crown, 1991).

Fein, Ellen, and Sherrie Schneider. *The Rules: Time-Tested Secrets for Capturing the Heart of Mr. Right* (New York: Warner Books, 1995).

Foner, Philip S. *Women and the American Labor Movement: From Colonial Times to the Eve of World War I.* (New York: Free Press, 1979).

Friedan, Betty. *The Feminine Mystique* (New York: W. W. Norton & Company, 1963).

Gerson, Kathleen. *Hard Choices: How Women Decide about Work, Career, and Motherhood* (Berkeley and Los Angeles: University of California Press, 1985).

Gilligan, Carol. *In a Different Voice: Psychological Theory and Women's Development* (Cambridge, Massachusetts: Harvard University Press, 1982).

Gleick, James. *Chaos: Making a New Science* (New York: Penguin Books, 1987).

Hawley, John Stratton, ed. *Sati, the Blessing and the Curse: The Burning of Wives in India* (New York and Oxford: Oxford University Press, 1994).

Helgesen, Sally. *The Web of Inclusion: Building an Organization for Everyone* (New York: Doubleday, 1995).

Hochschild, Arlie, and Ann Machung. *The Second Shift* (New York: Avon Books, 1989).

Kaminer, Wendy. *I'm Dysfunctional, You're Dysfunctional: The Recovery Movement and Other Self-Help Fashions* (Reading, Massachusetts: Addison Wesley, 1992).

Kotter, John P. *The New Rules: How to Succeed in Today's Post-Corporate World* (New York: The Free Press, 1995).

Kurian, George T. *Datapedia of the United States, 1790–2000: America Year by Year* (Lanham, Maryland: Bernan Press, 1994).

Mann, Judy. *The Difference: Growing Up Female in America* (New York: Warner Books, 1996).

Mintz, Steven, and Susan M. Kellogg. *Domestic Revolutions: A Social History of American Family Life* (New York: The Free Press, 1988).

Moody, Raymond A., Jr. *The Light Beyond* (New York: Bantam Books, 1988).

Olive, David. *Genderbabble: The Dumbest Things Men Ever Said About Women* (New York: Perigee Books, 1983).

Patterson, Orlando. *Slavery and Social Death: A Comparative Study* (Cambridge, Massachusetts: Harvard University Press, 1982).

Pride, Mary. *The Way Home: Beyond Feminism, Back to Reality* (Westchester, Illinois: Crossway Books, 1985).

Reis and Stone, eds. *The American Woman 1992–93: A Status Report* (New York: W. W. Norton & Co. 1992).

Ruth, Sheila, ed. *Issues in Feminism: A First Course in Women's Studies* (New York: Houghton Mifflin, 1980).

Schmittroth, Linda, and Mary R. McCall. *Women's Almanac* (New York: Newspaper Enterprise Association, 1977).

Sidel, Ruth. *Women and Children Last: The Plight of Poor Women in Affluent America* (New York: Penguin Books, 1986).

Sommers, Christina Hoff. *Who Stole Feminism? How Women Have Betrayed Women* (New York: Simon & Schuster, 1994).

Steers, Richard, and Stewart Black. *Organizational Behavior*, 5th ed. (New York: HarperCollins College Publishers, 1994).

Steinem, Gloria. *Revolution from Within: A Book of Self-Esteem* (Boston: Little, Brown & Co., 1993).

Tickle, Phyllis A. *Re-discovering the Sacred: Spirituality in America* (New York: Crossroad Press, 1995).

Weitzman, Lenore J. *The Divorce Revolution: The Unexpected Social and Economic Consequences for Women and Children in America* (New York: The Free Press, 1985).

Wolf, Naomi. *Fire with Fire: The New Female Power and How It Will Change the 21st Century* (New York: Random House, 1993).

Zelizer, Viviana A. *Pricing the Priceless Child: The Changing Social Value of Children* (New York: Basic Books, Inc., 1981).

Index

Abby (interviewee), 195

Abortion, 111, 116, 122, 169–72, 221, 236, 325

Abusive relationships, 264–65, 314, 368

Academia: as game, 324–25. *See also* Education; Harvard University

Achievement: and age factor, 193–94, 196, 197, 214; of Beck, 236–37, 267, 301; and caring for true self, 301, 335; and changing rules, 335; and emergent society, 365; and Harvard culture, 170–71; and "paradoxing" of women, 96–97; and reaching breaking point, 155, 165, 236–37; and *satori*, 267, 278

Adams, Abigail, 60, 61

Adrienne (interviewee), 213

African Americans, 37–45. *See also* Parks, Rosa; Race; Slavery; Woodman, Felicia

Age factor: and Beck's sister, 176–78; and betrayed, 189–97; "bridges" in, 197; and careers/work, 190, 191, 193–96, 197, 200–202, 204, 205, 206–7, 209, 210, 213–15, 219–20, 223; and cohorts, 179–208; and common characteristics of cohorts, 15, 225–26; and devalued, 183–88, 195; and double binds, 186–87, 190, 194, 209, 210, 215, 223, 224; and embattled, 208–16; and equality, 209, 217, 221; and expectations, 189–91, 206, 209, 220, 223, 225; and feminism, 178–79, 185, 187, 198–99, 205, 210, 211; and the future, 226; Generation X cohort, 208, 212–13, 214–16; and Holy War, 211–14, 221–22; and media, 189, 200, 205; and mother-daughter relationship, 199–200, 212–14; and no-win decisions, 210–11; and overwhelmed, 198–209, 214; and "real world," 222–25; and sacrifice without honor, 189–91; and social change, 186; and starting over,

Heidi (interviewee), 193
Helen (interviewee), 296–97
Helene (interviewee), 365
Helgesen, Sally, 371
"Herstory": and "Cult of True
    Womanhood," 65–66; in early
    U.S., 60–62; and family life, 81;
    and feminization of poverty, 86; of
    Industrial Revolution, 62–63; and
    lurching from left to right, 14,
    67–88; and role combination,
    79–80; and technology, 81–82;
    and unexpected patterns of role
    development, 58–62; and values,
    67. *See also* Feminist movement
Hierarchy, 26–33, 364–65
Higher education, 63–64, 219–22.
    See also Harvard University
"Historical moment," 354–57
Holt, Tamara (interviewee), 99–103,
    113–14
Holy War: and age factor, 211–14,
    221–22; and Beck's pregnancy,
    169–72; characteristics of, 14–15;
    civilians in, 15, 121–23, 124, 125,
    132–42, 143–44, 146–47, 211;
    and control of men, 126–32; and
    disinformation, 139–42; and
    double bind, 147; double jeopardy
    in, 142–43; as either-or conflict,
    14–15; and equality, 122; and
    feminine identity, 125–26; "filter"
    of, 134–36; and ideal society, 140;
    language in, 120–21, 132, 133,
    134, 136–42; and media, 125,
    126–27, 134, 136–37, 138; and
    morals, 122, 212; power as issue
    in, 126; and preconceptions,
    118–20; and silencing of women,
    15, 143–47, 213; and stereotypes,
    139, 145–46; and strange loops,
    147; warriors in, 15, 121–23, 124,
    125–26, 132, 134–44, 211,

213–14, 221–22, 376; and women
    as traitors, 134–42, 143–44; and
    work, 127–32, 145, 146, 213–14.
    See also Feminist movement
Honesty: and caring for true self, 17,
    289–95, 296–98, 299, 304–6,
    318, 329; and cruelty of lies,
    304–5; and emergent society, 18,
    346, 361, 365; and favorite lies of
    women, 291; and games, 17–18,
    325, 326, 329, 331, 332, 341; and
    hard truths, 296–98; intersection
    of compassion and, 304–6; and
    "polite" lying, 291–95; and re-
    creation, 289–90, 342, 346. *See
    also* Disinformation

In a Different Voice (Gilligan), 124
Individual, 31–32, 270–73, 363–64.
    See also True self
Industrial Revolution, 45–50, 52–54,
    62–63
Infantilization, 42
Infertility, 83, 210
"Inner Child," 351
Inner lizard, 160–63
Insanity. *See* Transferring insanity
Invisible women, 25–26, 32, 33,
    34–37, 52–53, 55, 56
Irene (interviewee), 239
Iris (interviewee), 308–9
Isabelle (interviewee), 76
Isolation, 279–81, 345–46, 376–77

Jacquée (interviewee), 223
Jade (interviewee), 328
Jamie (interviewee), 369
Jane (interviewee), 330
Janice (interviewee), 190–91
Jeanette (interviewee), 197
Jenny (interviewee), 6–7, 158
Jesse (friend), 366
Jessie (interviewee), 146

About the Author

Martha Beck lives in Phoenix, Arizona, where she teaches "Life Design" seminars. Beck has done sociological research on the relationship between modernization and gender roles in both Asian and Western cultures. During her education at Harvard, where she earned her B.A., M.A., and Ph.D. degrees, Beck taught courses in the departments of foreign cultures and studio art. She has also worked at a variety of jobs in the "real world," ranging from book illustration to economic development work in Cambodia. Beck has written books and articles on a variety of topics, including labor management in China, the Japanese employment system, the position of women in American religion, the social dynamics of sexual abuse, and the ethics of new medical technologies. She and her husband, John, have two daughters, one son, a beagle, and two guinea pigs. Her primary recreational pursuit is napping.